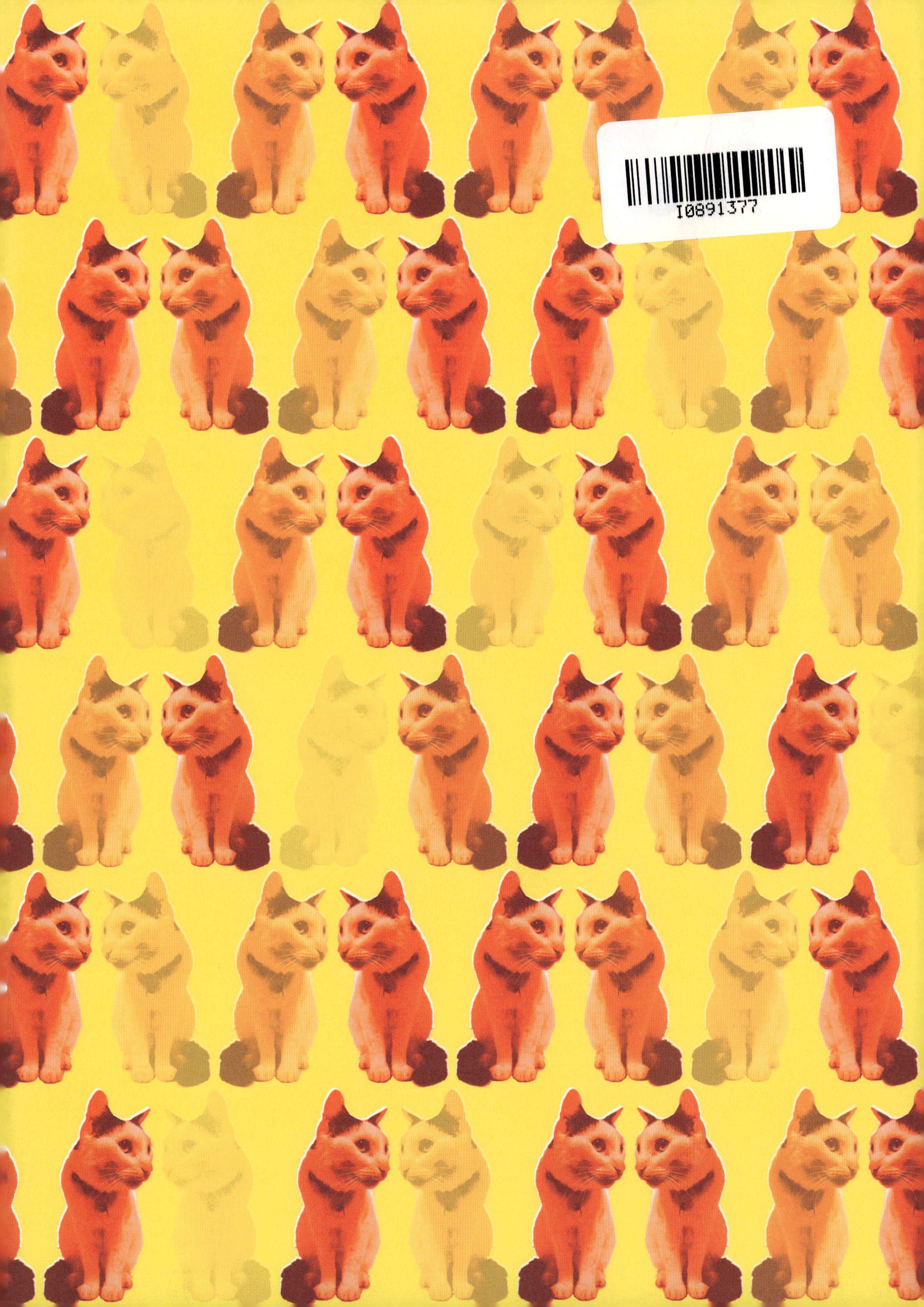

'To the memory of my sweet angel **Barnabé** (Christmas 2008 - 30 March 2022), my soul mate, my companion, my irreplaceable cat. He contributed to creating this book by his boundless love and constant supervision of my work over 13 years. I had cats all my life but never one like him. I will miss him eternally.'

Fabrice

STILLS

THE CURE

PHOTOGRAPHY PAUL COX

CONCEPT & DESIGN FABRICE COUILLEROT

EYES ON ROBERT SMITH

ACC ART BOOKS

FOR AROUND TWENTY YEARS 'THE PAUL COX SHOOT' WAS AN ANNUAL DATE IN THE CURE DIARY – NEW PHOTOGRAPHS WERE REQUIRED FOR NEW RELEASES, INTERVIEWS, T-SHIRTS, TOUR PROGRAMMES, CALENDARS – A MINIMUM SEVEN DIFFERENT BACKDROPS, SEVEN DIFFERENT OUTFITS, BAND PICTURES, SOLO PICTURES, B&W, COLOUR, WEIRD AND 'NORMAL' – AND ALL USUALLY TO BE ACHIEVED IN A DAY…

WITH HINDSIGHT IT WAS A TOTALLY INSANE SCHEDULE! BUT WITH A MINIMUM OF FUSS, PAUL COX WAS THE PHOTOGRAPHER THAT INVARIABLY GOT IT DONE.

I WOULD GENERALLY HAVE A CONVERSATION (AND/OR EXCHANGE FAXES!) WITH PAUL PRIOR TO ANY SHOOT, TO TALK OVER BASIC IDEAS FOR THE OVERALL 'LOOK' – LIGHTING, PROJECTION, PROPS, BACKDROP IDEAS AND STUFF – AS WELL AS CONFIRM WHO WAS IN THE BAND(!) AND WHAT THE VIBE OF ANY NEW MUSIC WAS.

SHOOT DAY IN PAUL'S LONDON STUDIO WOULD USUALLY START AROUND 2PM – A STAGGERED BAND ARRIVAL FOR COFFEE, MAKE-UP AND POLAROIDS – AND I WOULD ROLL IN AROUND 3PM. WE WOULD THEN GLOOM, GURN AND GRIN OUR WAY THROUGH THE ENSUING TWELVE HOURS – BAND SHOT, BAND GETS CHANGED WHILE I DO A FEW ON MY OWN, I GET CHANGED, FIVE MINUTES FOR REFRESHMENTS – A FEW GLUGS OF SOMETHING COLD, A QUICK POWDERING OF NOSES (AHEM) AND… BAND SHOT, BAND GETS CHANGED WHILST I DO A FEW ON MY OWN…

AND ALL THE WHILE PAUL, CALM, TOTALLY IN CONTROL OF PROCEEDINGS – A GENTLE SOUNDTRACK OF HIS VOICE WHISPERING IN THE BACKGROUND, A MURMURED SUGGESTION HERE, A GENTLE CAJOLE THERE, A VERY FEW RAISED CRIES IMPLORING US TO STOP FUCKING TALKING FOR A FEW SECONDS…

AS THE SHOOT PROGRESSED THE BAND WOULD INEVITABLY BECOME MORE DISHEVELLED, SULLEN AND UNPROFESSIONAL, AND IT REQUIRED ALL PAUL'S NOUS TO GET ANYTHING REMOTELY USABLE OUT OF THE HOURS AROUND MIDNIGHT… I WAS ALWAYS GENUINELY ASTONISHED WHEN I GOT THE SESSION CONTACT SHEETS TO LOOK AT THE FOLLOWING WEEK – THE QUALITY AND CHOICE WAS OFTEN OVERWHELMING – I COULD NEVER QUITE FIGURE OUT HOW HE DID IT!

LOOKING AT THEM NOW, I REALISE PAUL COX'S PHOTOGRAPHS OF THE CURE – AND OF ME – ARE INSTANTLY RECOGNISABLE. AMONG MY FAVOURITES ARE P30'S 'FINGER GUN', P124-125'S 'CANDLES' AND P162'S 'BIRDS NEST' – BUT THEY ALL HAVE AN INDEFINABLE 'SOMETHING' ABOUT THEM, AND MANY IN THIS COLLECTION HAVE BECOME 'ICONIC' IN THE VISUAL HISTORY OF THE BAND.

AS THIS BOOK SHOWS, THE 'LOOK' OF THE VARIOUS INCARNATIONS OF THE CURE, THROUGH MANY DIFFERENT PERIODS, IS INEXTRICABLY LINKED TO PAUL'S PICTURES; HIS VISION, EXPERTISE AND PATIENCE PLAYED A HUGE PART IN PORTRAYING US, NOT JUST AS WE WANTED TO BE, BUT AS WE REALLY WERE.

AN EXCELLENT PHOTOGRAPHER, AND AN EXCELLENT MAN… AND A VERY GOOD JOB HE WASN'T PUT OFF BY THE VERY WEIRD JOB THAT WAS THE CURE ON *TOP OF THE POPS* IN 1980!

ROBERT SMITH
LONDON, JUNE 2021

'I can honestly say that Robert Smith is my favourite person to photograph; he is very clever, astute, knows what looks good – and he writes great songs.'

It is therefore not very surprising that Paul Cox felt the desire to make a picture book about The Cure.

After leaving school in the mid 1970s, Paul studied Art at Amersham College in Buckinghamshire where he discovered an interest in photography. LFI, an established picture agency, offered Paul a job as an apprentice but, wary of not finishing his course, he declined their offer. A few months later, LFI asked for a second time, and despite still not having completed his studies, Paul embarked on an adventure, photographing live bands at venues in London. Artists such as Blondie, Sid Vicious, Ian Drury – to name a few – were photographed by Paul at iconic venues such as the Marquee, Hope and Anchor pub and the Electric Ballroom. He definitly got bashed about by the fans whilst taking photos! During this period Paul did a lot of live shoots, but also worked for a number of music magazines and record companies. After three years, Paul left the agency and set up a partnership with a fellow photographer from LFI, Simon Fowler. They set up a studio in an amazing rundown building in Belgravia. After a few years there, they moved to the studio in Fulham, going their separate ways in the mid-eighties.

Paul's strategy was simple and efficient. In between working on commissions from record companies, he looked for new up-and-coming bands on the verge of success. It worked with Adam and the Ants and Duran Duran for example, who exploded in the charts weeks after doing a session with Paul. It definitely worked with The Cure.

On most weeks in the early 1980s Paul went to the BBC studios for *Top of the Pops* to photograph the bands. This is where Paul first encountered The Cure in 1980. He had a commission in 1981 from the bizarre pop magazine *Flexipop!*. At this time, The Cure had three band members, and Paul made it his mission to get a proper studio session with the band. This finally took place in 1984. A trusting relationship was established over the years, despite the band's line-up changing several times. Paul photographed the band on many occasions at his studio in Fulham, often starting late in the day and going on very late into the night. These sessions were always busy and incredibly productive. Paul also went on many location shoots with the band, getting inspiration from Robert and the many interesting surroundings they found themselves in. Many commissions were directly from Robert, a rare situation in the music business, and for many years Paul appreciated the exchange of ideas with Robert, his dedication to his art, and even his occasional eccentricity!

The proof is in this book.

Lydie Barbarian & Helen Cox
London, April 2021

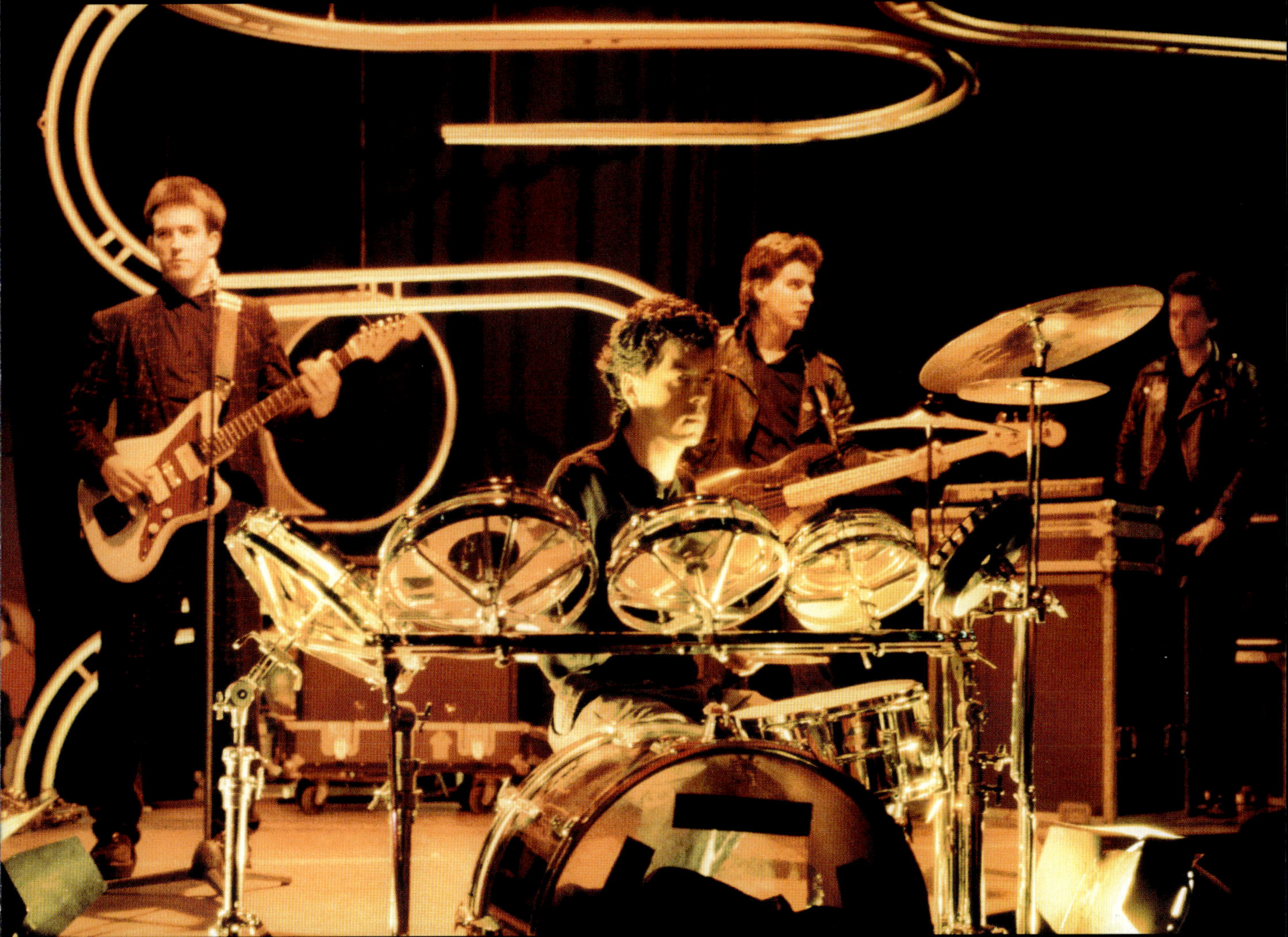

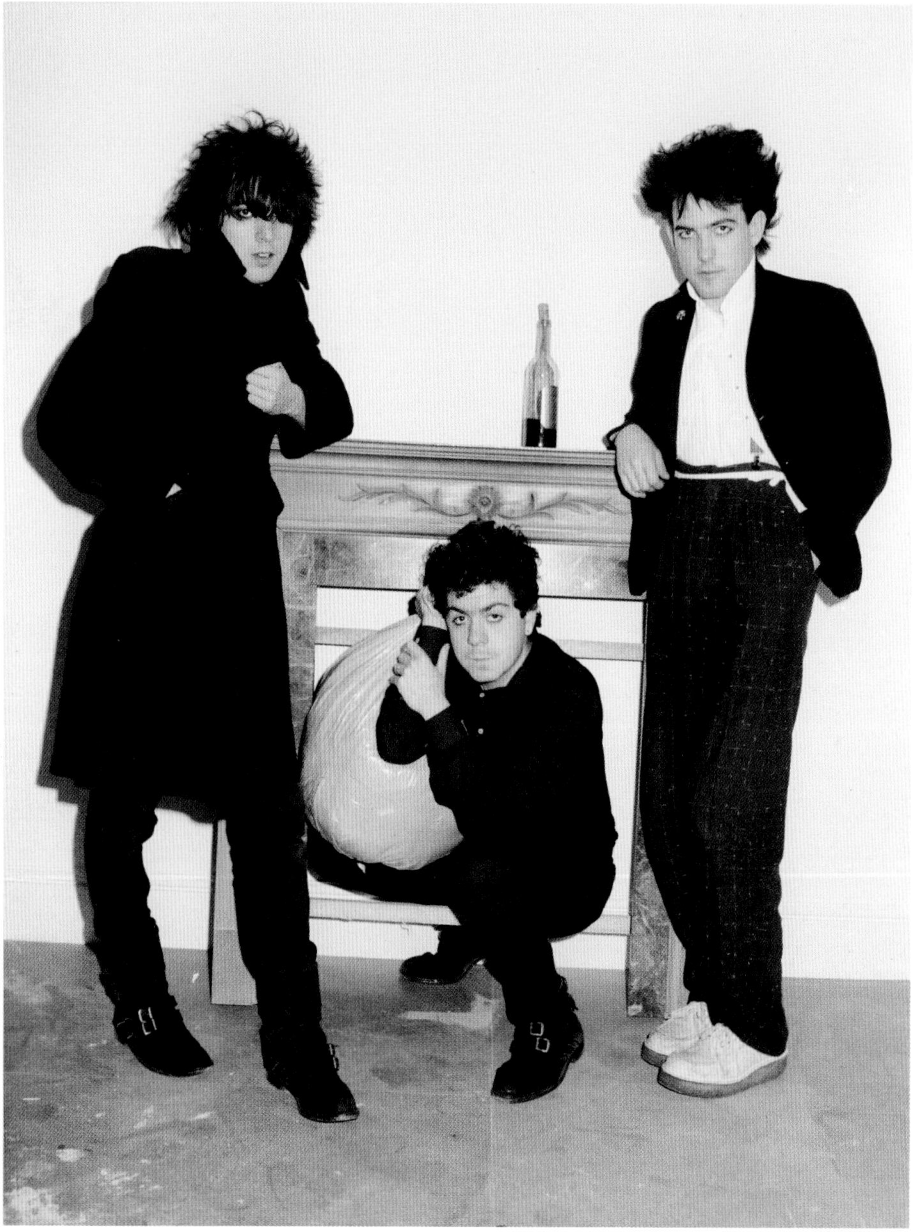

FICTION RECORDS
London W1
1981

Paul: I started doing a few jobs for *Flexipop!* magazine, and one of the commissions was to take photographs of The Cure, which I jumped at as I had been trying to set up a session through Polydor Records with no luck. I met the band at Fiction Records and had just half an hour to get something on film. This was a bit of a pressure, especially as the band members weren't overly co-operative at this time. It made me want to get more though, as they had a certain presence!

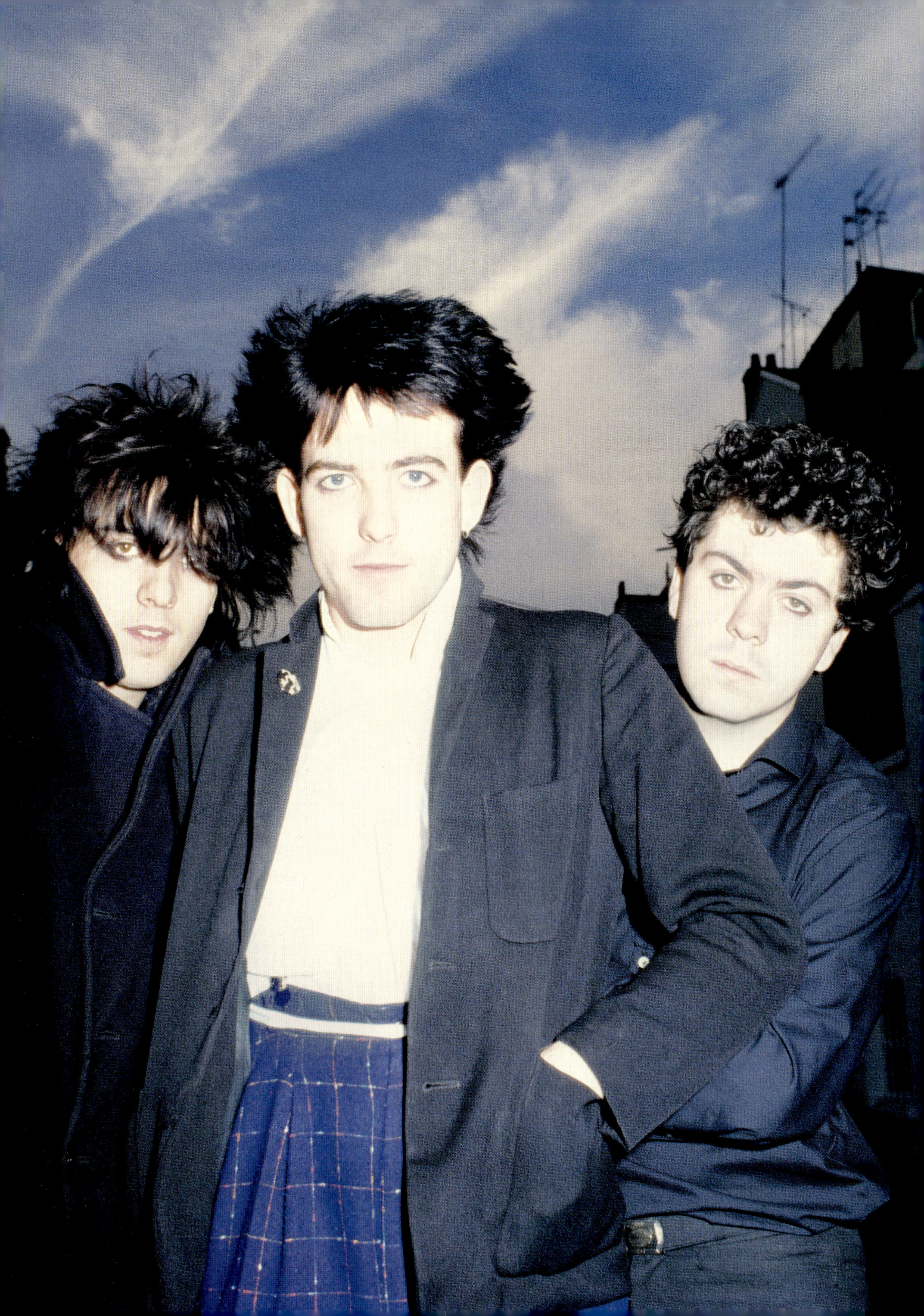

TOP OF THE POPS
'Primary'
16th April 1981

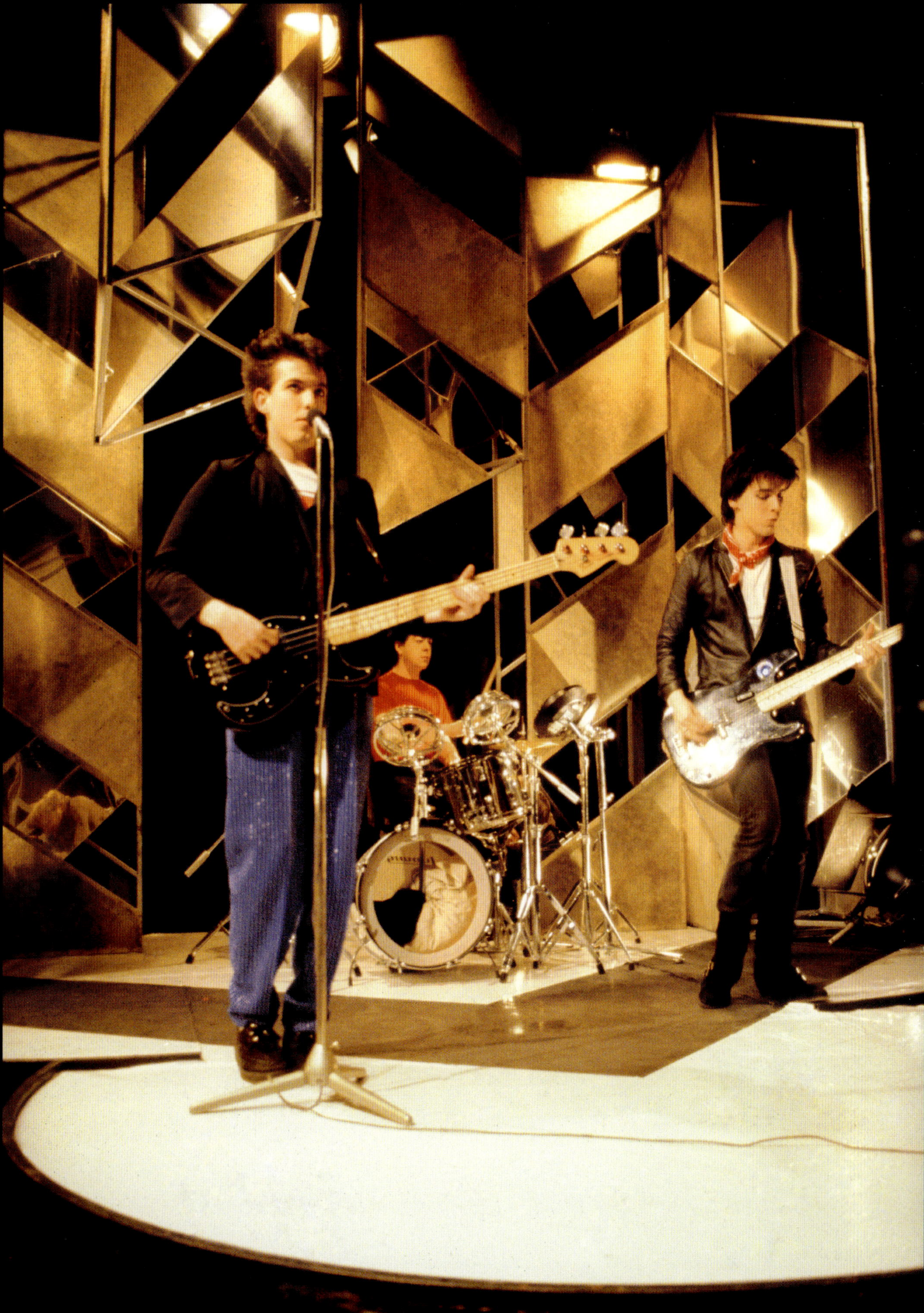

FULHAM STUDIO
[p. 12 to 19]
1984

ROBERT: THIS WAS MY/OUR FIRST VISIT TO YOUR FULHAM STUDIO – PRESS/PROMO SHOTS FOR *THE TOP* ALBUM/TOUR 1984 – FUNNY THAT WE DID A FEW DUO PICTURES, JUST IN CASE THE TOP BAND IMPLODED!

Paul: Finally, through Polydor Records, I managed to set a session. I instigated this off my own back as I wanted to photograph the band in the studio. The understanding was that the band would have total approval of the images. As it happened, the session went well, and this started the beginning of a trusting relationship between me and the band. Once they had reviewed the pictures, they came back to me, and I was surprised to see some of them with hole-punches in them. This meant I could only use the ones without hole-punches; I had never experienced this sort of feedback before! All was well as enough of the pictures were approved.

My studio in Farm Lane, Fulham, was always a bit tricky for people to find because they had to walk up a two-storey ramp to the top of a building which was originally used to keep horse-drawn buses. The building has sadly since been demolished for redevelopment in 2013. Many bands were photographed there.

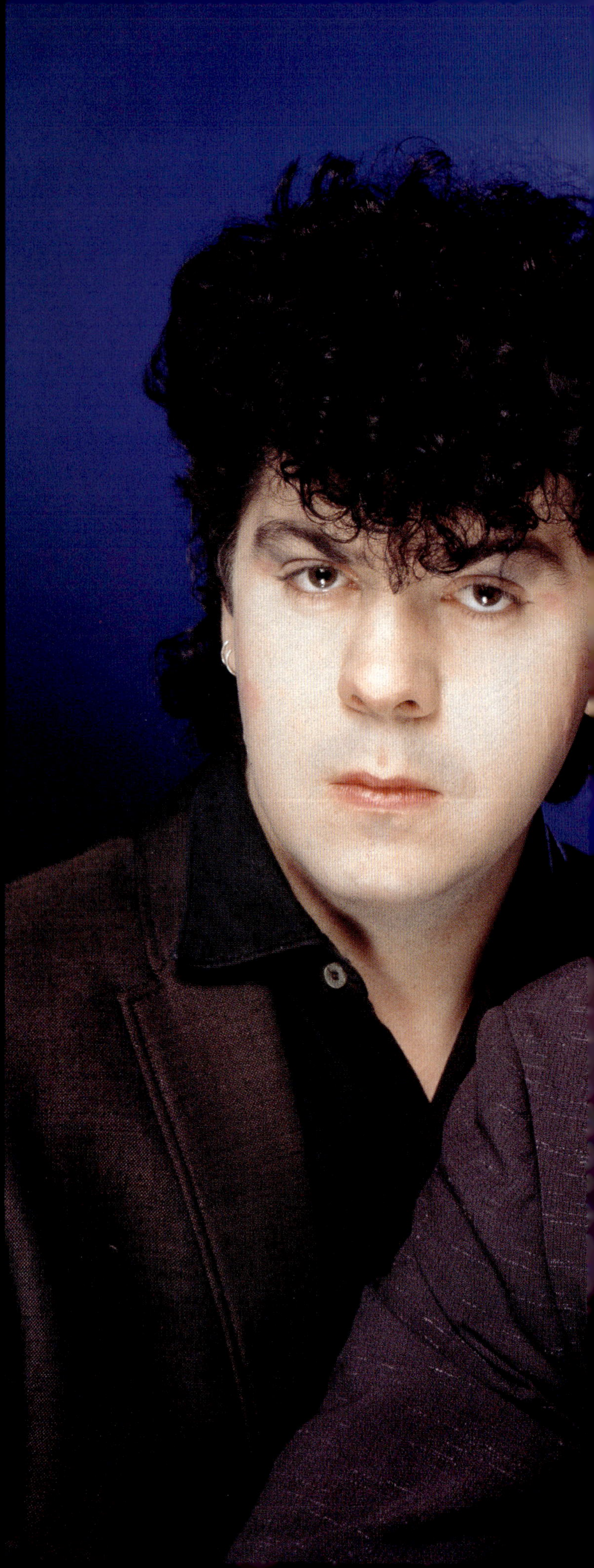

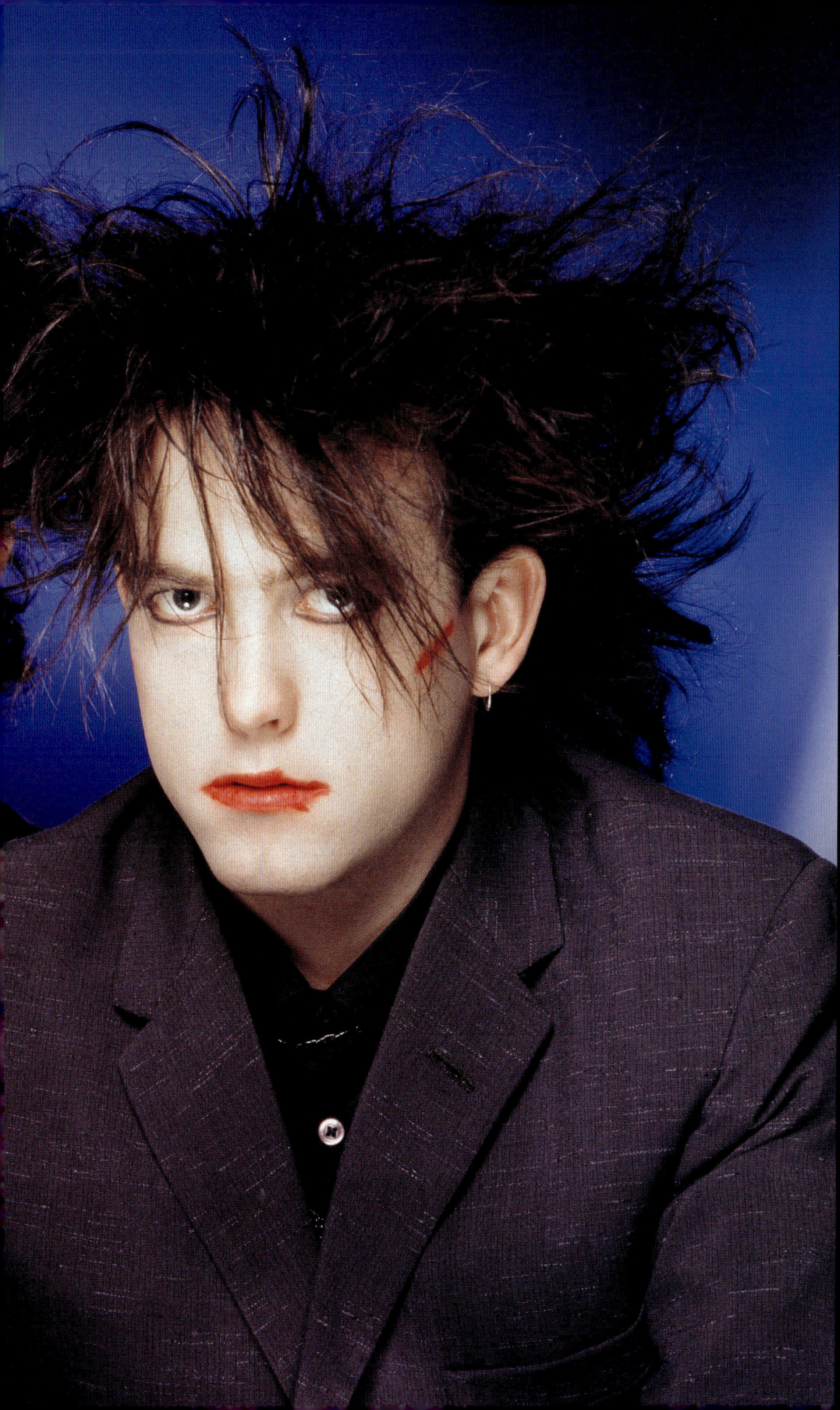

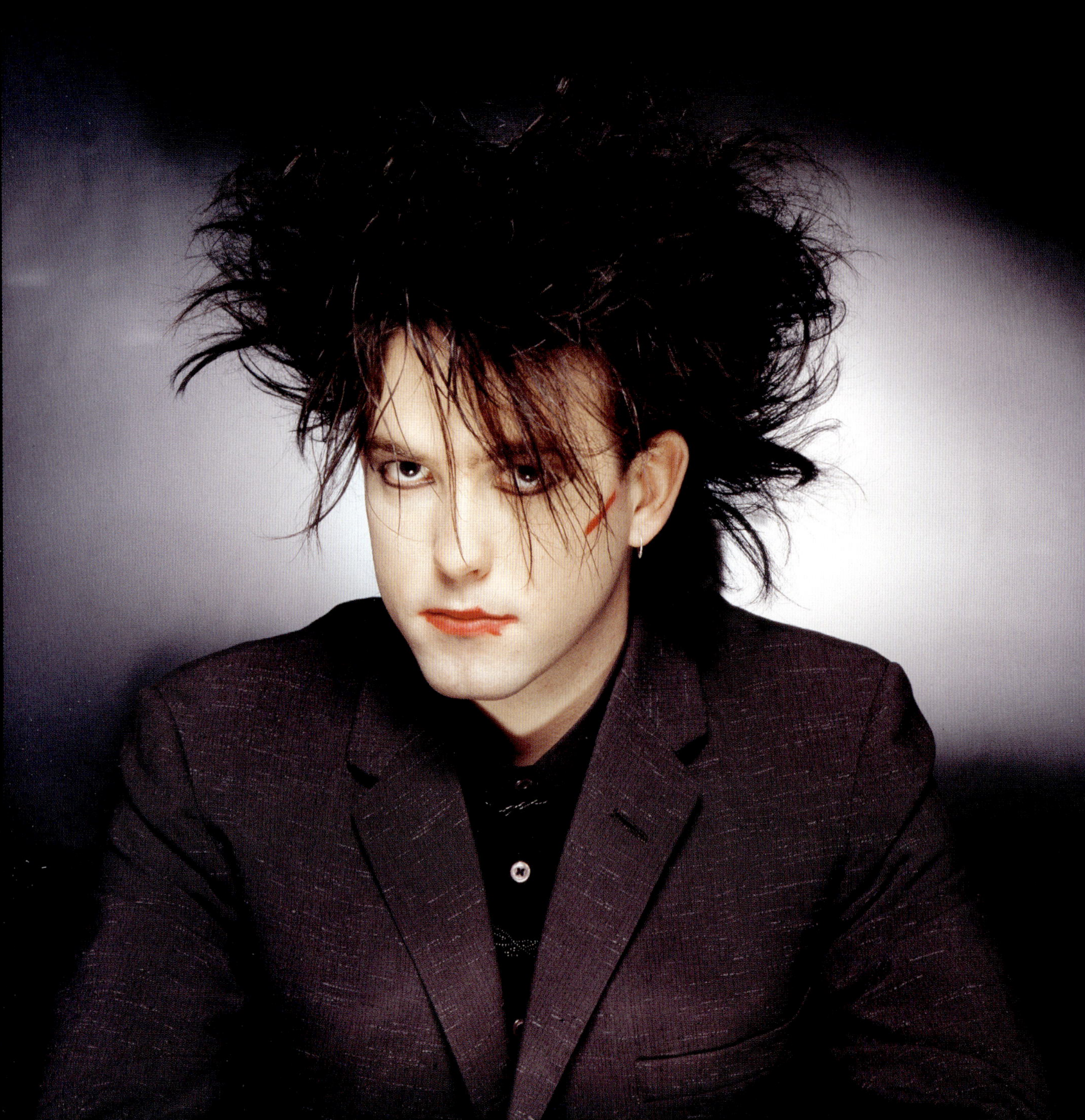

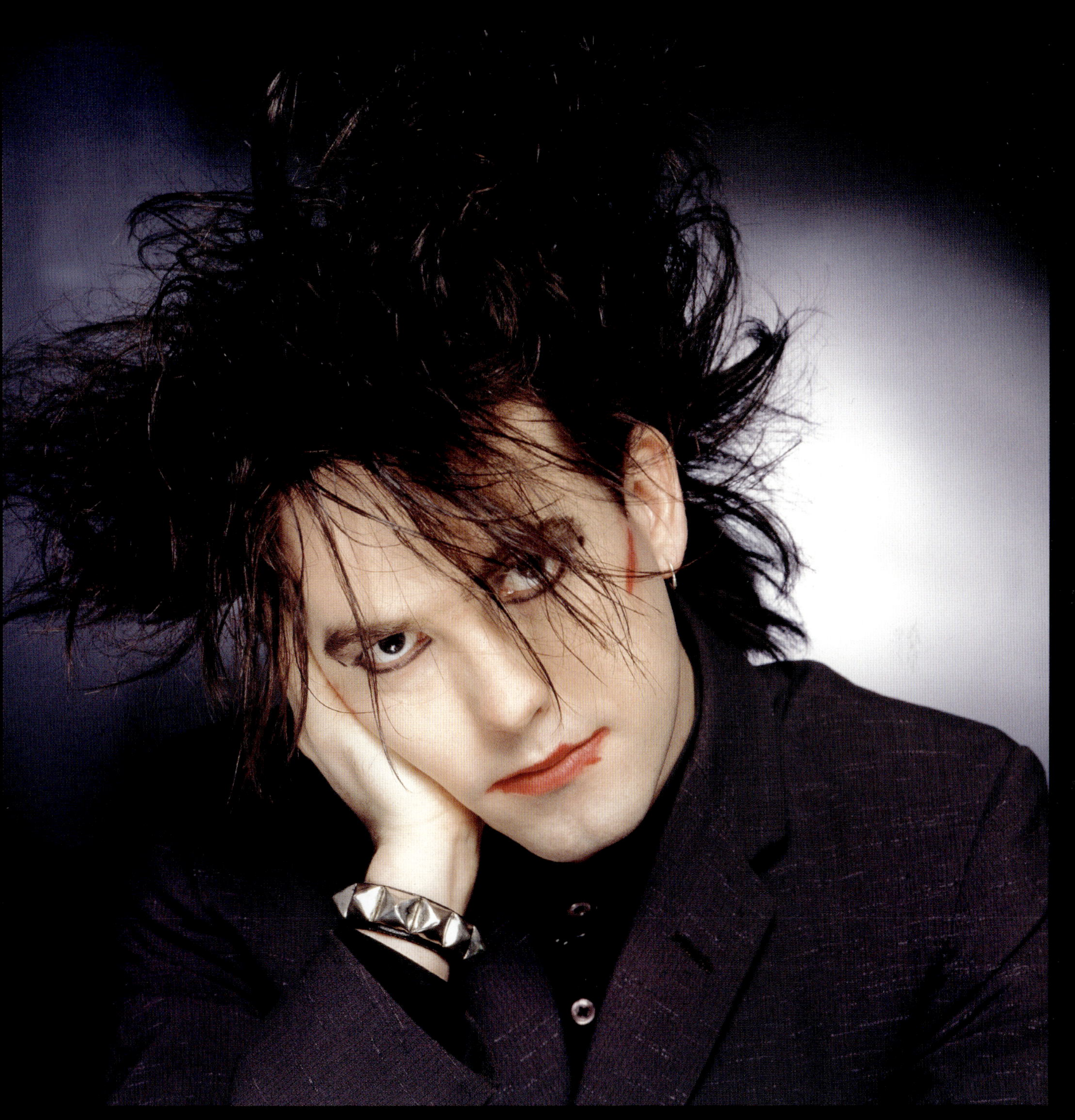

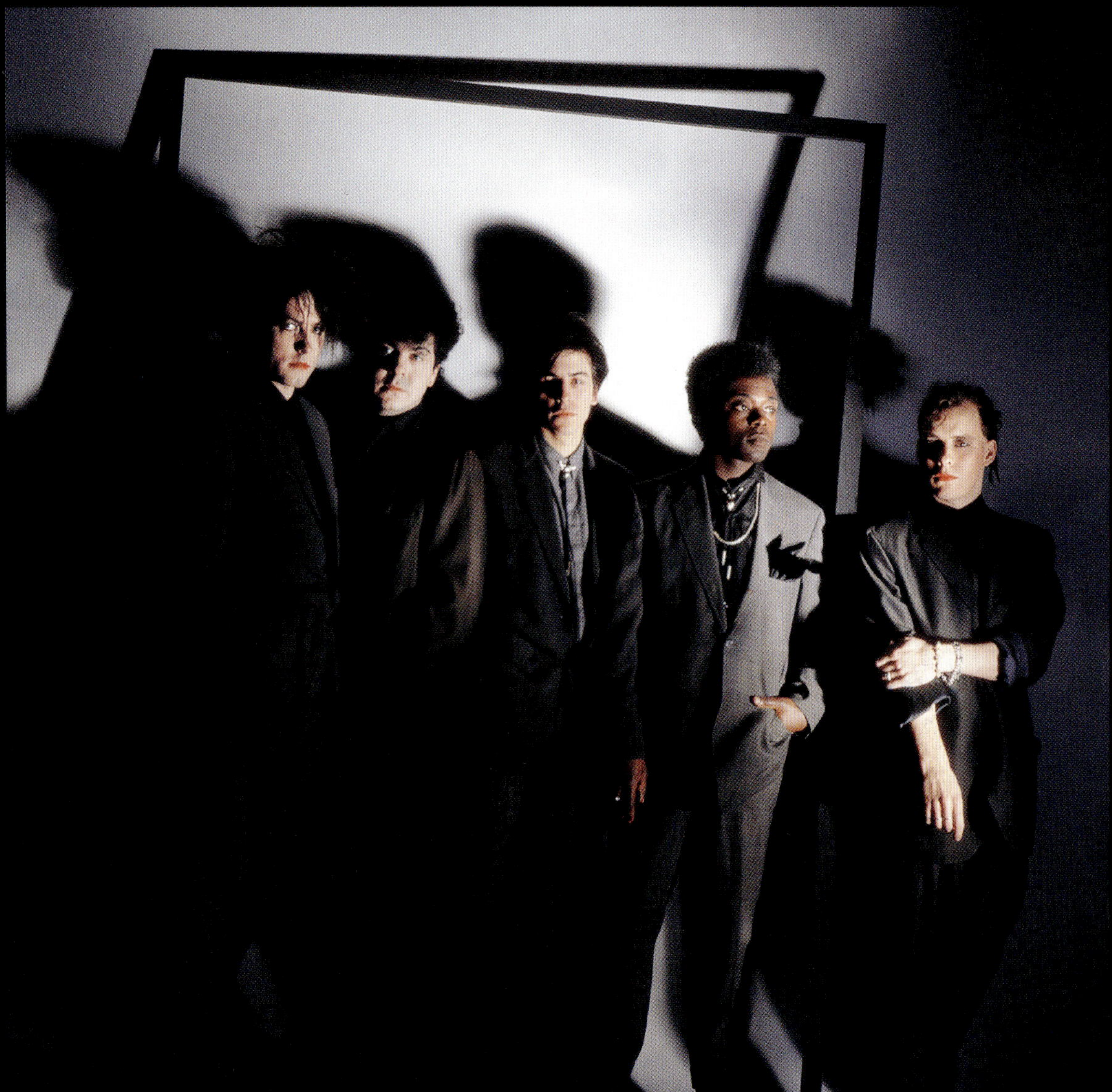

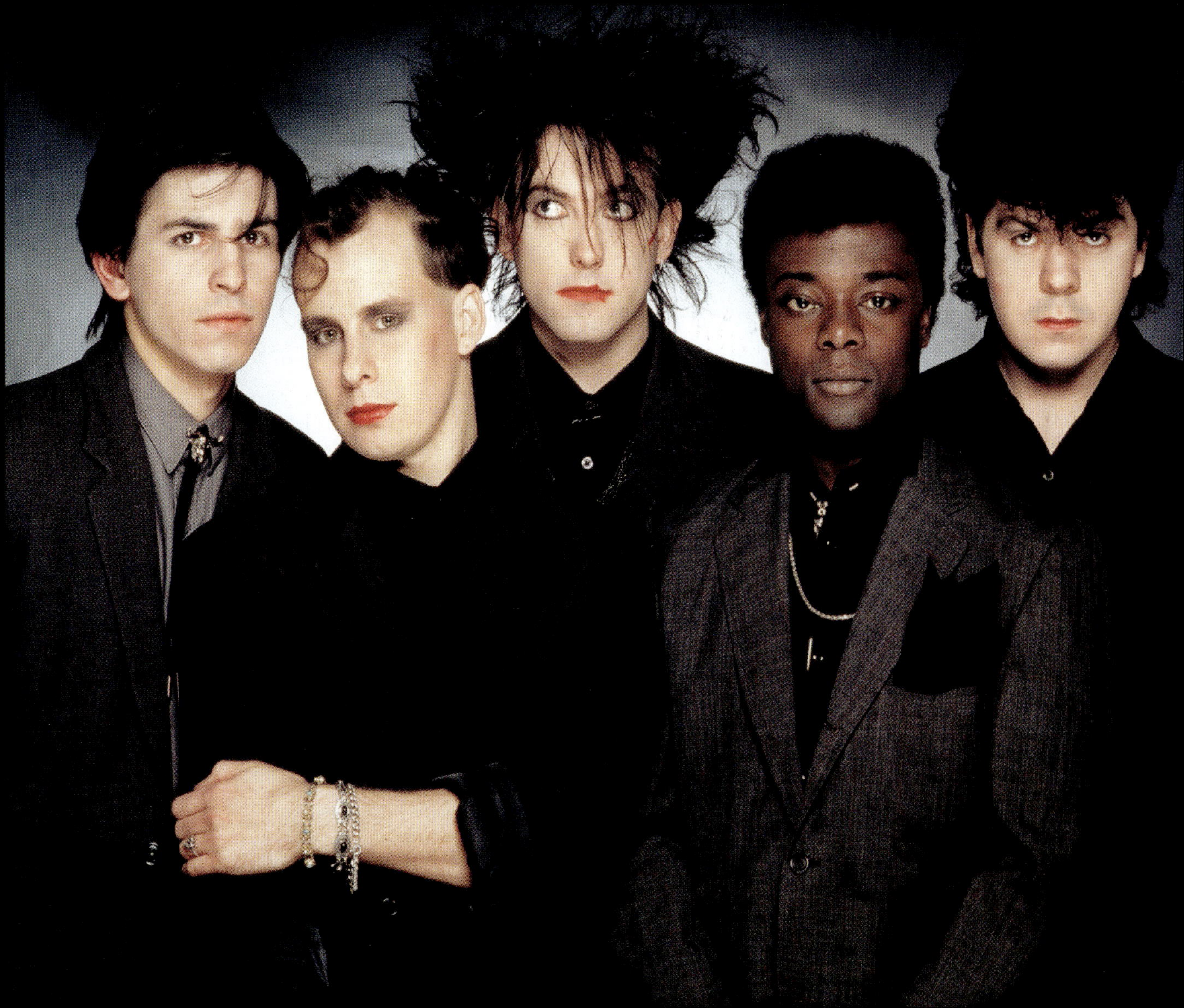

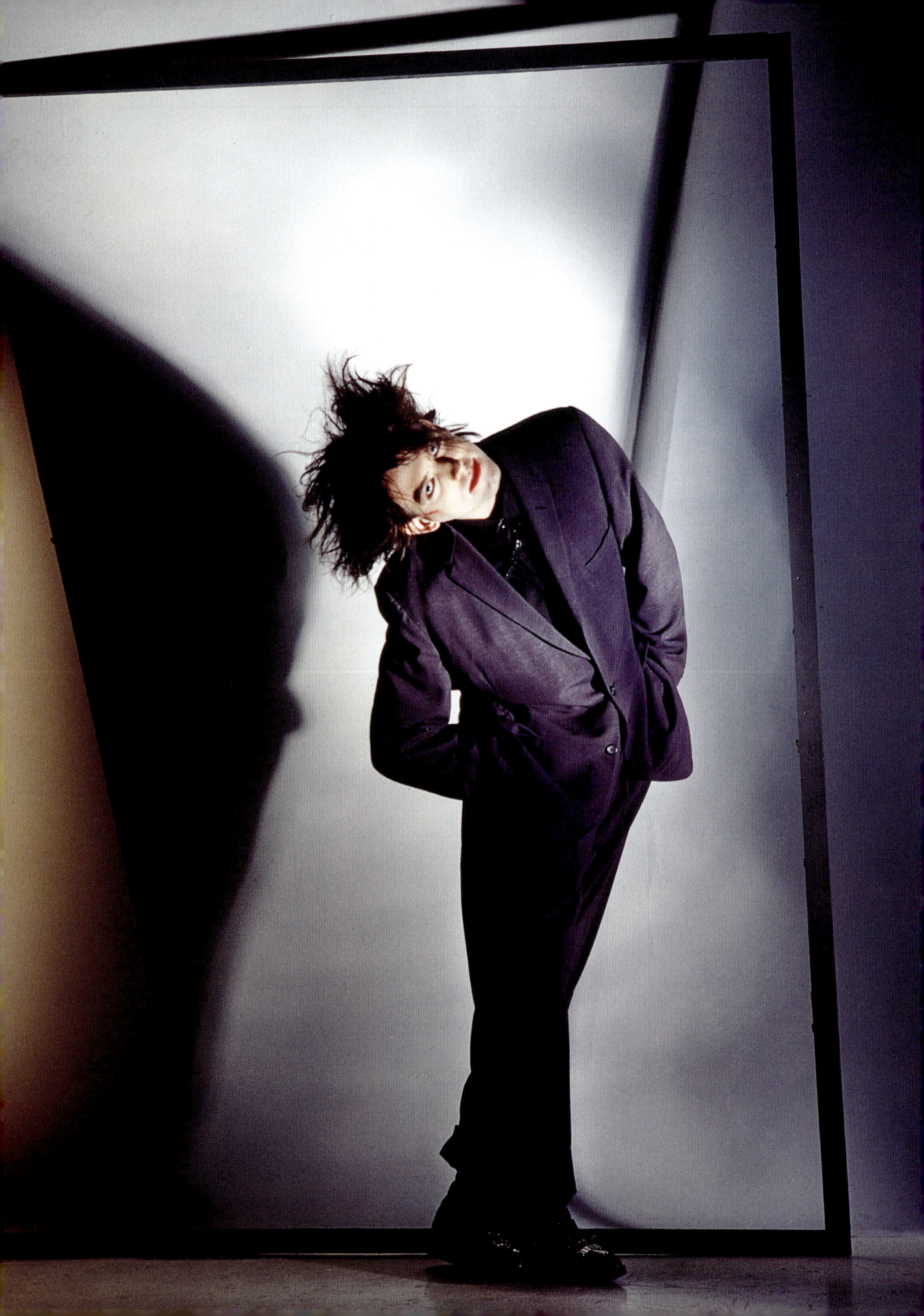

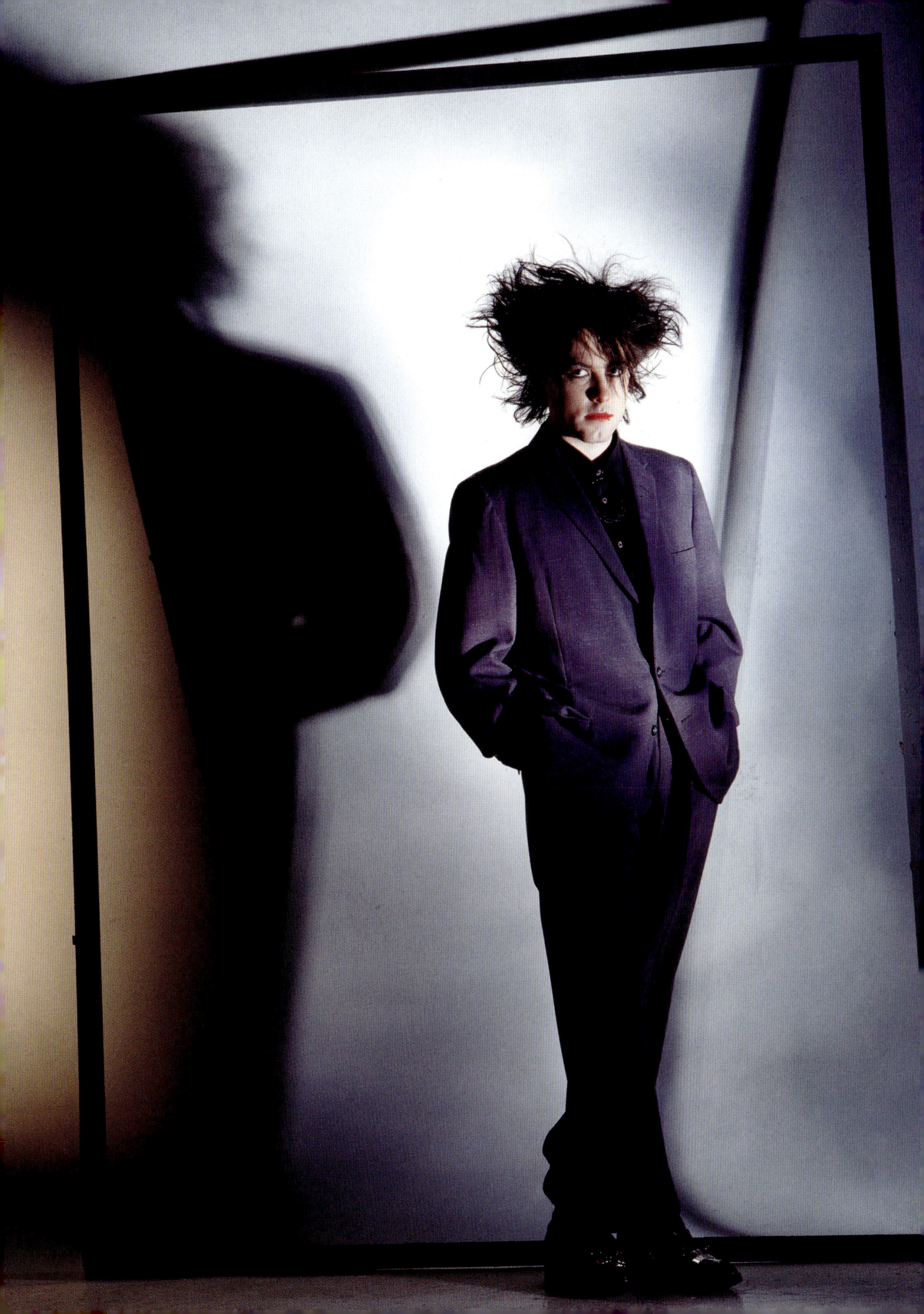

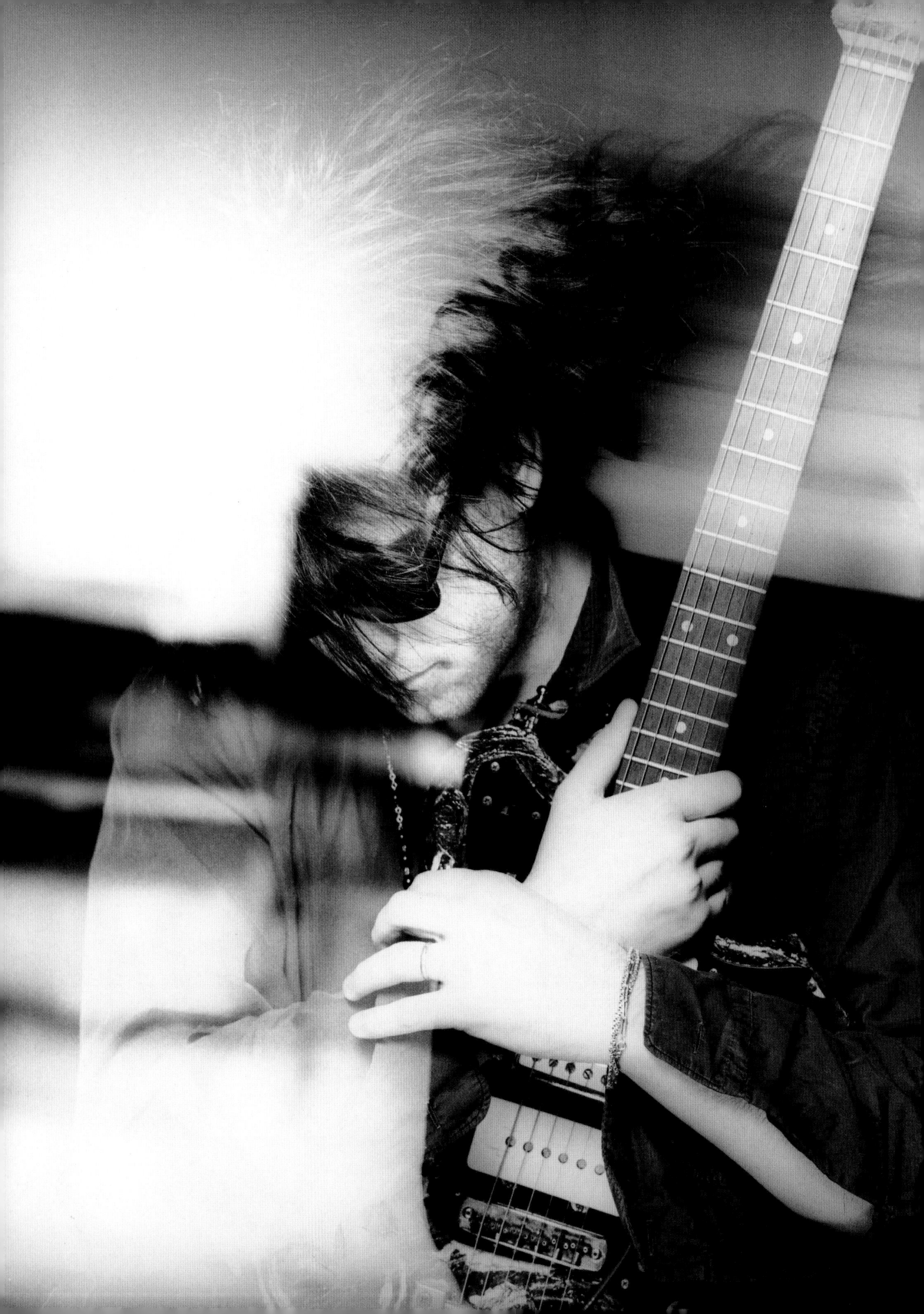

WIMBLEDON THEATRE

Rehearsal for 1984 tour

(p. 20 to 23)

1984

ROBERT: VERY RARE PICTURES OF MY TREASURED FENDER 'FISH' – A VINTAGE JAZZMASTER THAT WAS TURNED INTO 'ART' SOMEWHERE ALONG THE WAY... AND YOU CAN ALMOST HEAR MY 'COOL' SHADES SCREAMING 'VERY HEAVY NIGHT BEFORE – PLEASE KEEP BACK'!

Paul: I had a phone call from Fiction Records asking me to photograph Robert for *Guitar Magazine*. The band were rehearsing at Wimbledon Theatre for their forthcoming tour. I went up into the 'gods', looking back towards the stage, which gave an interesting perspective. At this point it seemed like I was being commissioned through the band even though this was for a third party.

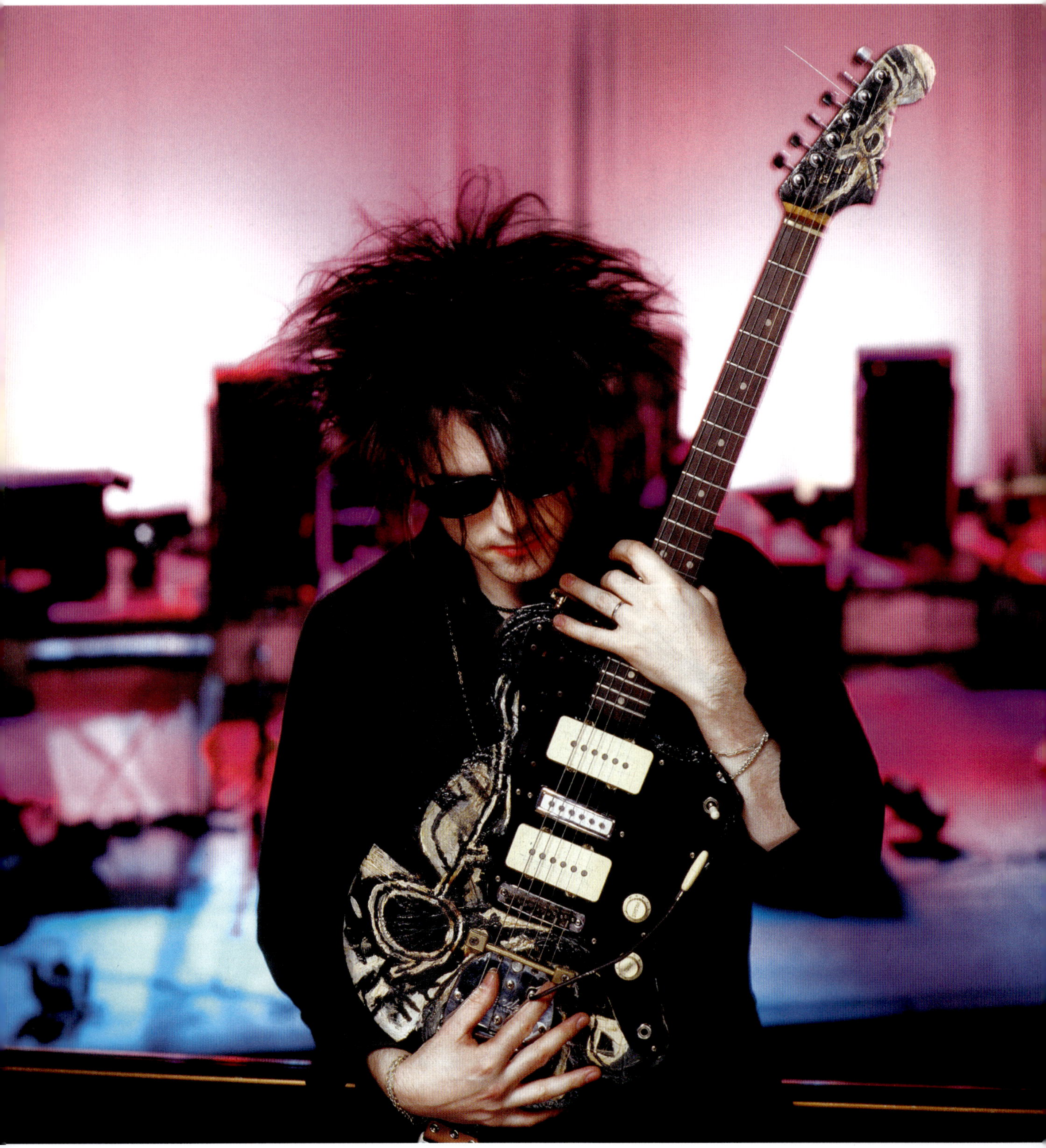

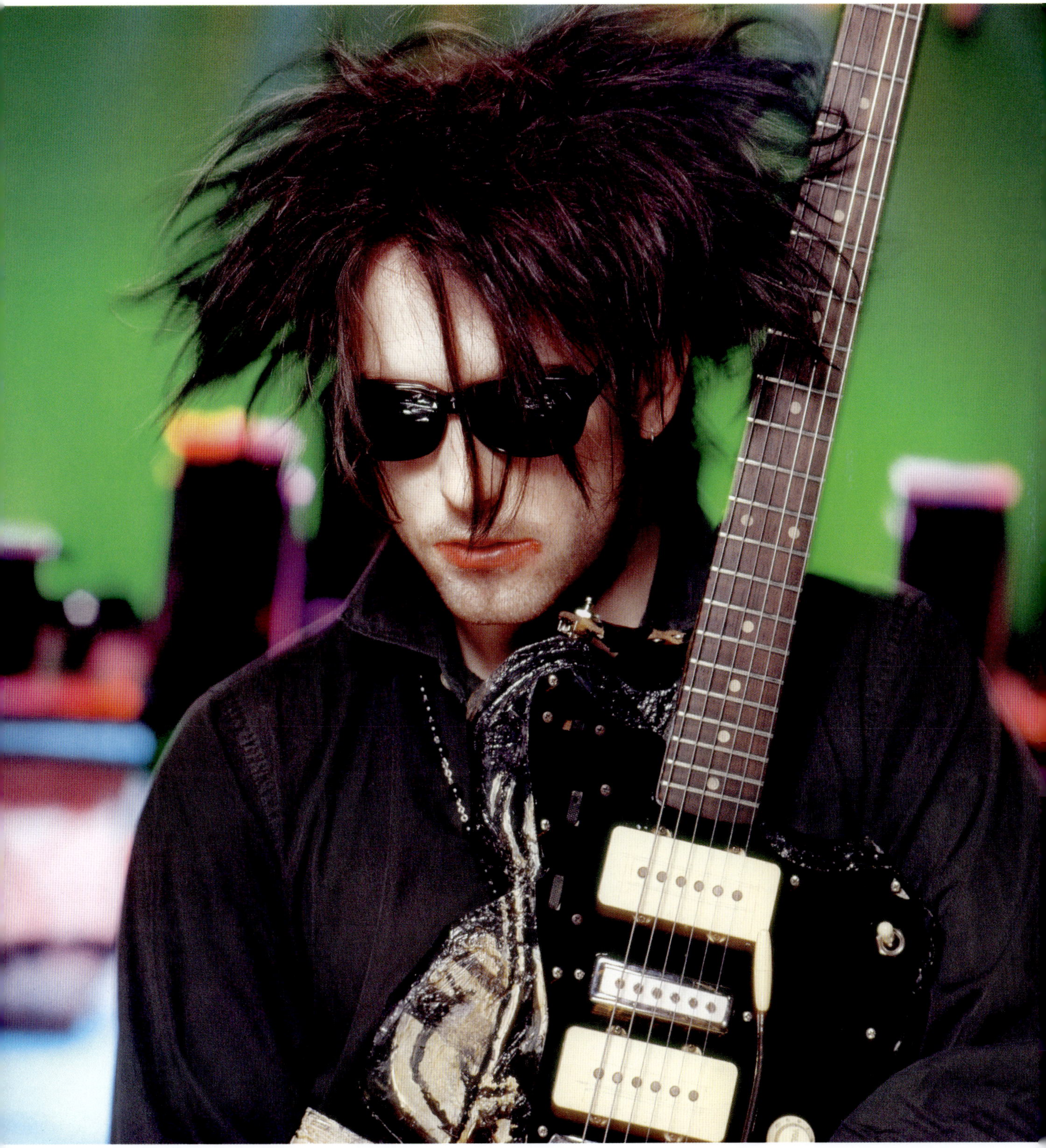

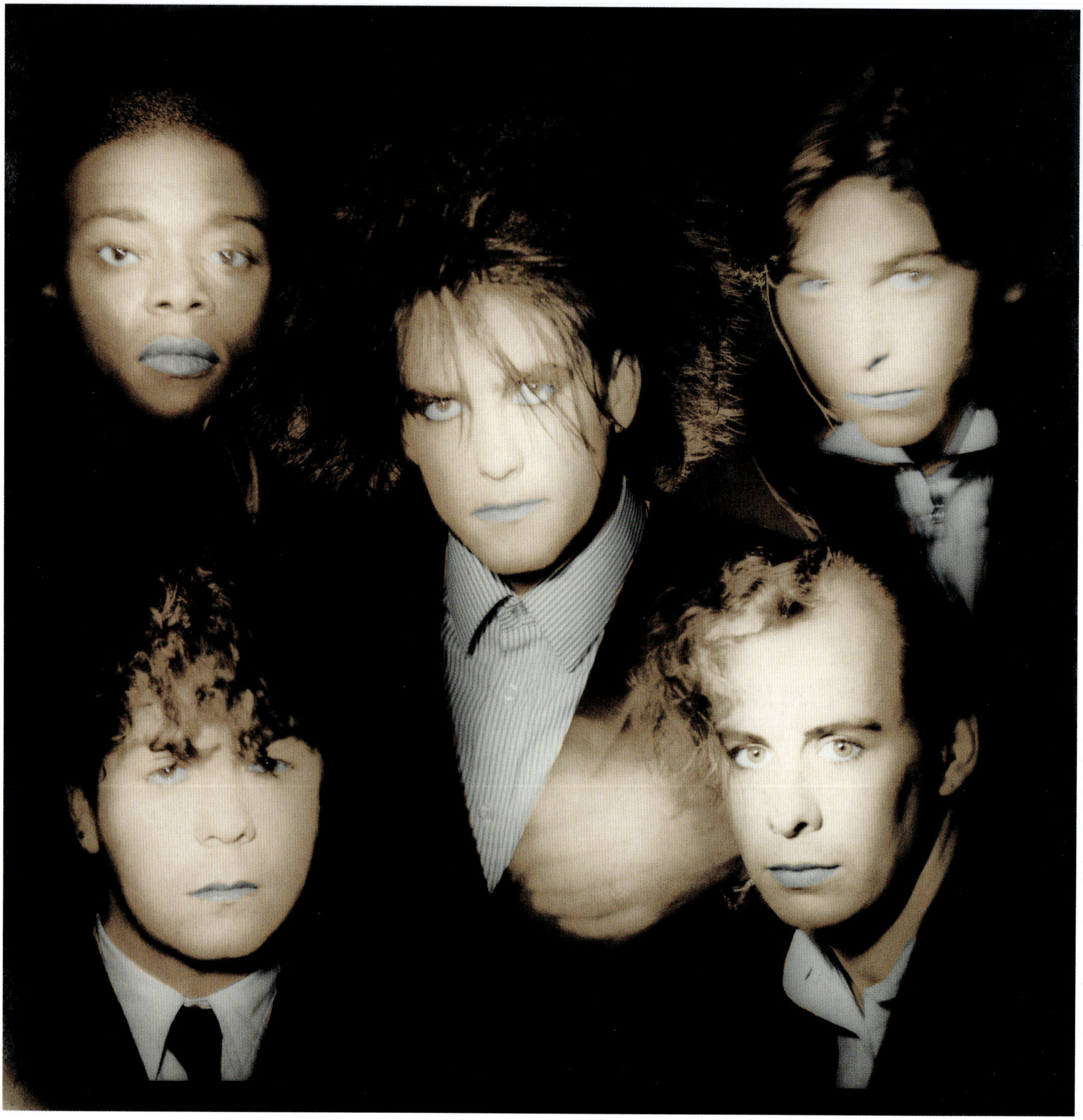

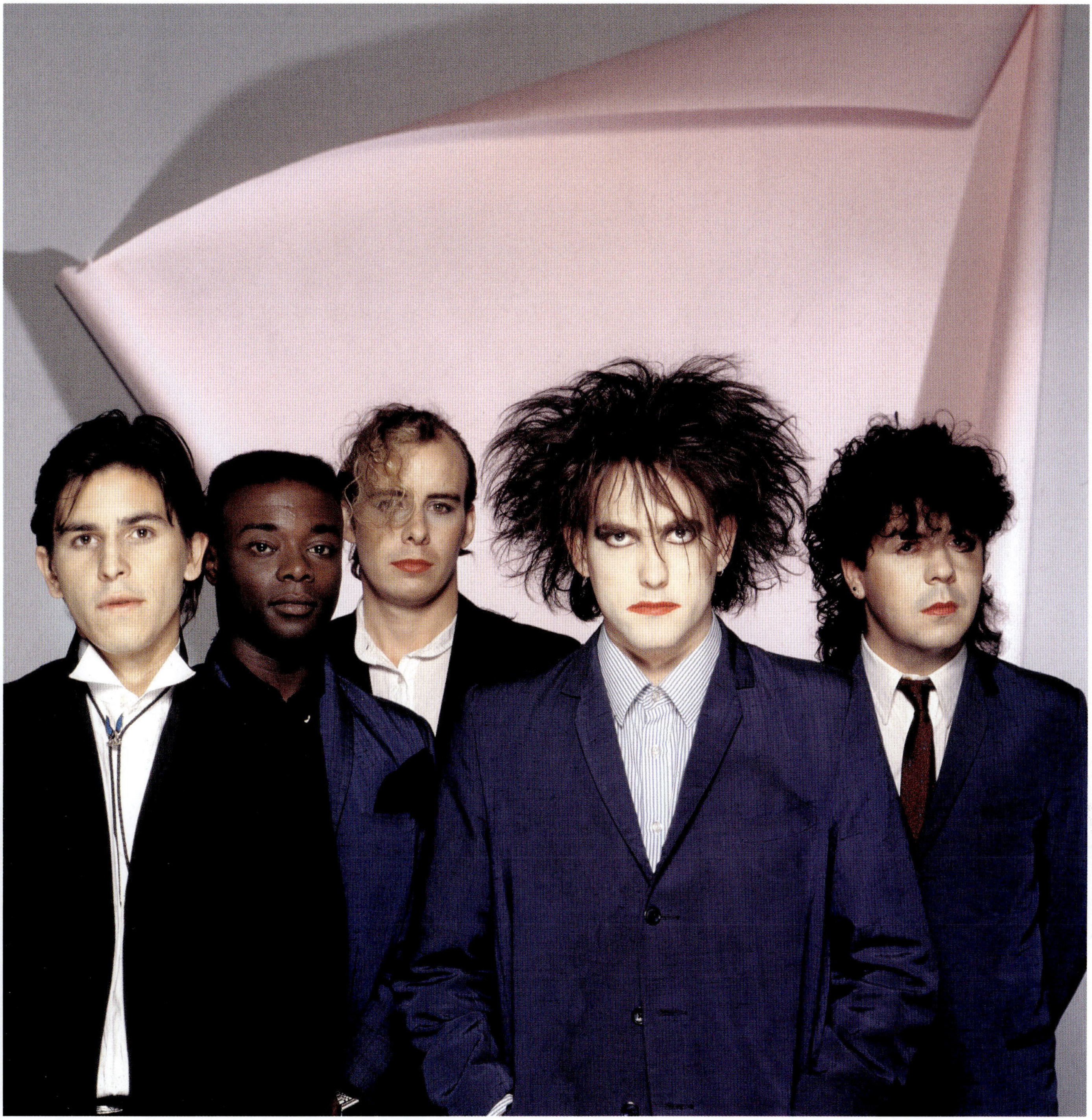

FULHAM STUDIO

(p.24 to 35)

1984

ROBERT: THIS WAS MY/OUR SECOND VISIT TO YOUR FULHAM STUDIO – MORE PRESS/PROMO SHOTS FOR *THE TOP* ALBUM/TOUR 1984 – WE NOW HAVE SUAVE MATCHING SUITS – SHAME ABOUT THE TIES…

Paul: By this time I have been commissioned by the band to do another session, which I was chuffed about. One of my strengths was to photograph a number of people to get the best out of all of them. Robert was always an interesting muse who kept everyone on their toes.

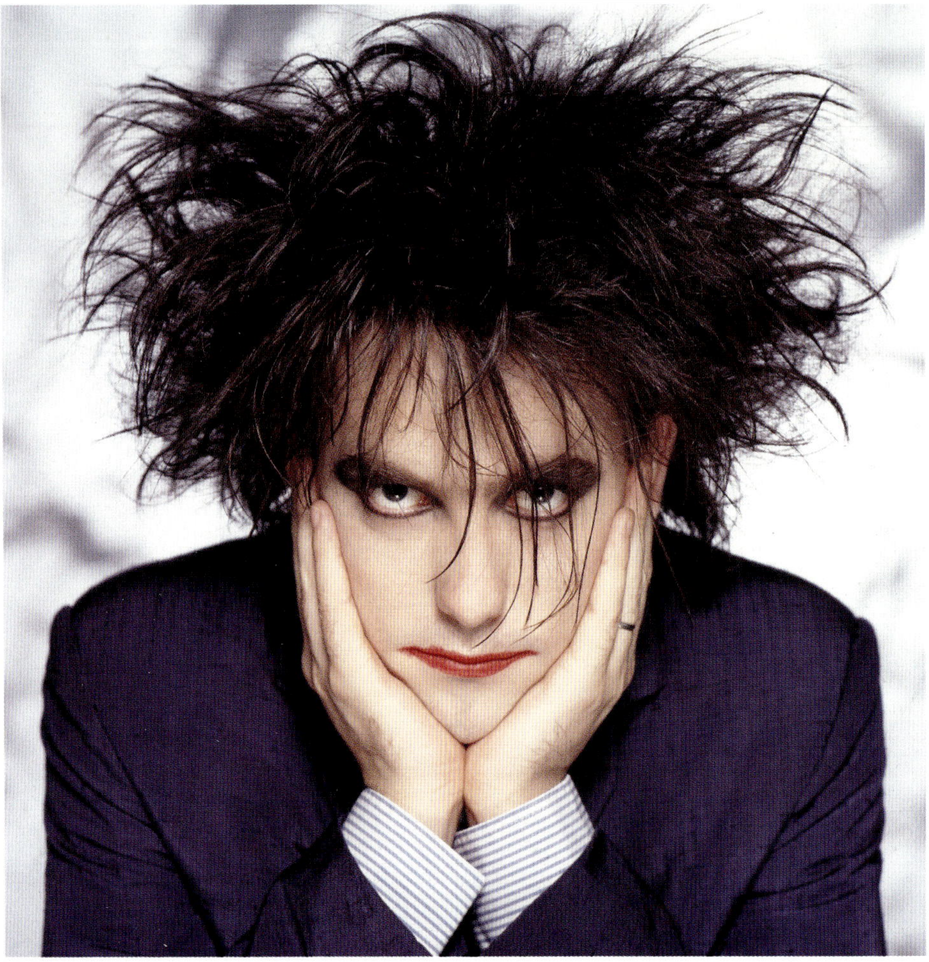

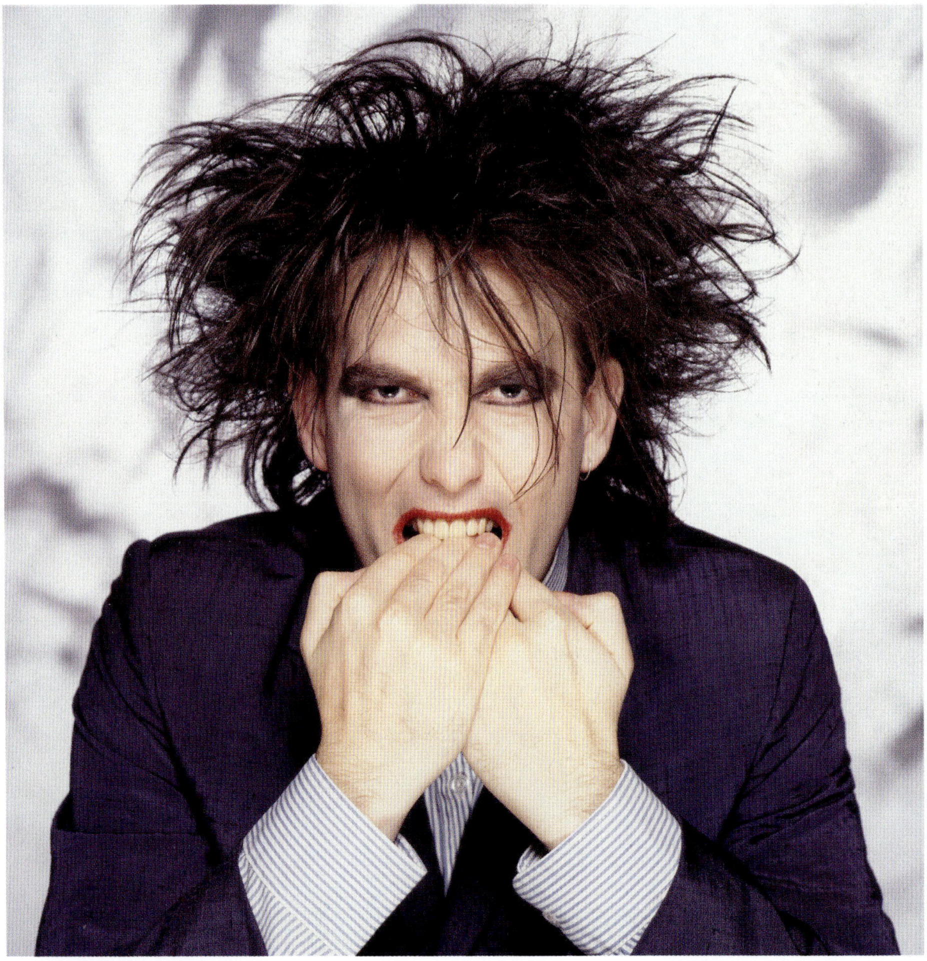

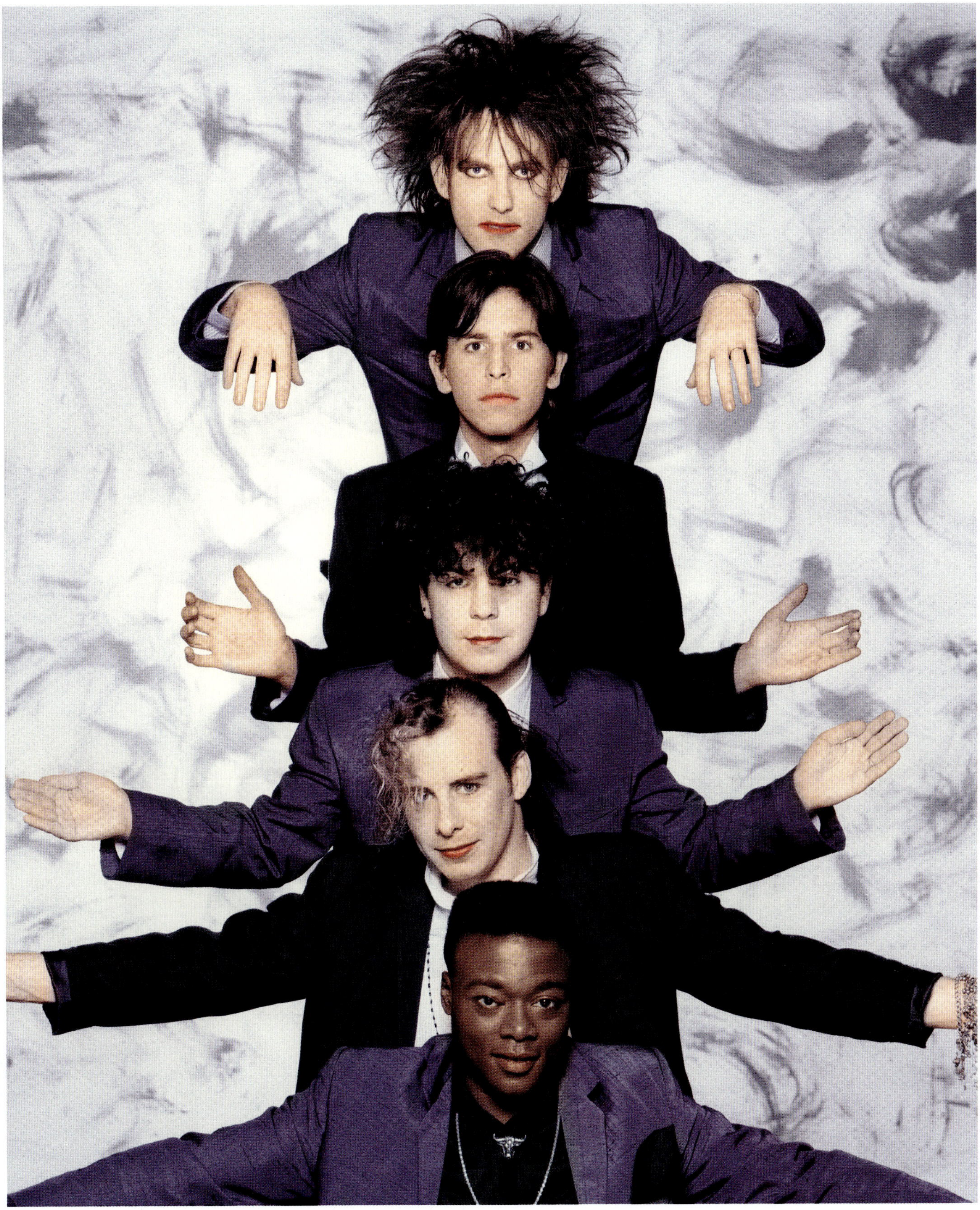

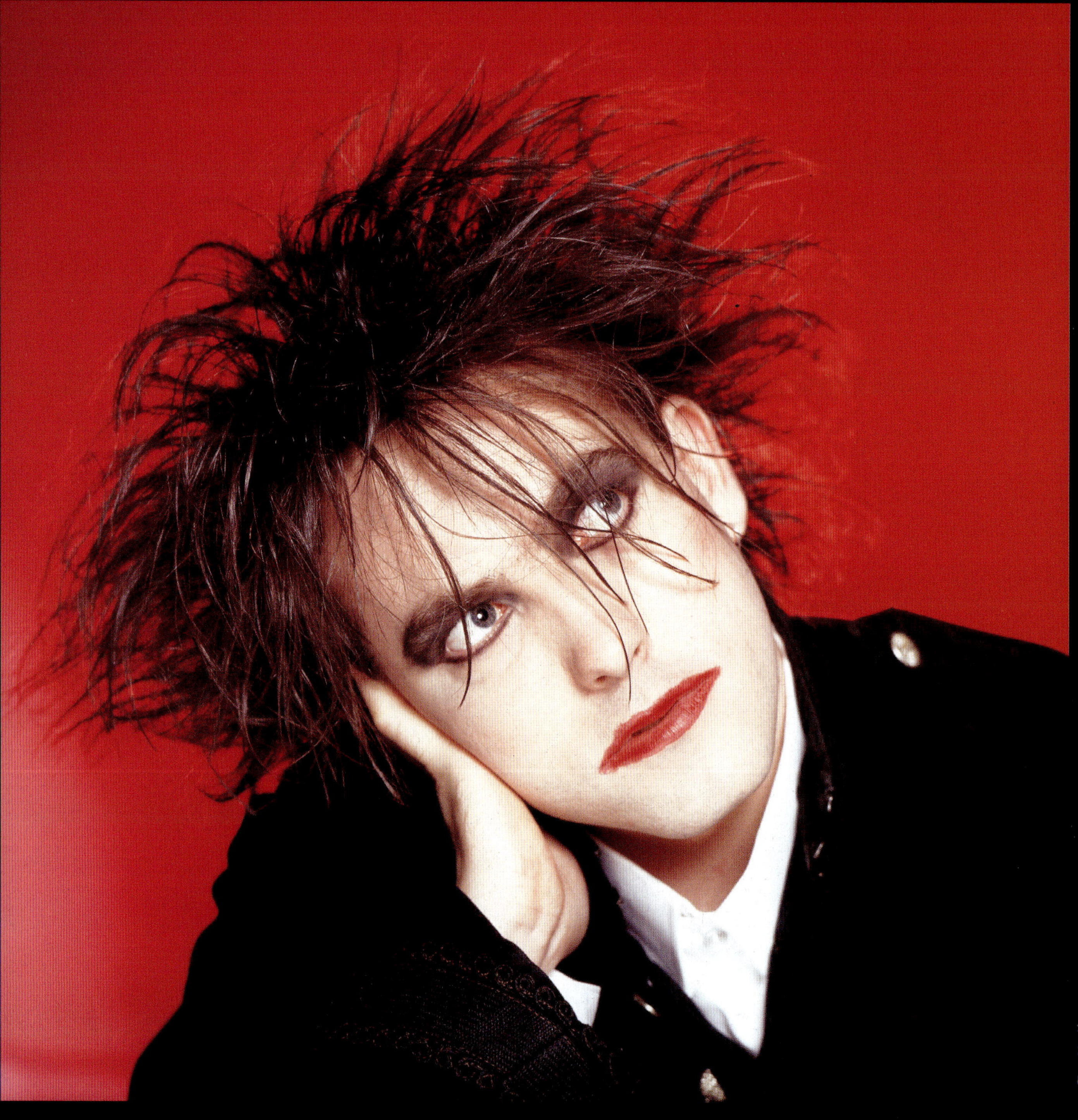

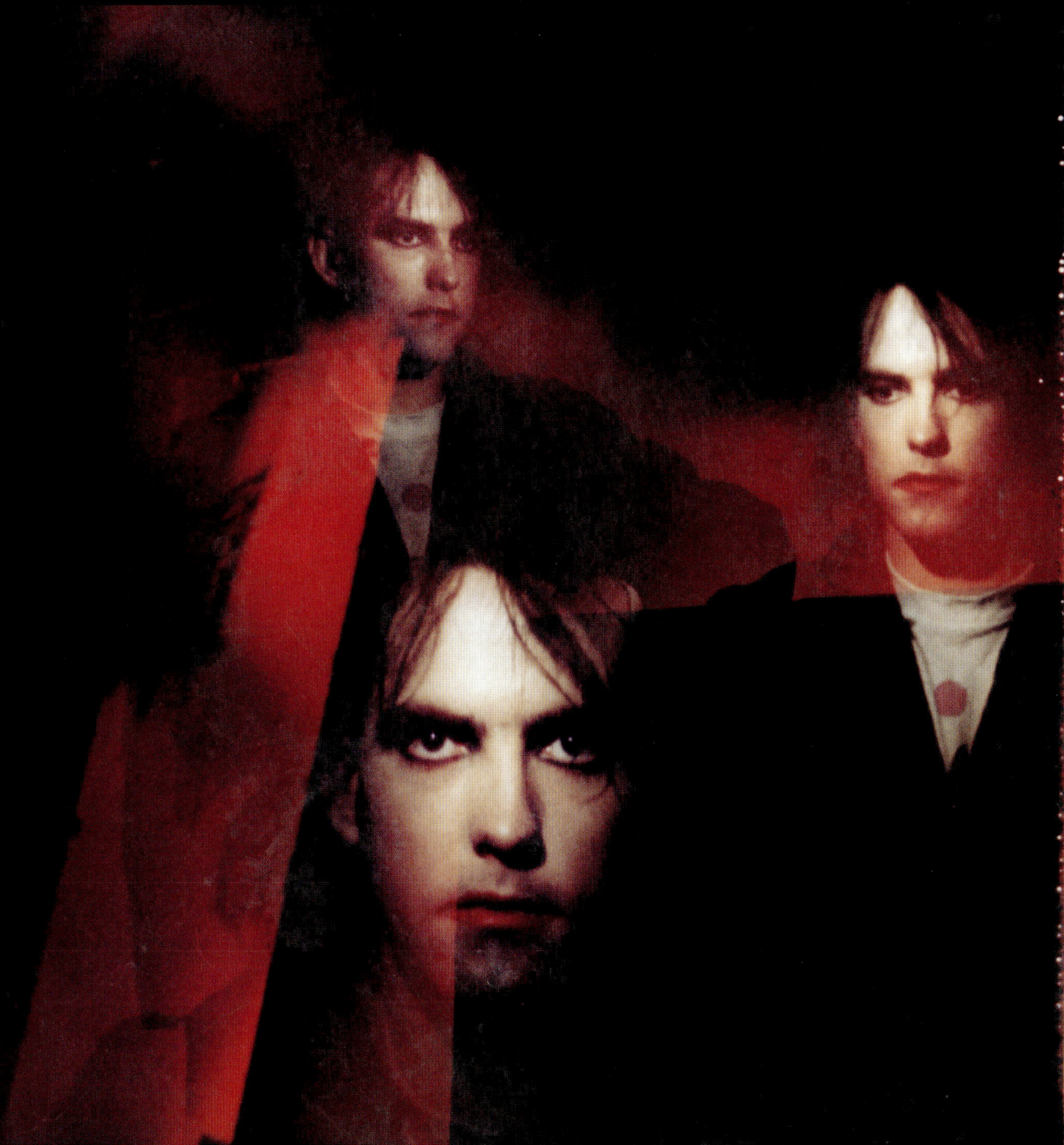

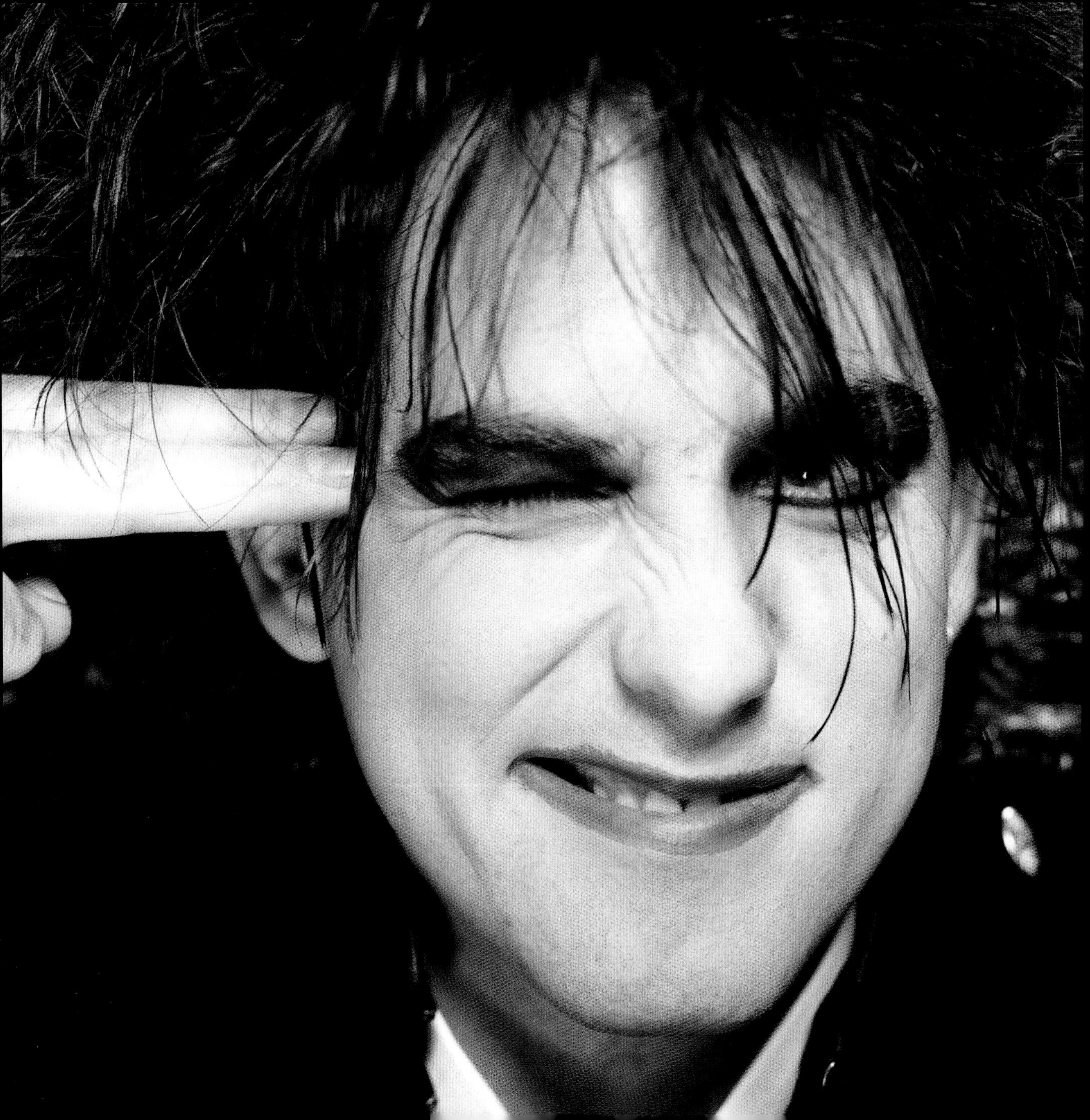

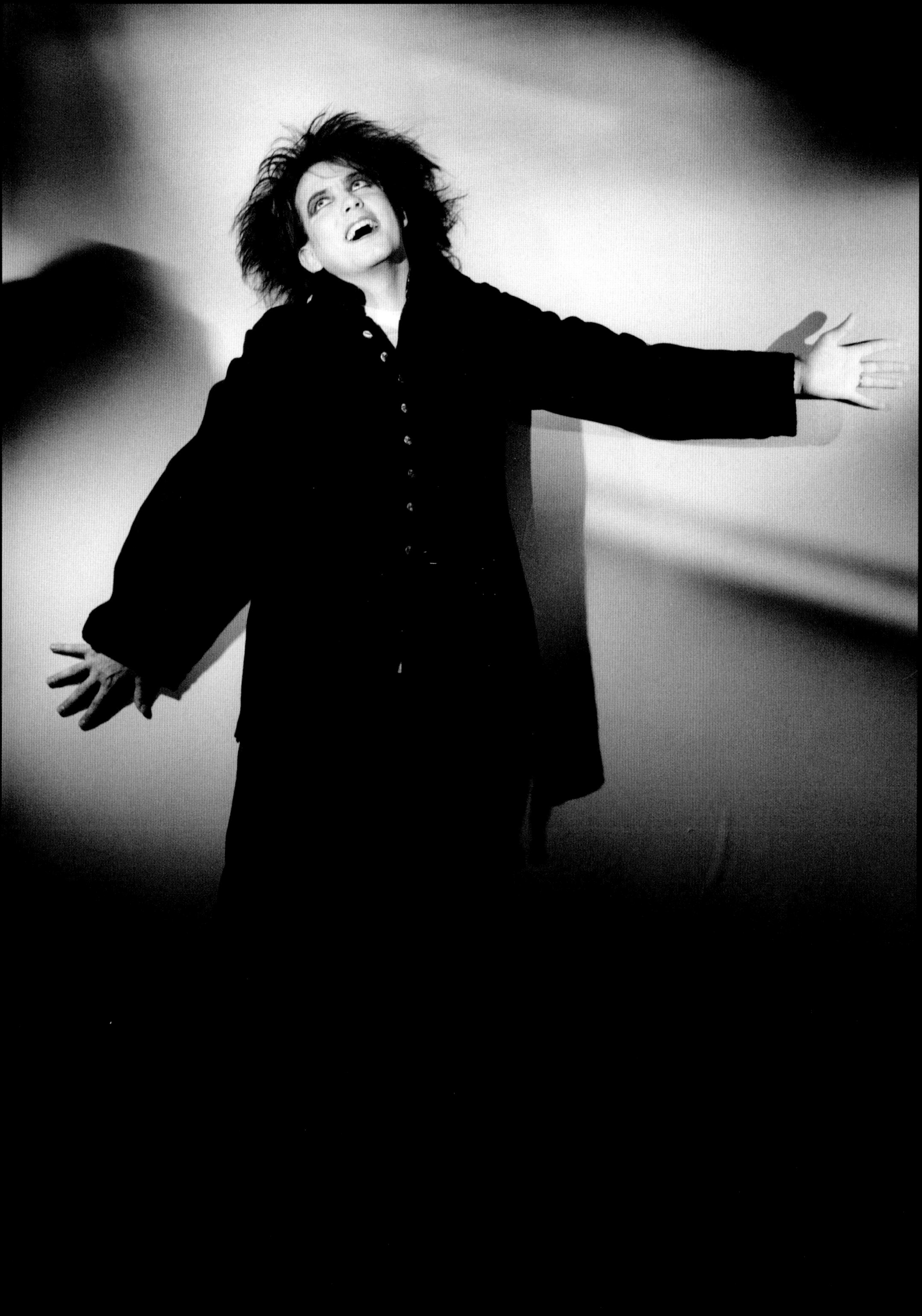

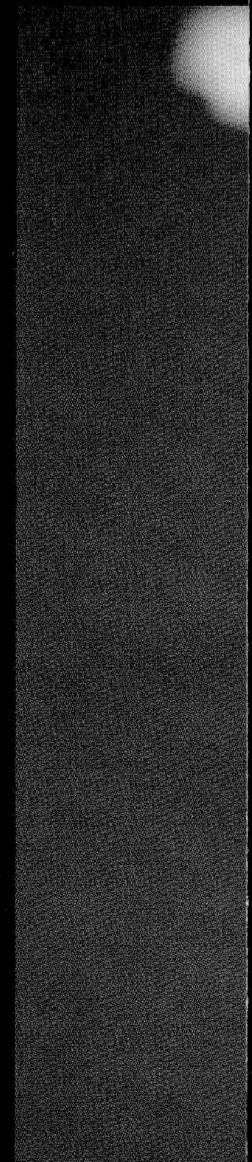

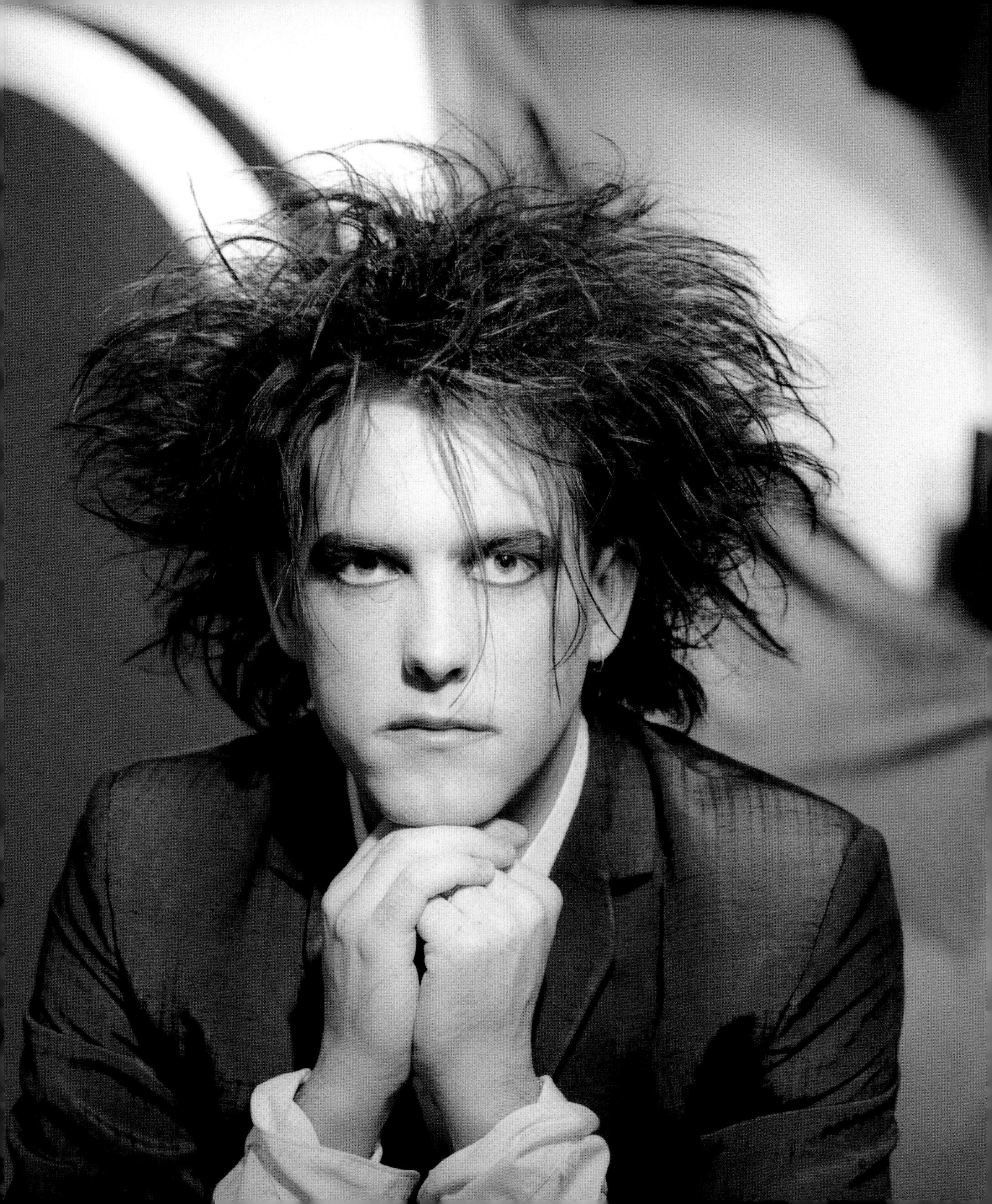

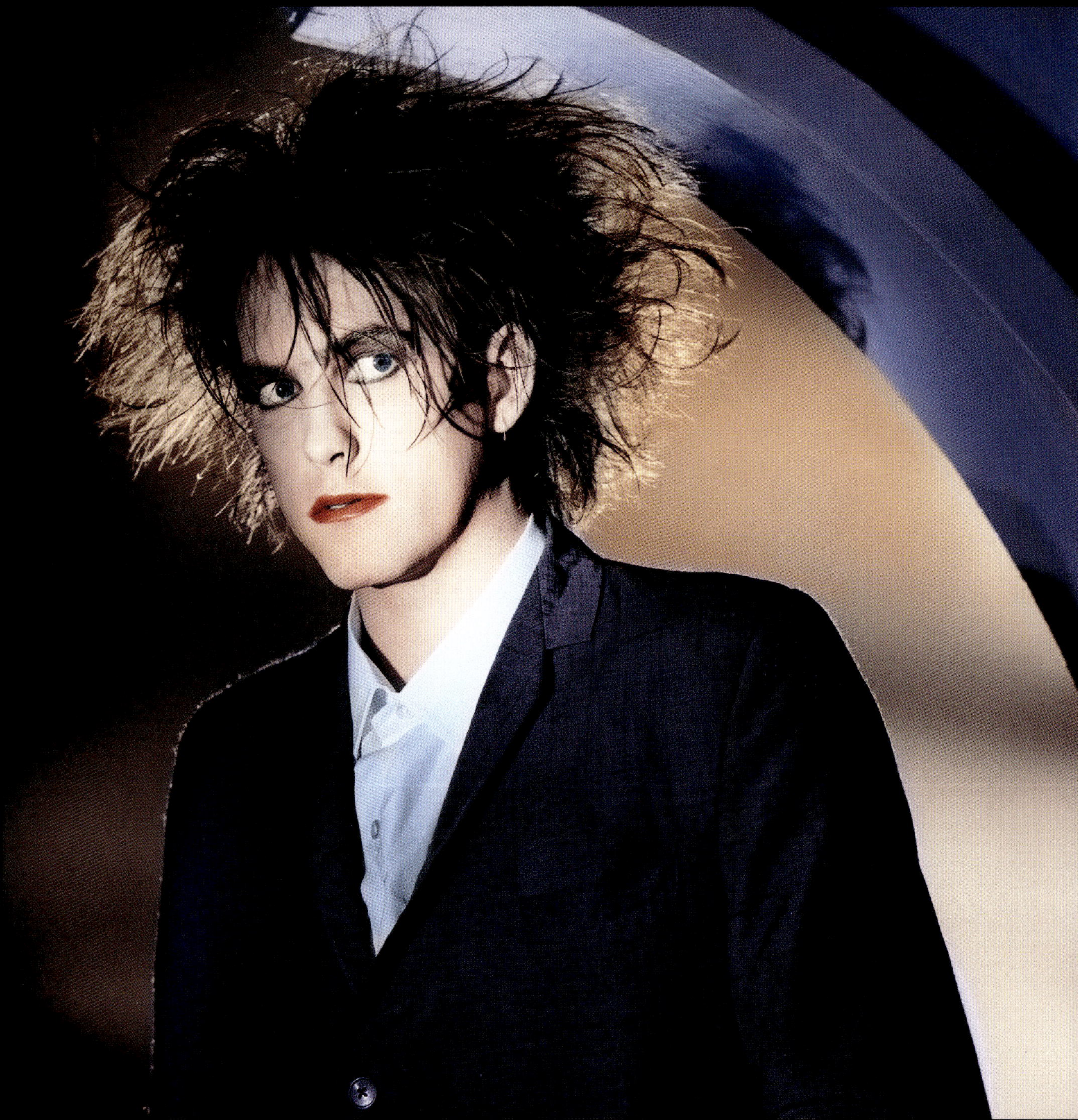

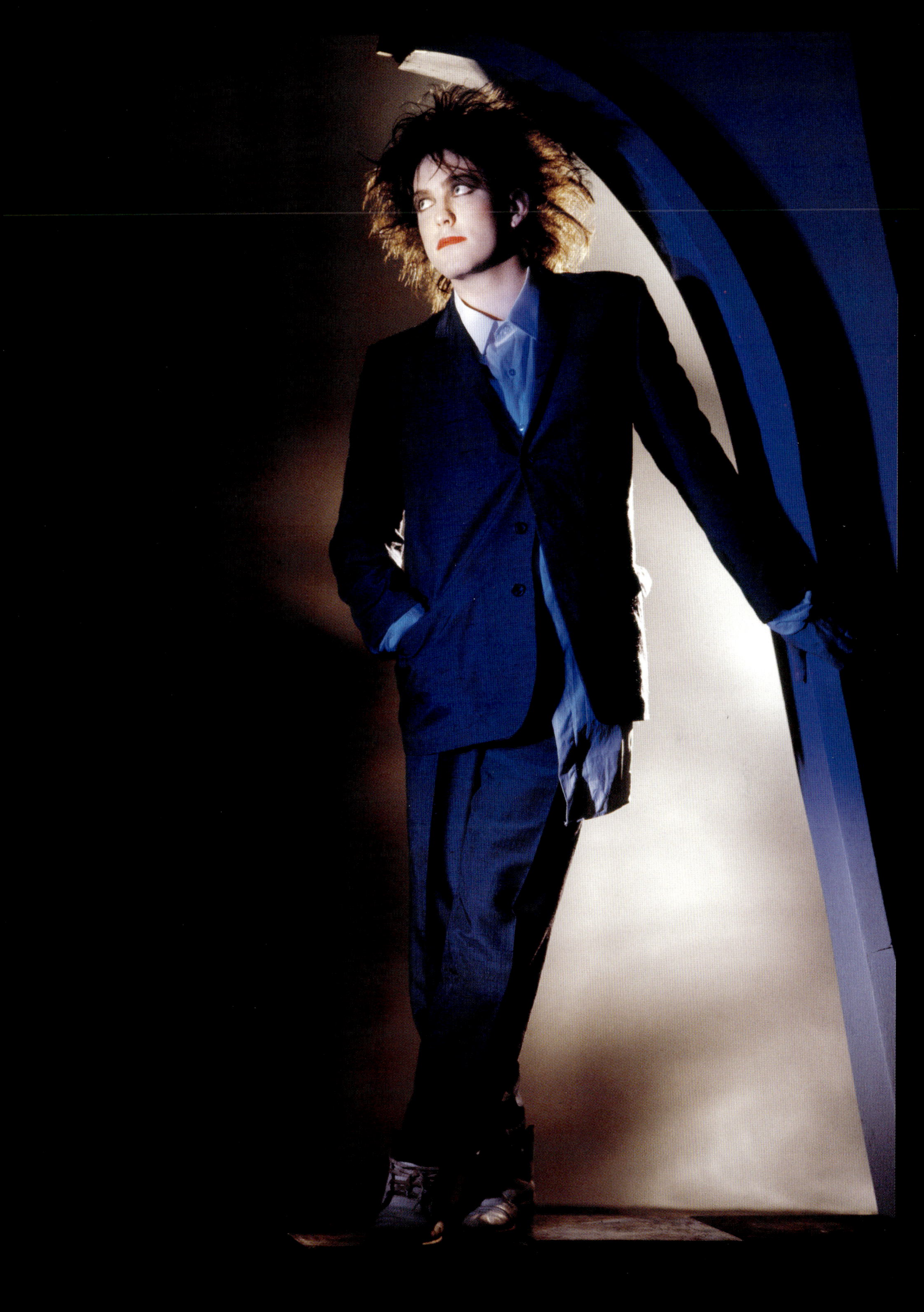

FULHAM STUDIO
(p.36 to 45)
1985

ROBERT: THIS WAS MY/OUR THIRD VISIT TO YOUR FULHAM STUDIO – PHIL AND ANDY ARE GONE – SIMON IS BACK – AND BORIS IS THE NEW DRUMMER – THIS SESSION WAS FOR PRESS/PROMO SHOTS FOR *THE HEAD ON THE DOOR* ALBUM/TOUR 1985 – I AM HAPPY TO SEE THE 'SAME BUT DIFFERENT' BESPOKE SUITS... AND ARE THOSE REAL SILK SHIRTS? WE ARE DEFINITELY GOING UP IN THE WORLD!

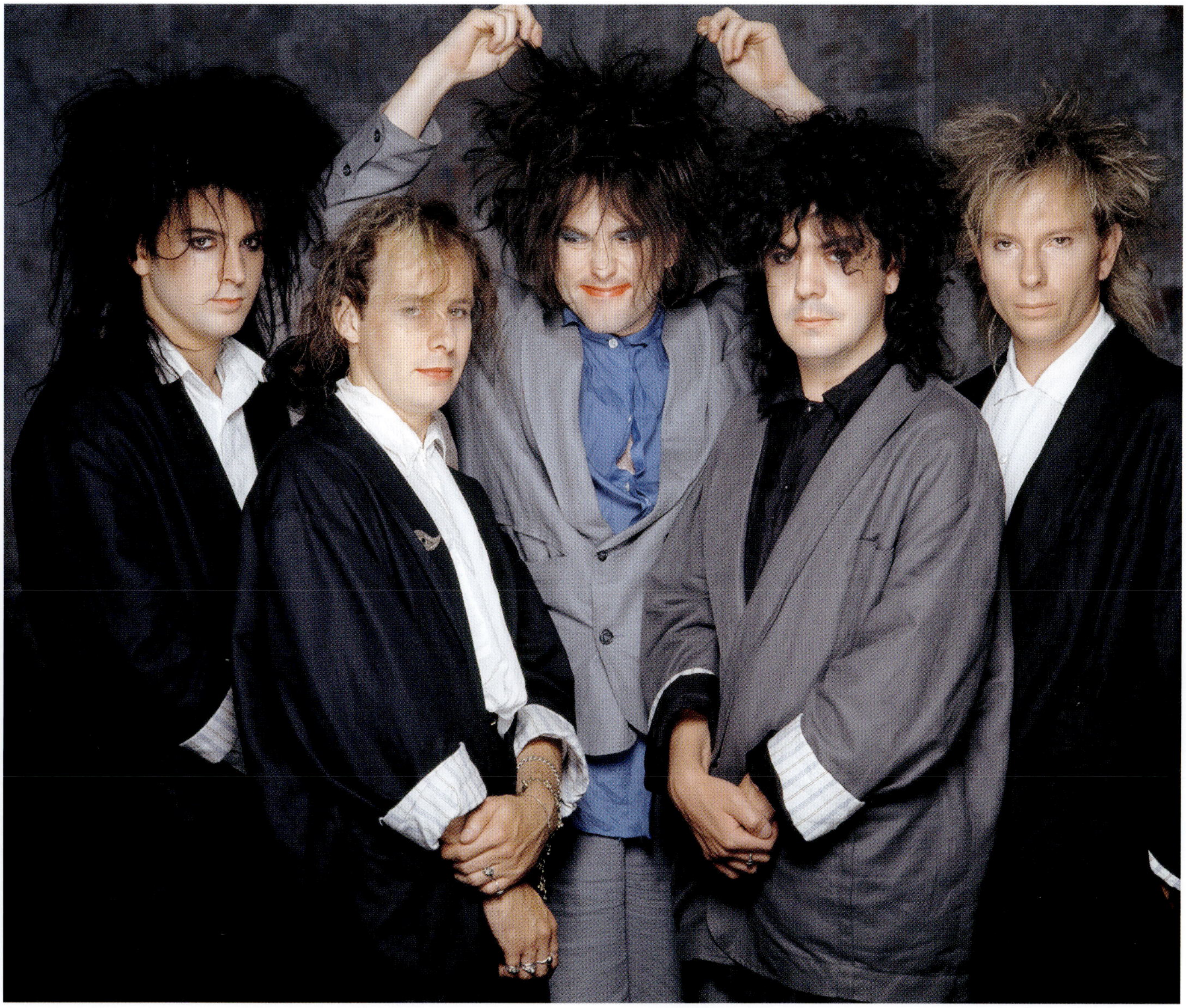

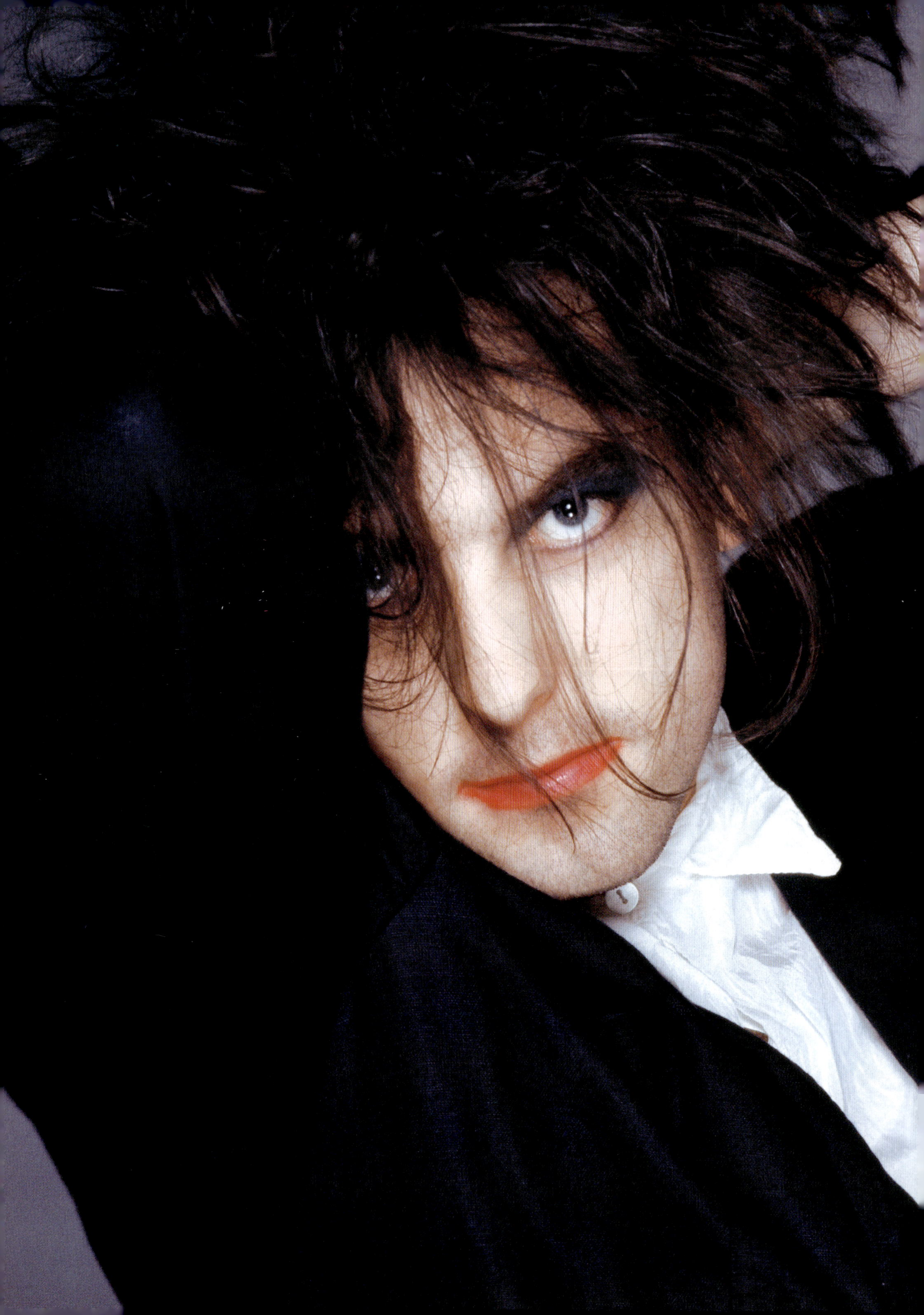

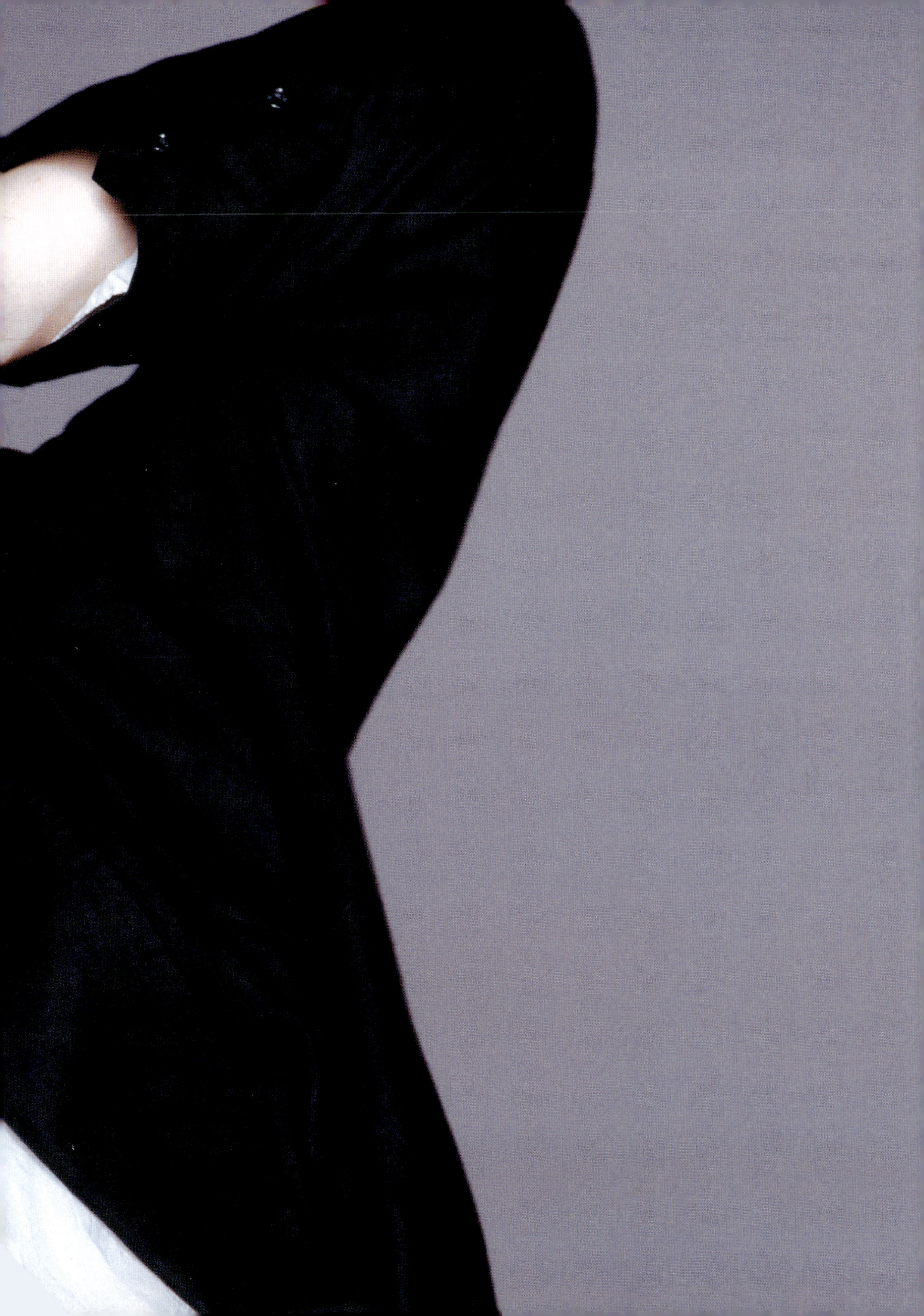

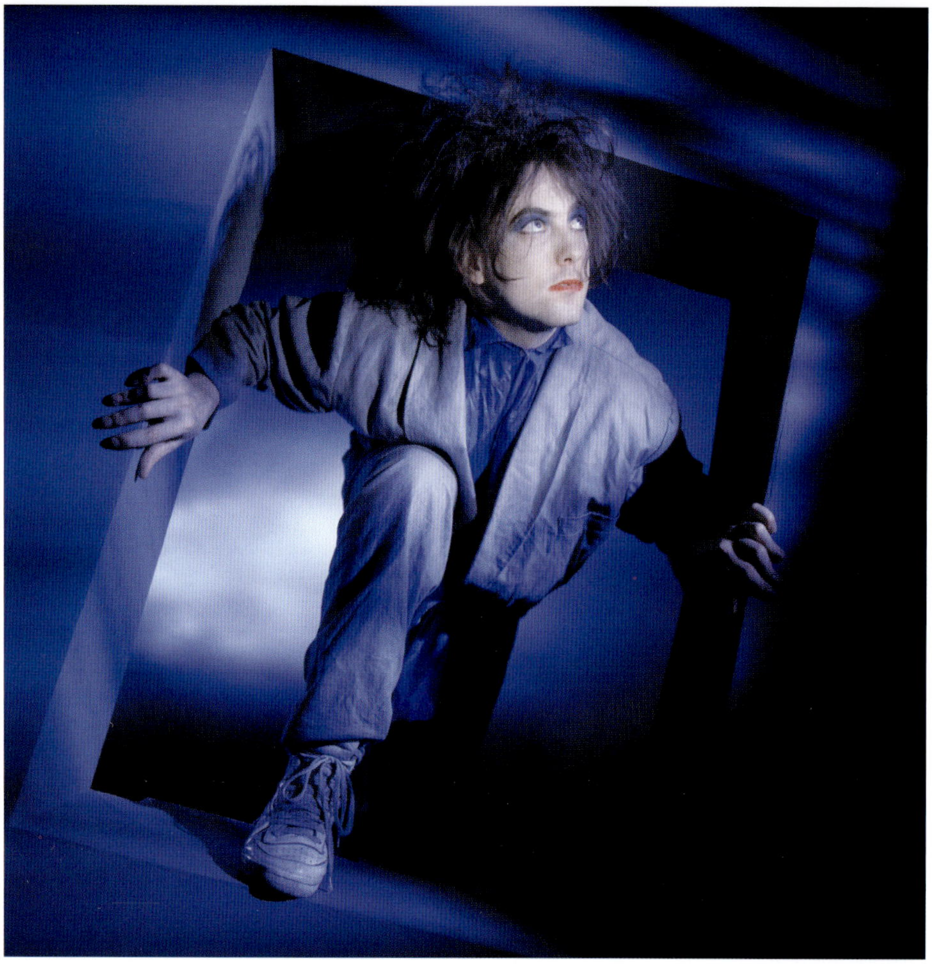

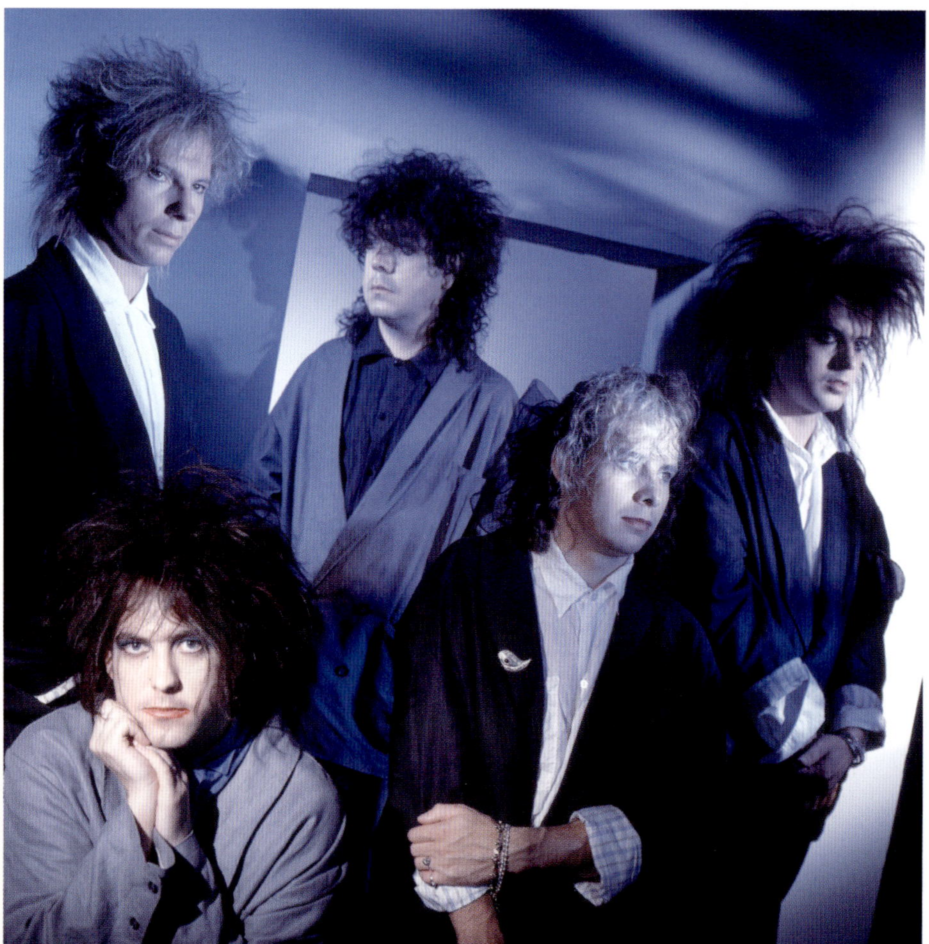

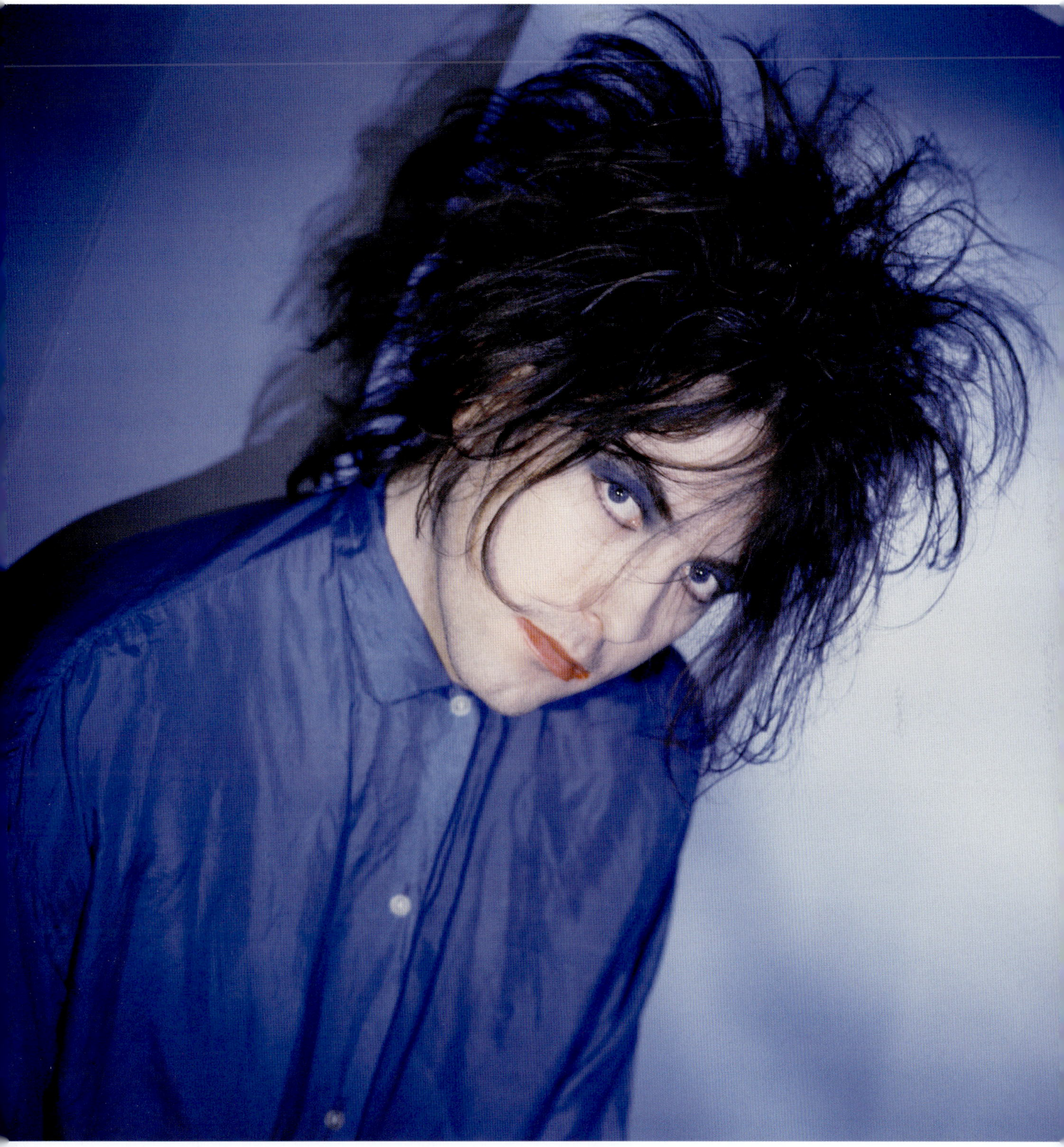

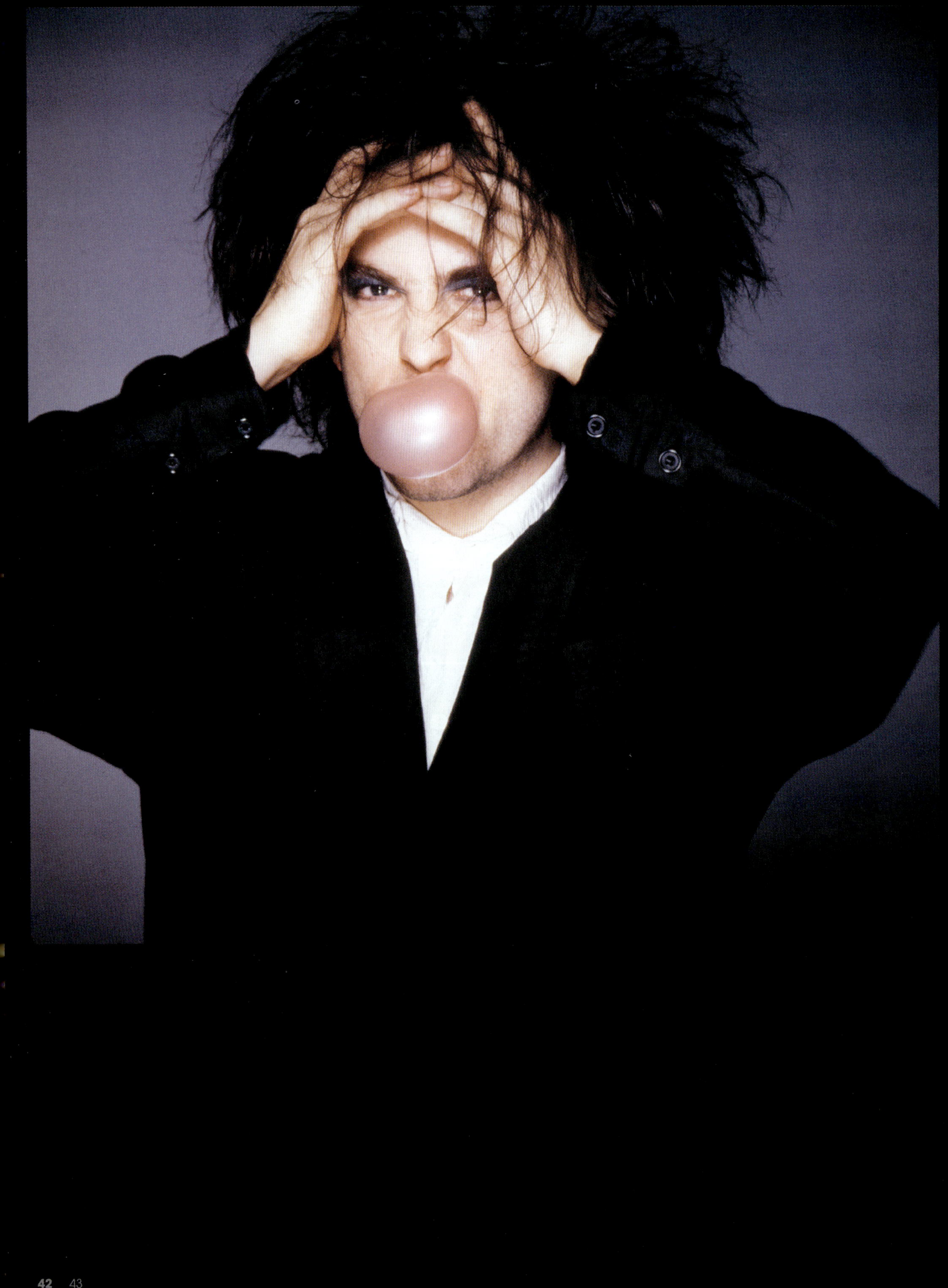

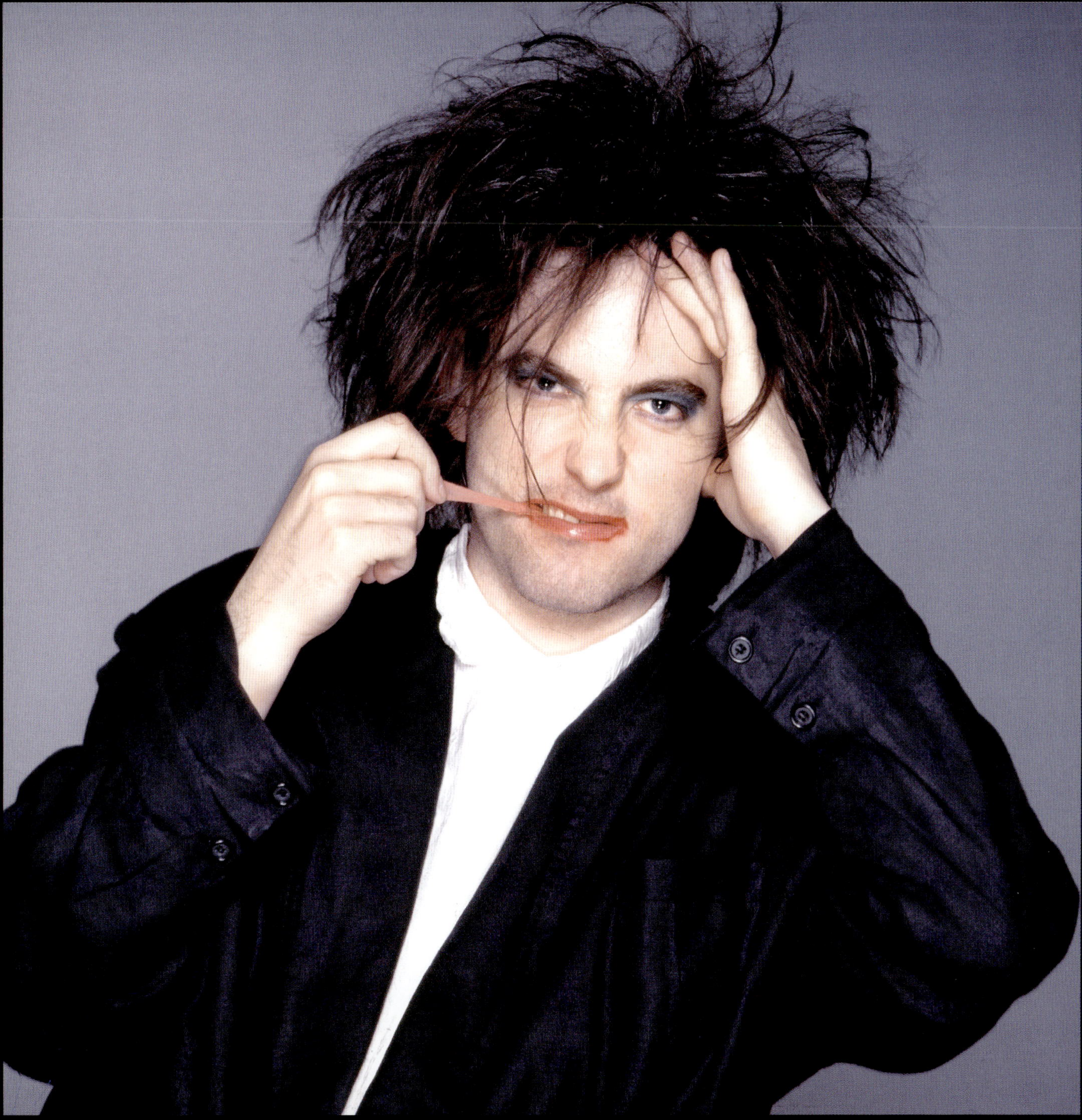

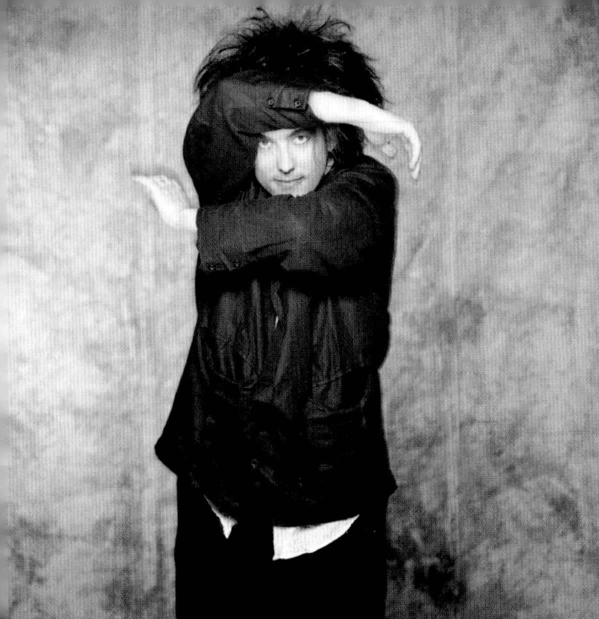
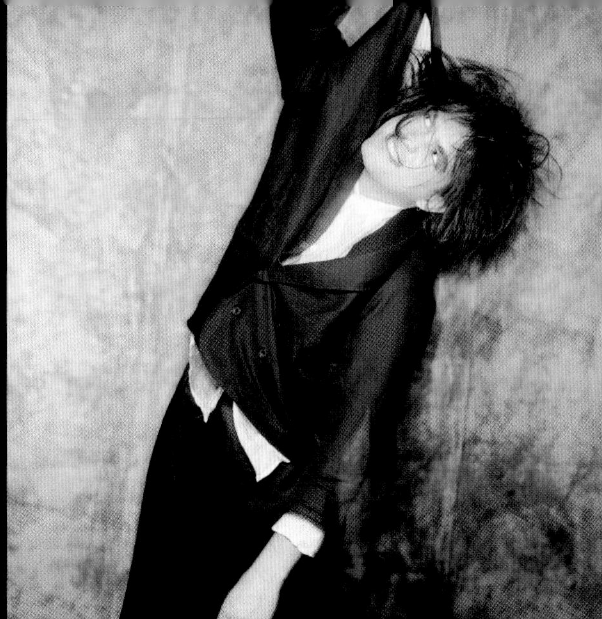
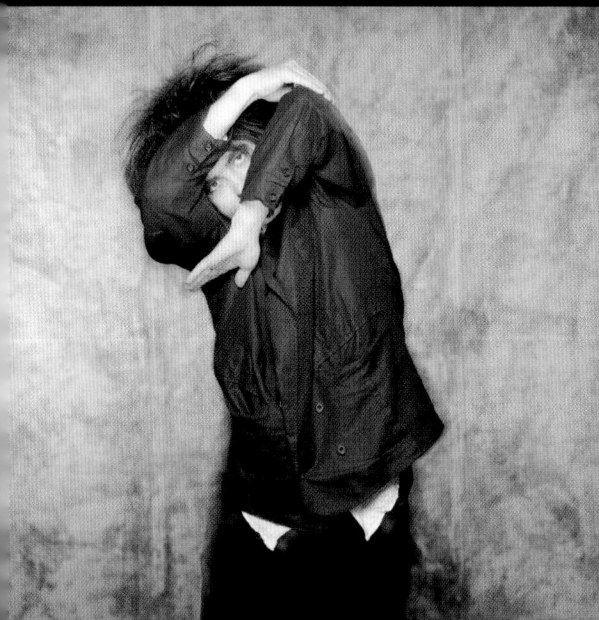
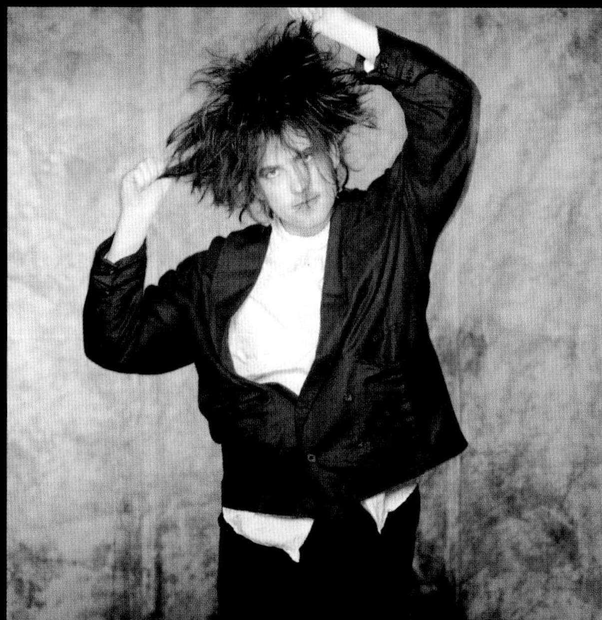
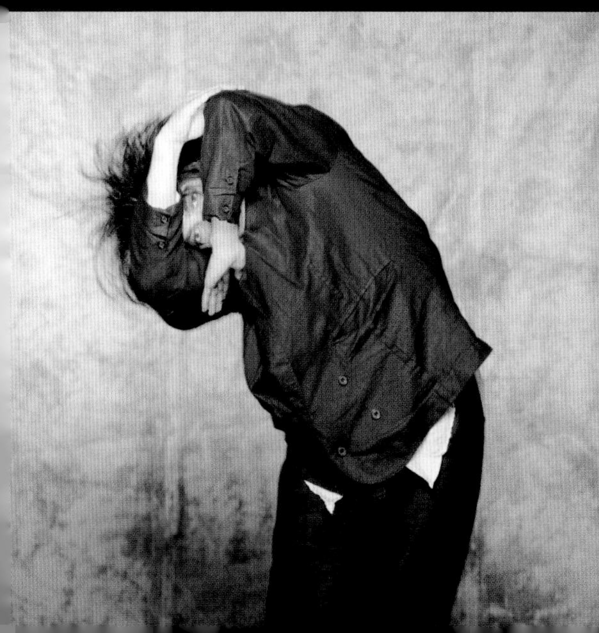
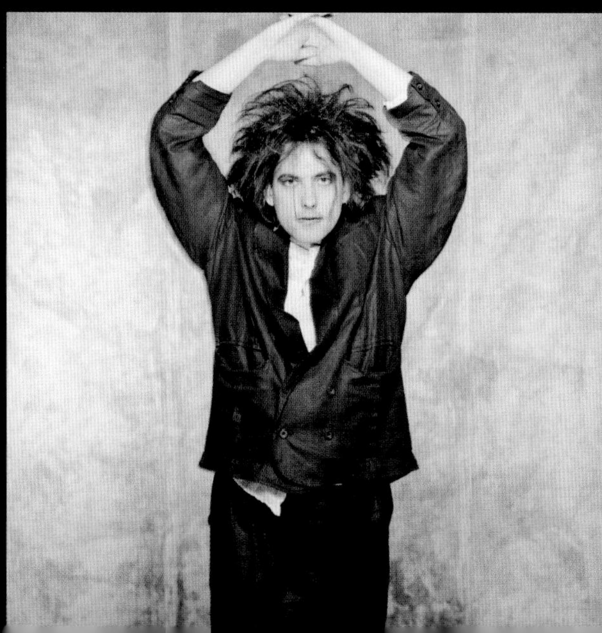

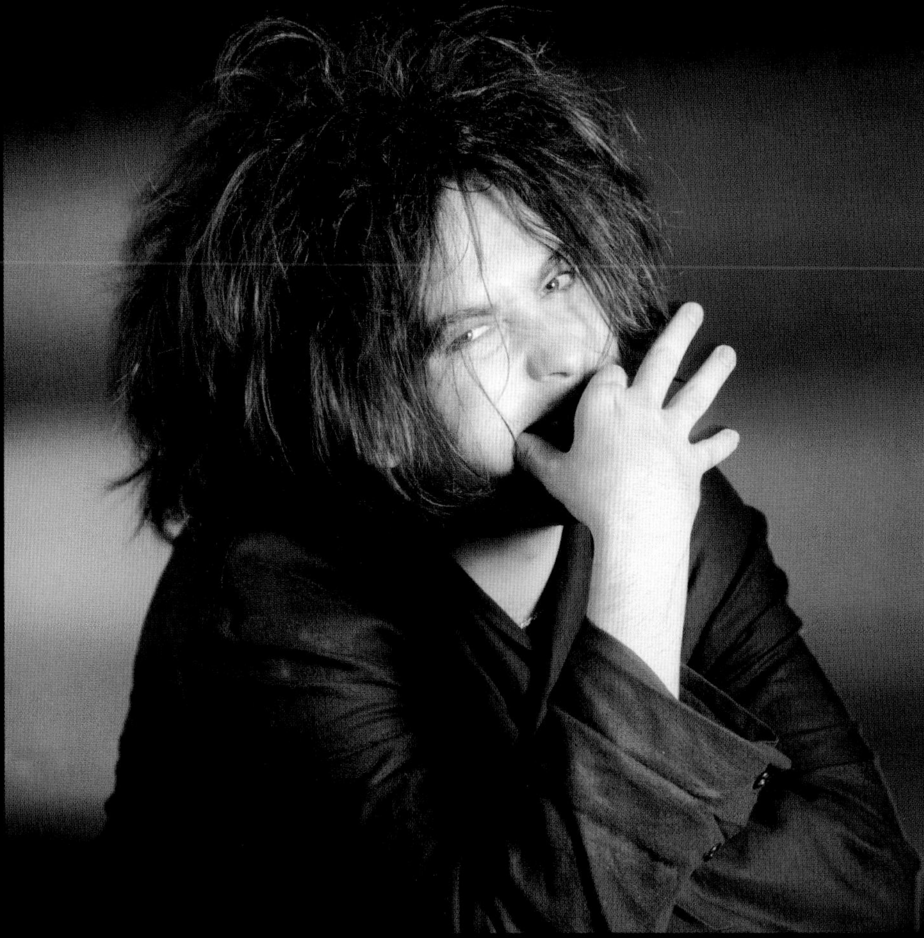

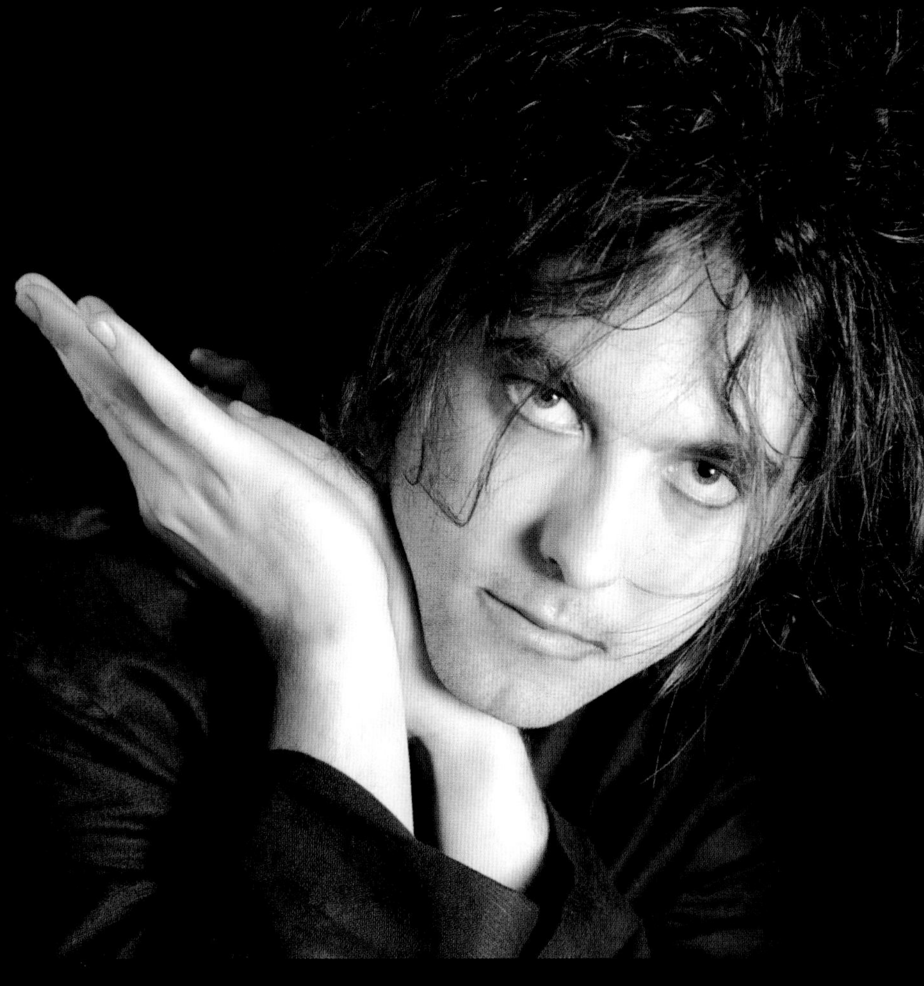

FULHAM STUDIO
(p.46 to 55)
1986

ROBERT: THIS SESSION WAS FOR PROMOTIONAL AND 'ART' PICTURES RELATING TO THE RE-RELEASE OF THE 'BOYS DON'T CRY' SINGLE AND THE *STANDING ON A BEACH* SINGLES COLLECTION ALBUM.

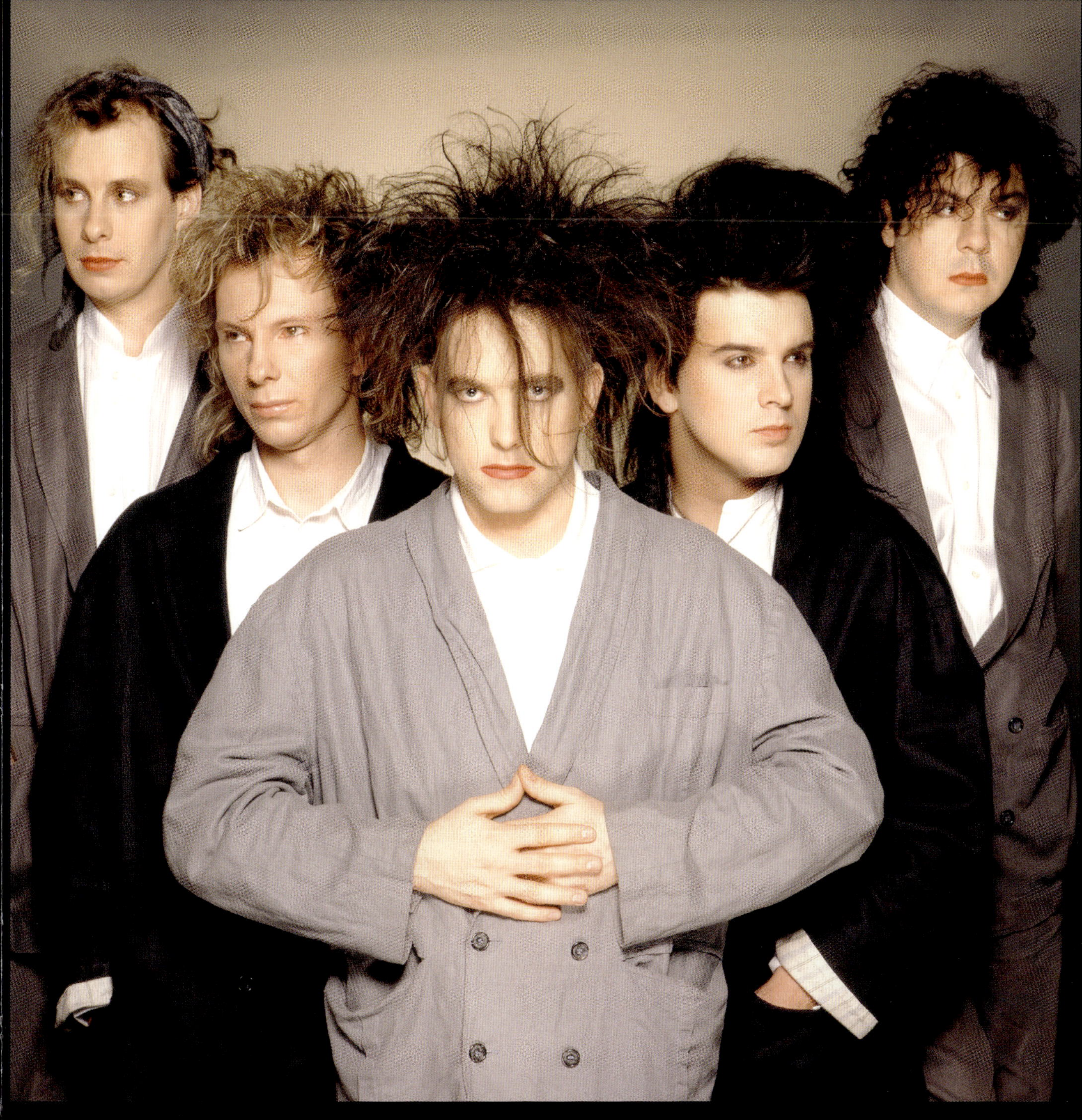

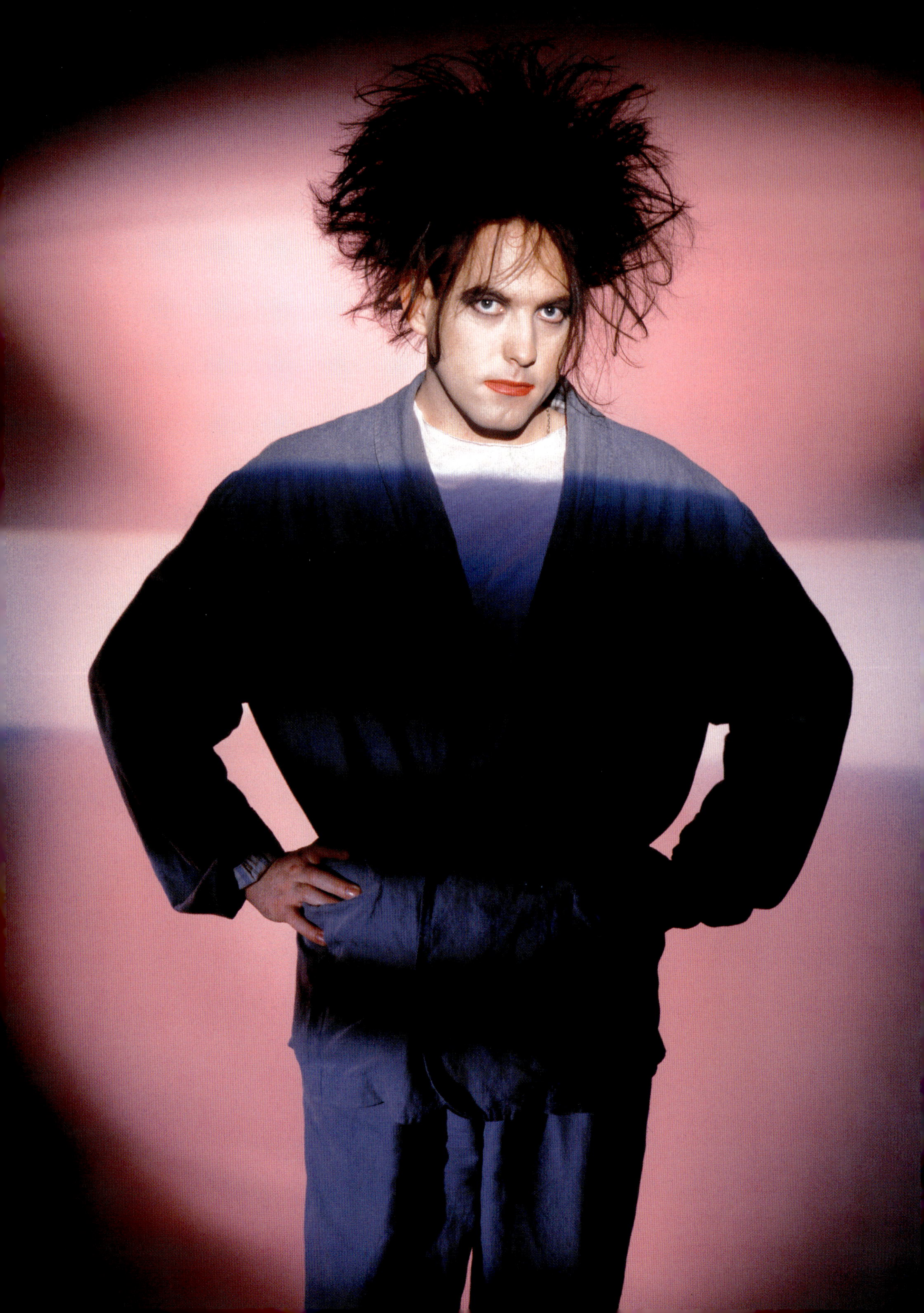

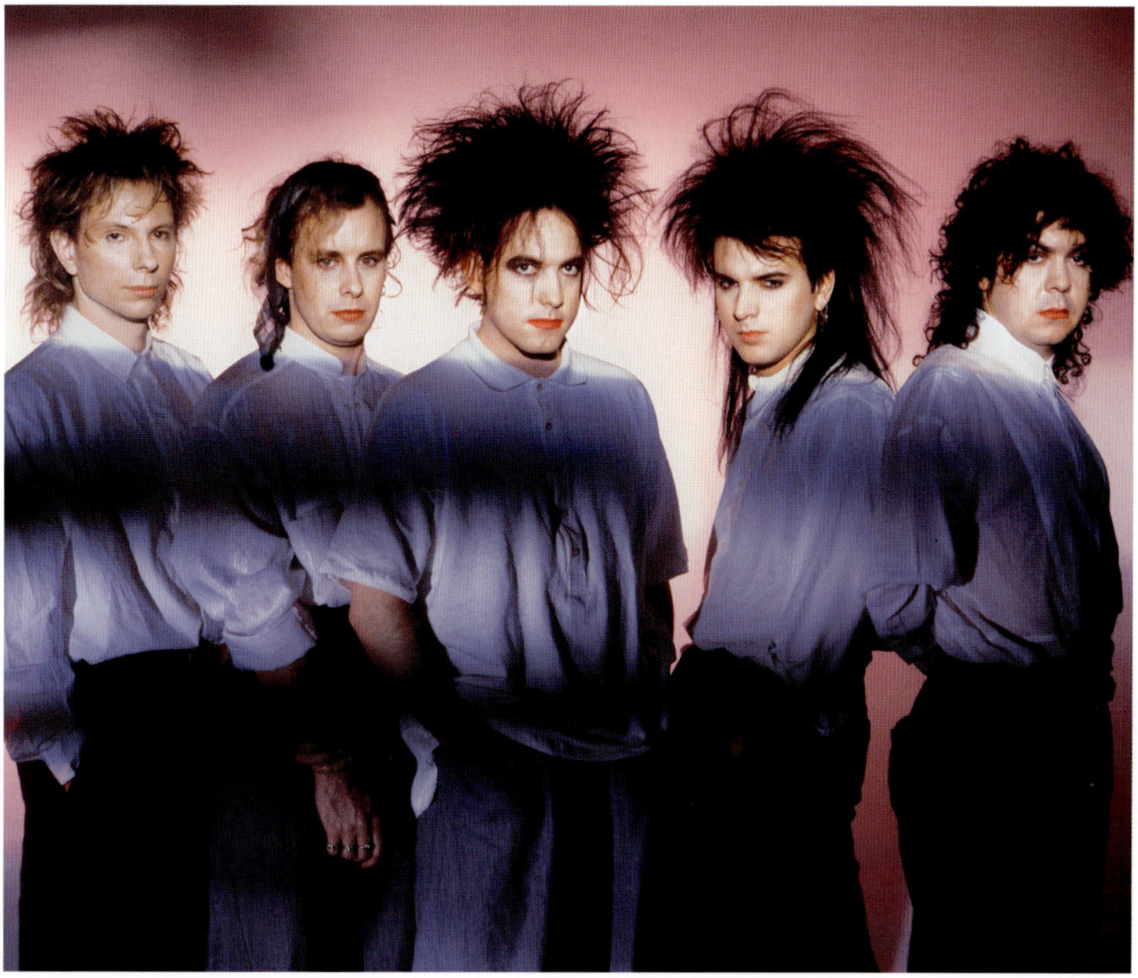

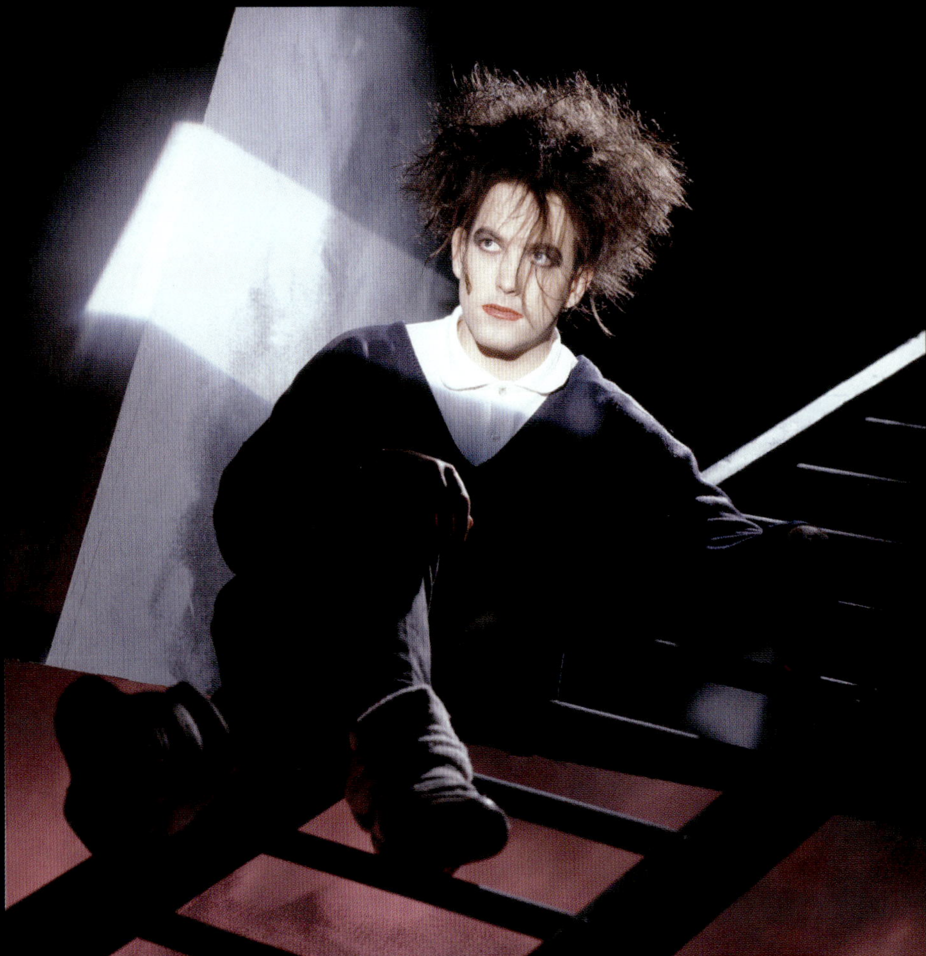

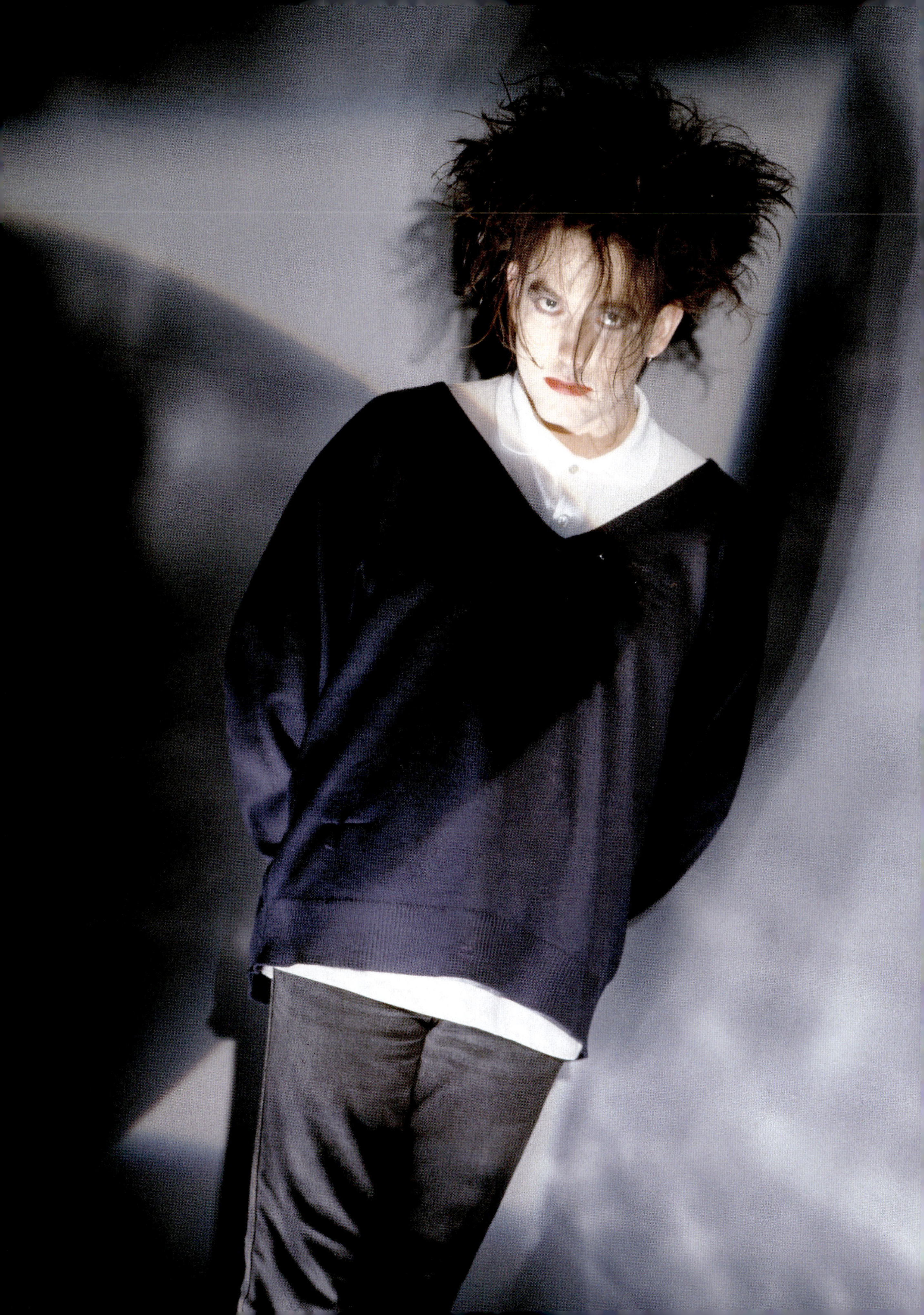

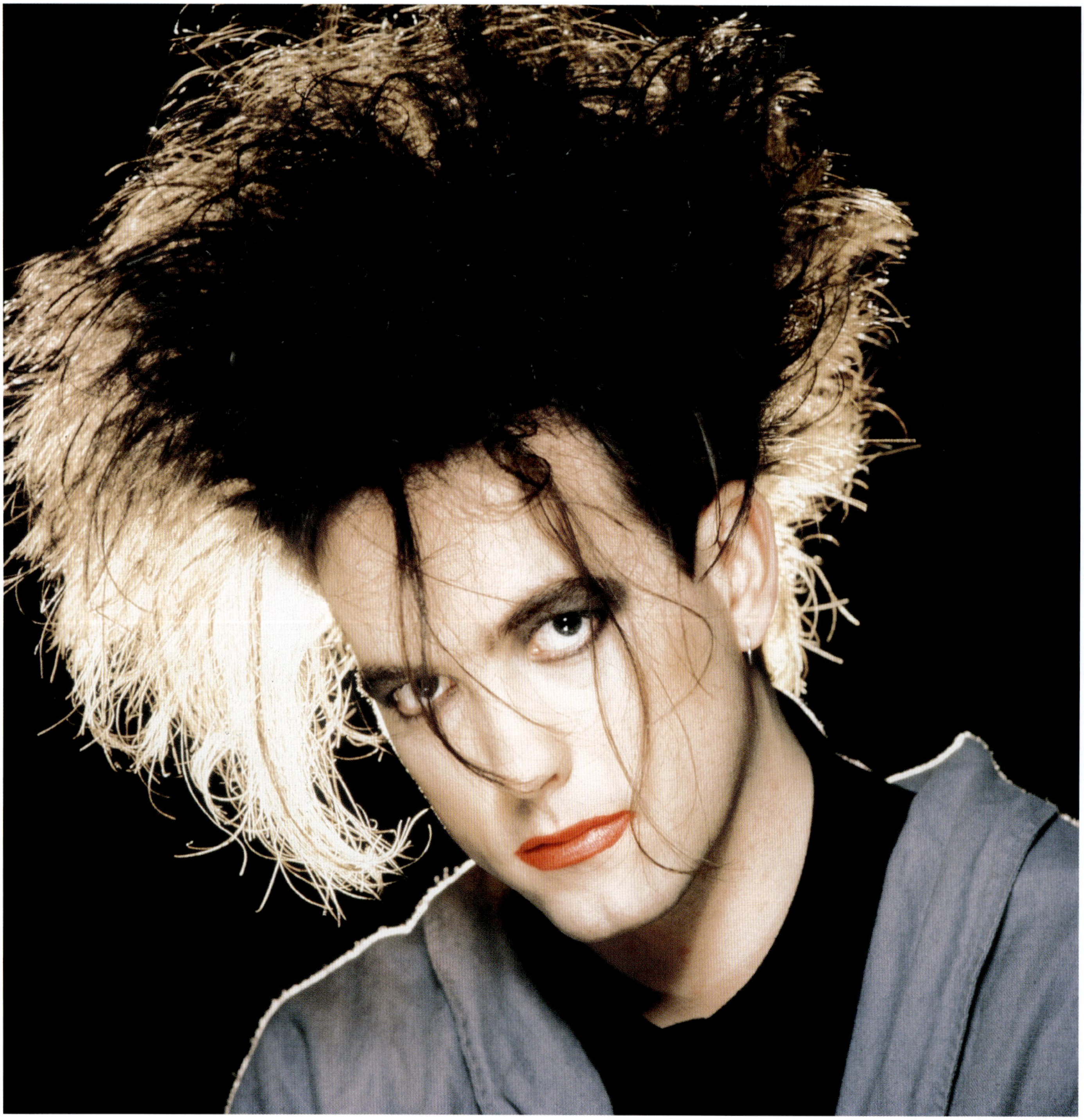

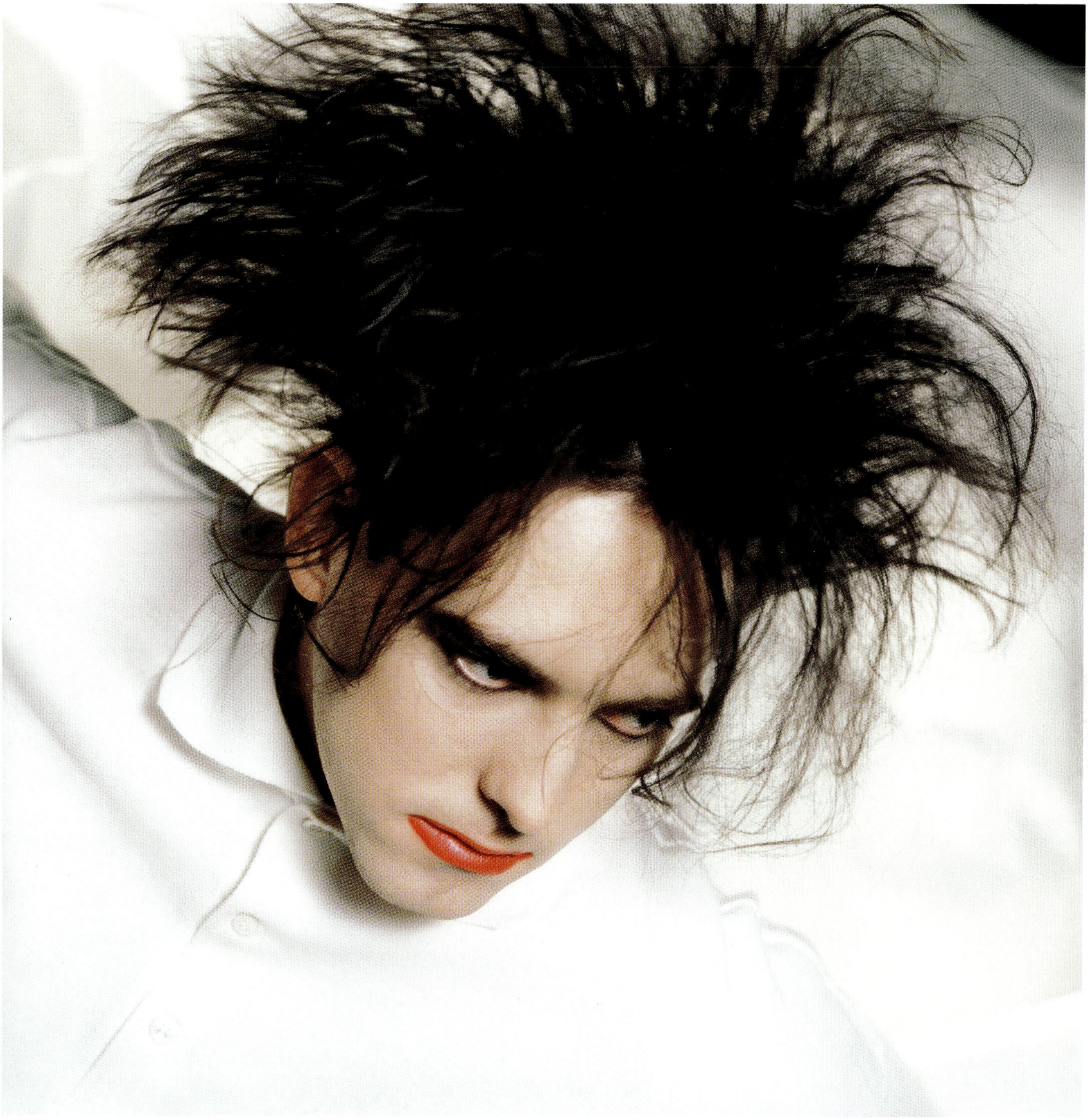

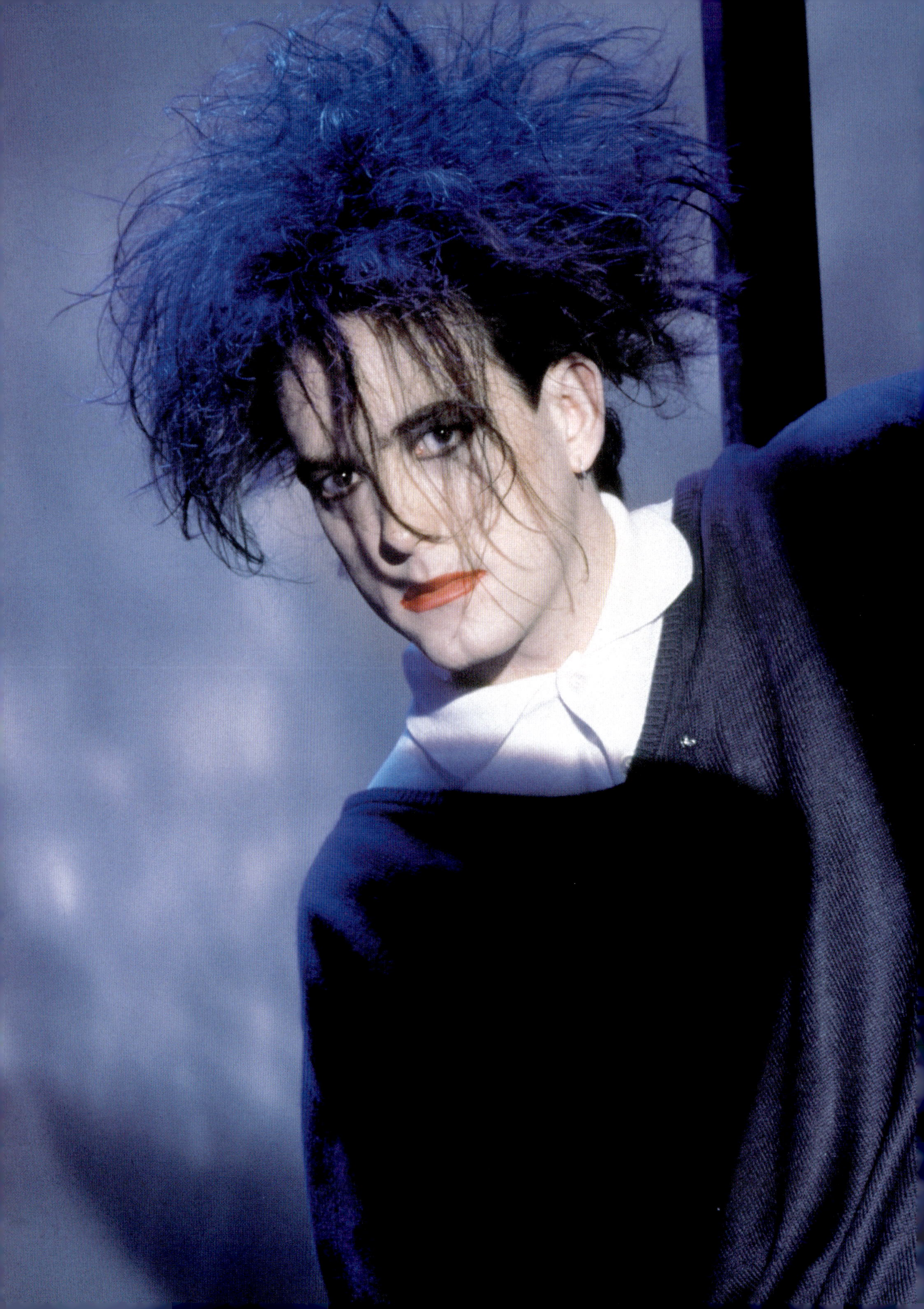

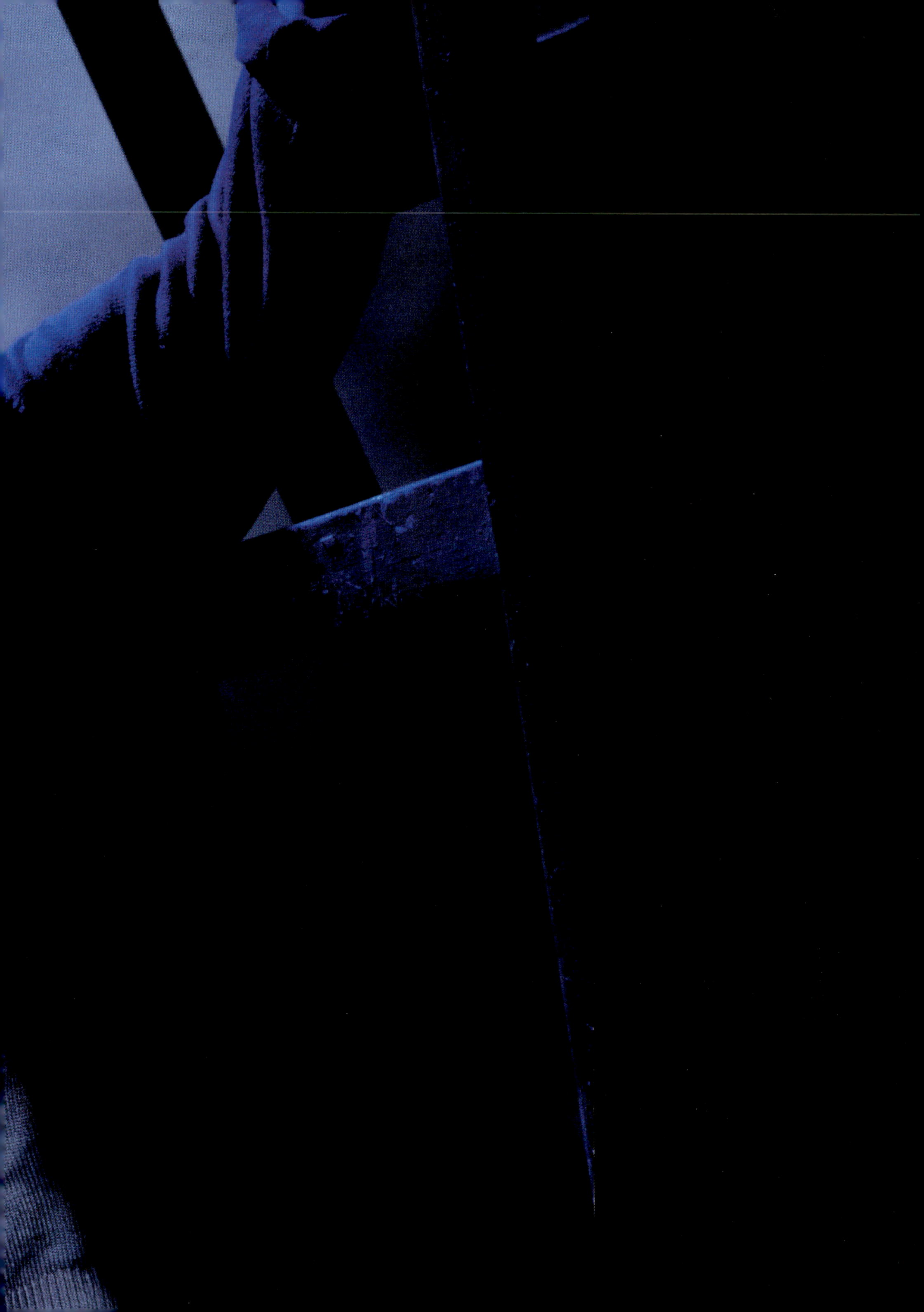

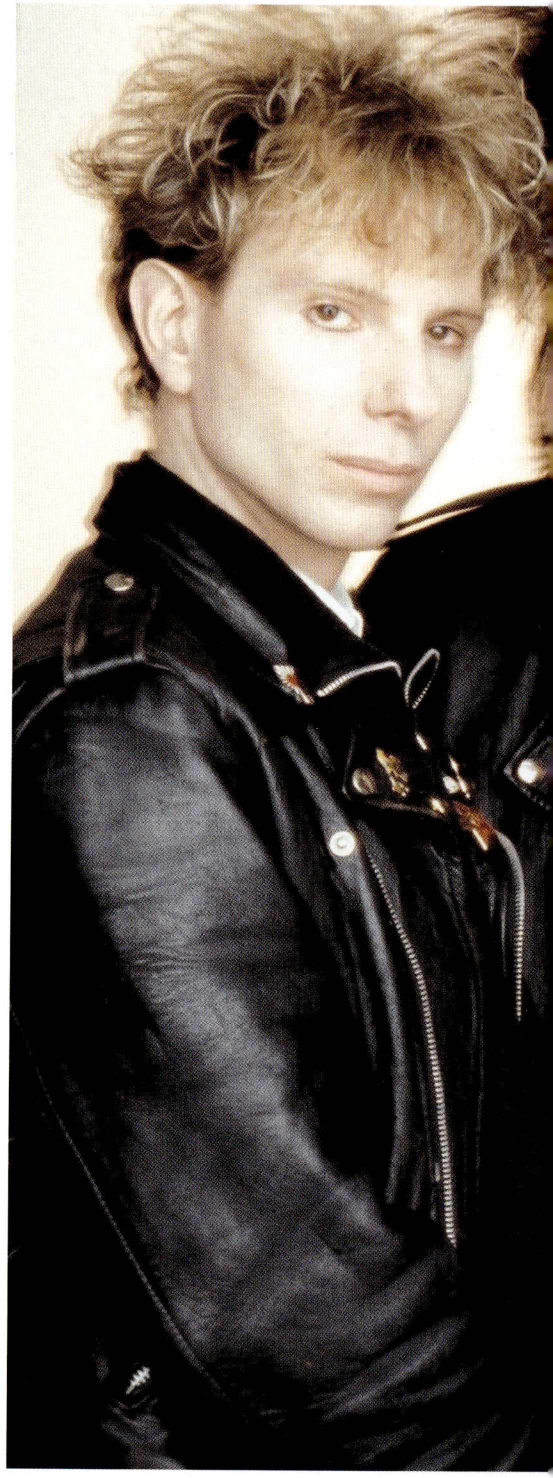

DUBLIN
[p.56 to 61]
March 1987

ROBERT: WE WERE IN DUBLIN MAKING A VIDEO FOR *WHY CAN'T I BE YOU?* BEFORE STARTING REHEARSALS FOR THE IMMINENT 'HONEYMOON/KISSING' TOUR – THESE 'QUINTET' SHOTS WERE USED AS PROMOTIONAL SHOTS FOR THE *KISS ME KISS ME KISS ME* ALBUM AND SINGLES.

Paul: A session for press and the forthcoming tour. I turned up in Dublin and went straight to the rehearsal rooms where the shoot was due to take place, not knowing what to expect. We couldn't do any location shots outside as it was March and by the time everyone was ready it was dark! So I set up a make-shift studio in the rehearsal room and found an interesting space in the loft to utilise.

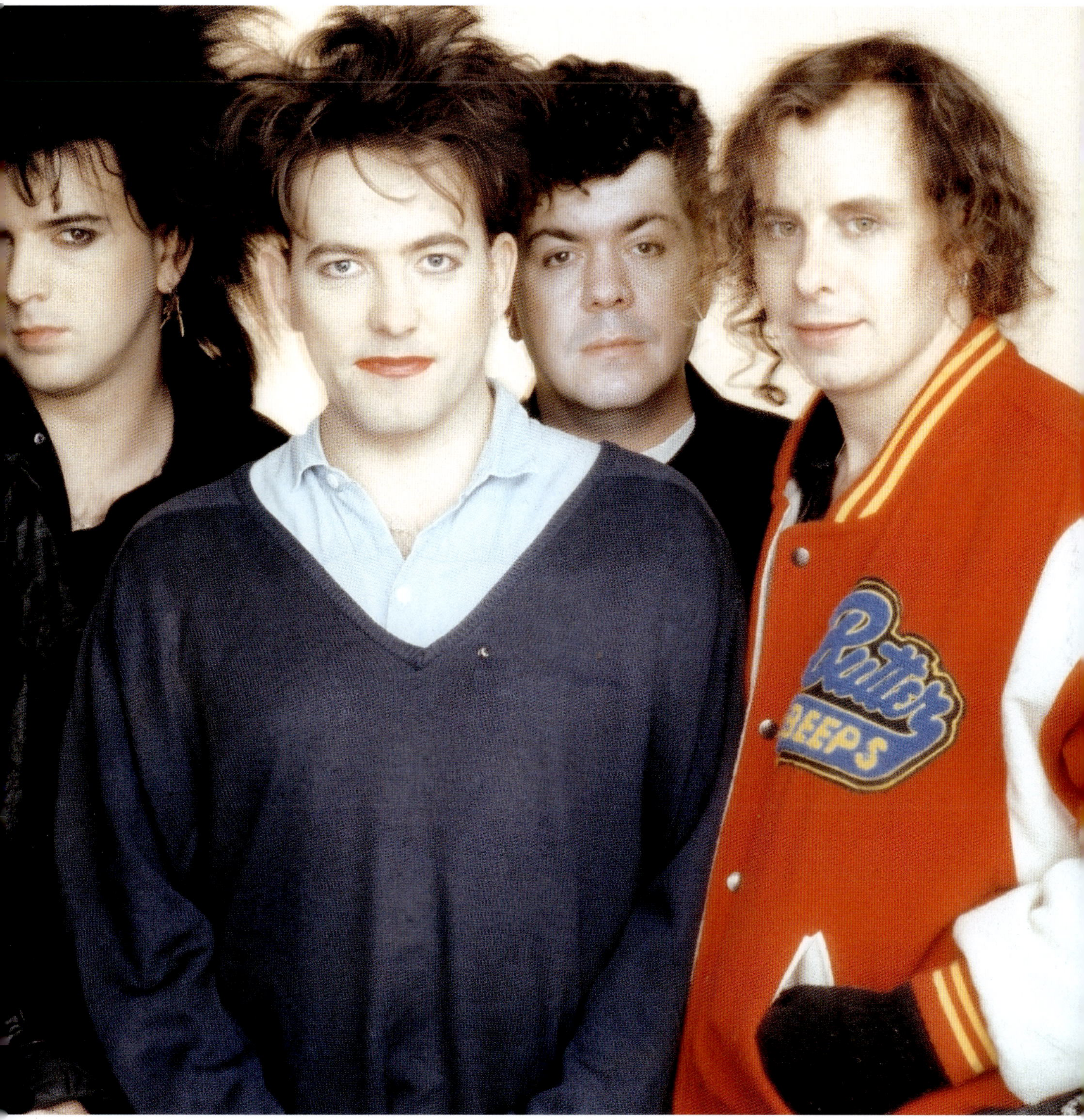

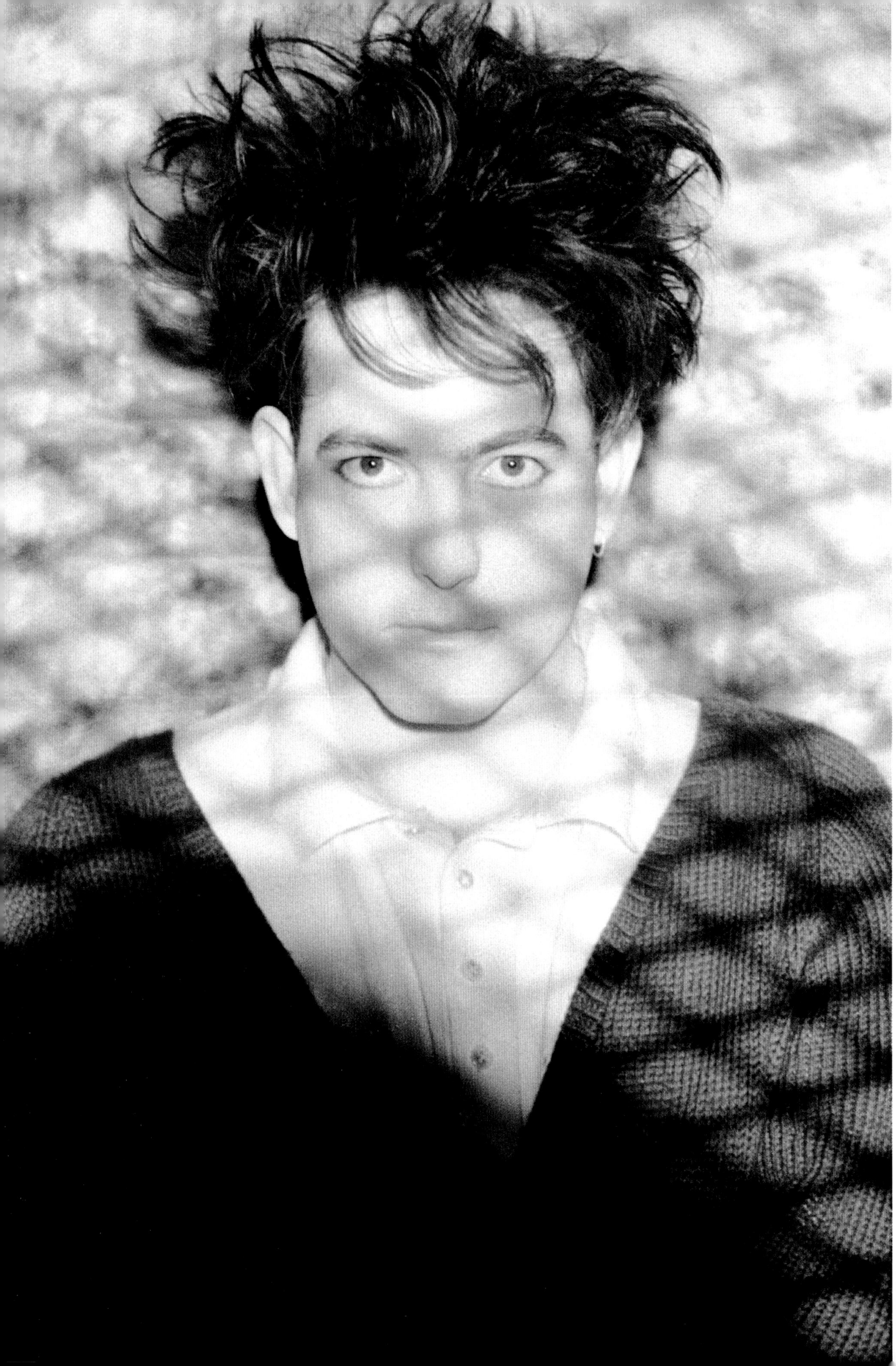

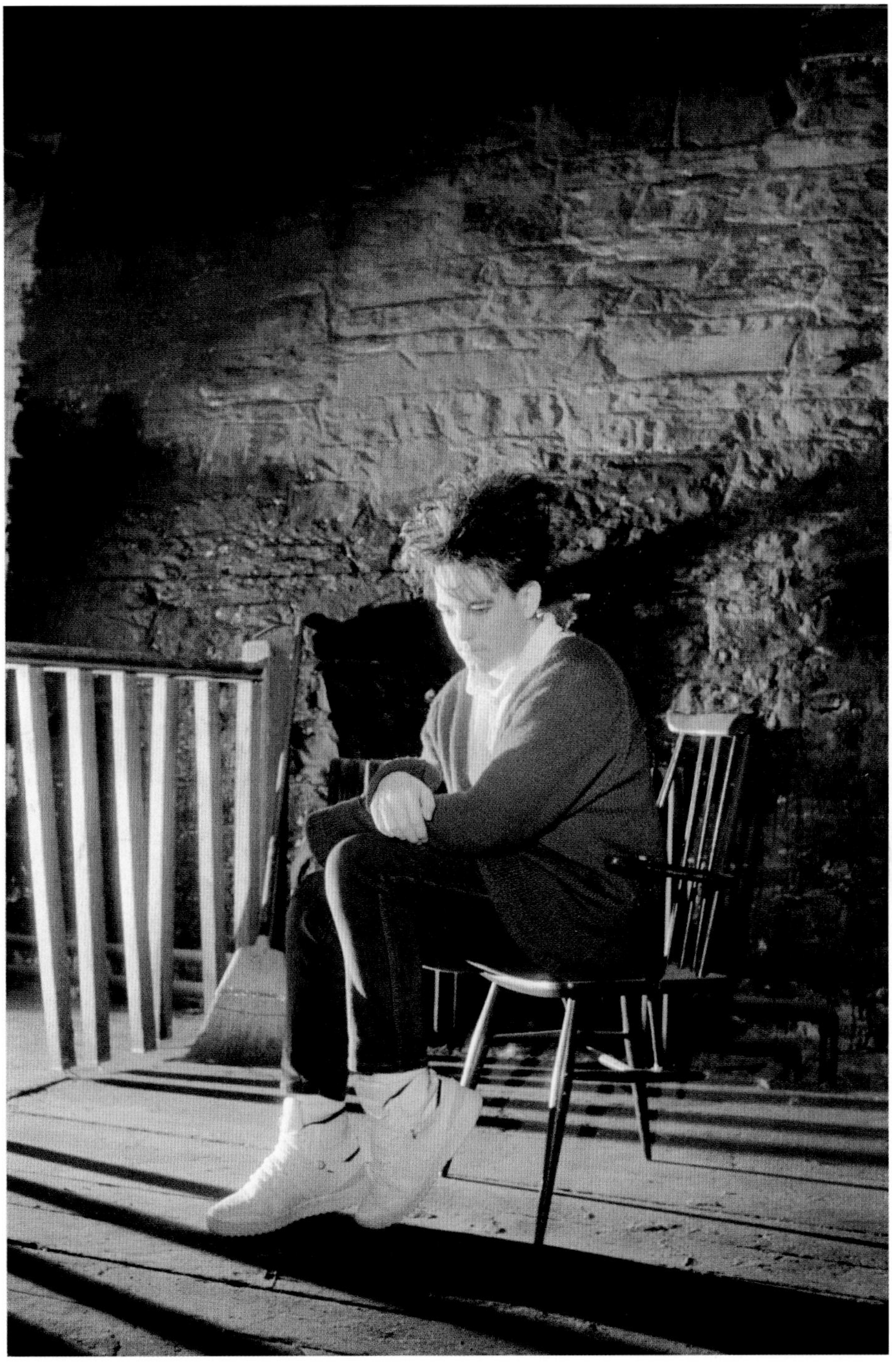

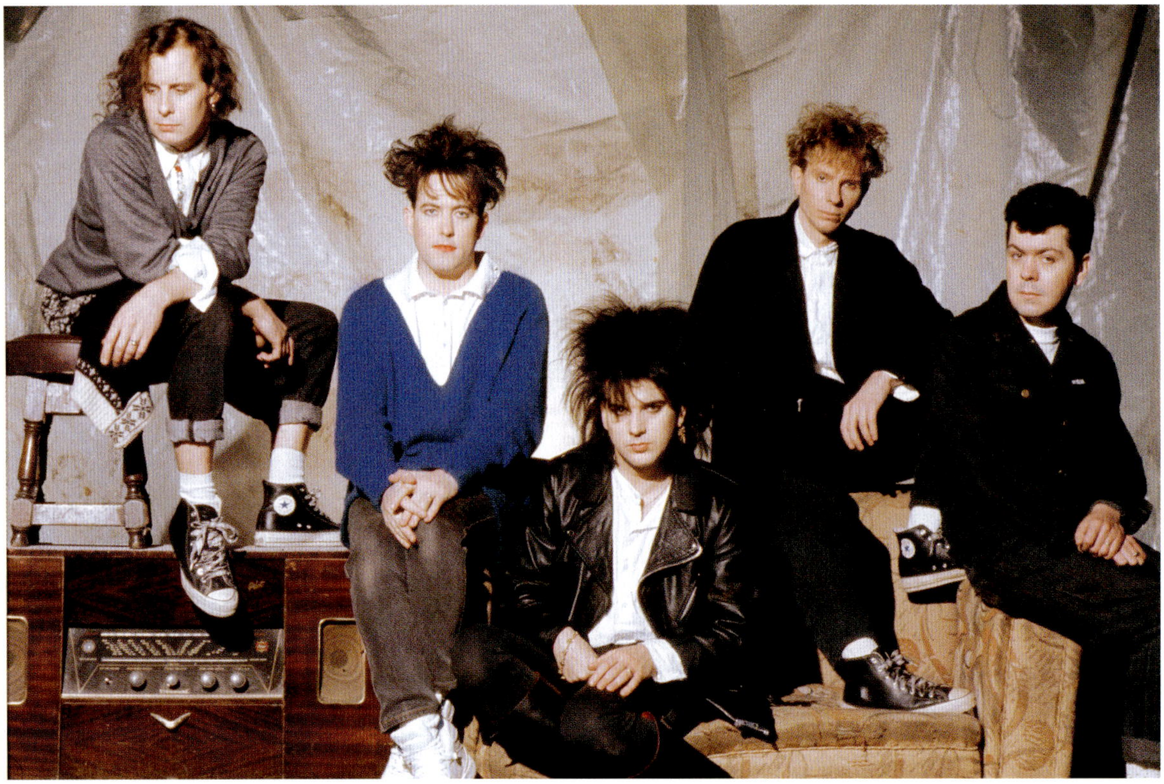

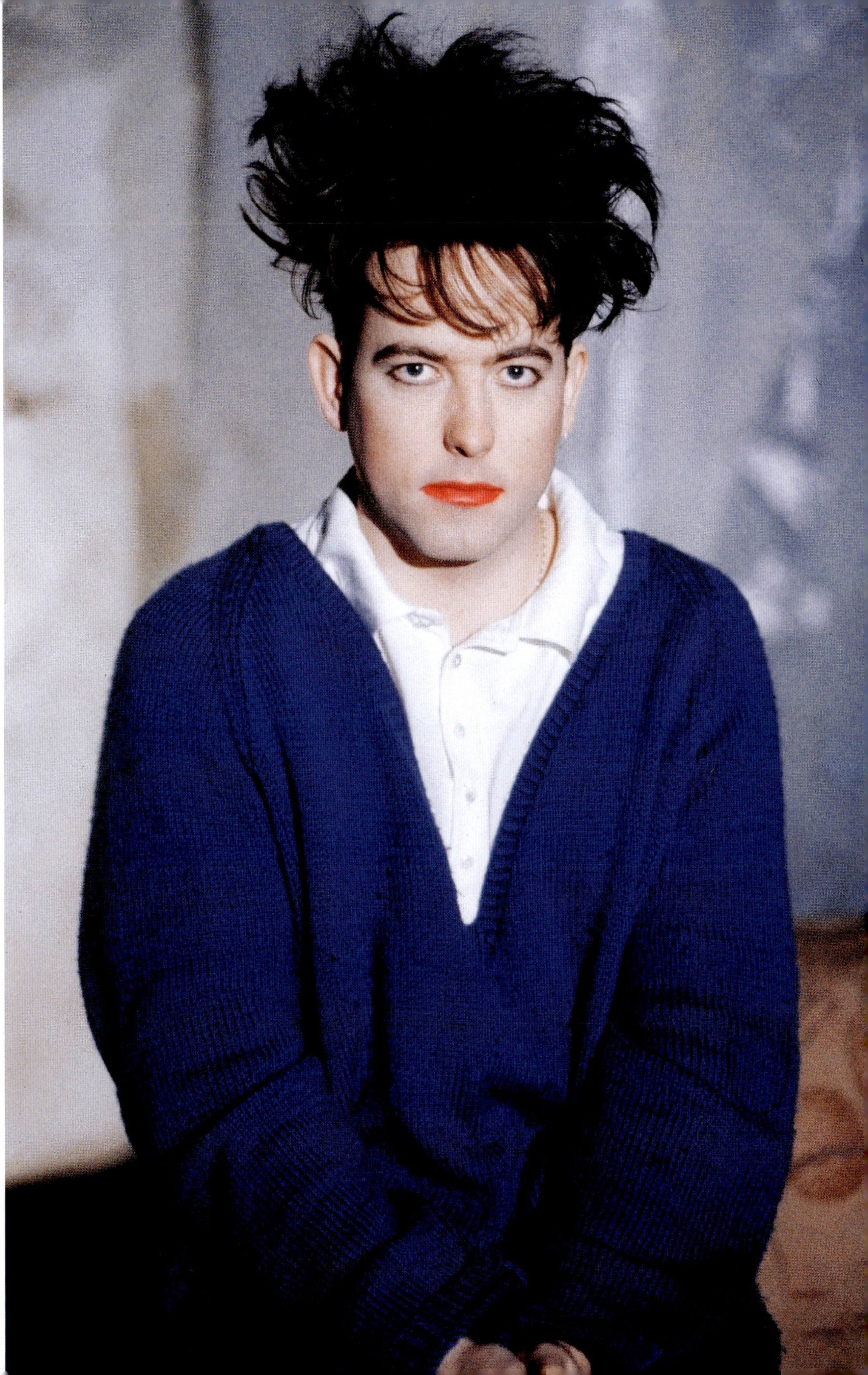

DUBLIN
(p.62 to 73)
June 1987

ROBERT: OUR NEW KEYBOARD PLAYER ROGER JOINED US FOR THE TOUR, AND THE CURE EXPANDED INTO A SEXTET FOR THE FIRST AND ONLY TIME... P68-69 SHOWS US AT OUR SWEETEST! DURING THIS PERIOD I WAS SPENDING QUITE A LOT OF TIME IN IRELAND – THE SHAKING DOGS BELONGED TO ONE OF MANY NEW IRISH FRIENDS!

Paul: I went back to Ireland for another session, as Roger had joined the band, to get some up-to-date pictures. We did the outdoor locations in Dalkey, just outside Dublin, near where Robert was staying. This took a lot of organising and juggling of logistics, with the band and equipment driving to a couple of different spots. The dogs were a bonus!

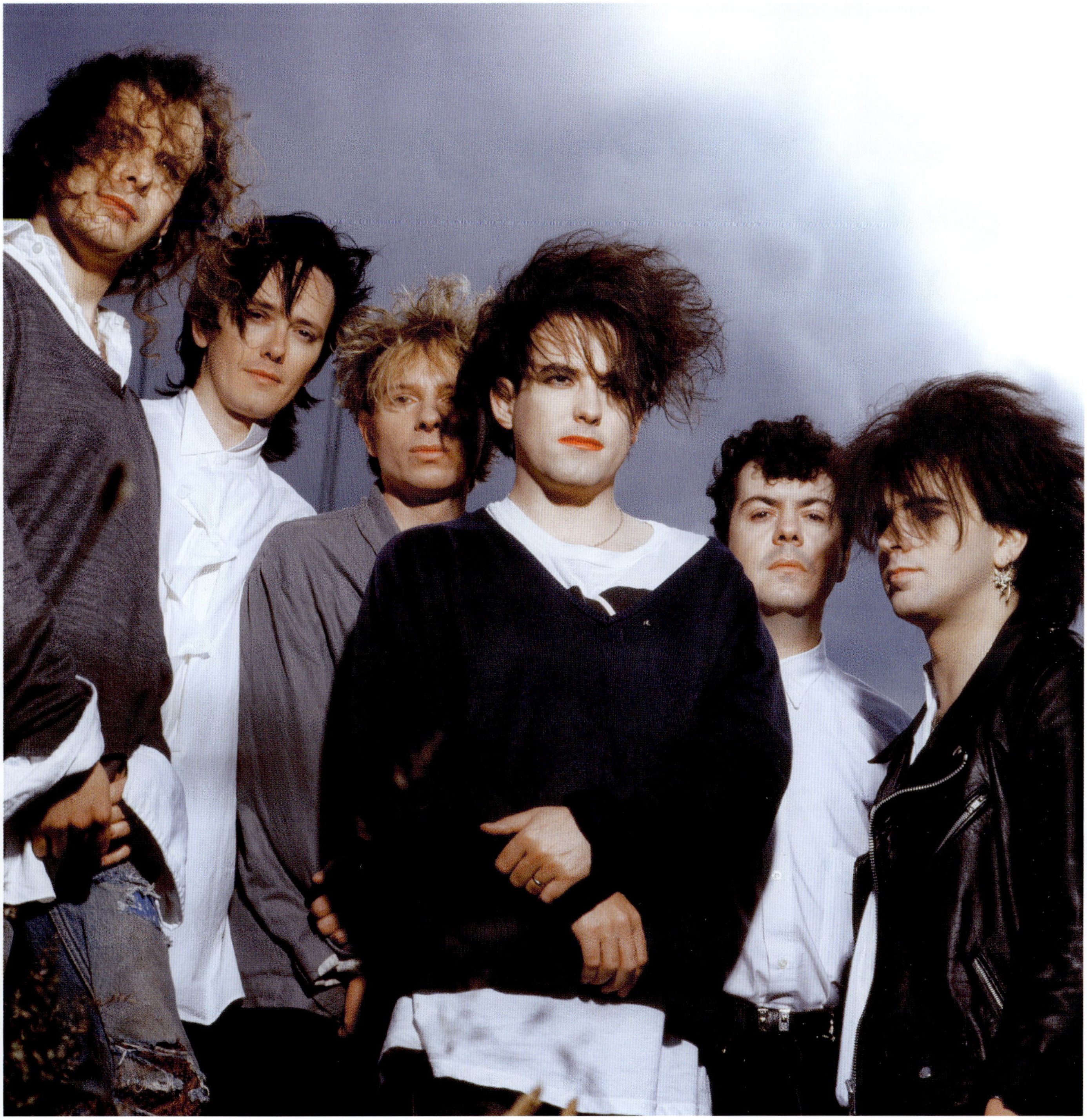

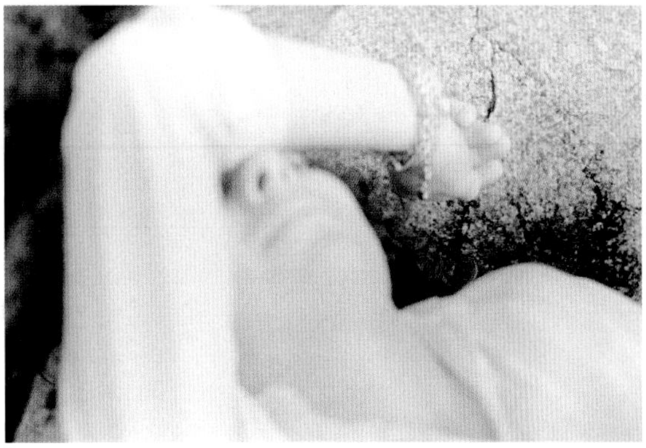
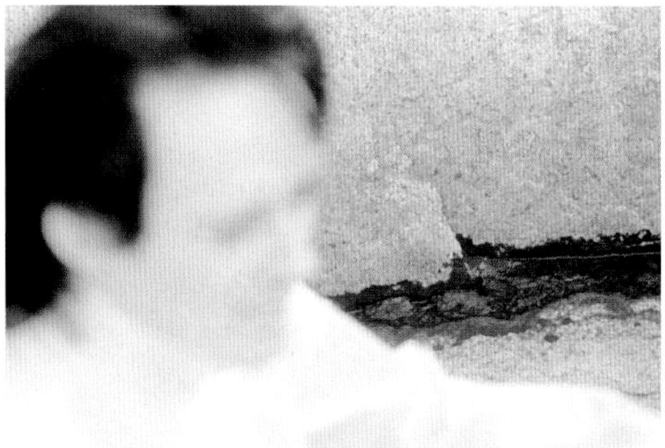
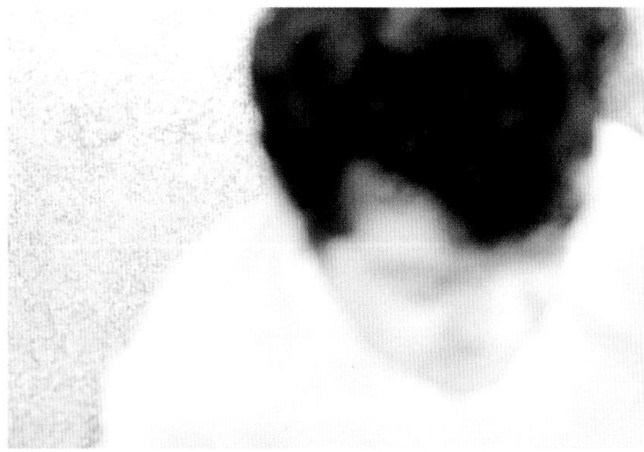
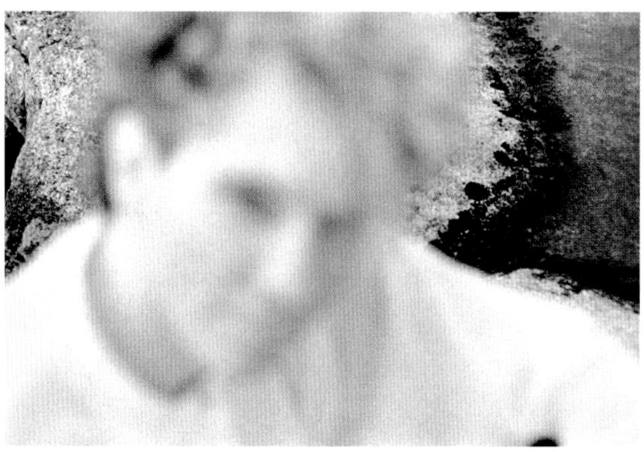
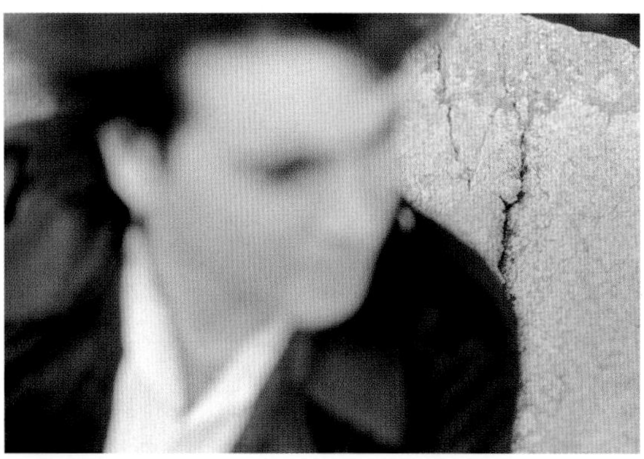

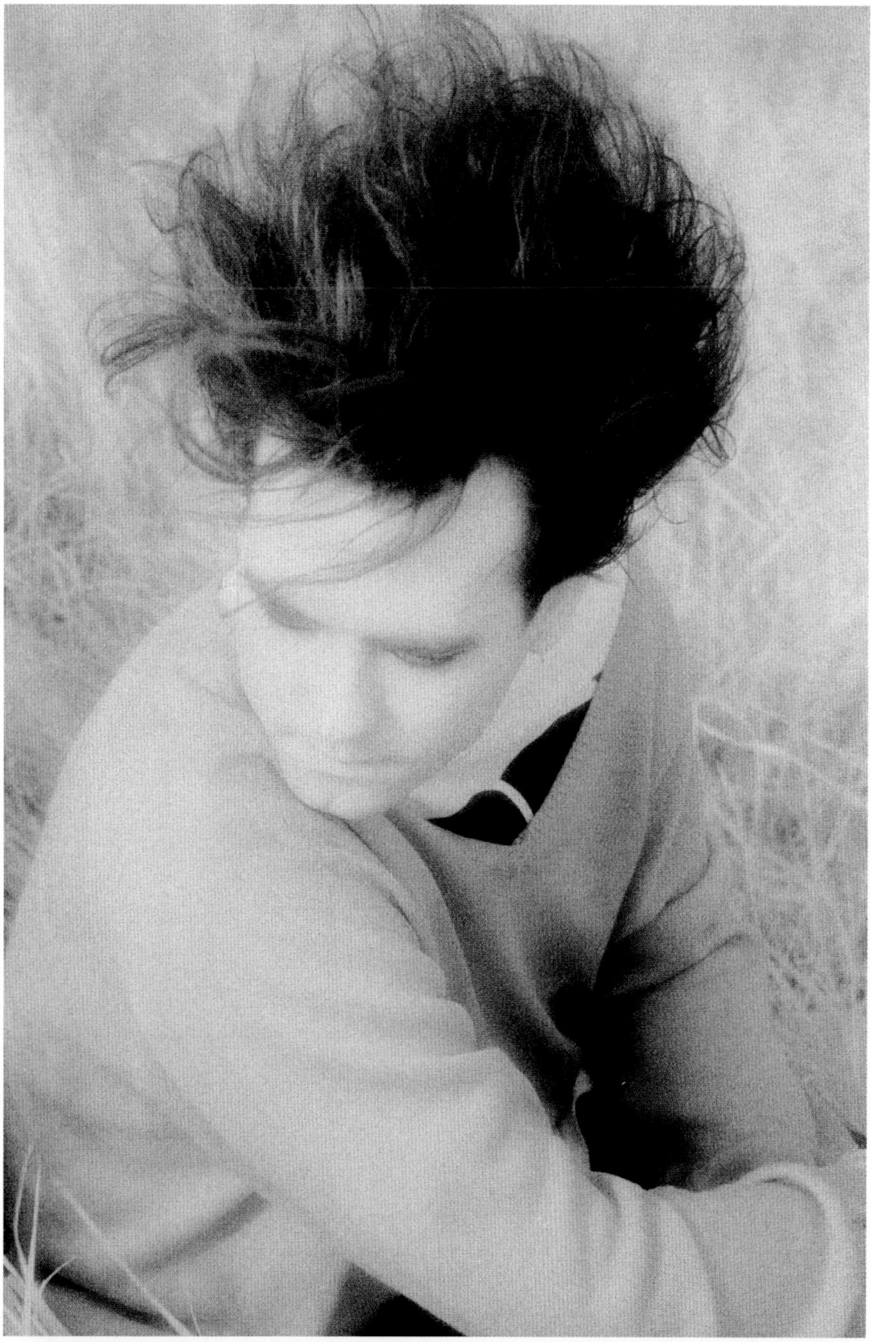

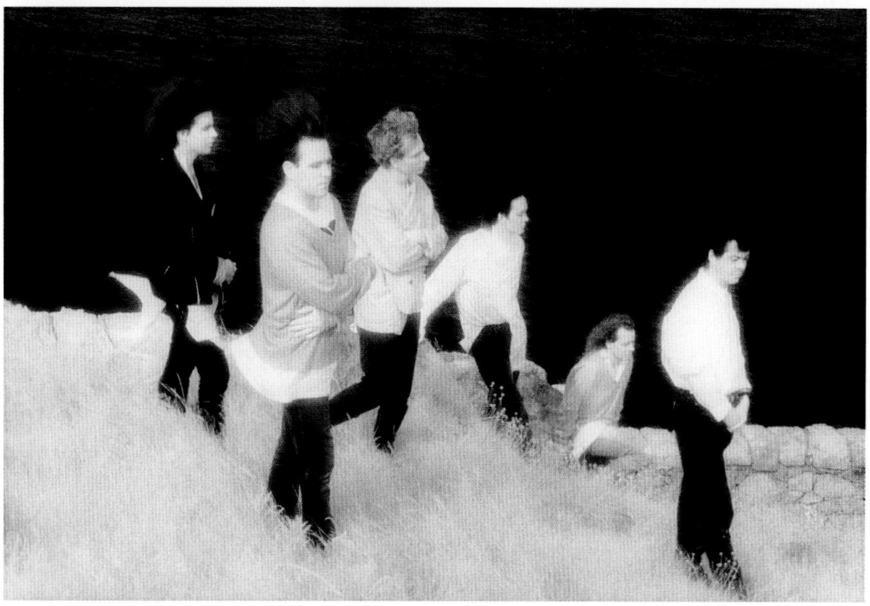

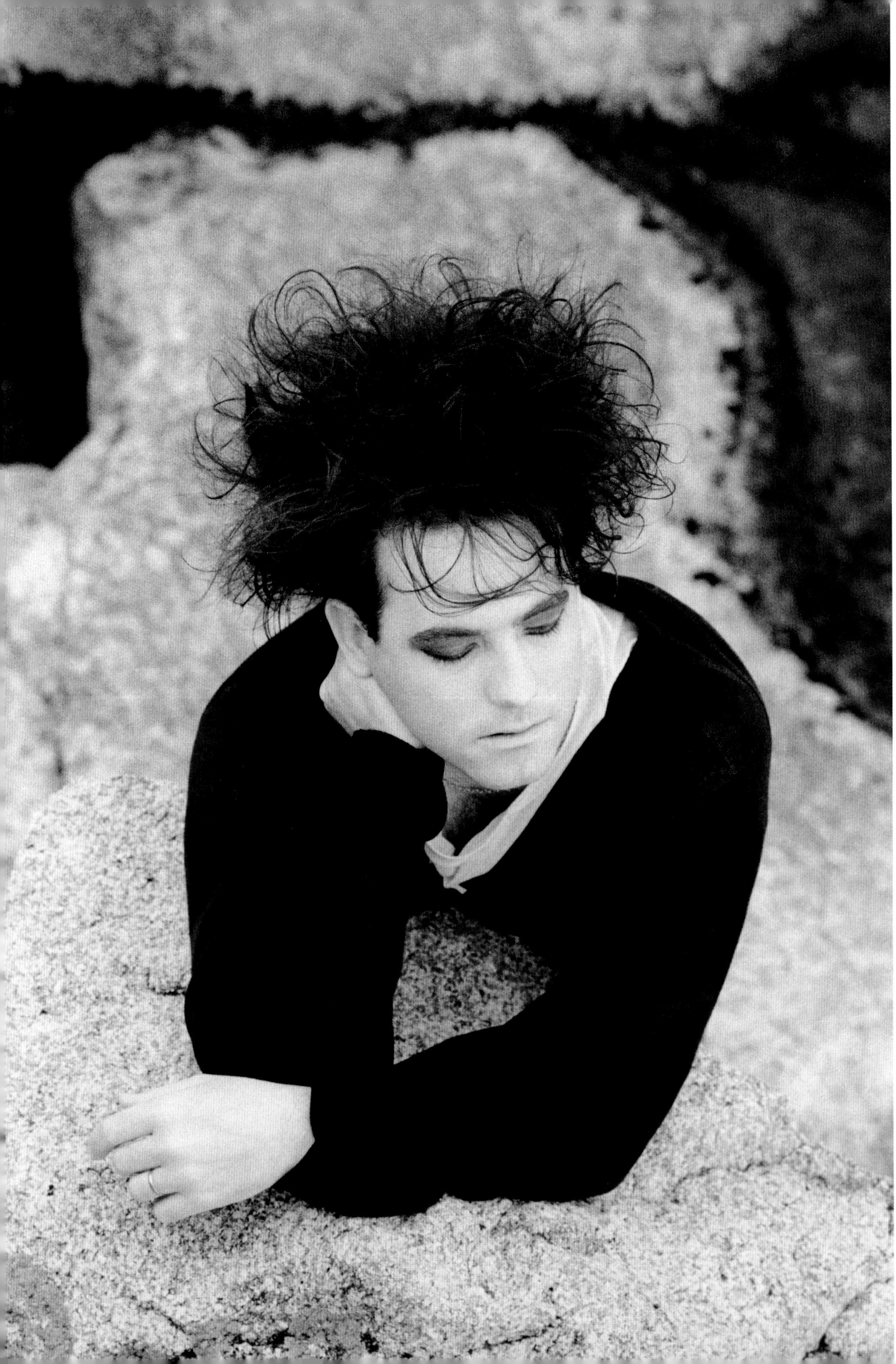

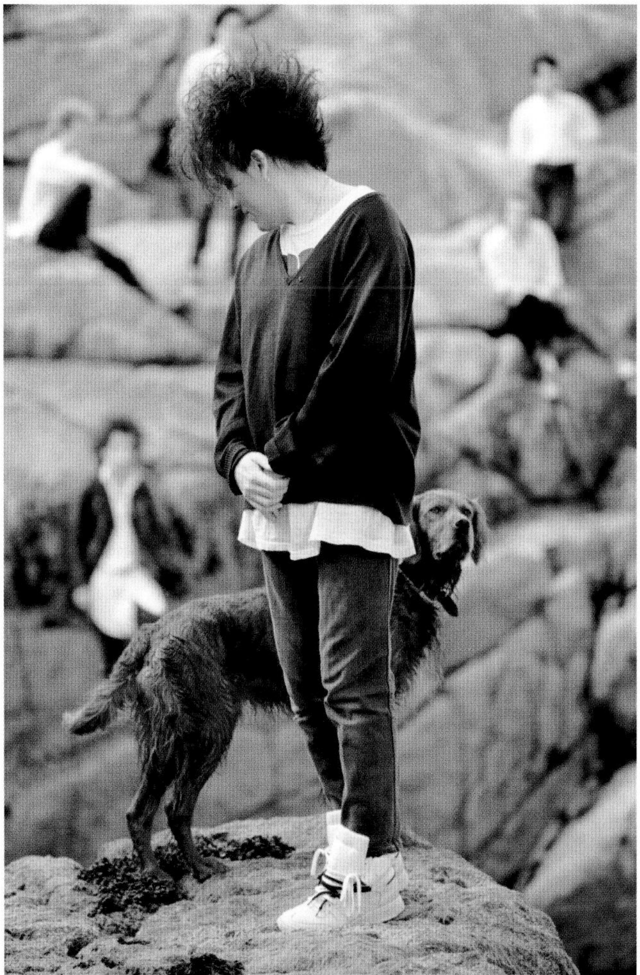

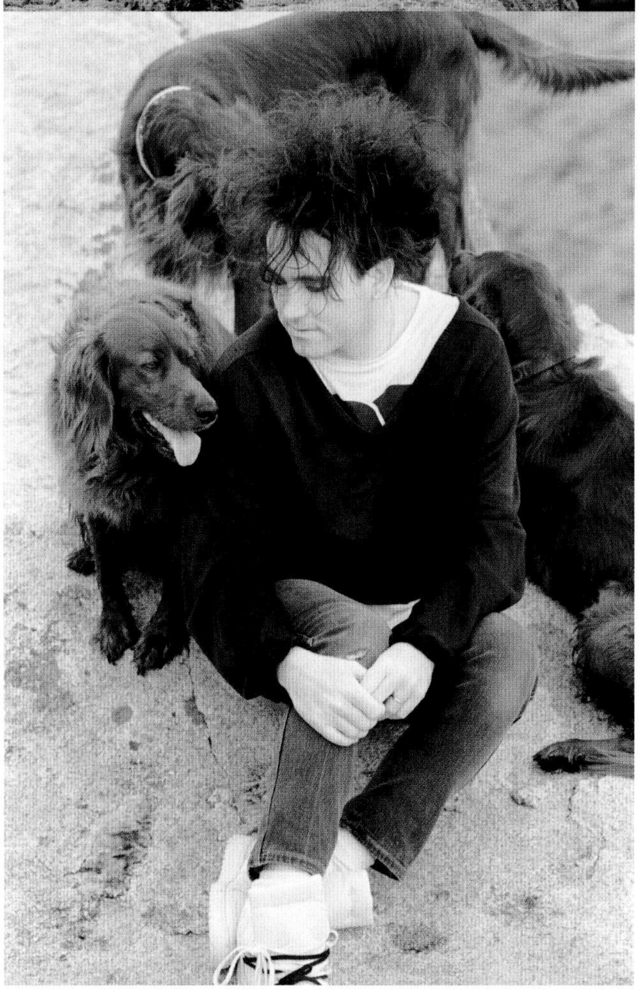

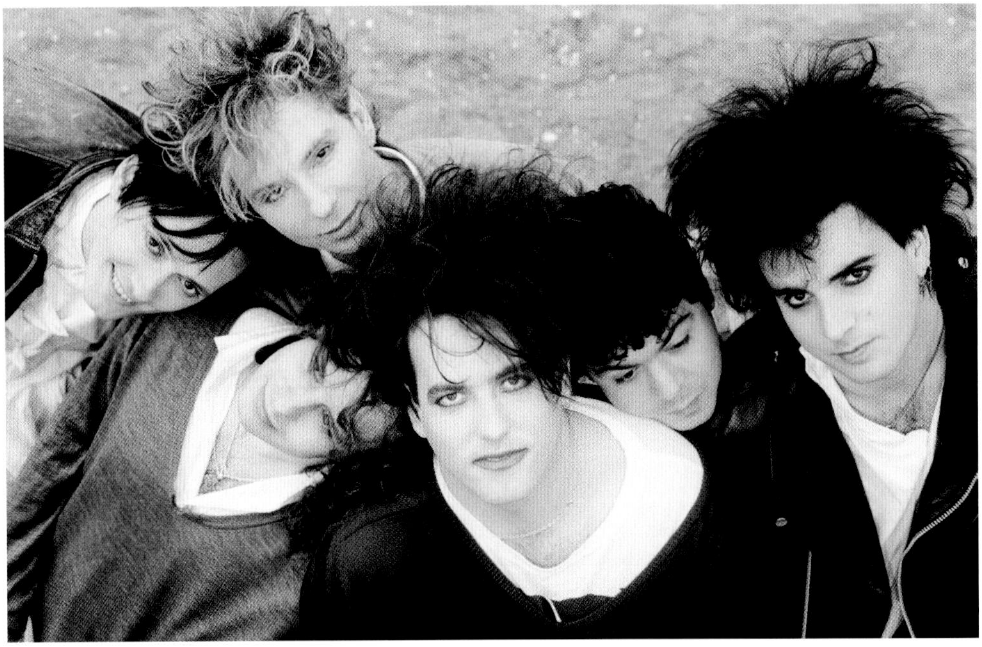

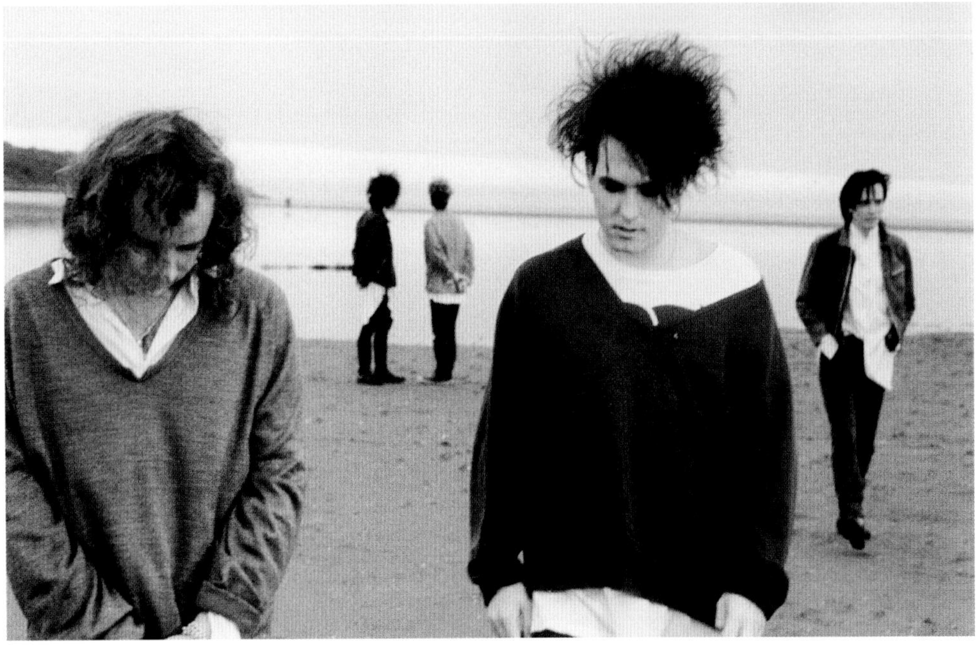

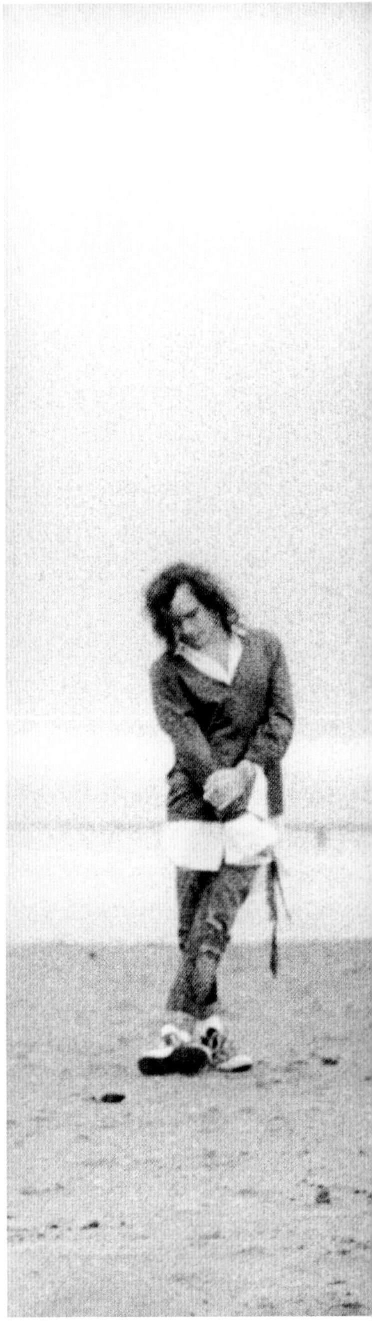

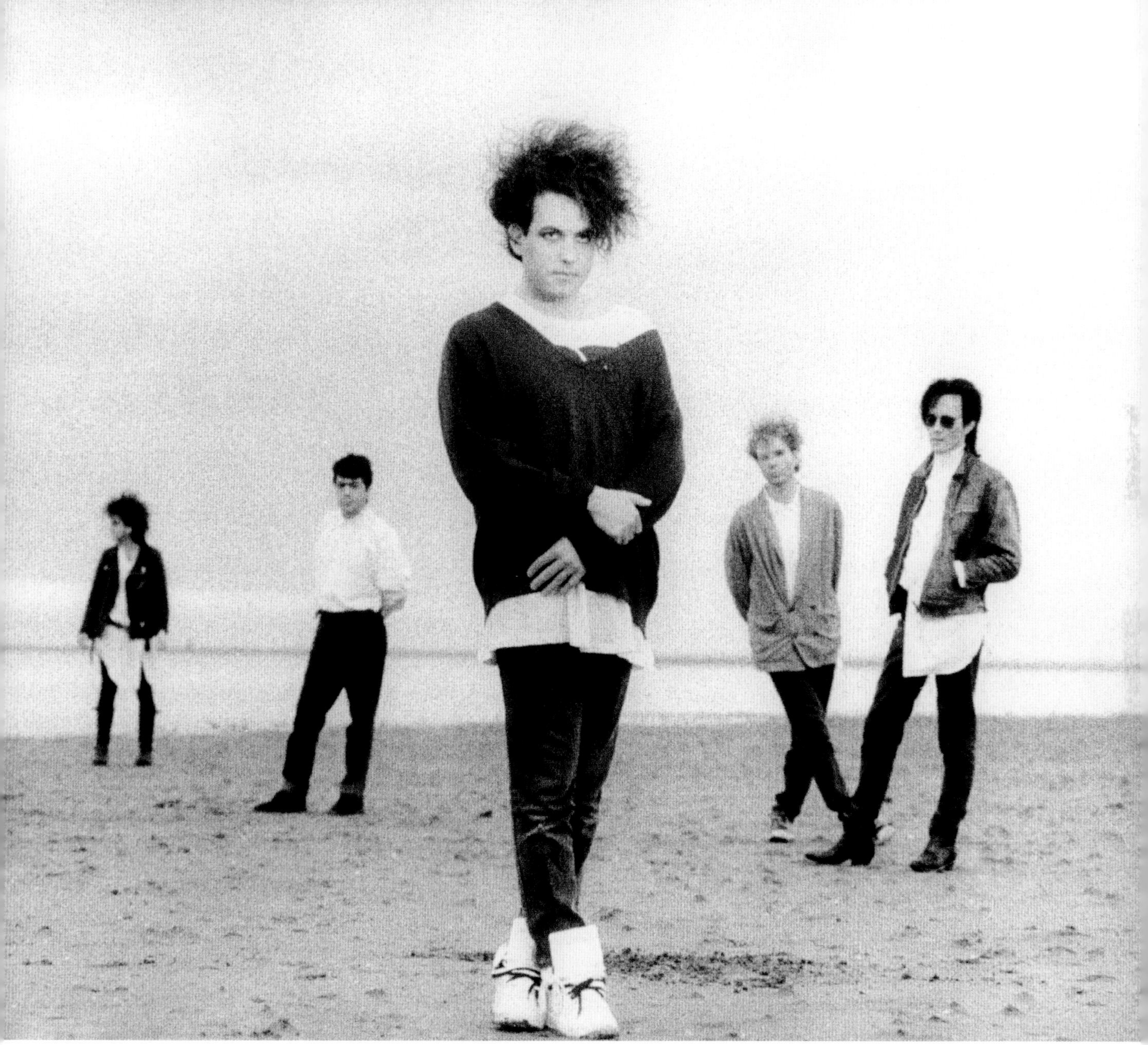

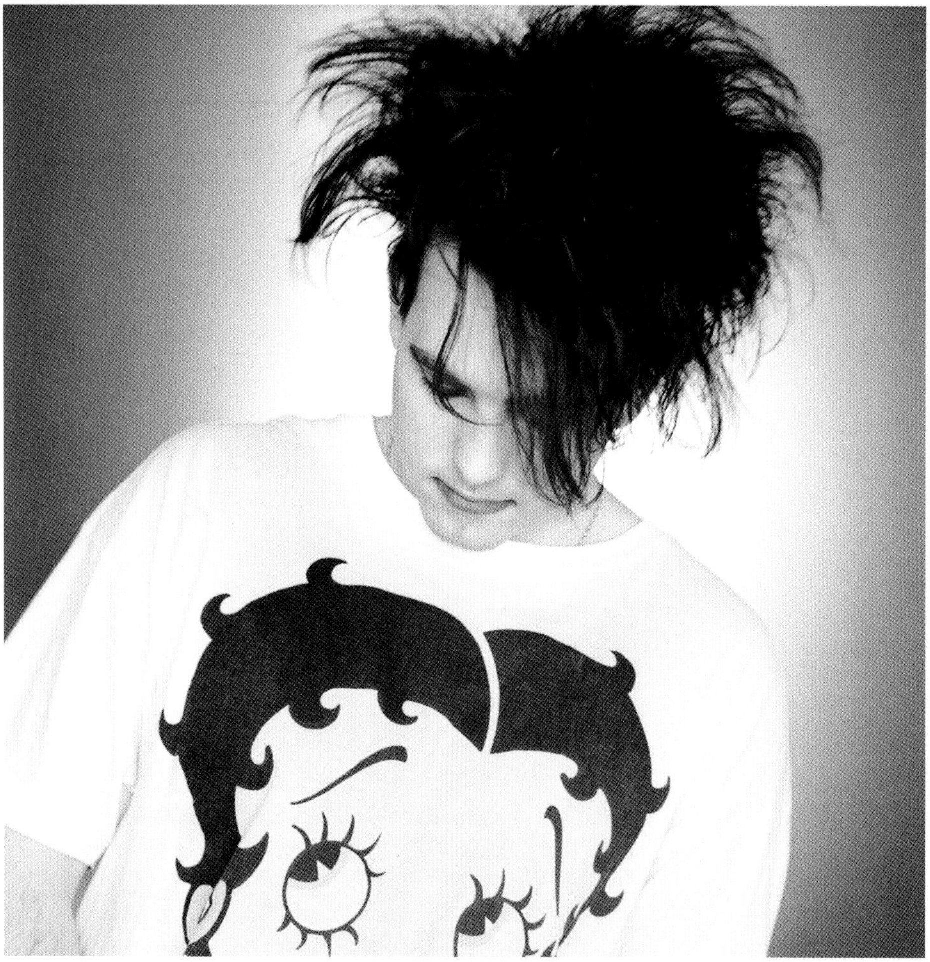
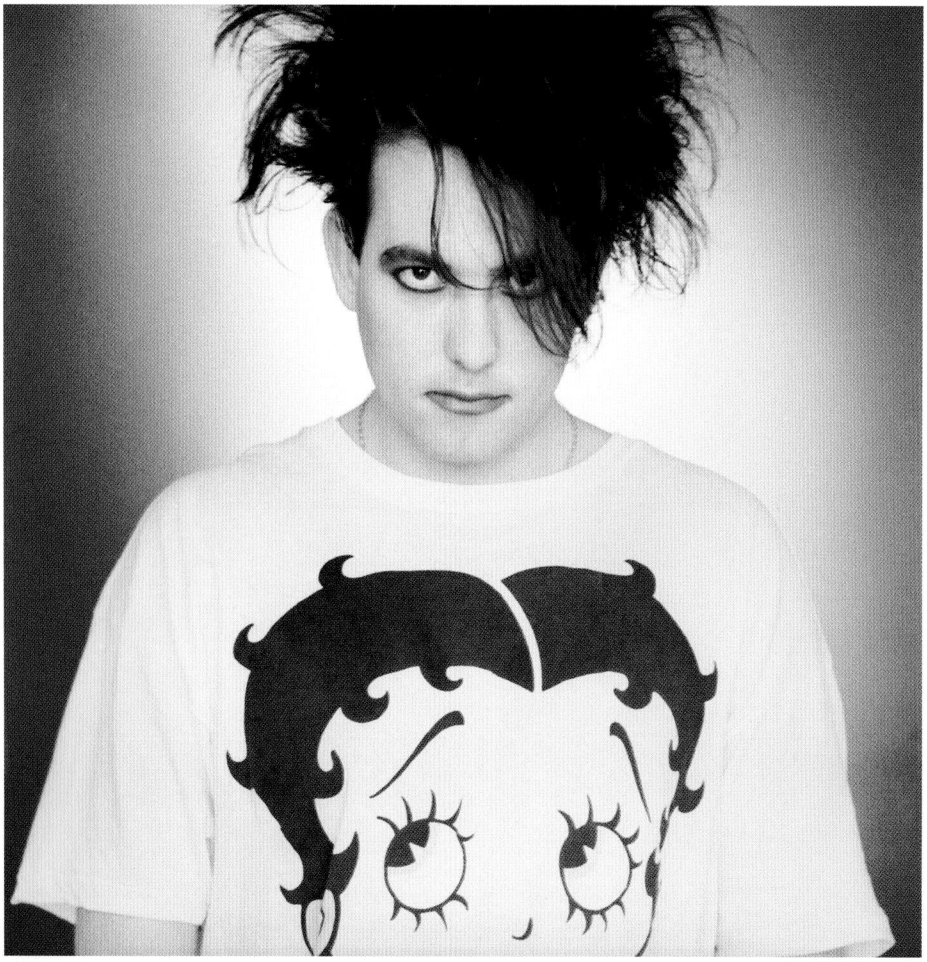

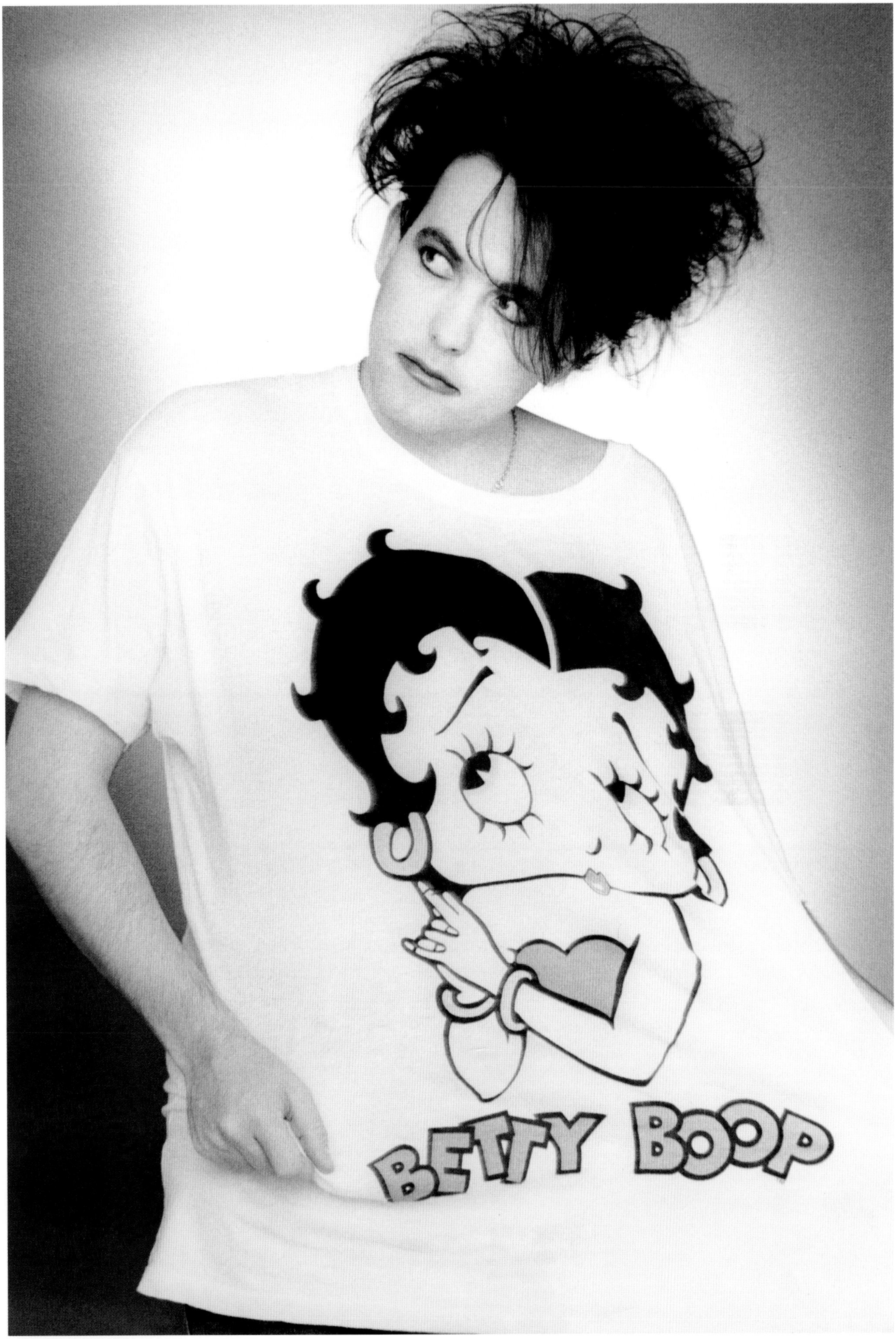
BETTY BOOP

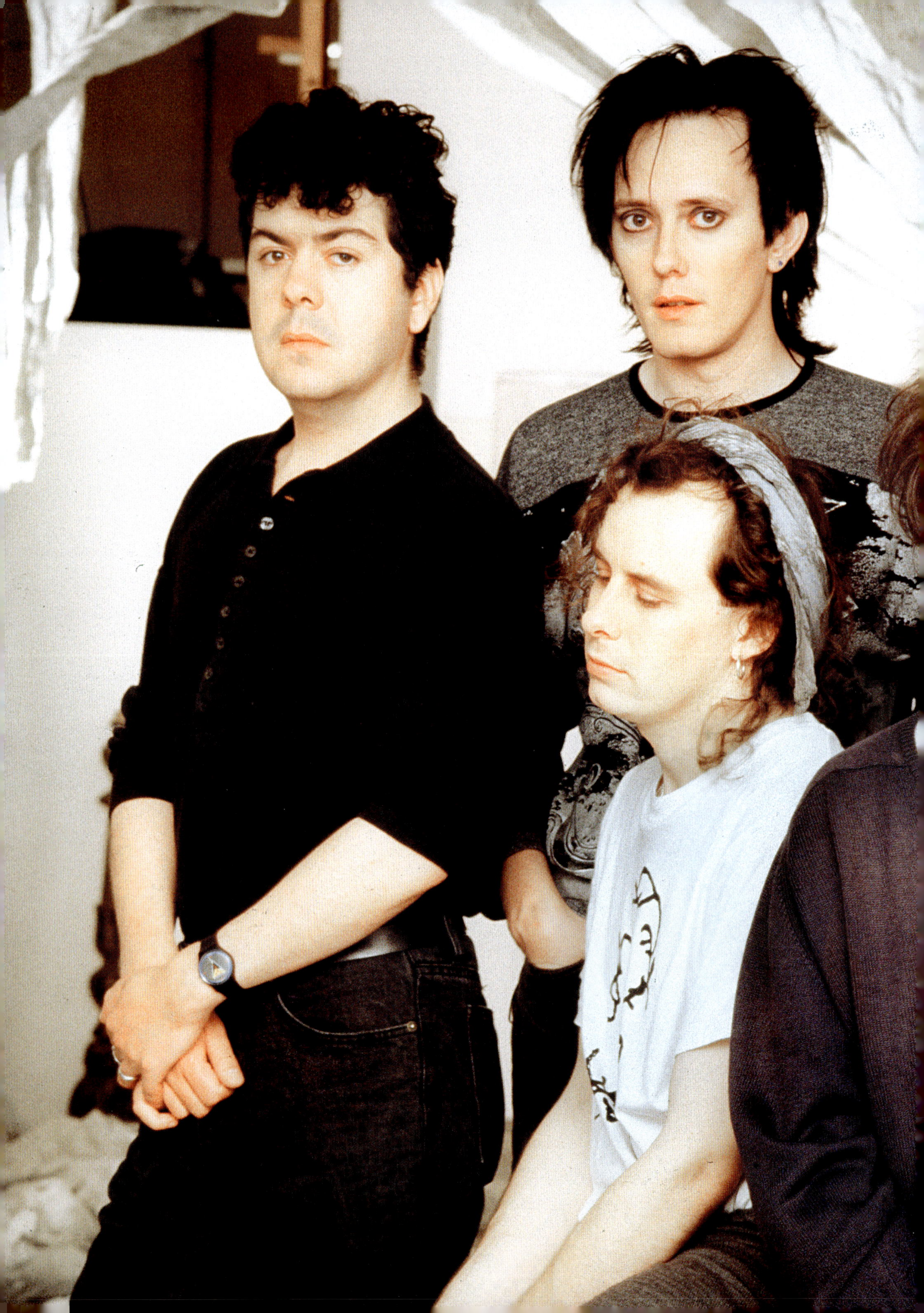

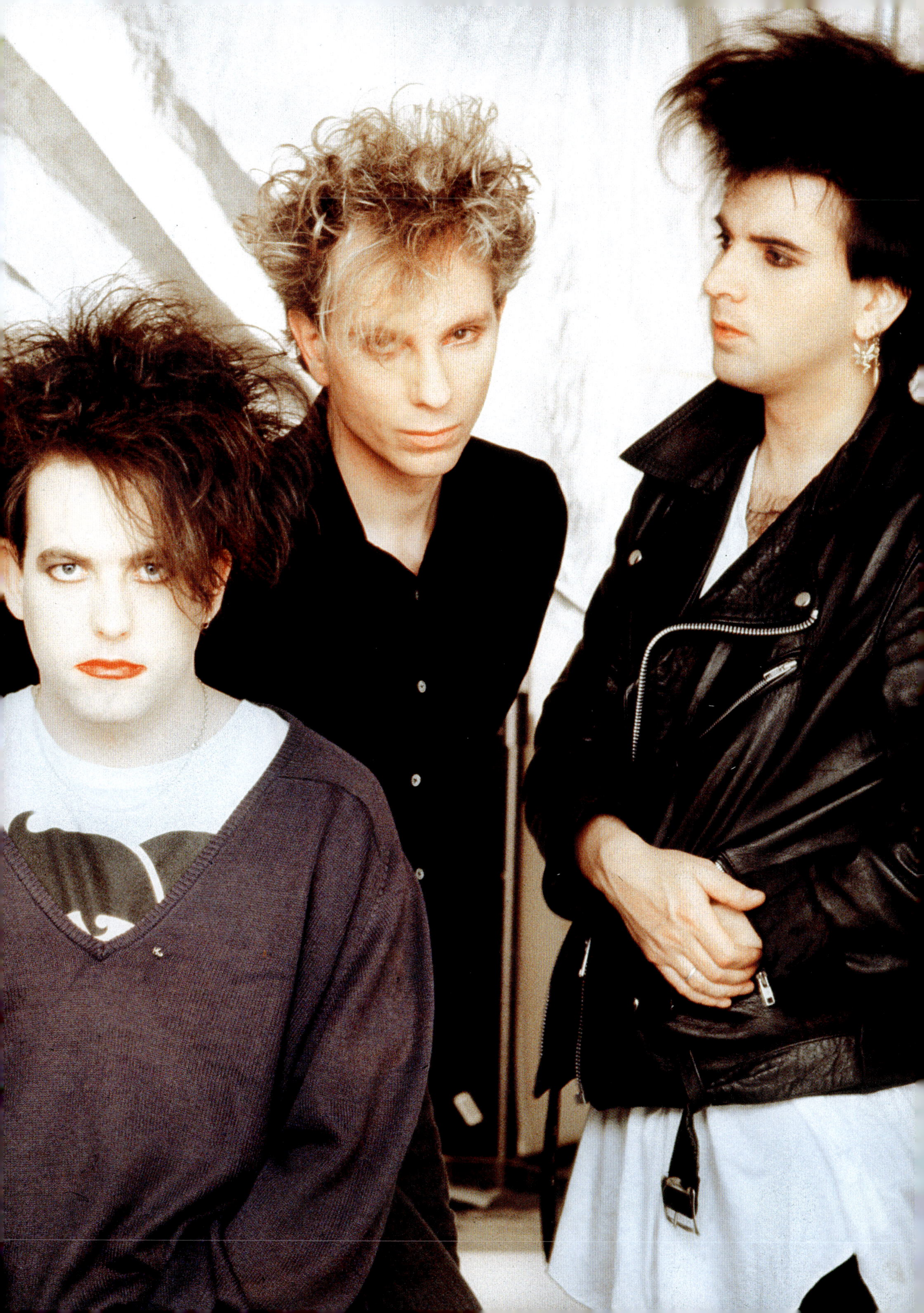

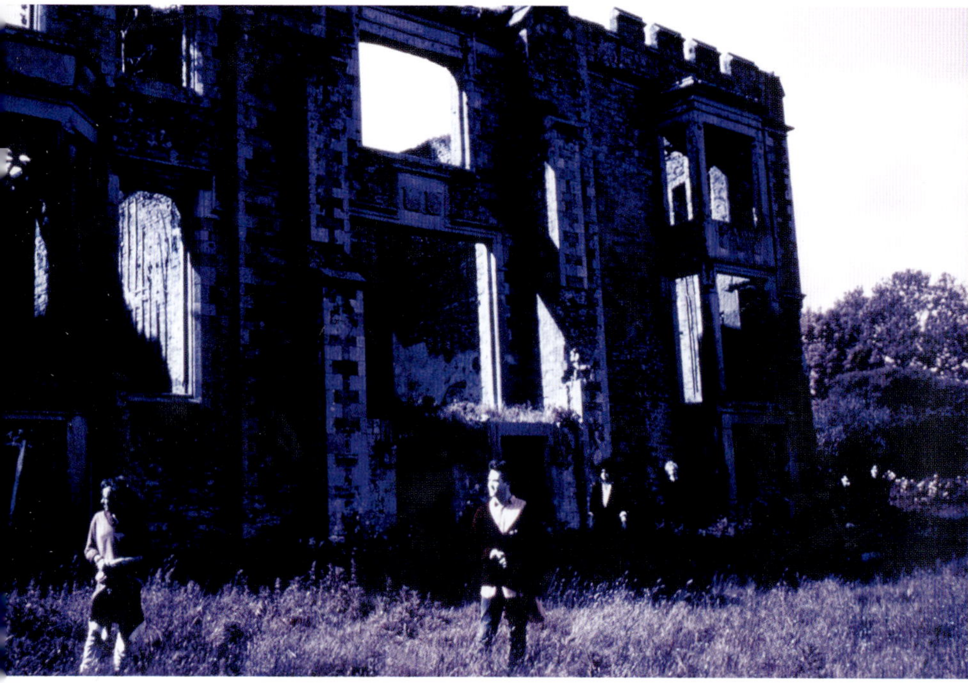
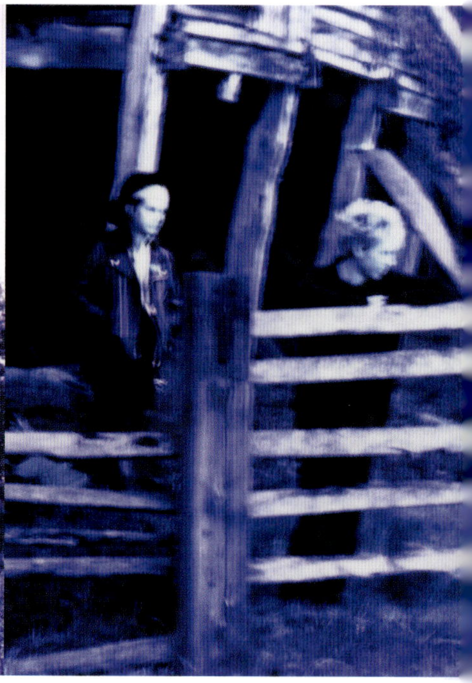

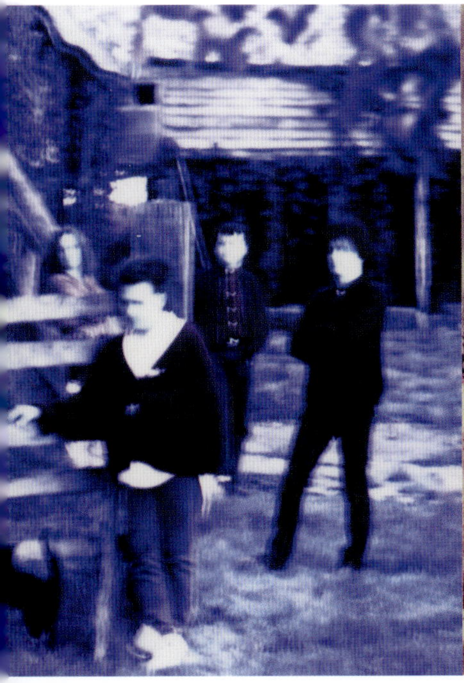

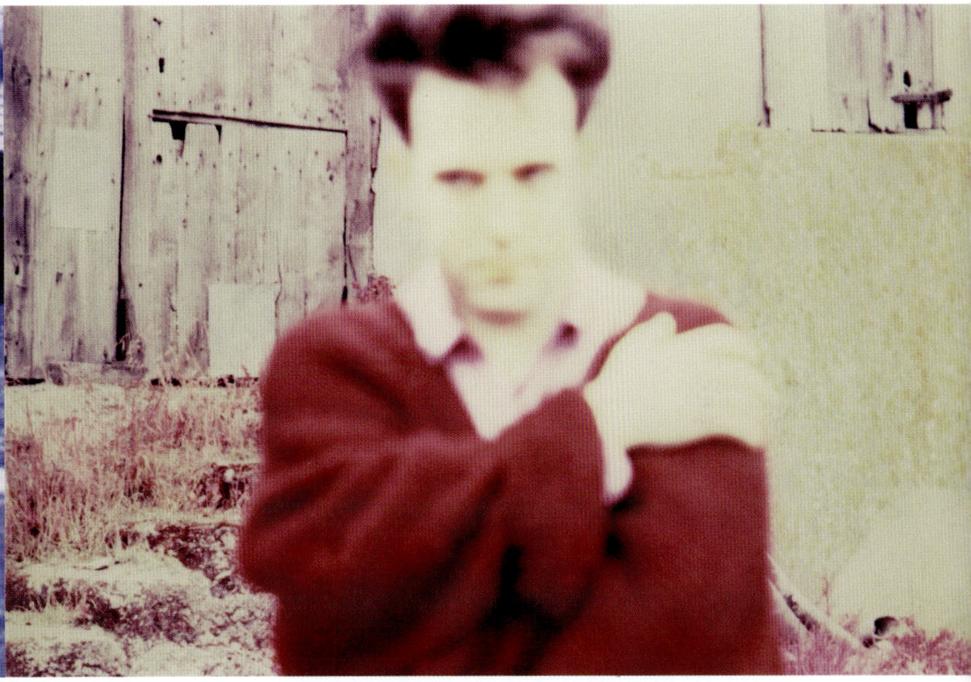

BORIS'S HOUSE
Devon
(p. 74 to 93)
1988

ROBERT: REHEARSING FOR *DISINTEGRATION* THE UP-COMING ALBUM RECORDING SESSION. SHAME I HAD MY HAIR CUT DRUNKENLY SHORT BEFORE THE SESSION – IT DEFINITELY HURTS THE GOTHIC VIBE… WELL, THAT AND THE DENIM SHIRT! P89 IS PRETTY MOODY THOUGH…

Paul: We turned up at Boris's house where the band were staying and rehearsing, once again not knowing what we would find. It turned out to be a great outdoor location, with lots of rambling outbuildings and a nearby derelict folly. The surrounding moors contributed to the atmospheric feel.

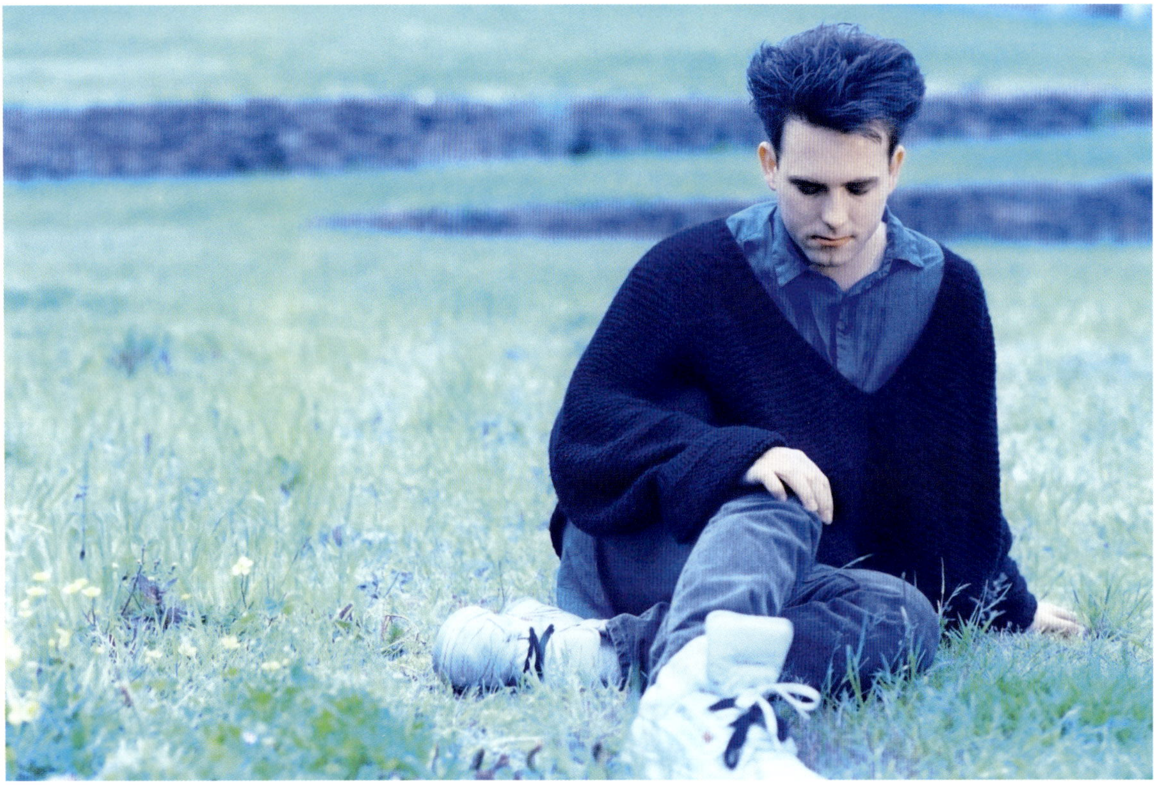

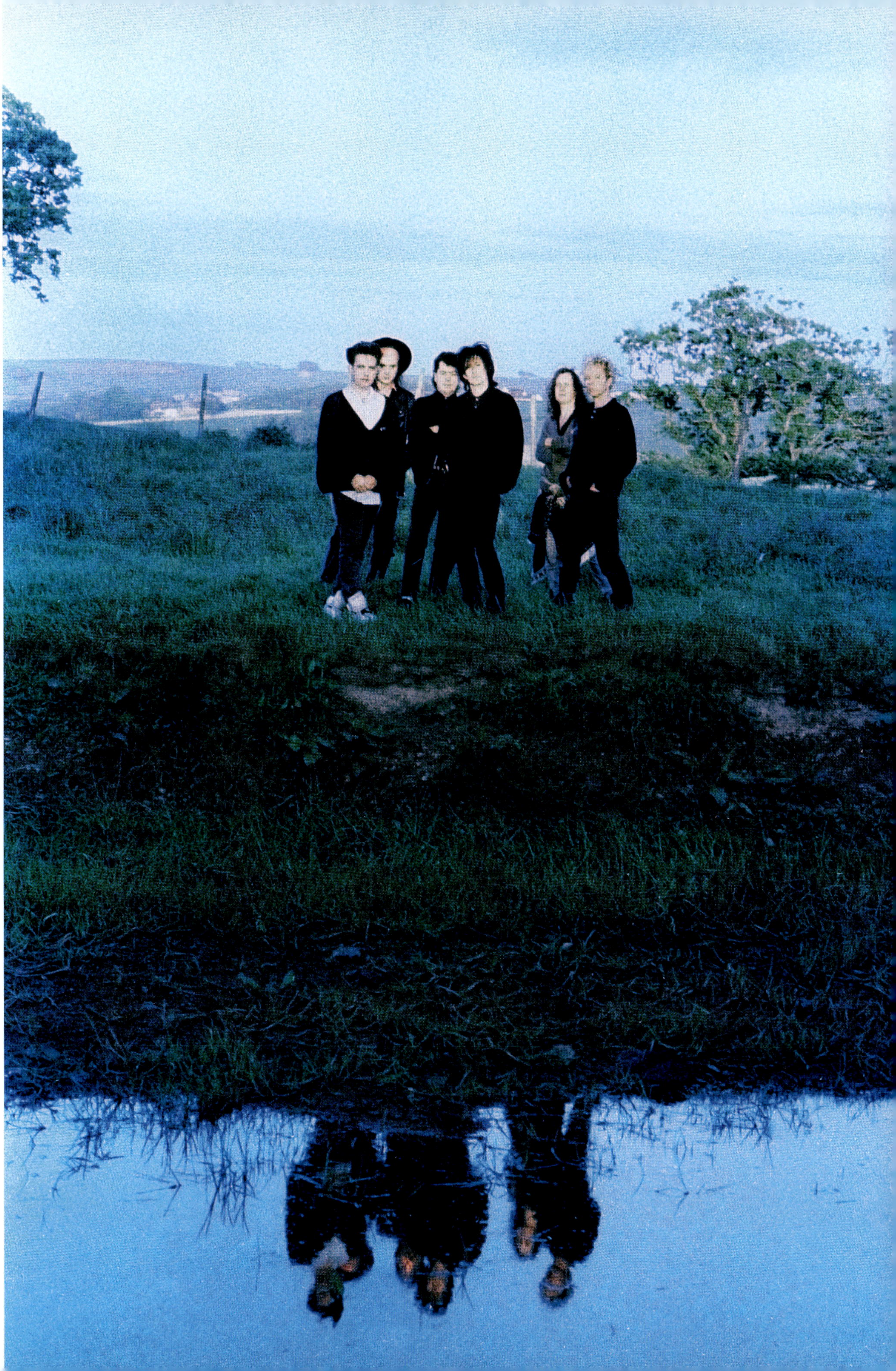

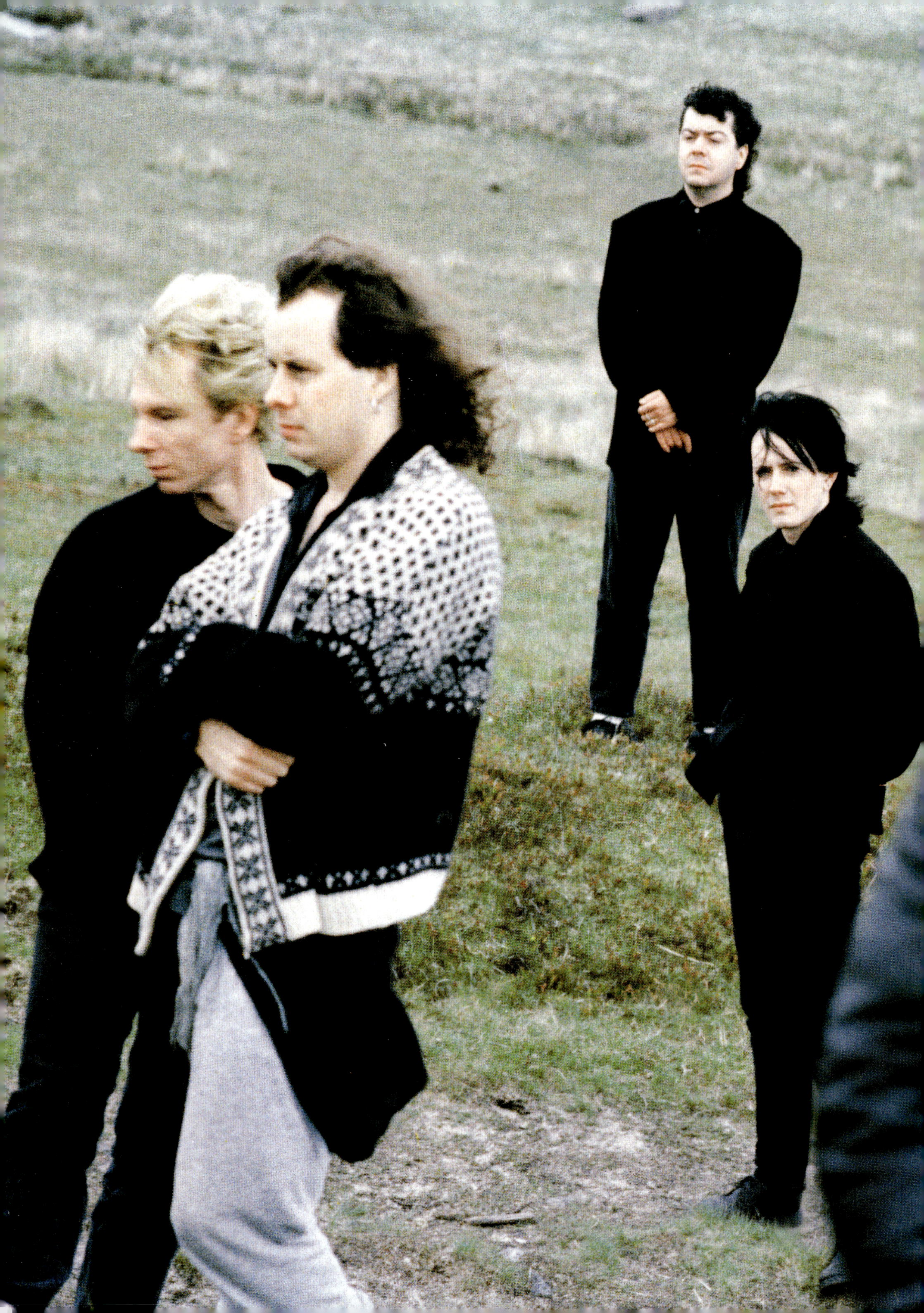

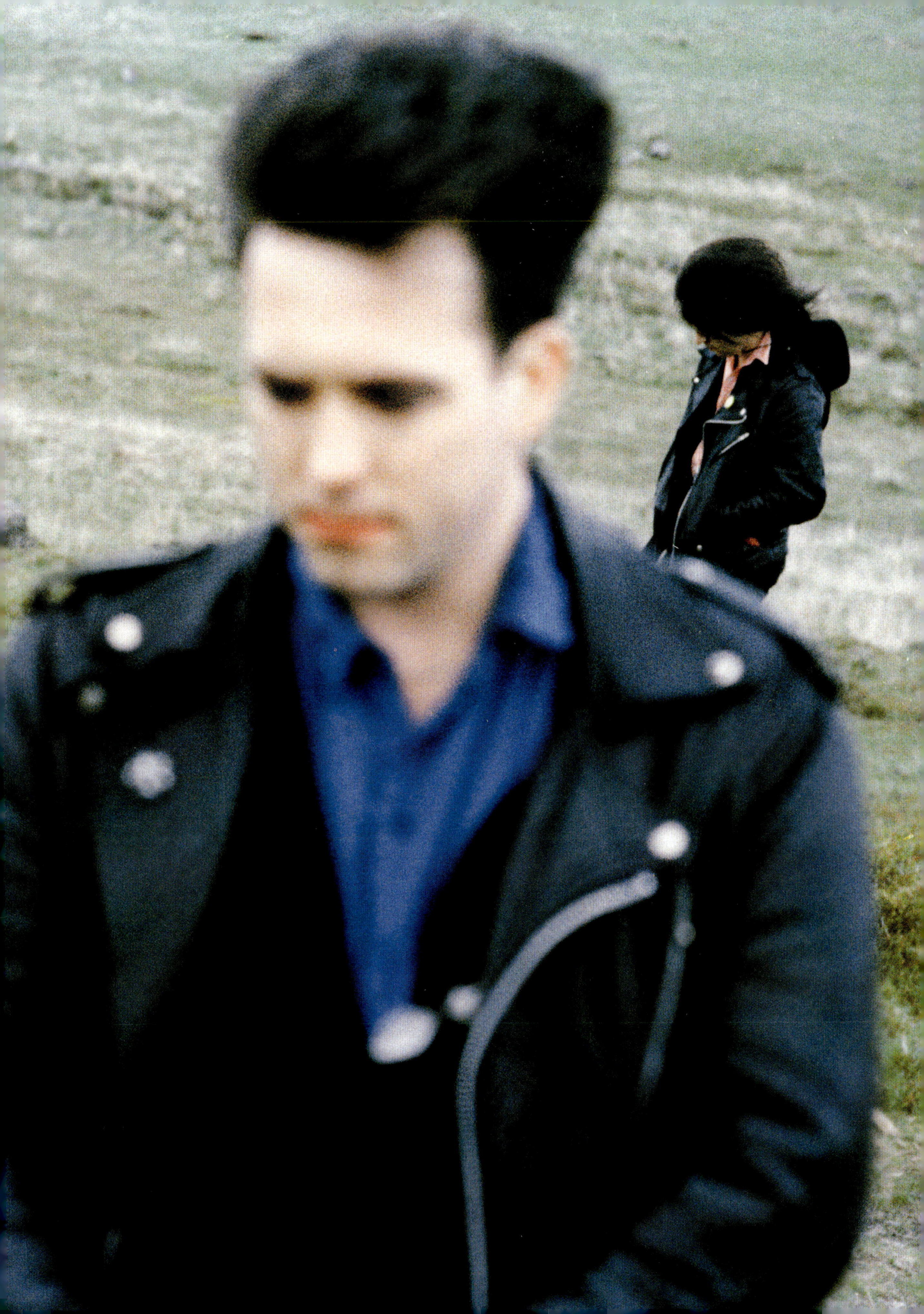

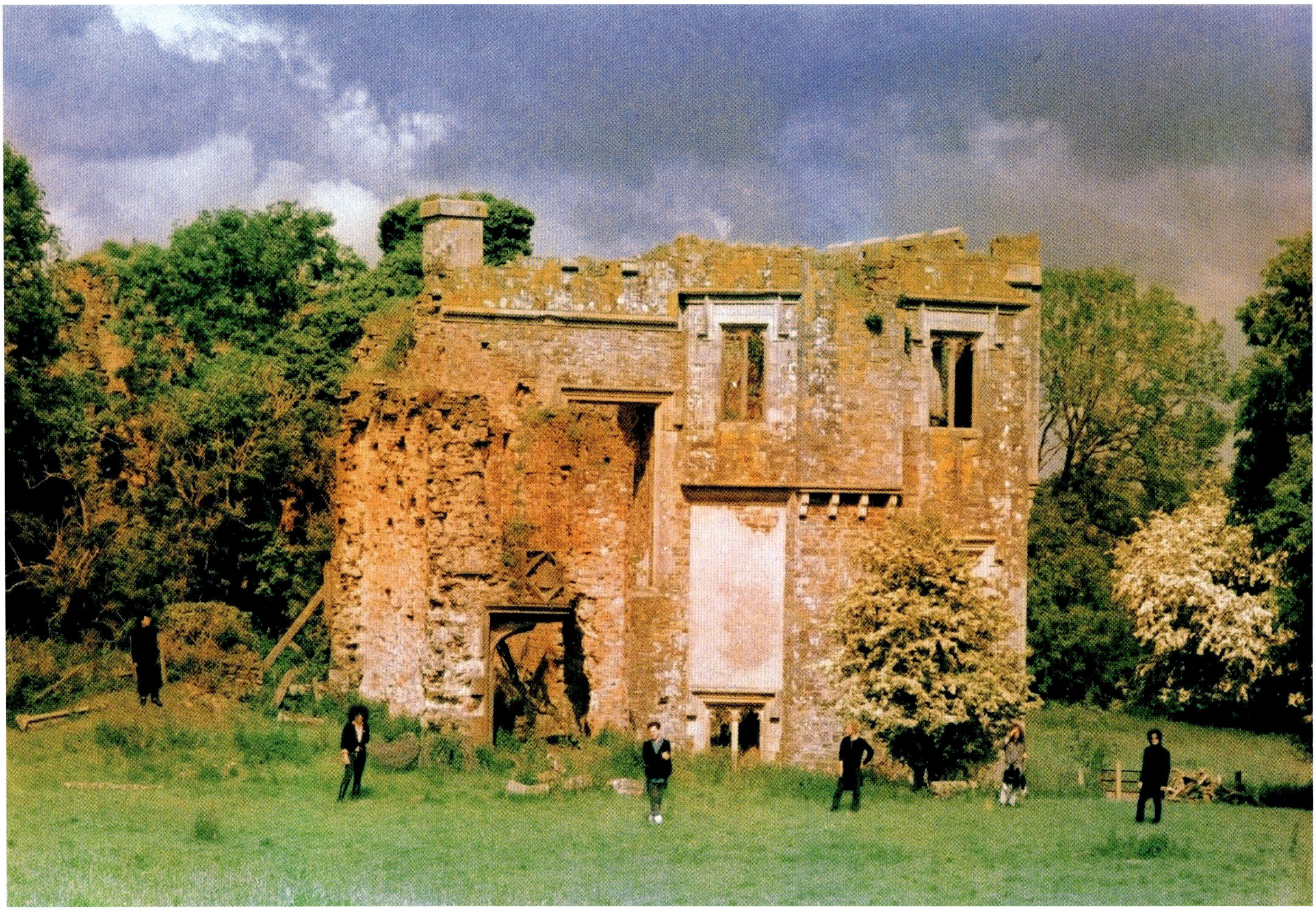

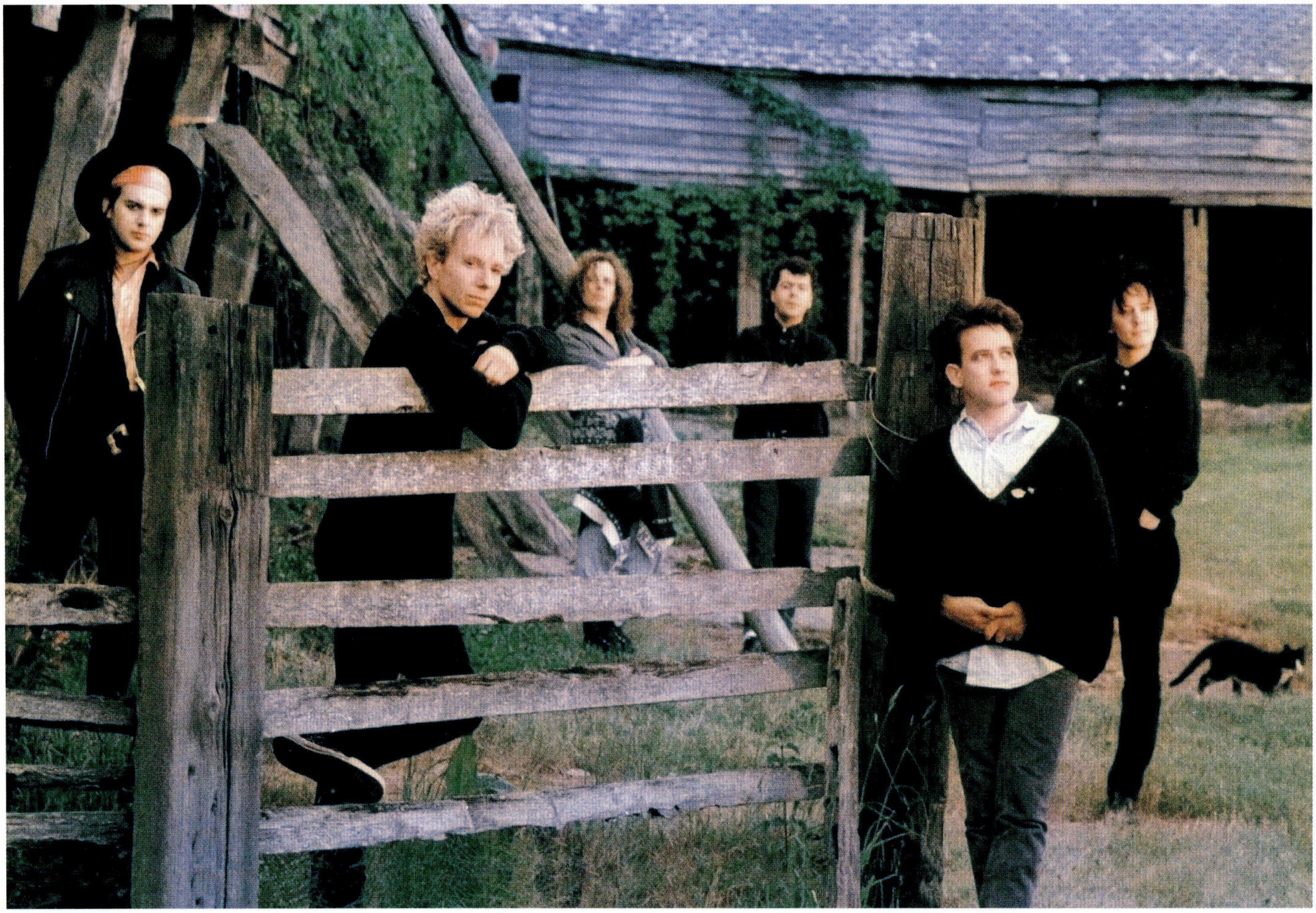

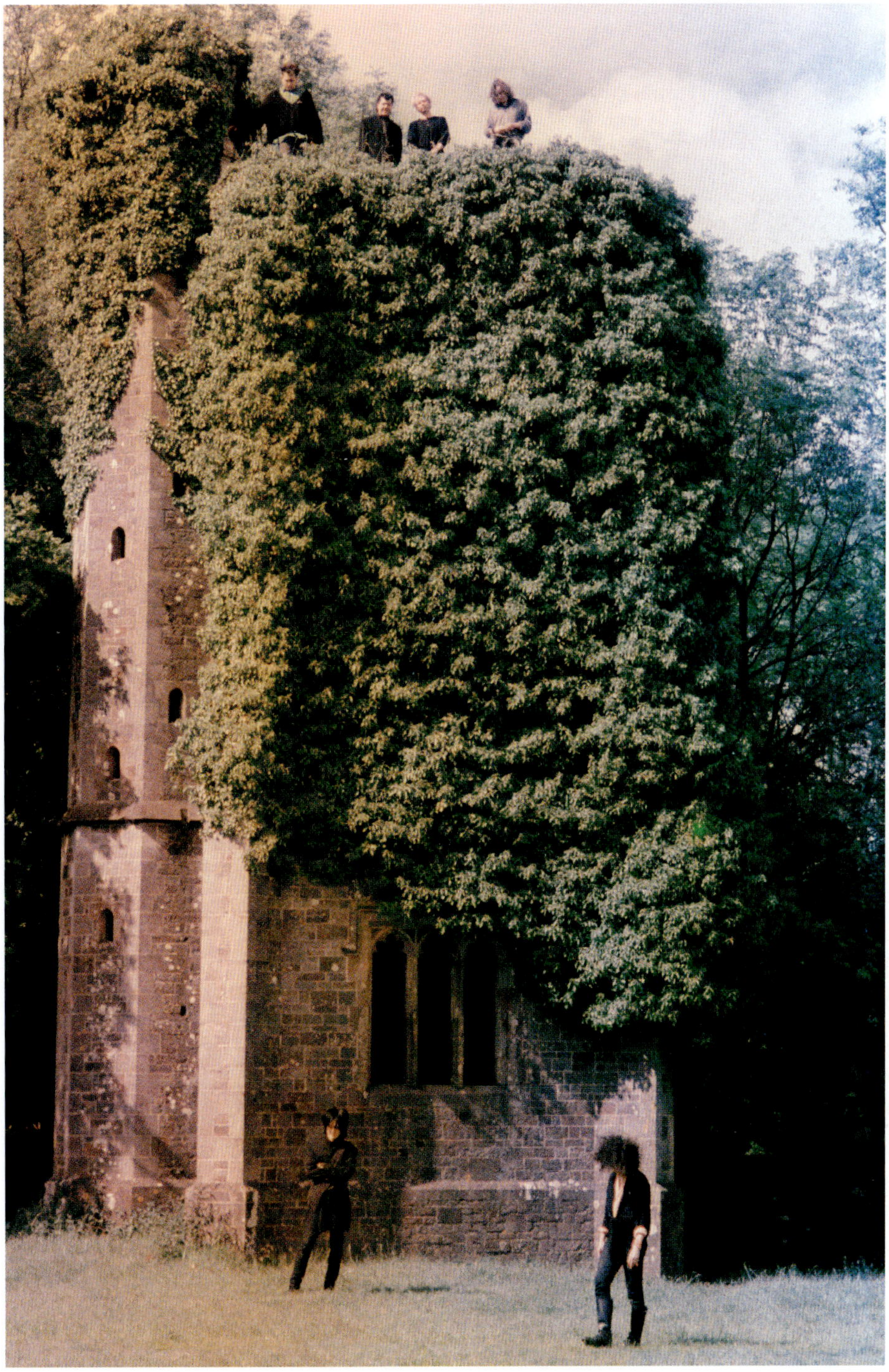

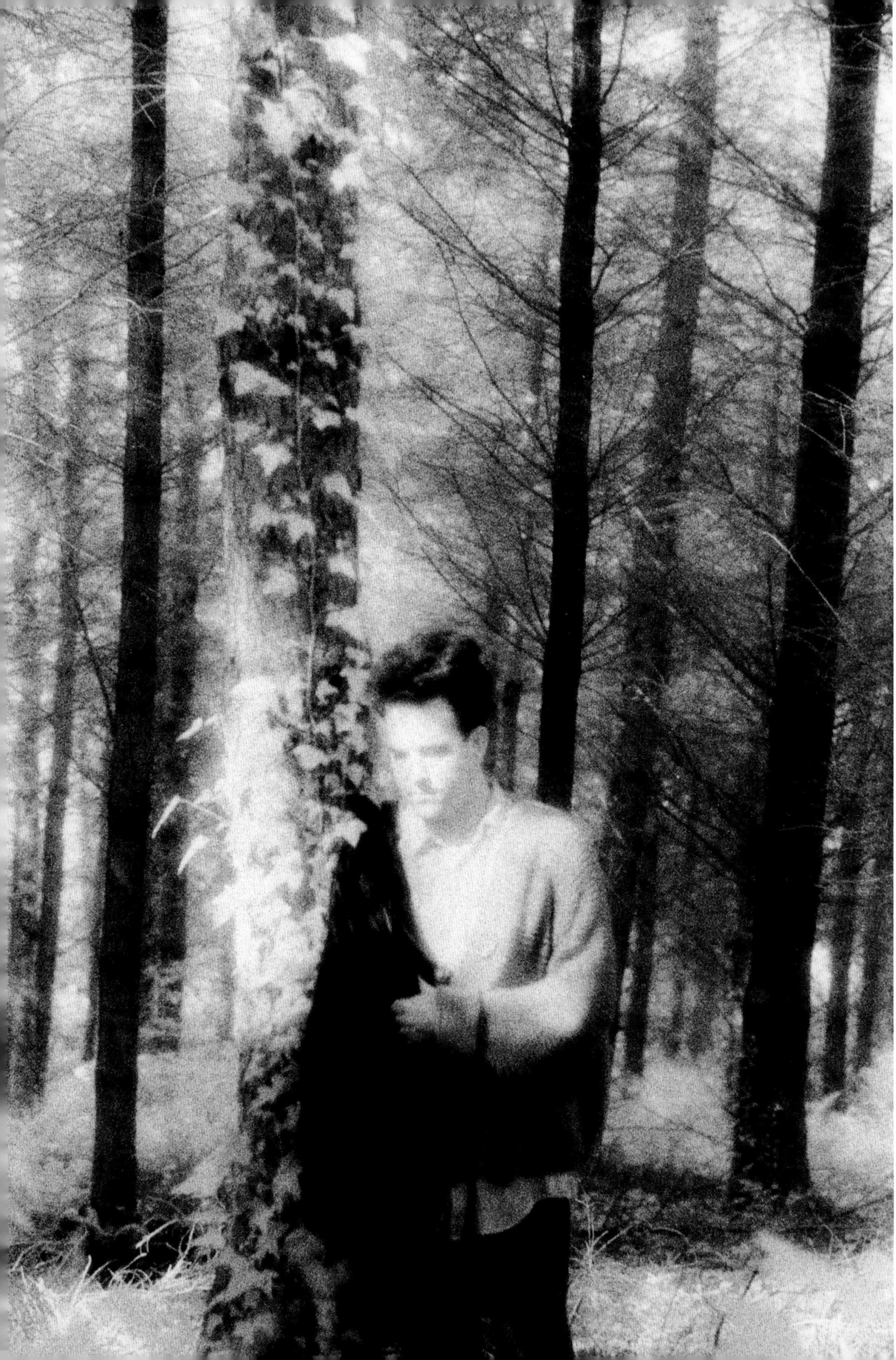

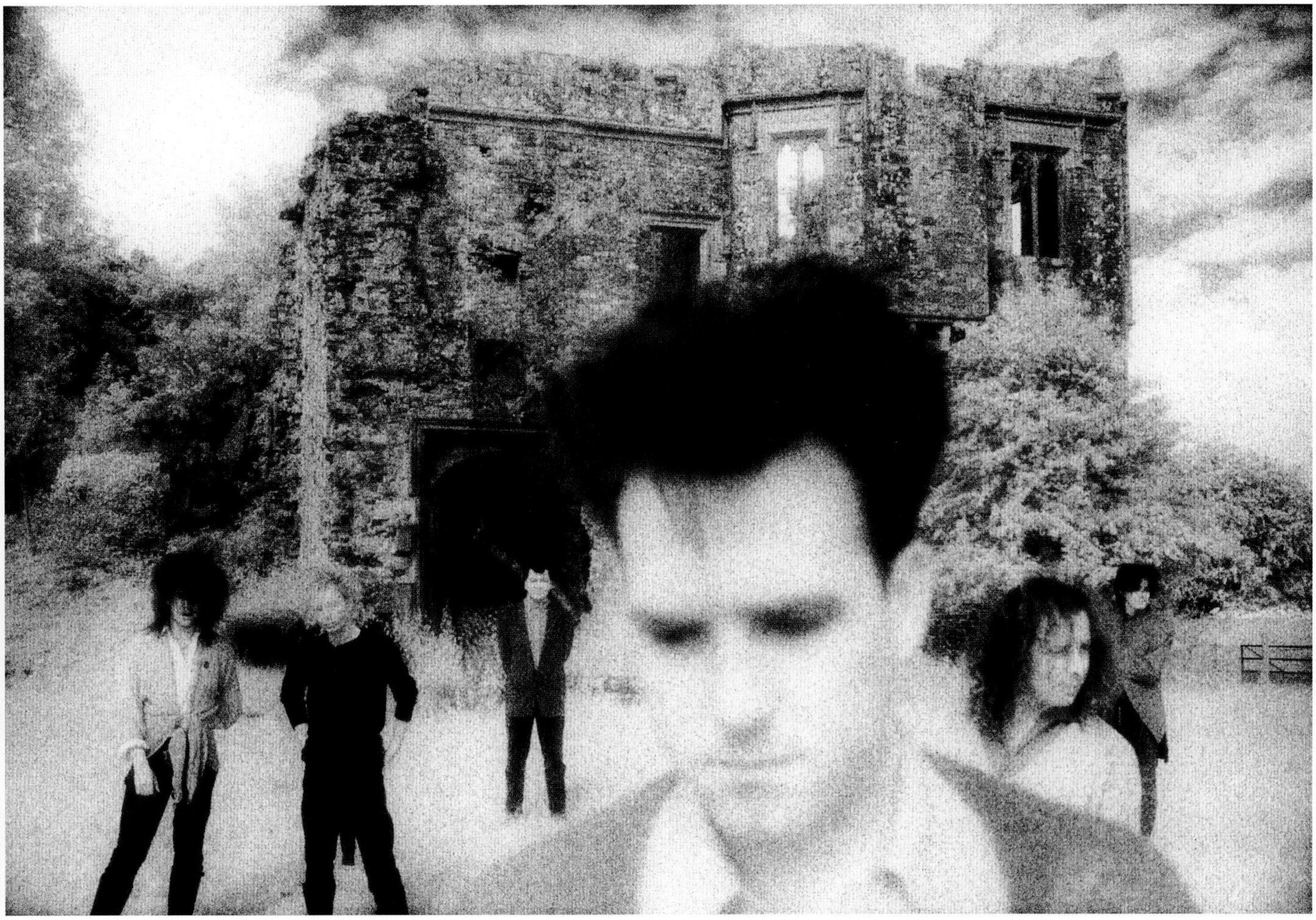

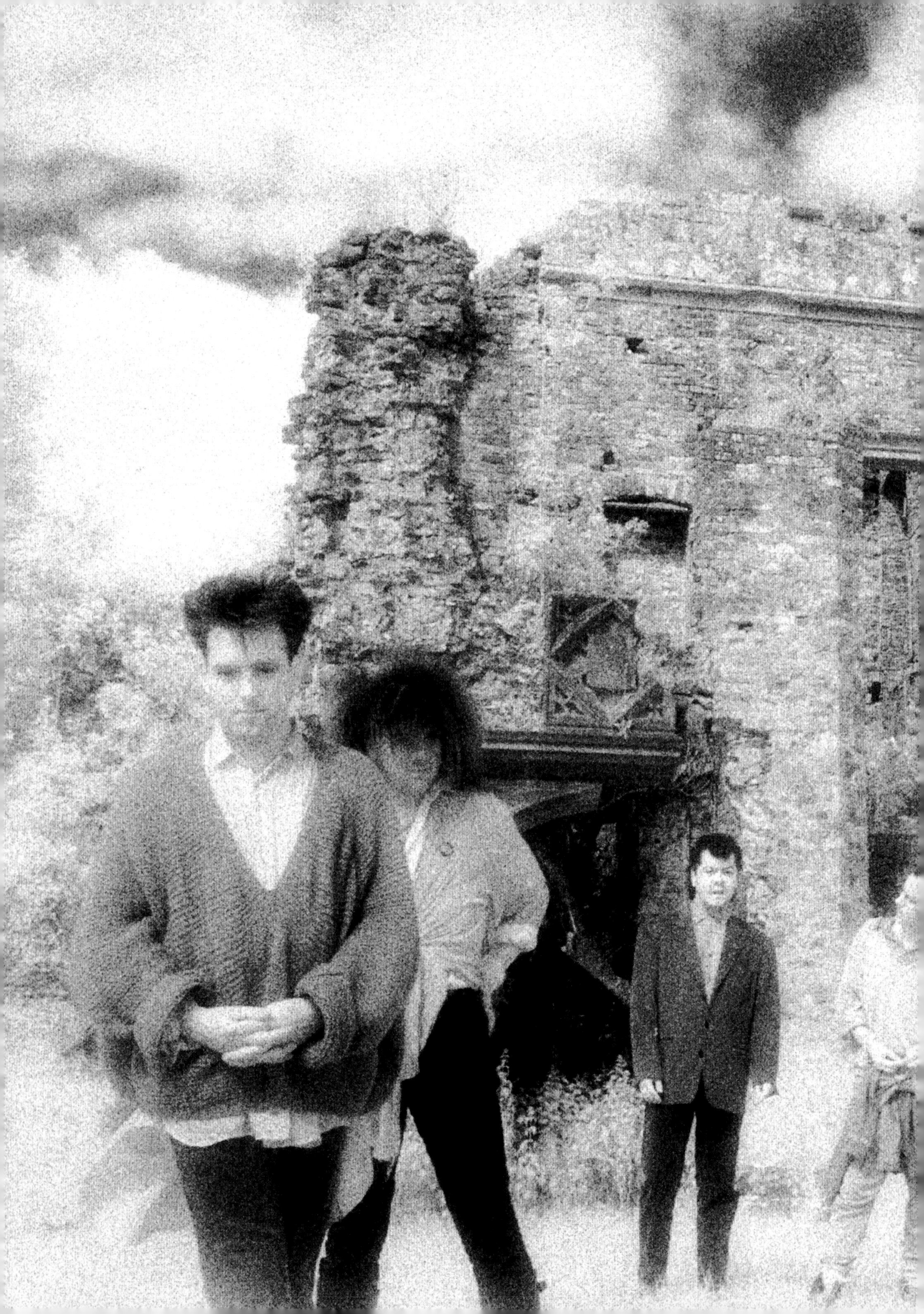

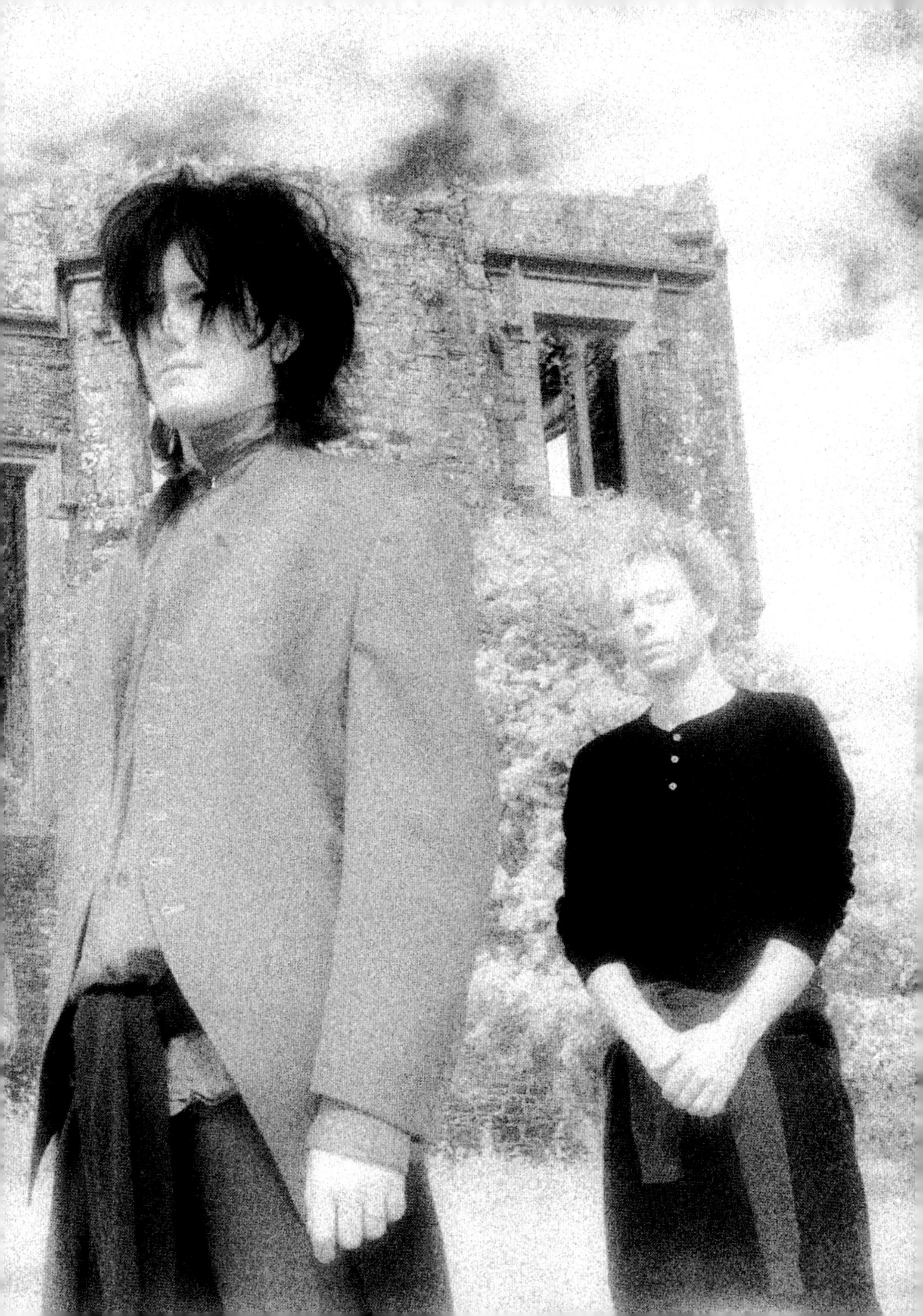

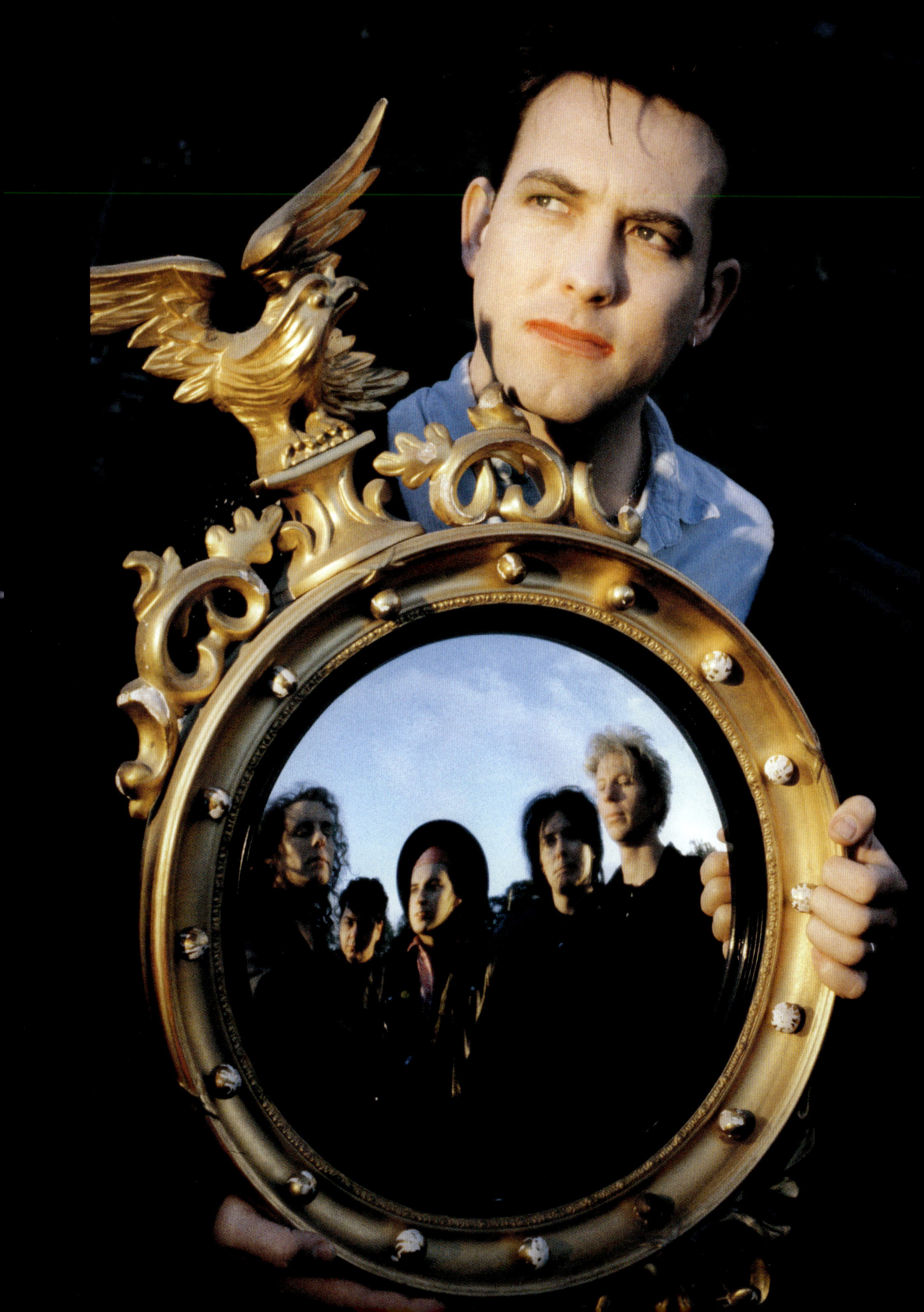

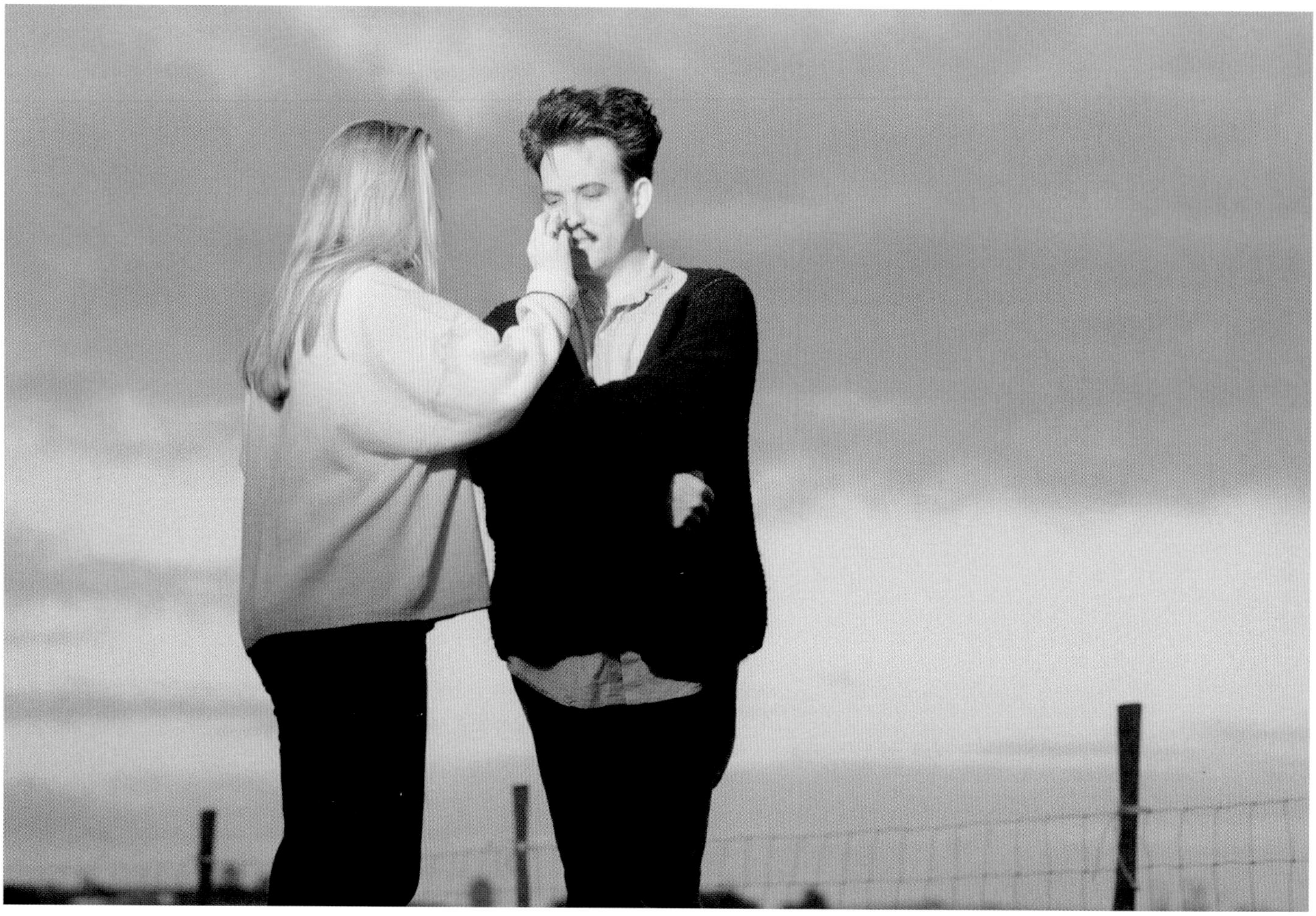

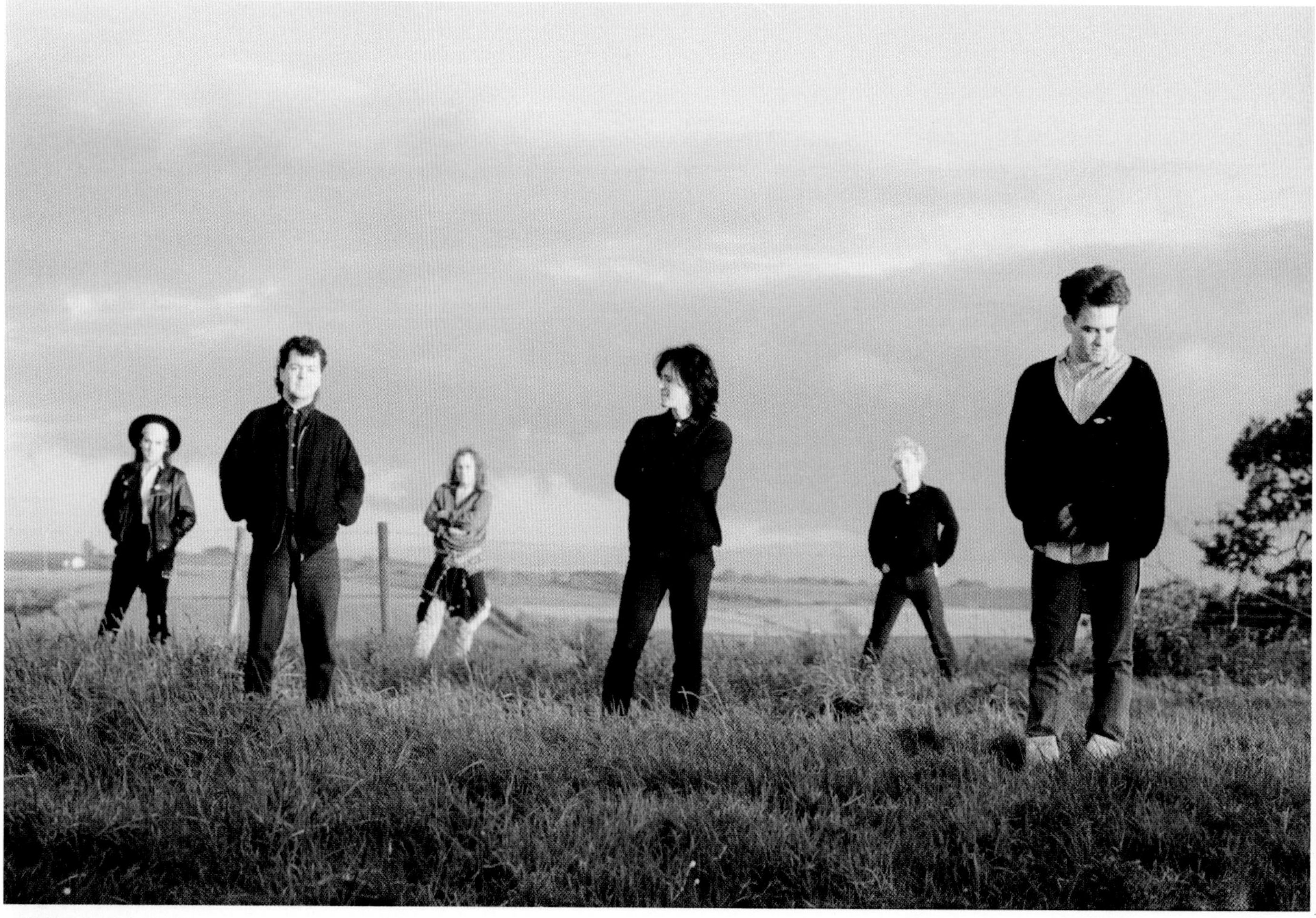

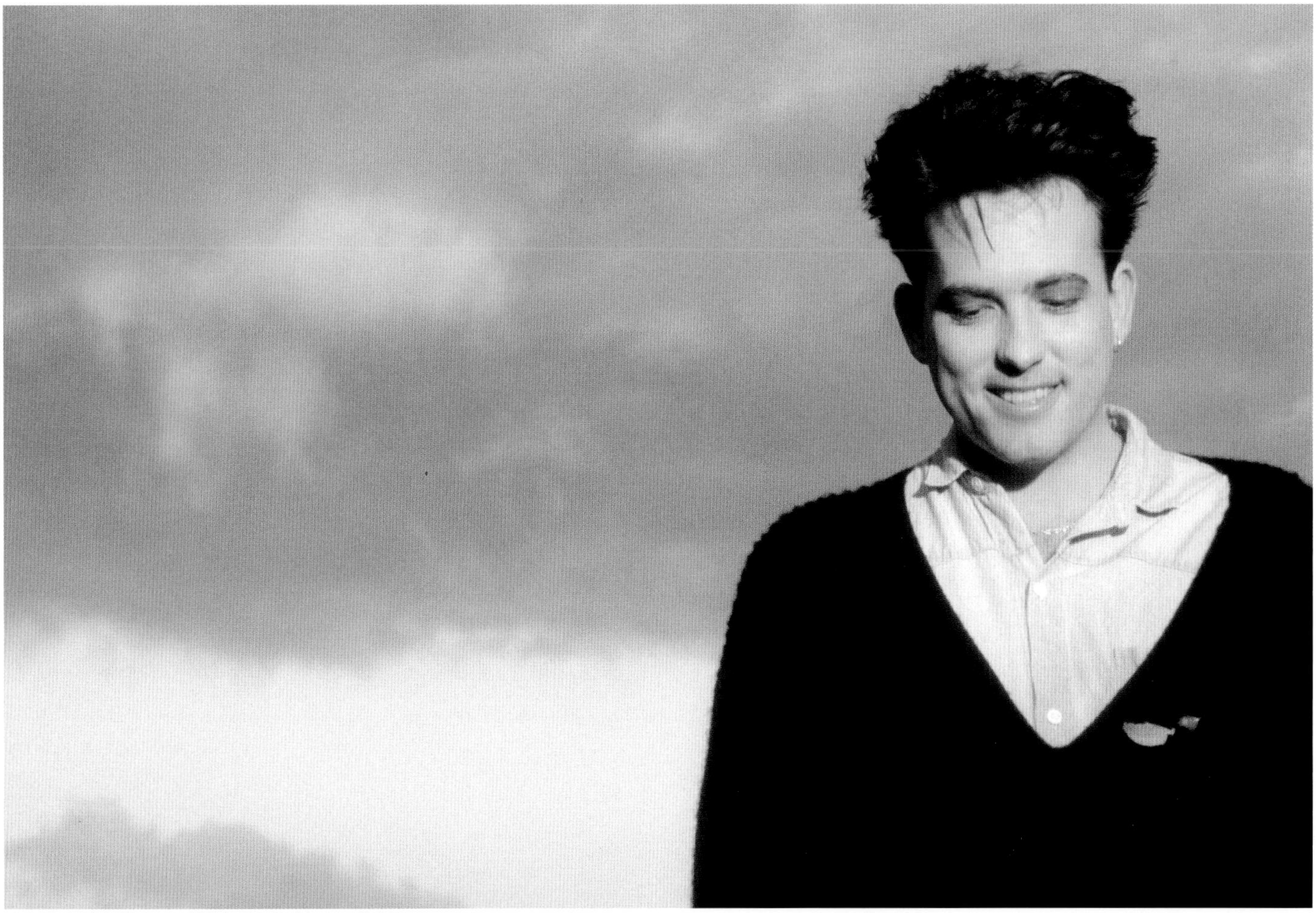

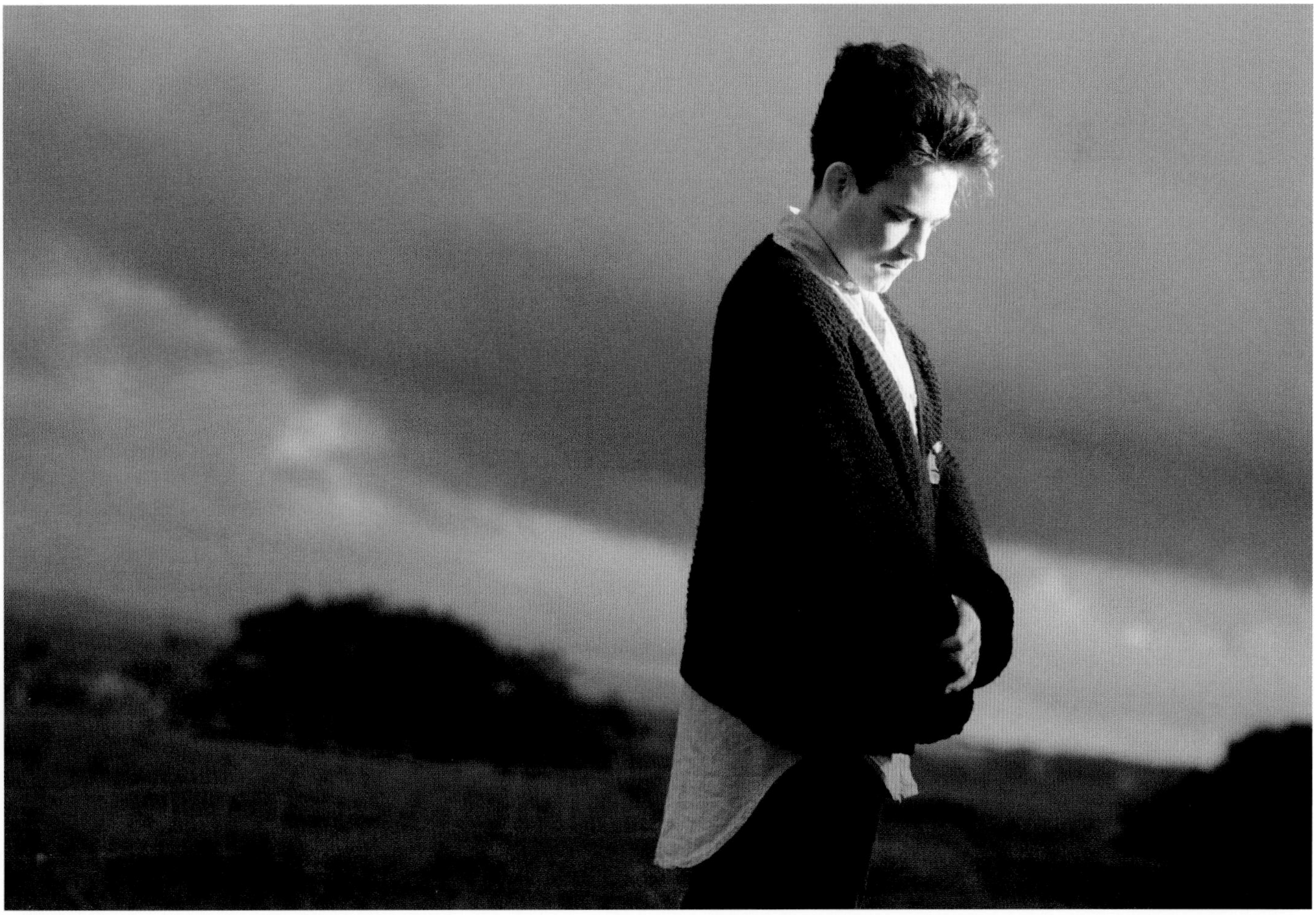

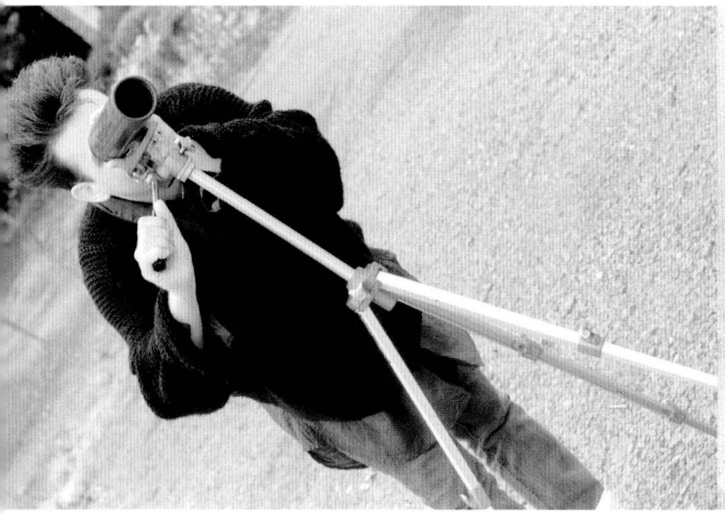
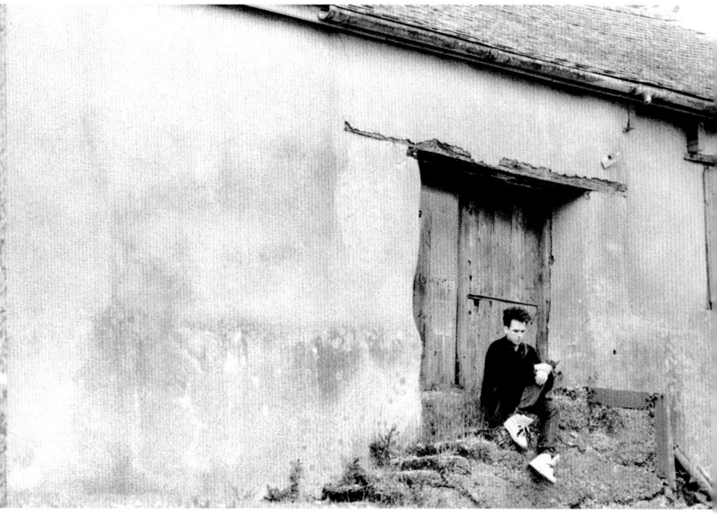

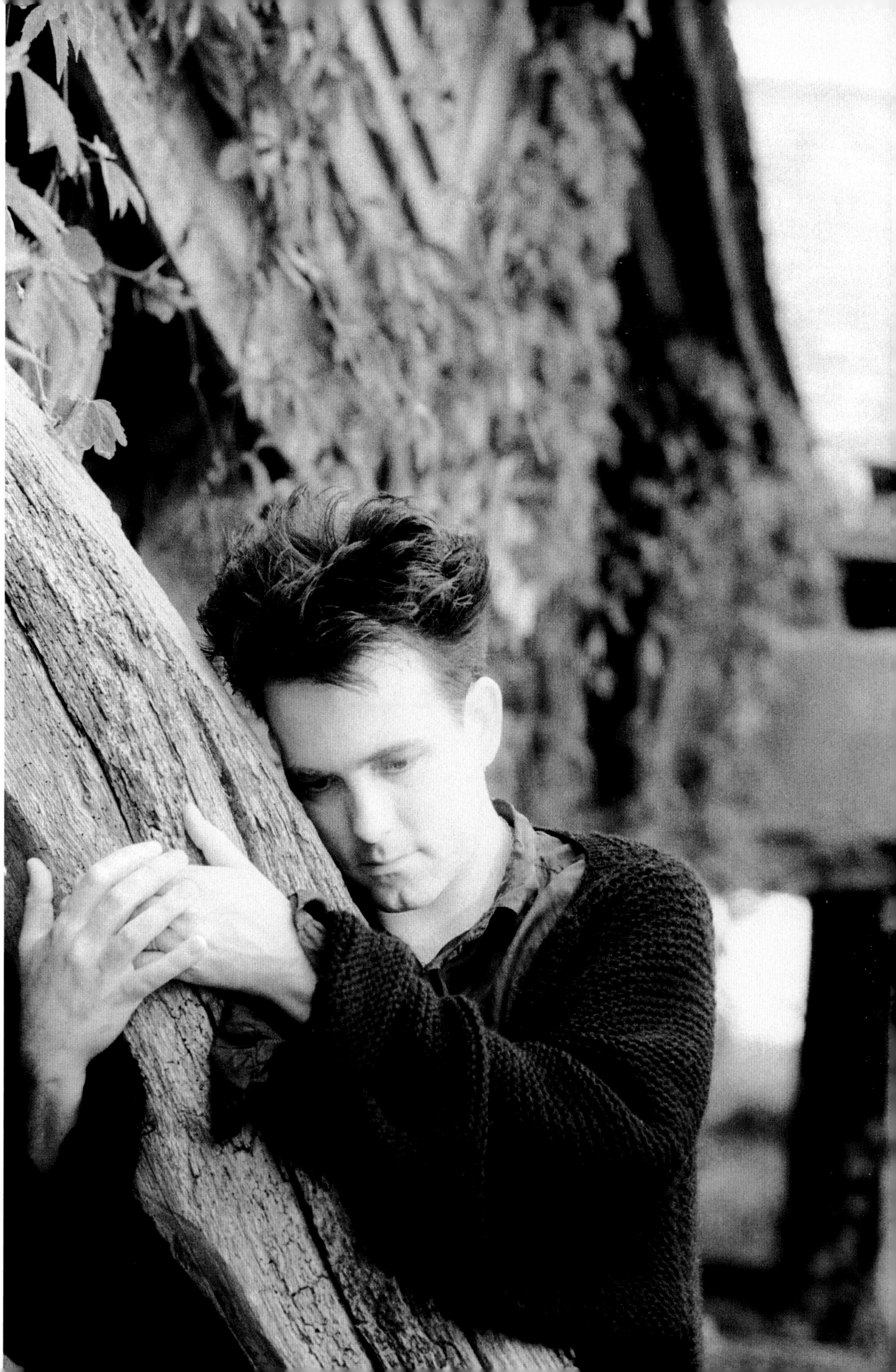

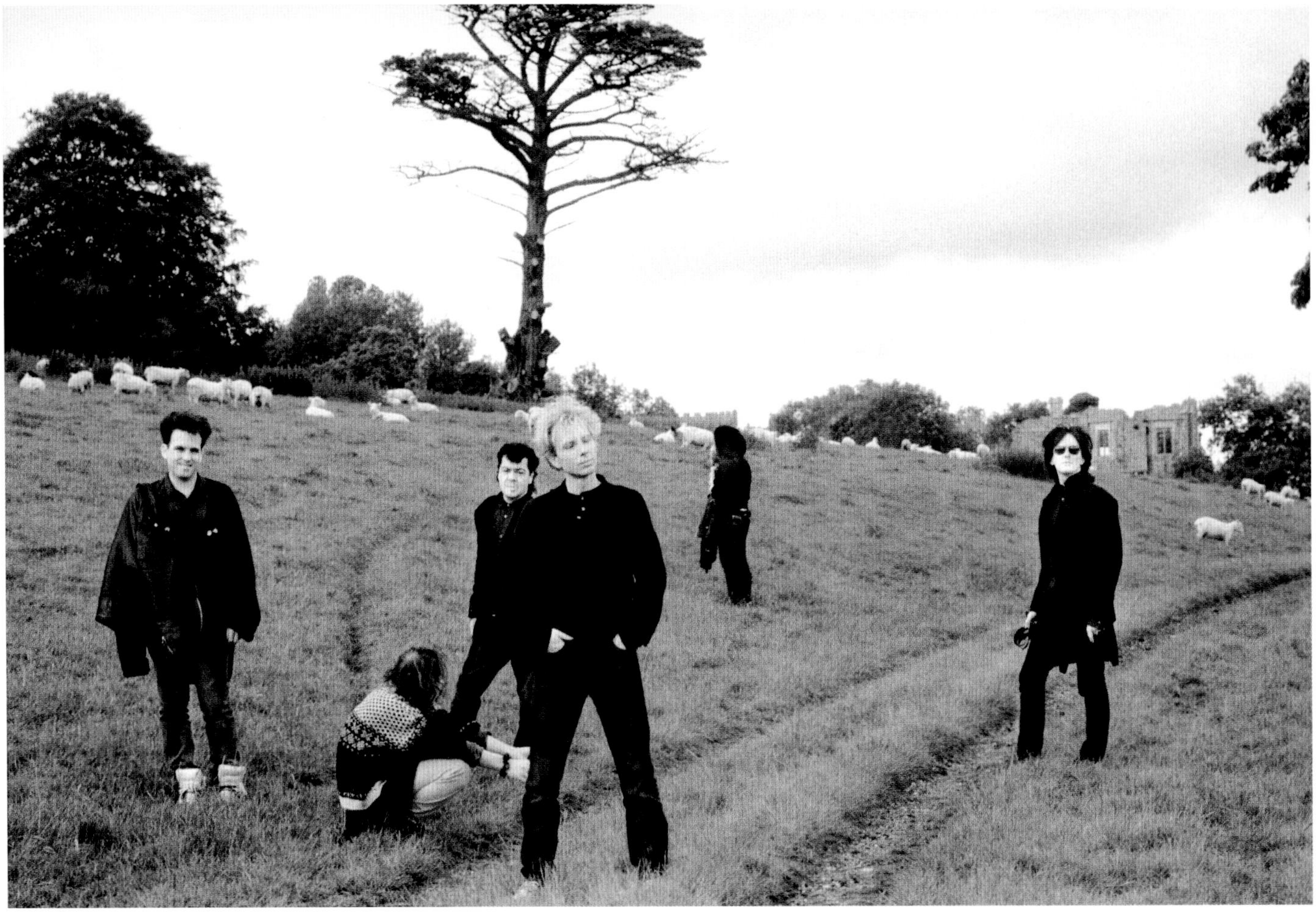

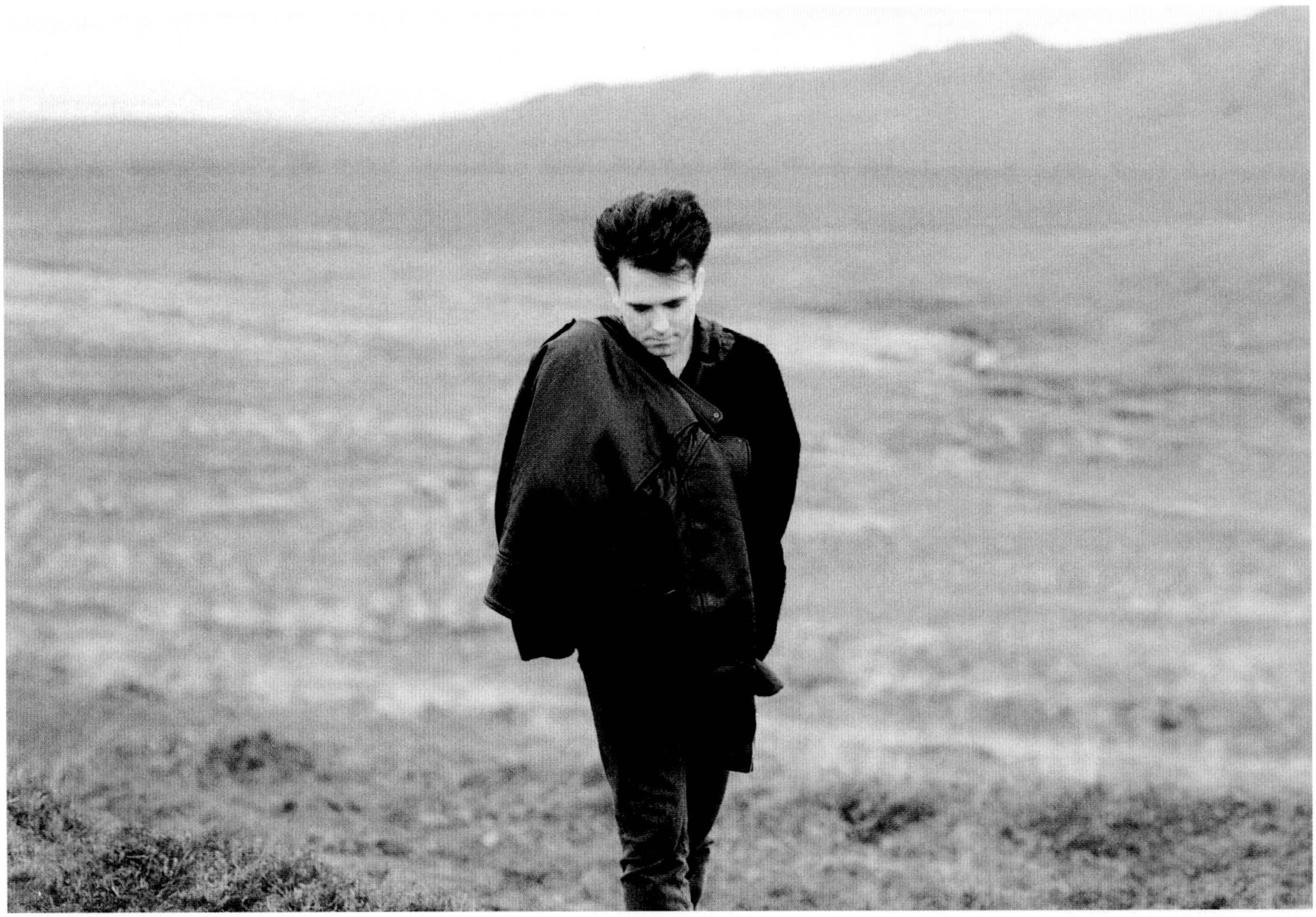

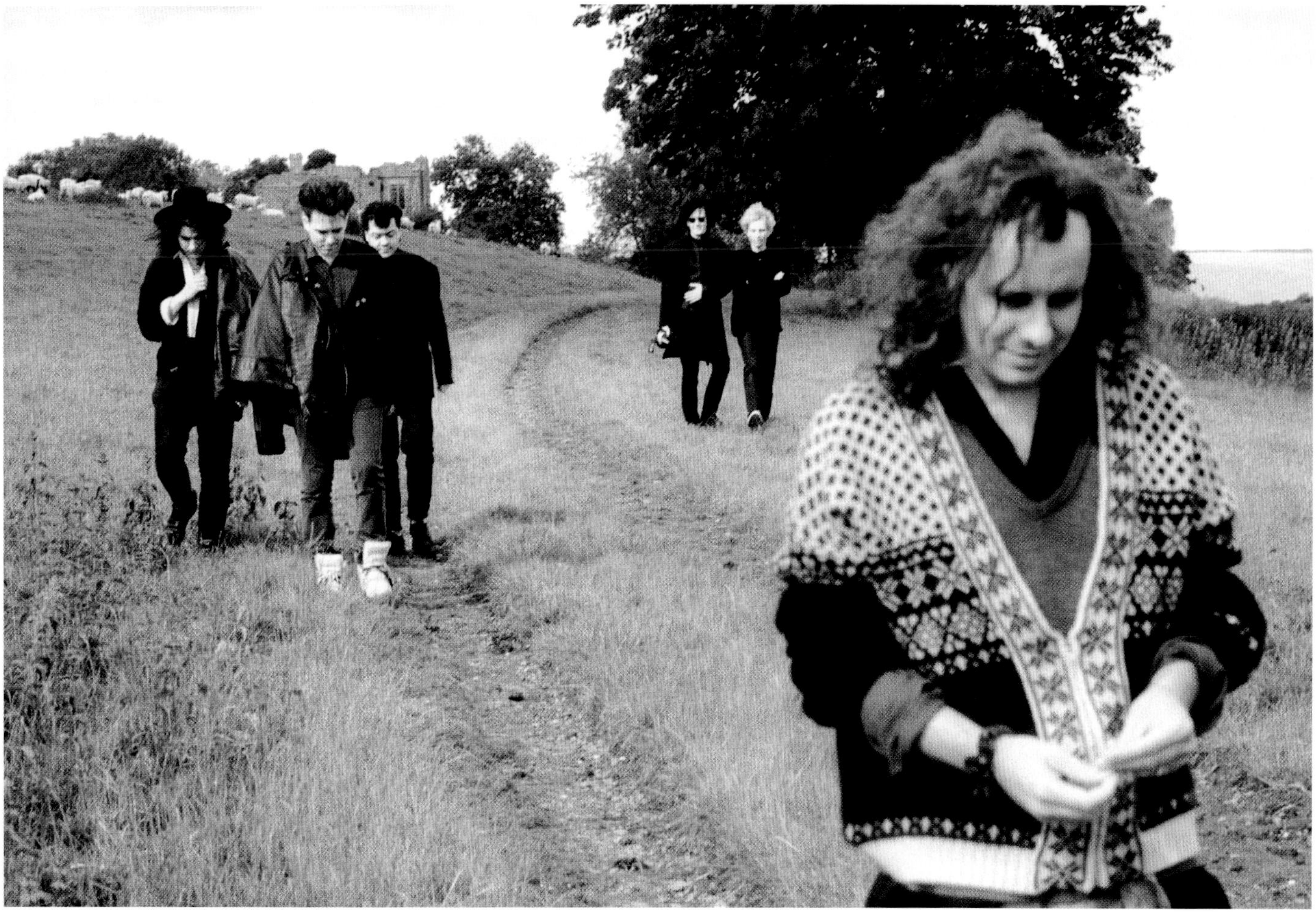

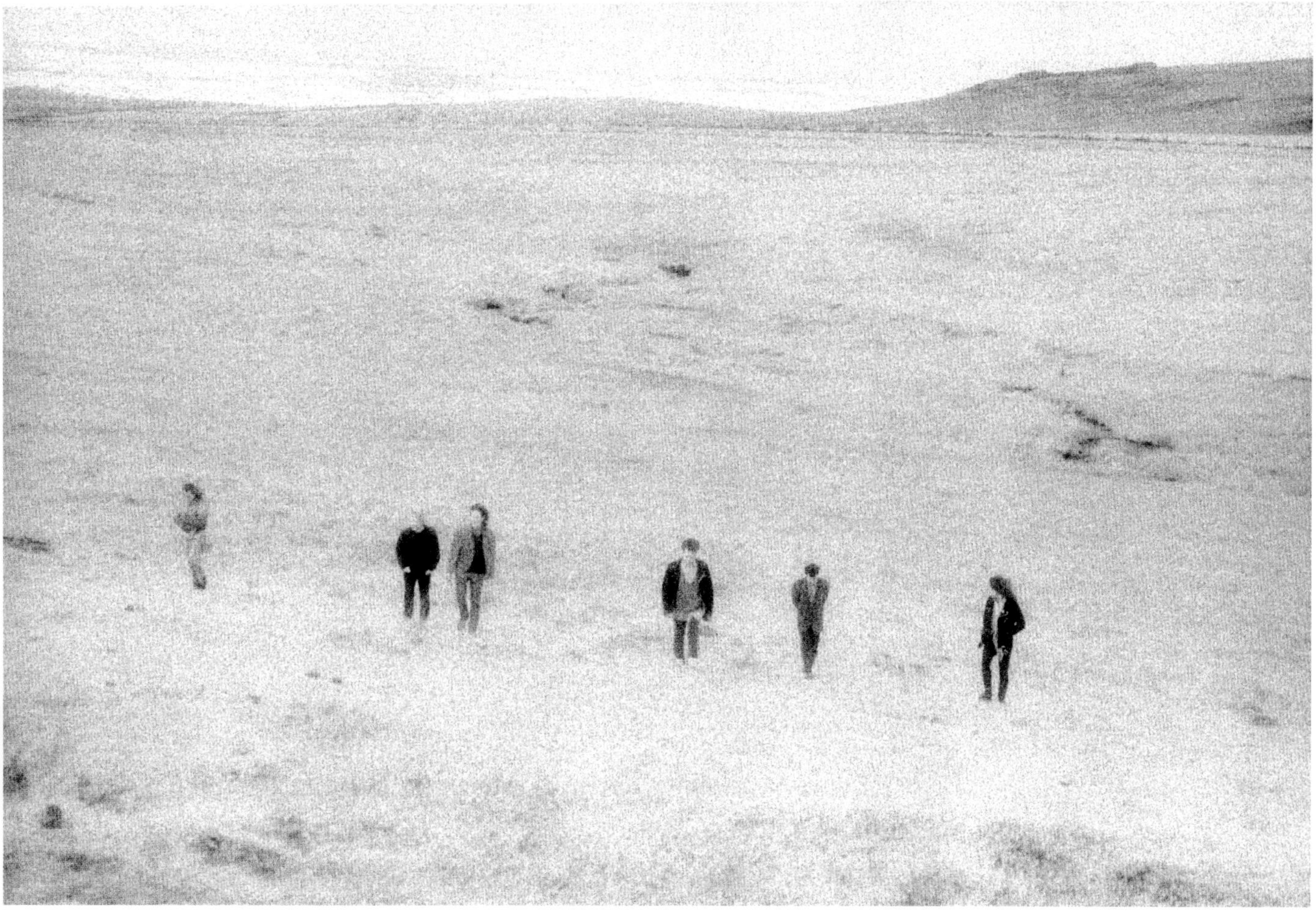

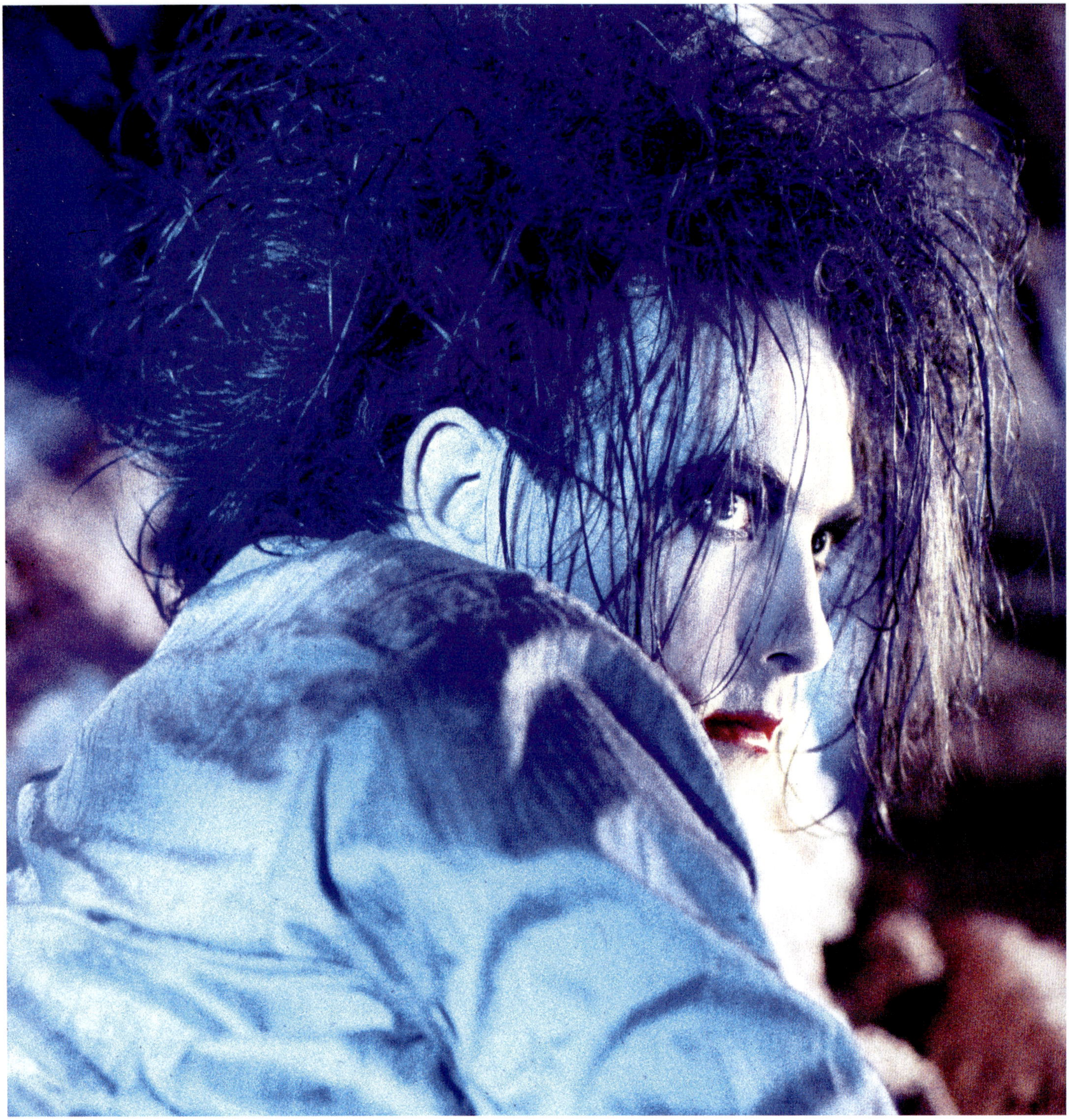

VIDEO FILMING
'Lovesong'
(p.94 to 101)
3rd August 1989

ROBERT: THE 'LOVESONG' VIDEO SHOOT – A VERY STRANGE DAY...

Paul: 'Lovesong' video shoot. Talking to Ita at Fiction Records, she said The Cure were about to do a video shoot somewhere near London. I went down for the day, just to cover, not for a particular use, but the images ended up appearing in a number of magazines – with the band's approval!

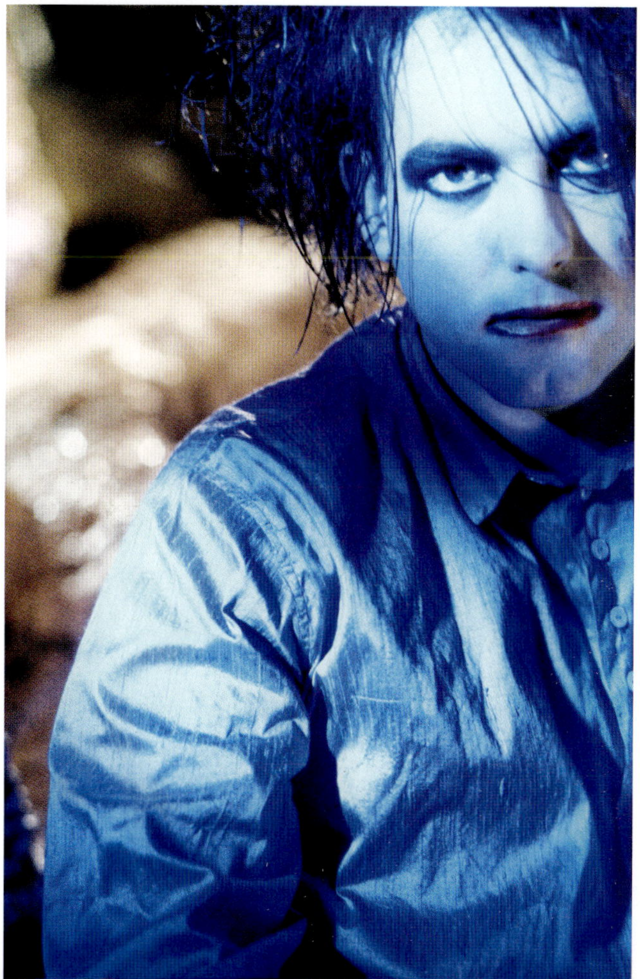

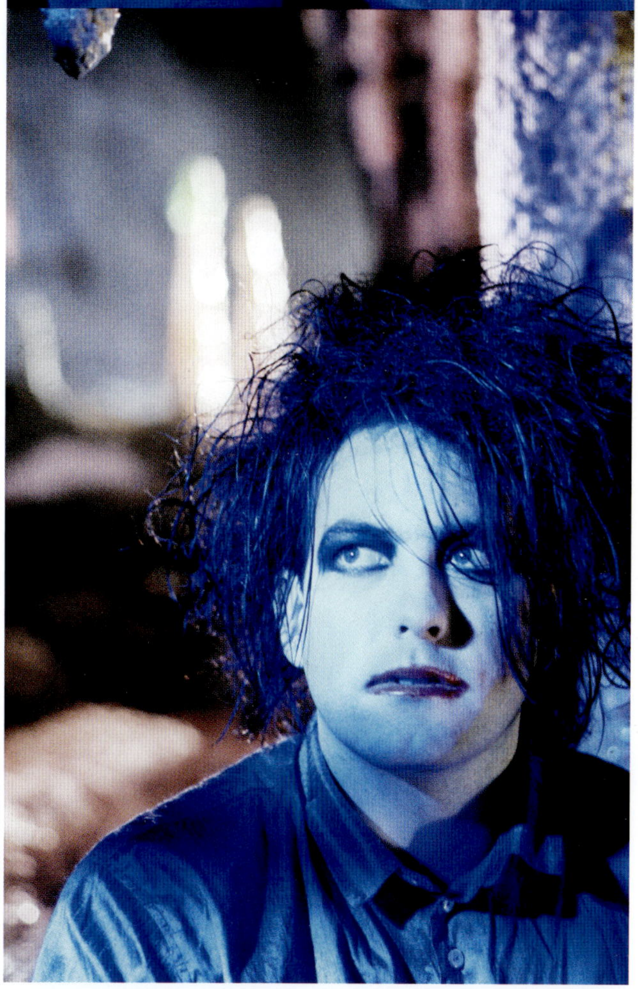

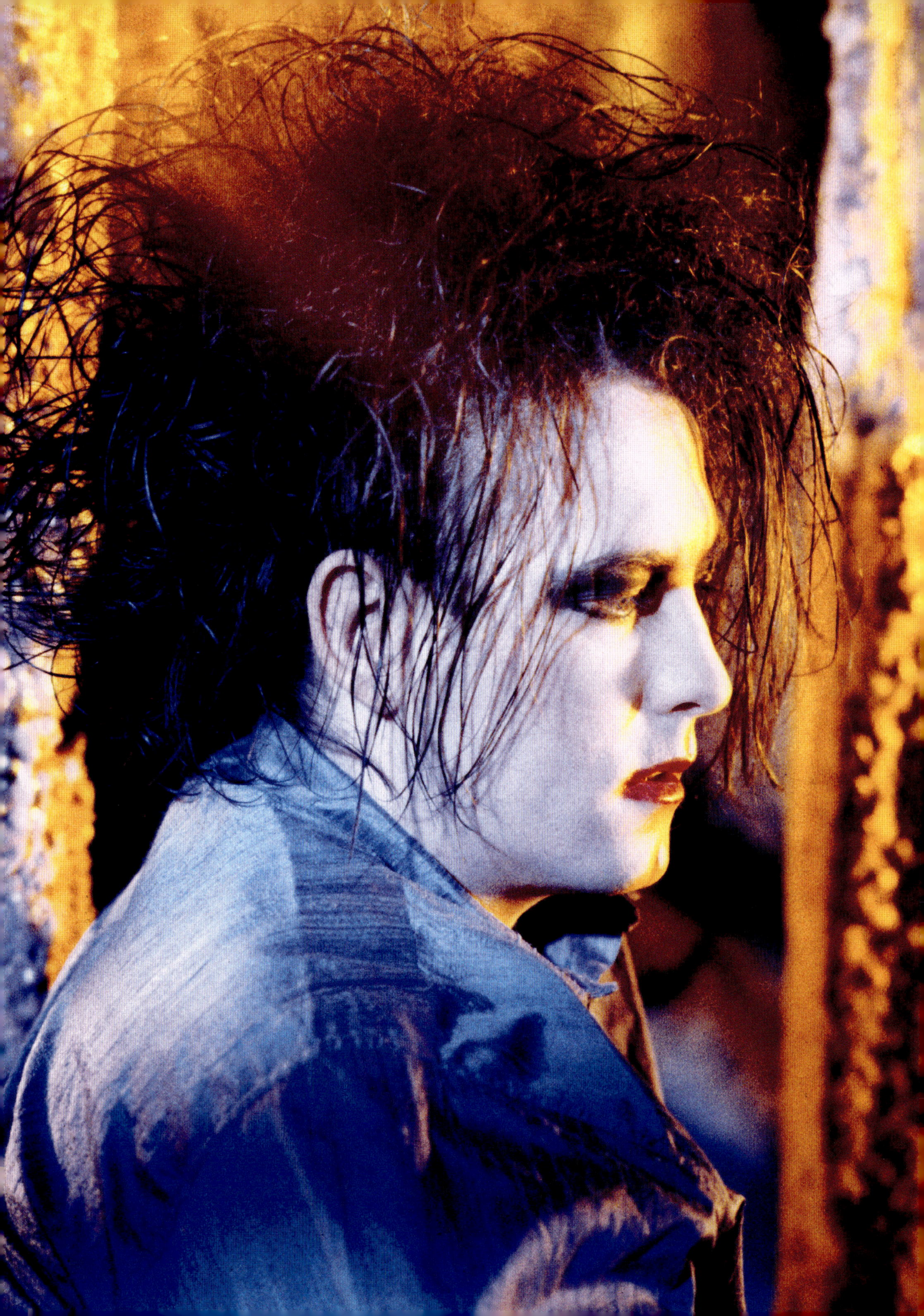

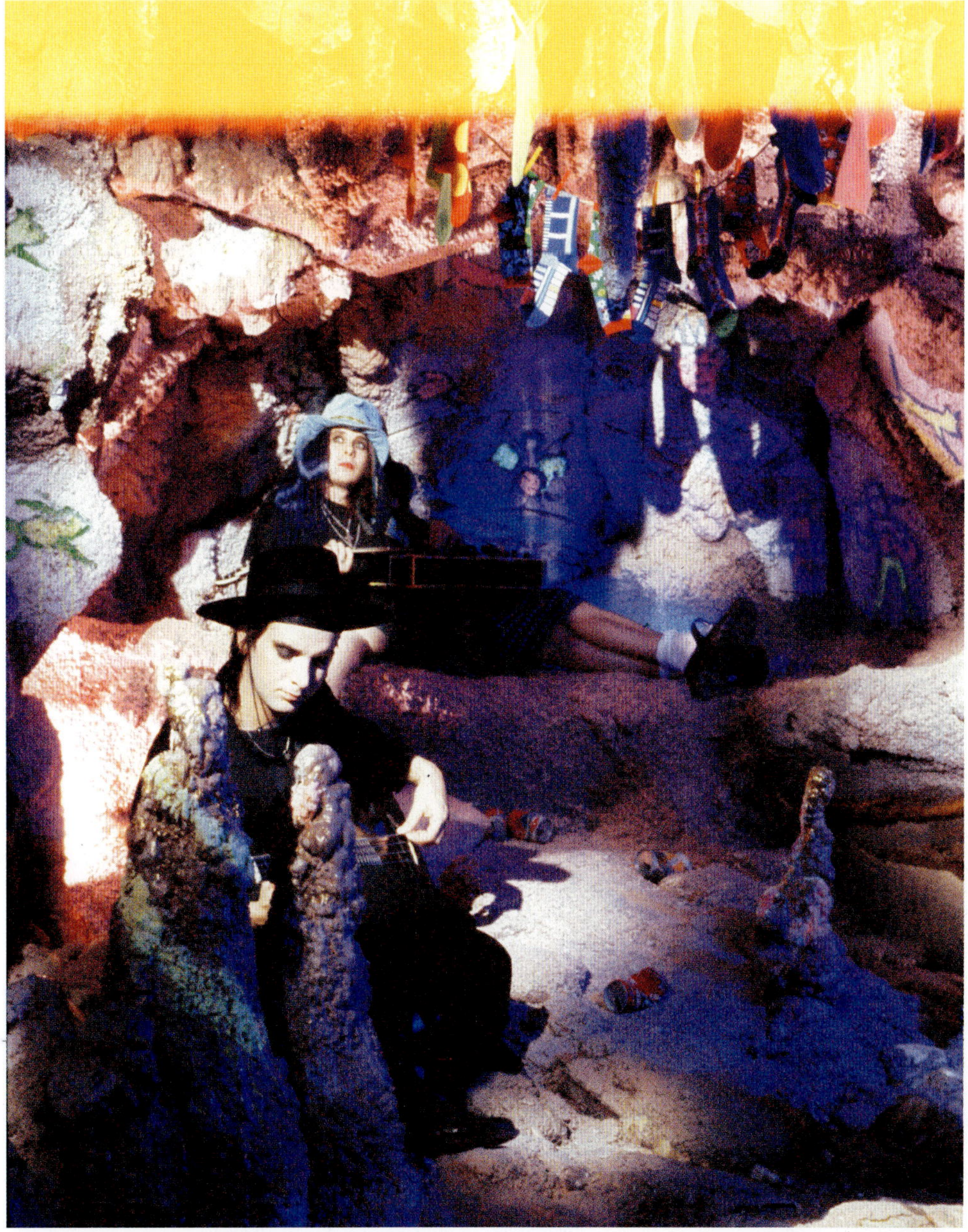

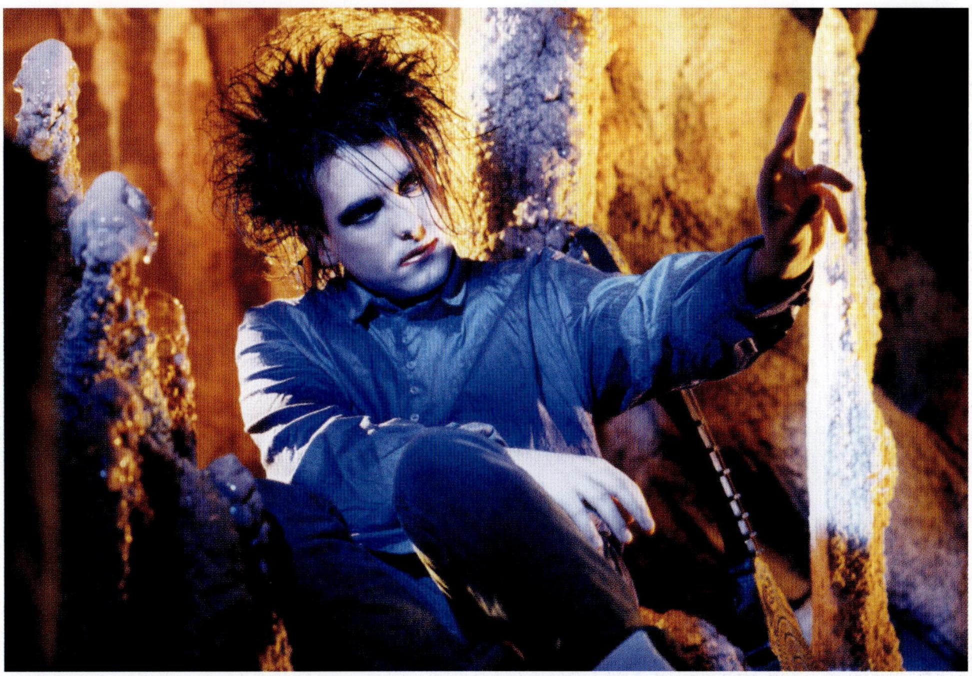

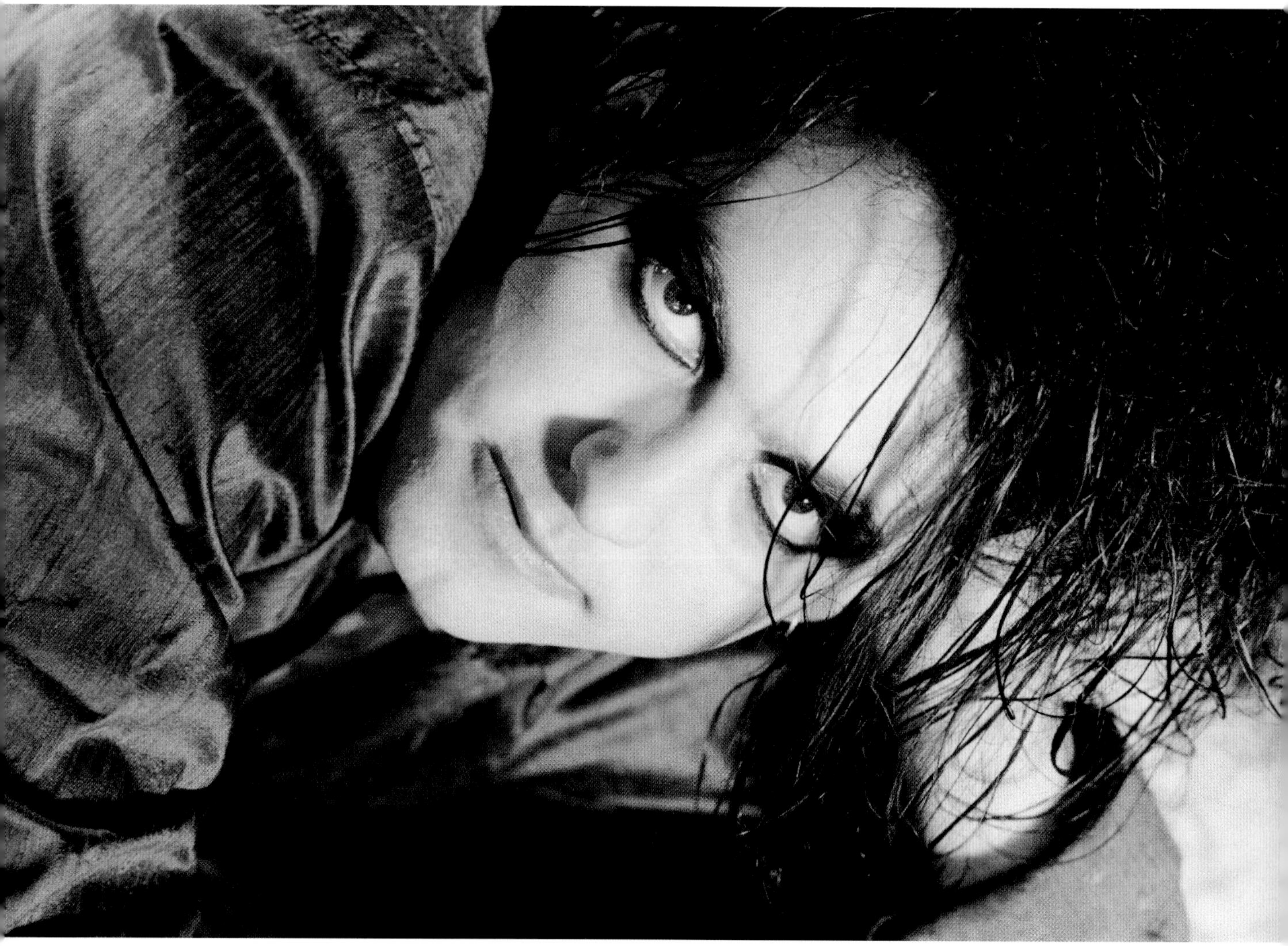

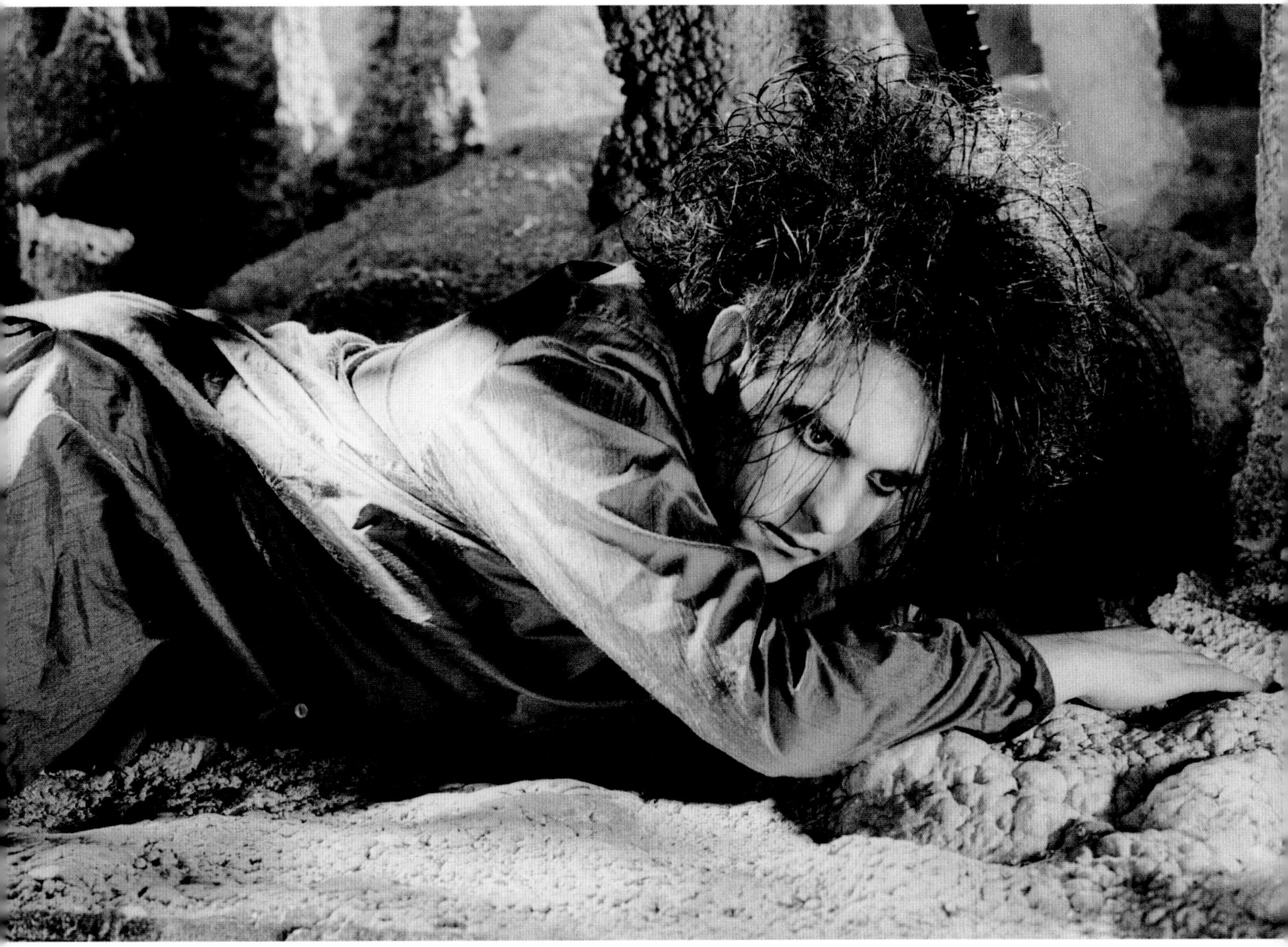

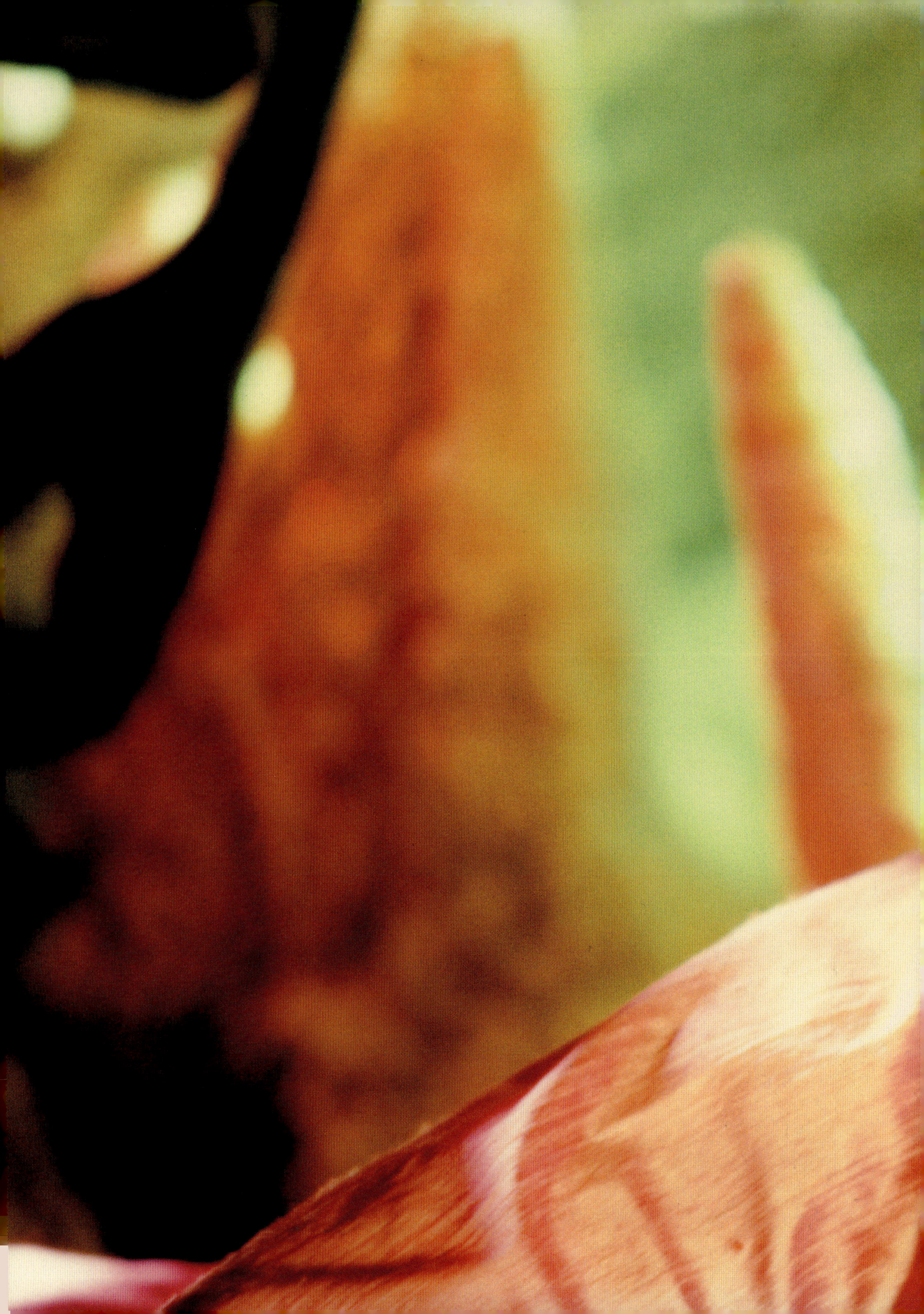

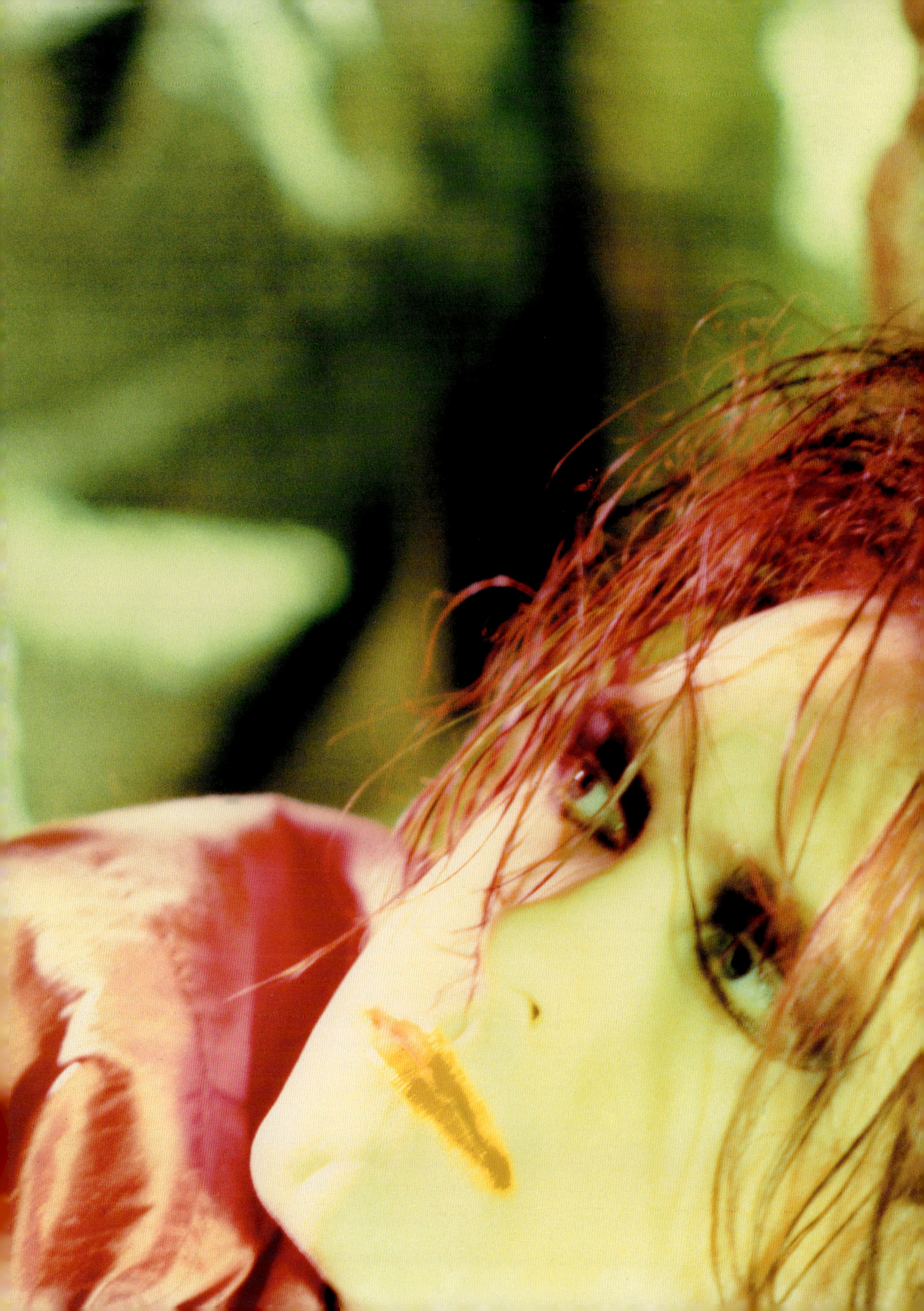

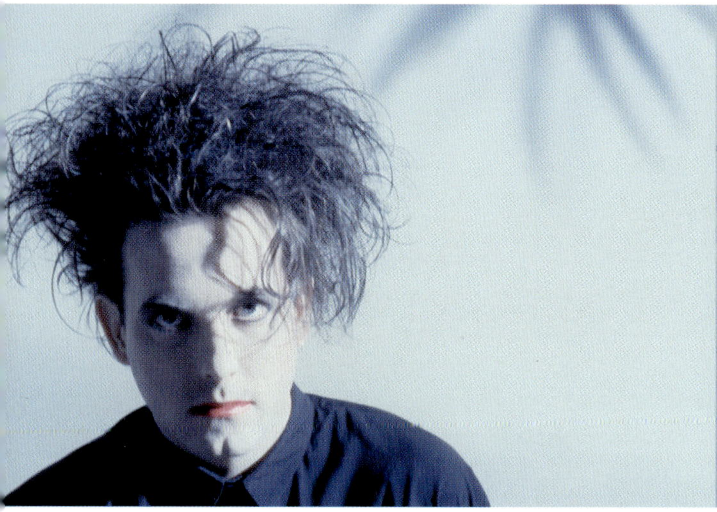

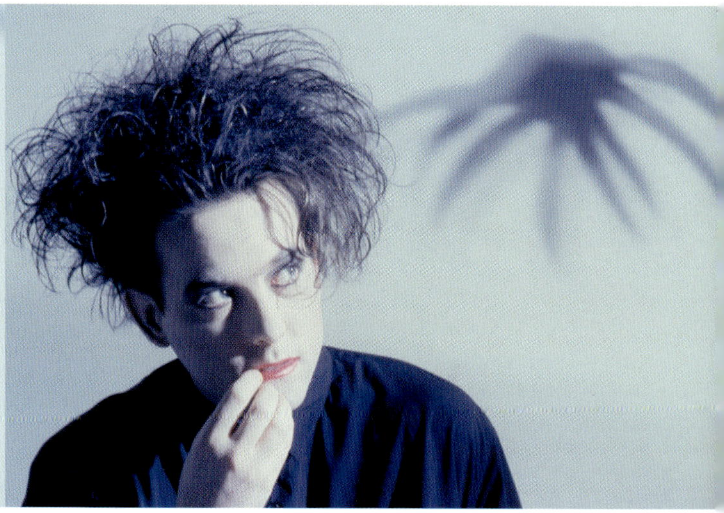

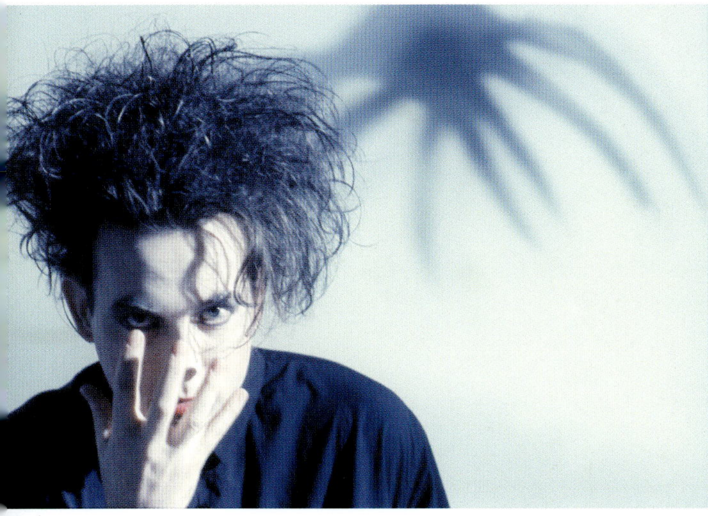

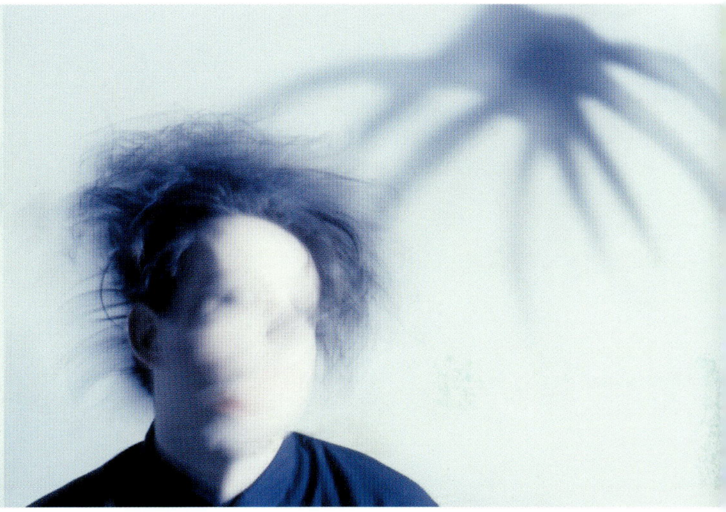

FULHAM STUDIO

[p. 102 to 137]

14th August 1989

ROBERT: ONE OF THE MORE MEMORABLE SESSIONS – AND ONE OF THE LONGEST – SHOTS TO PROMOTE THE RELEASE OF *DISINTEGRATION* – POLKA DOTS, CARDIGANS, FLOPPY HATS, SILK SHIRTS, BIG COATS, MOHAIR, PROJECTIONS, CANDLES, DOUBLE EXPOSURES… THE LATE '80S WORKS!

Paul: In the pre-digital age, talking on the landline phone really helped us to come up with inspiration and imagery relating to various tracks on an album, hence the props, projections and the spiders. Always starting at 3.00pm and finishing in the early hours! Fond memories. This was a two-day shoot, solo with Robert and then with the band.

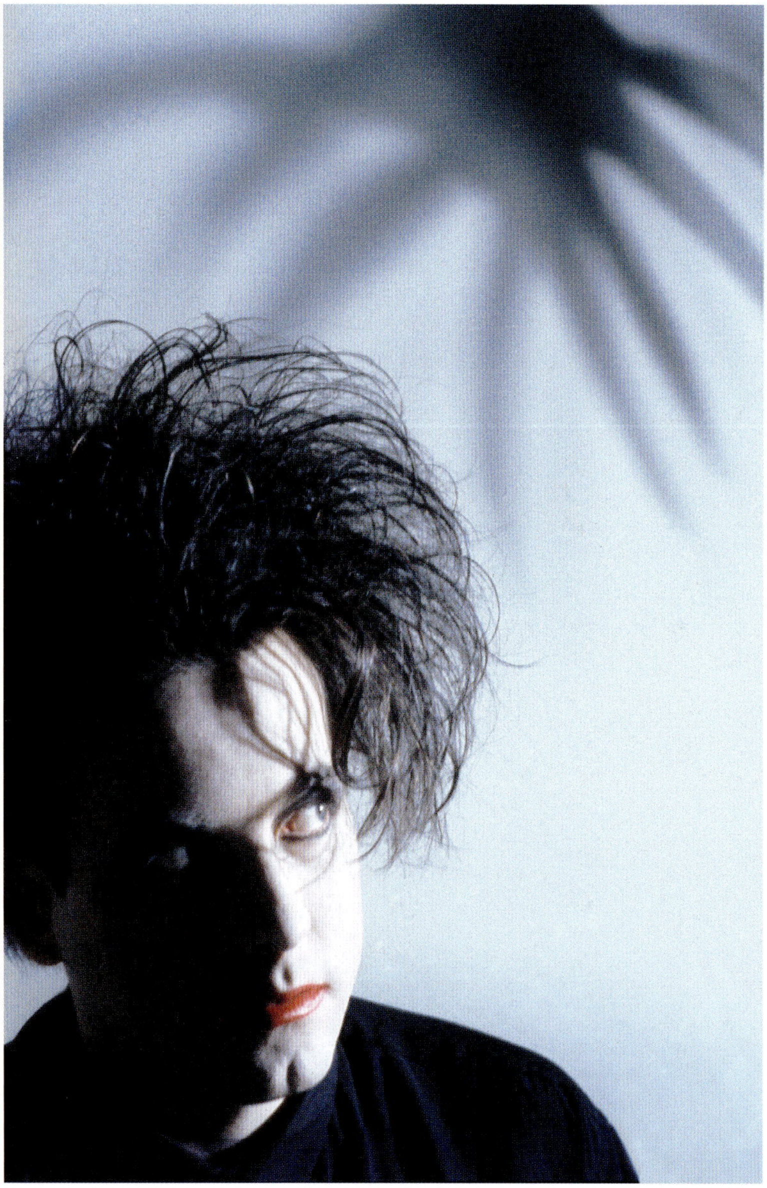

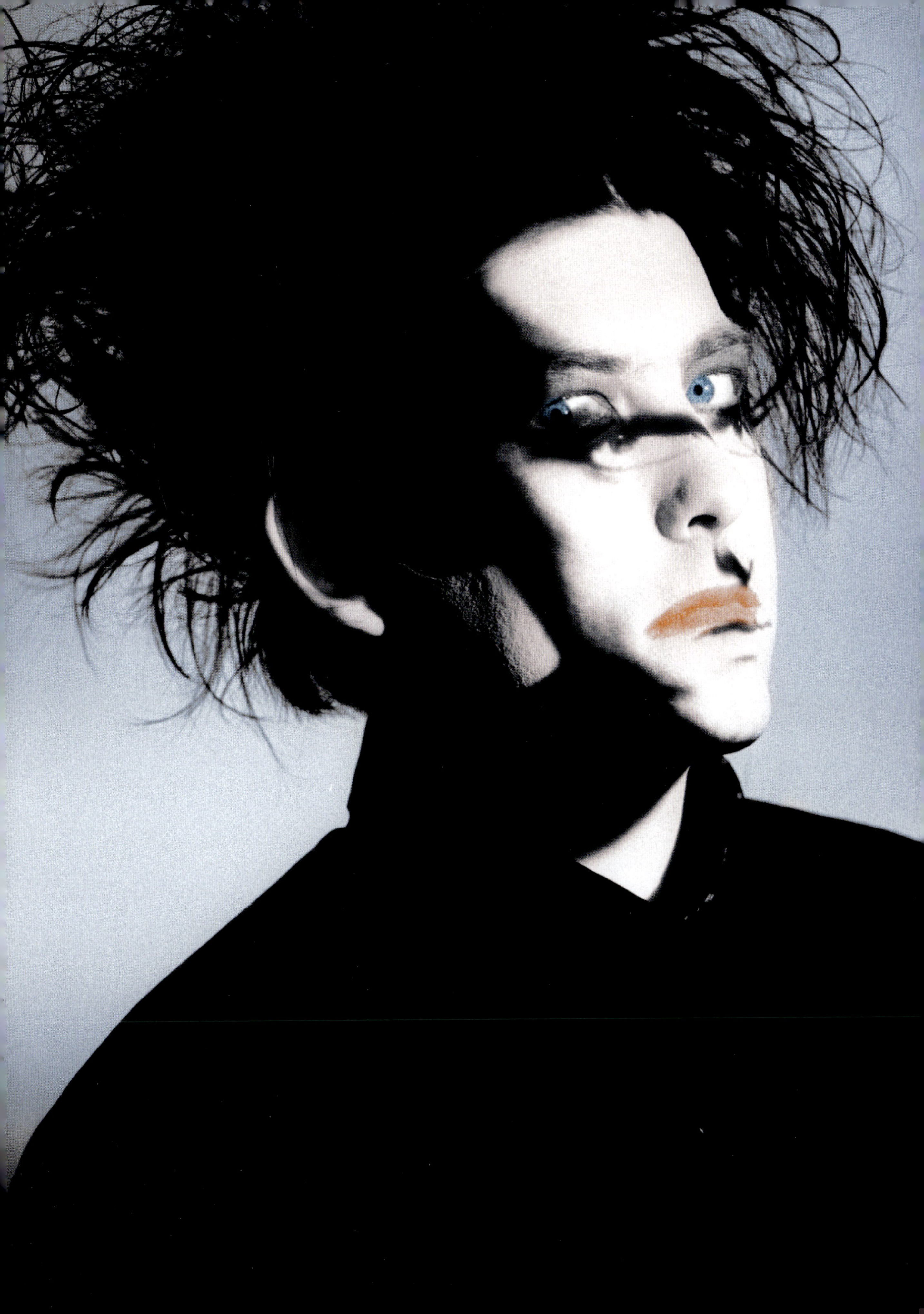

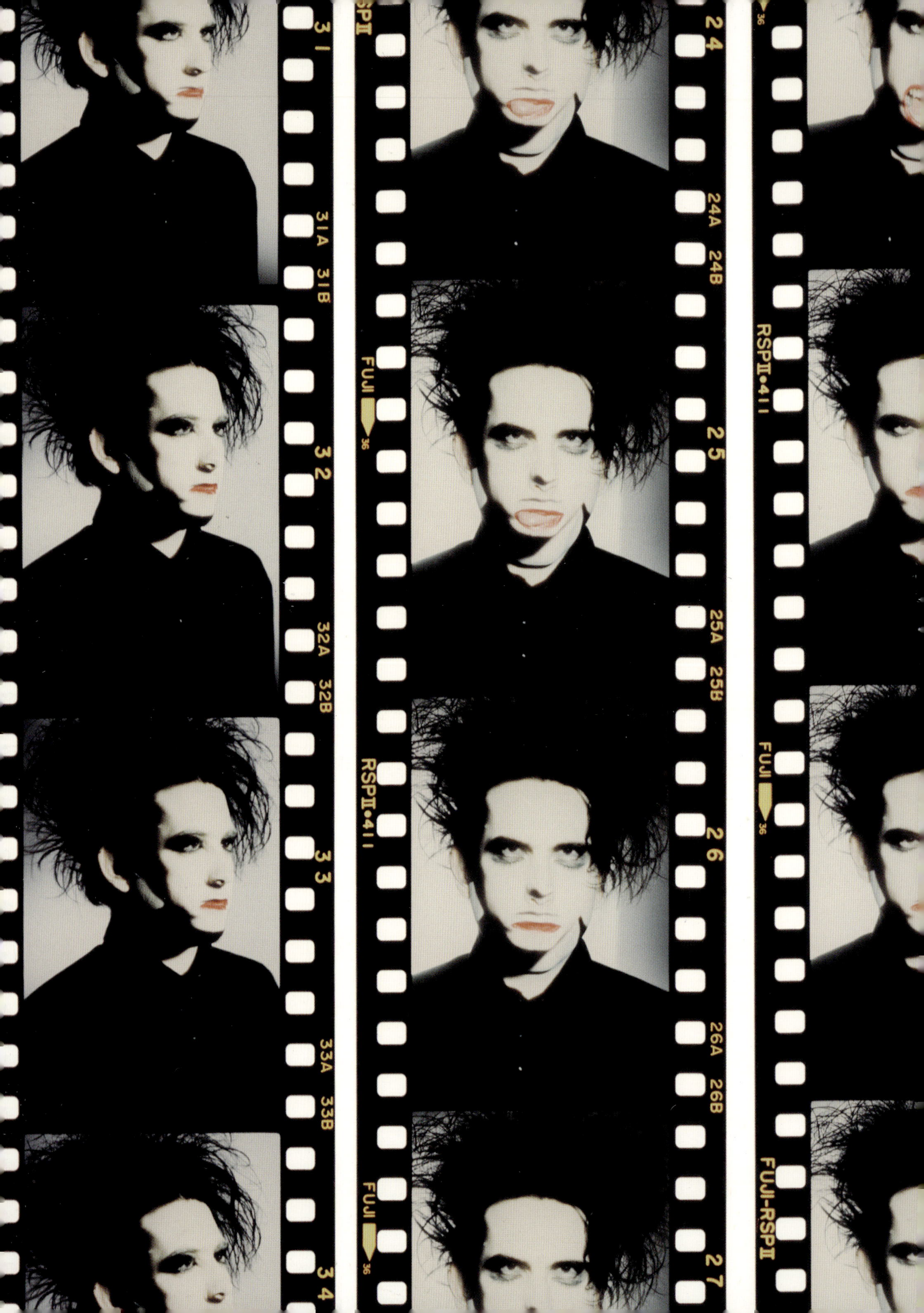
31
31A
31B
32
32A
32B
33
33A
33B
34
24
24A
24B
25
25A
25B
26
26A
26B
27
FUJI
RSPII•411
FUJI-RSPII

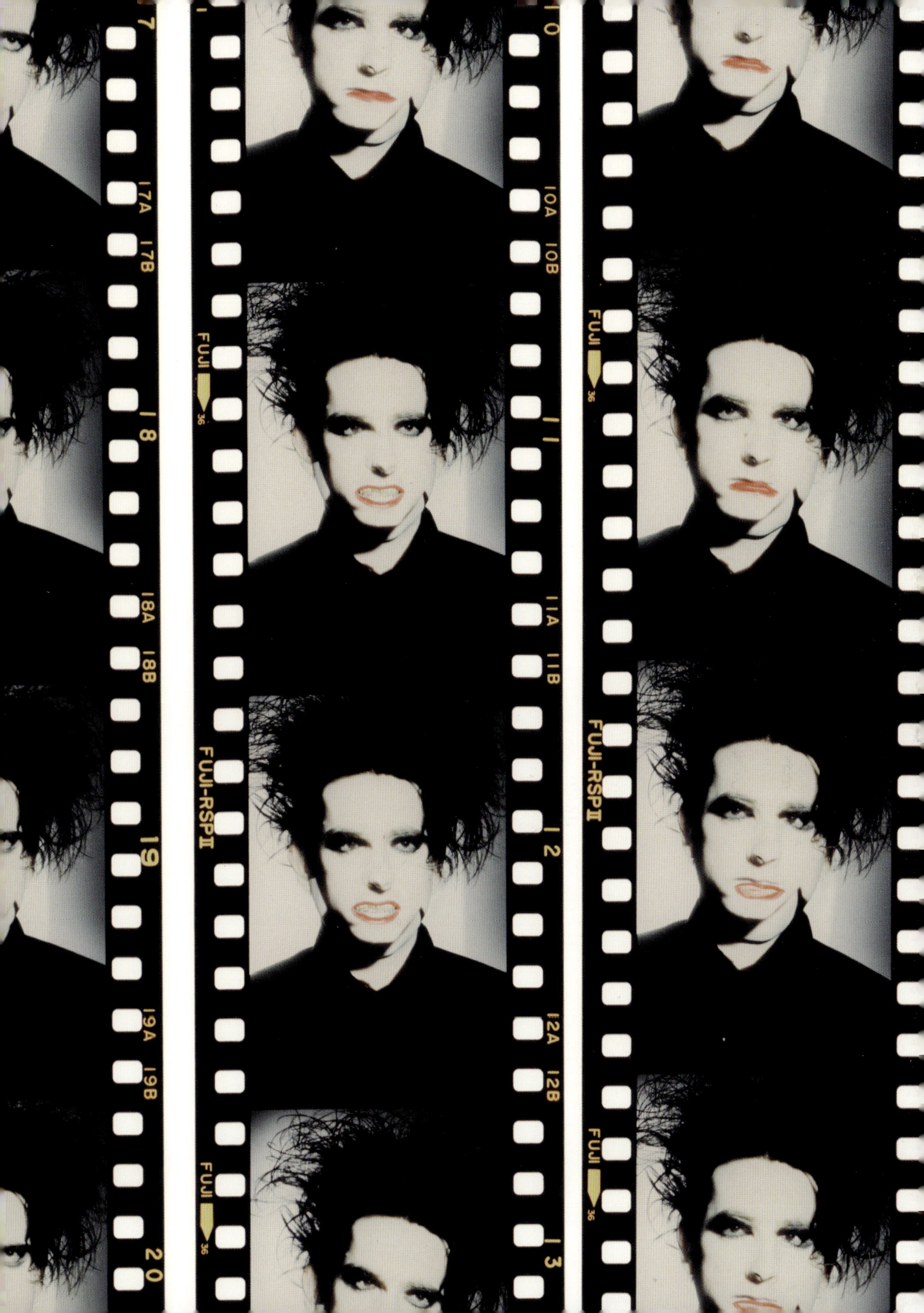

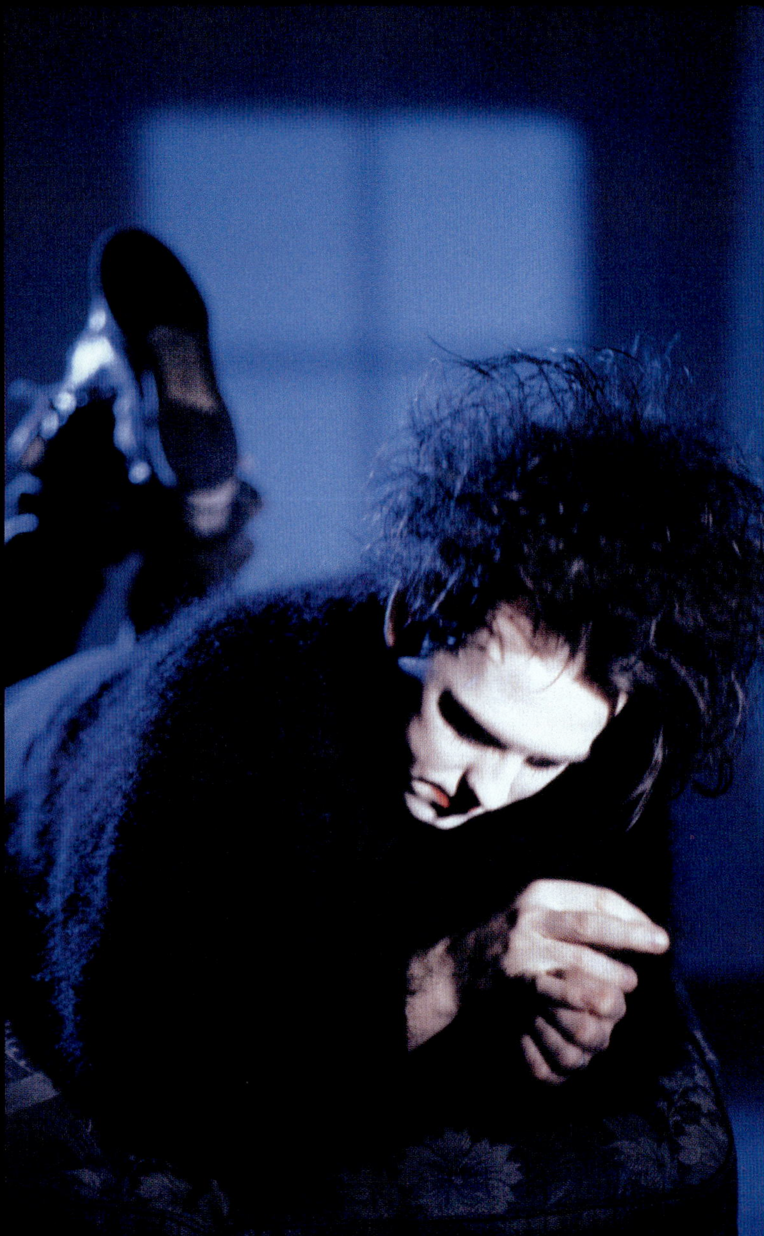

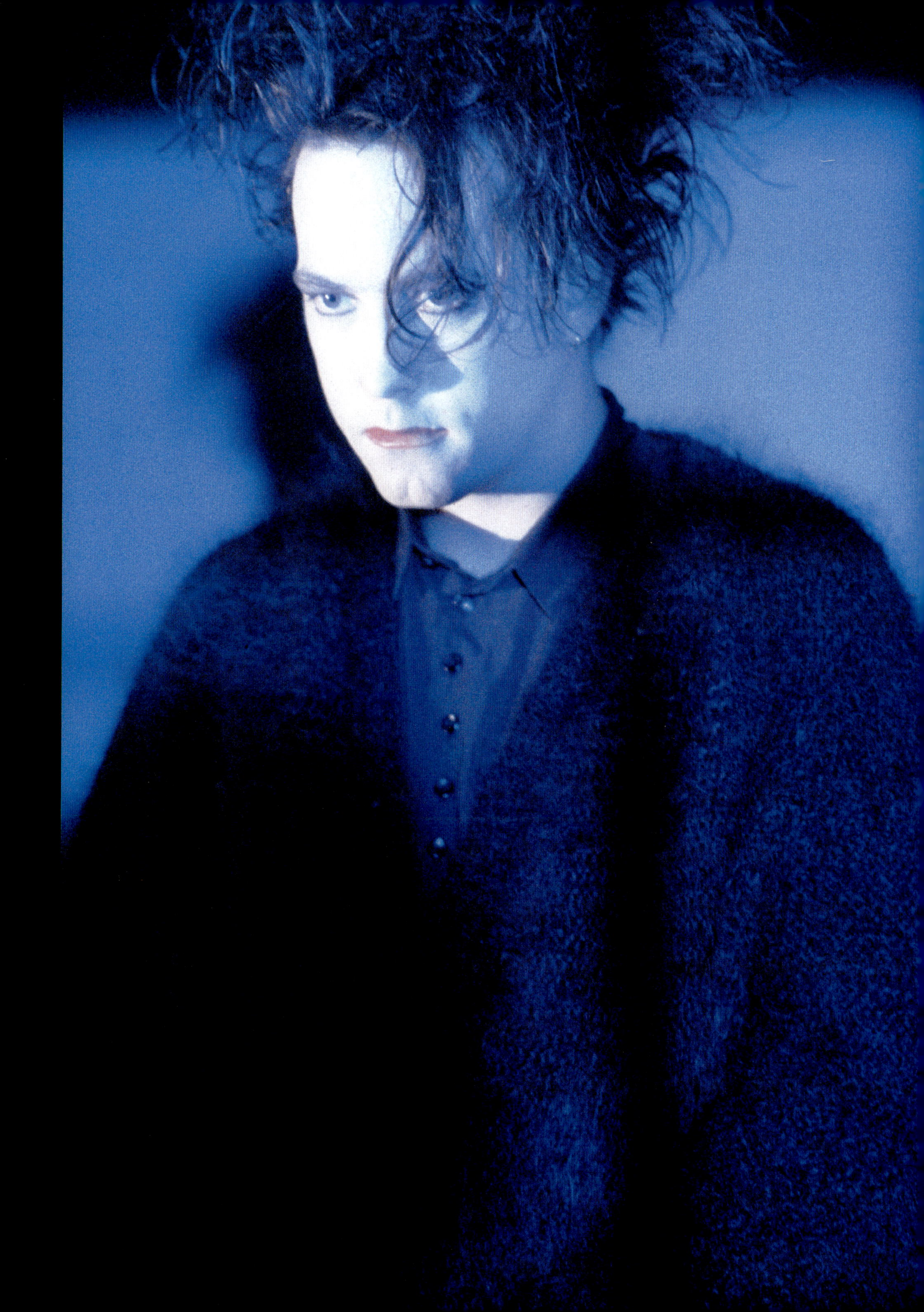

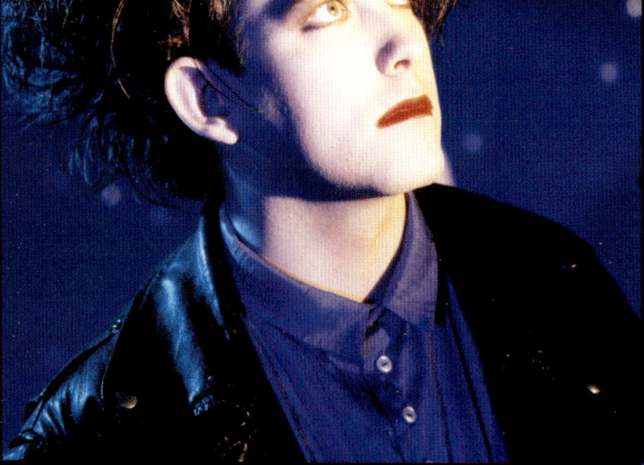

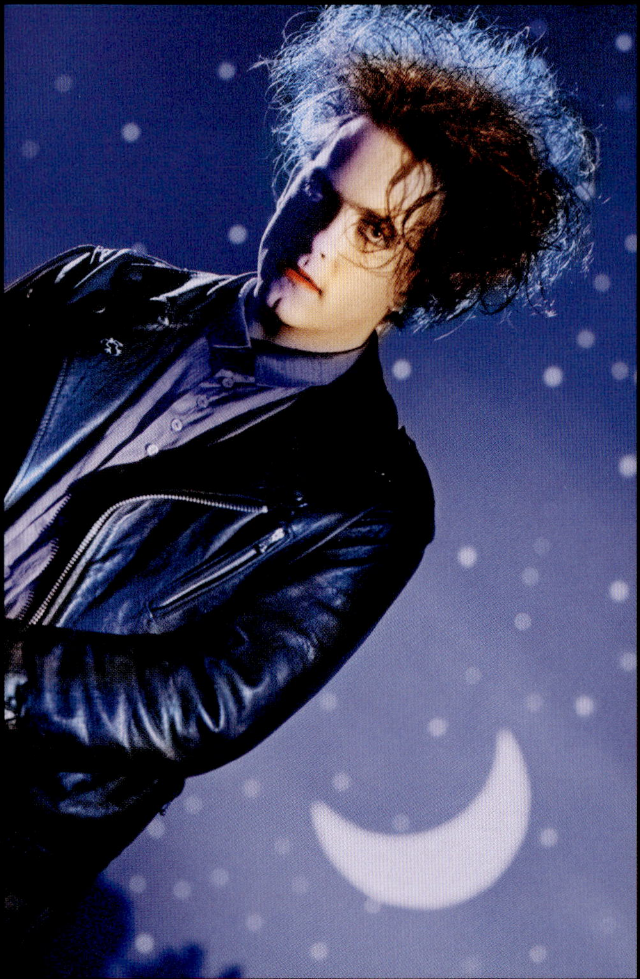

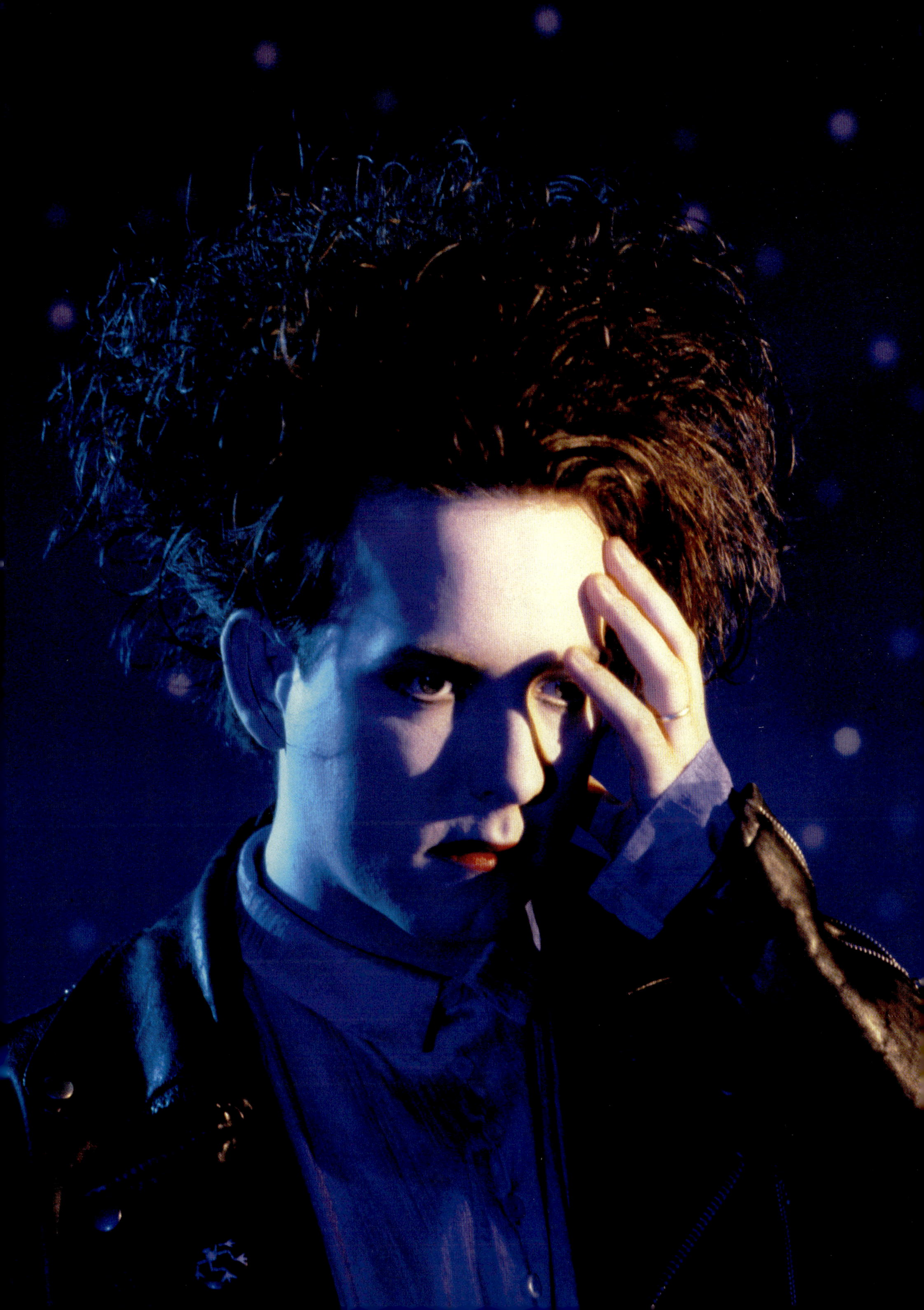

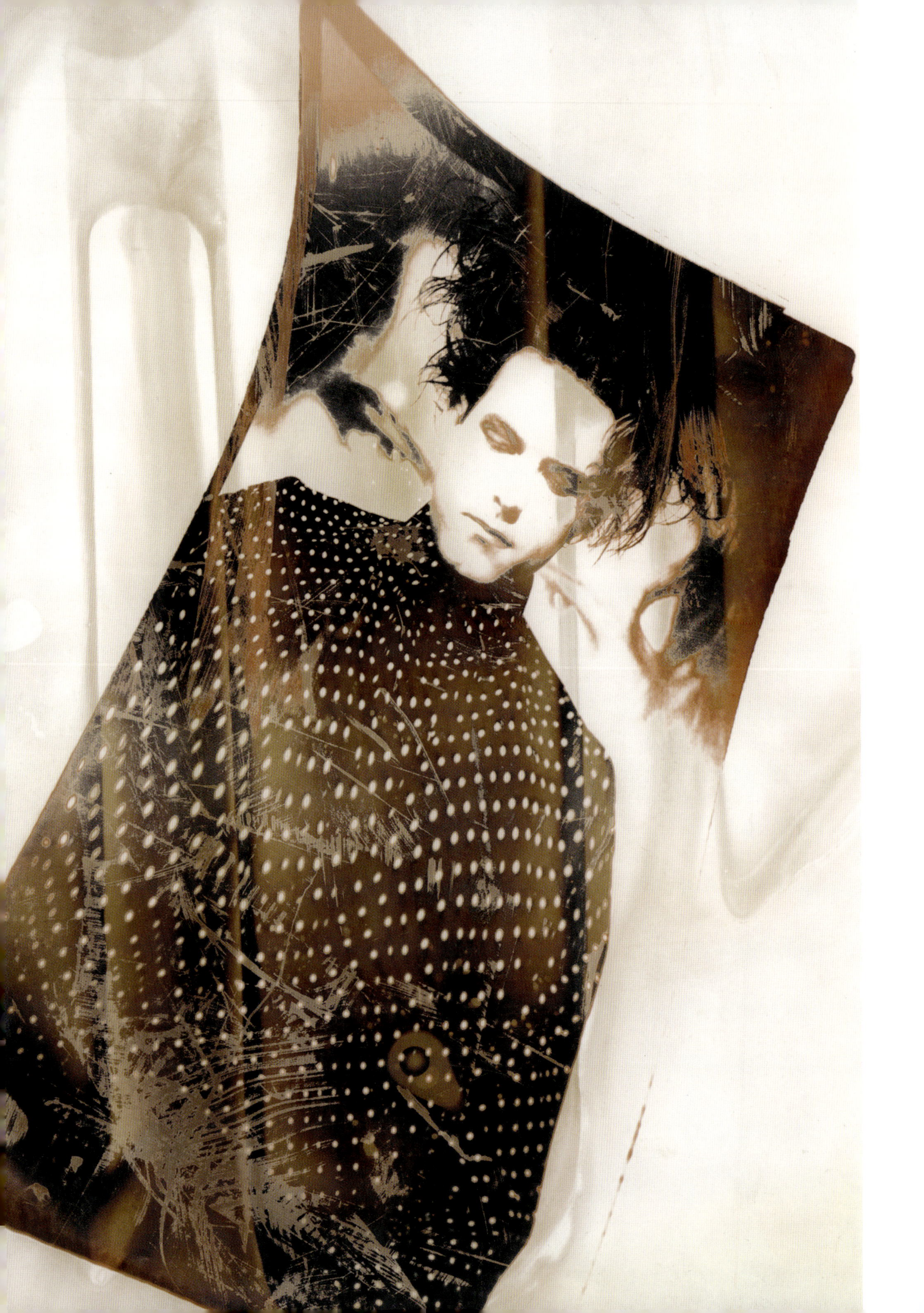

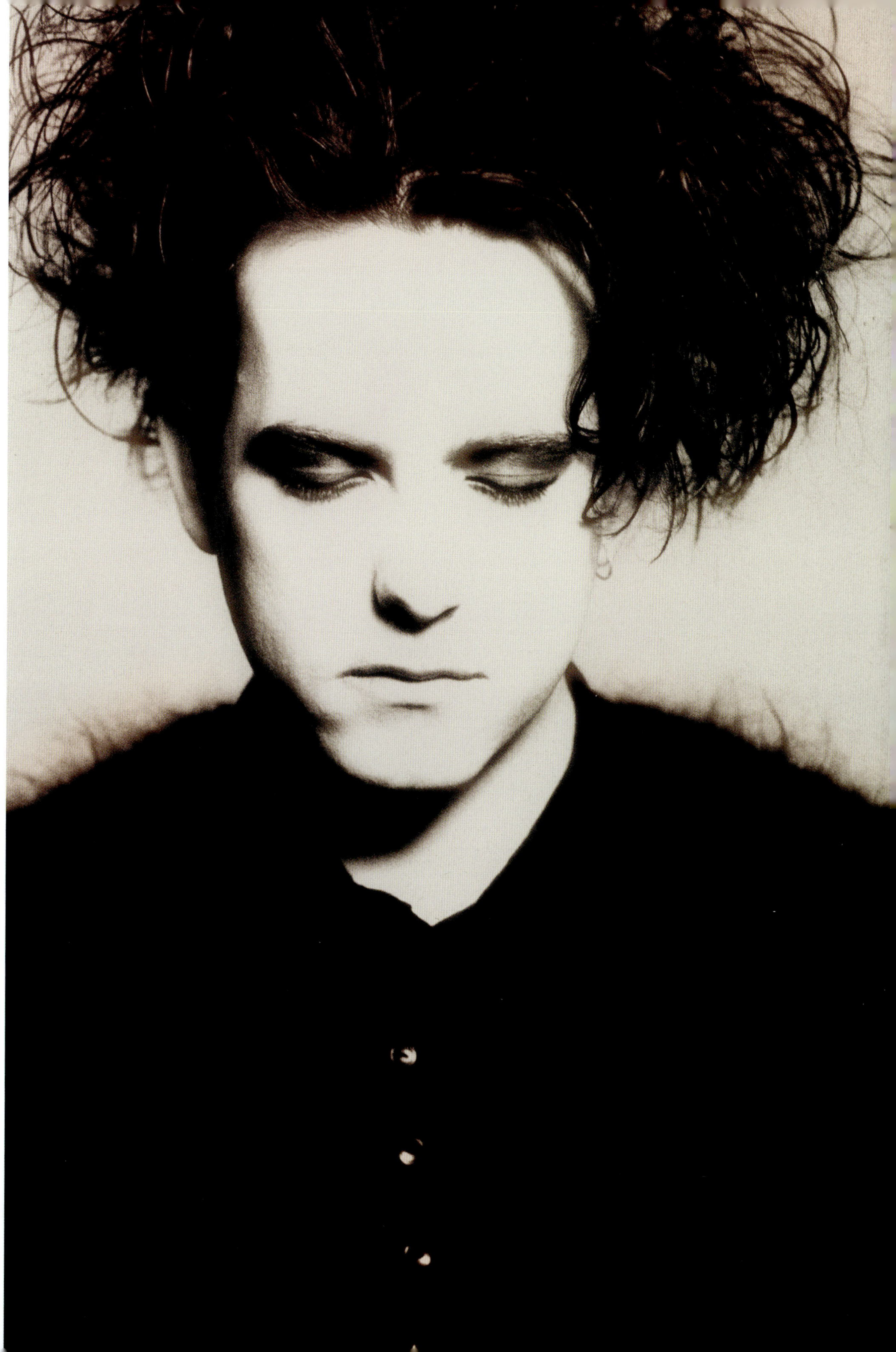

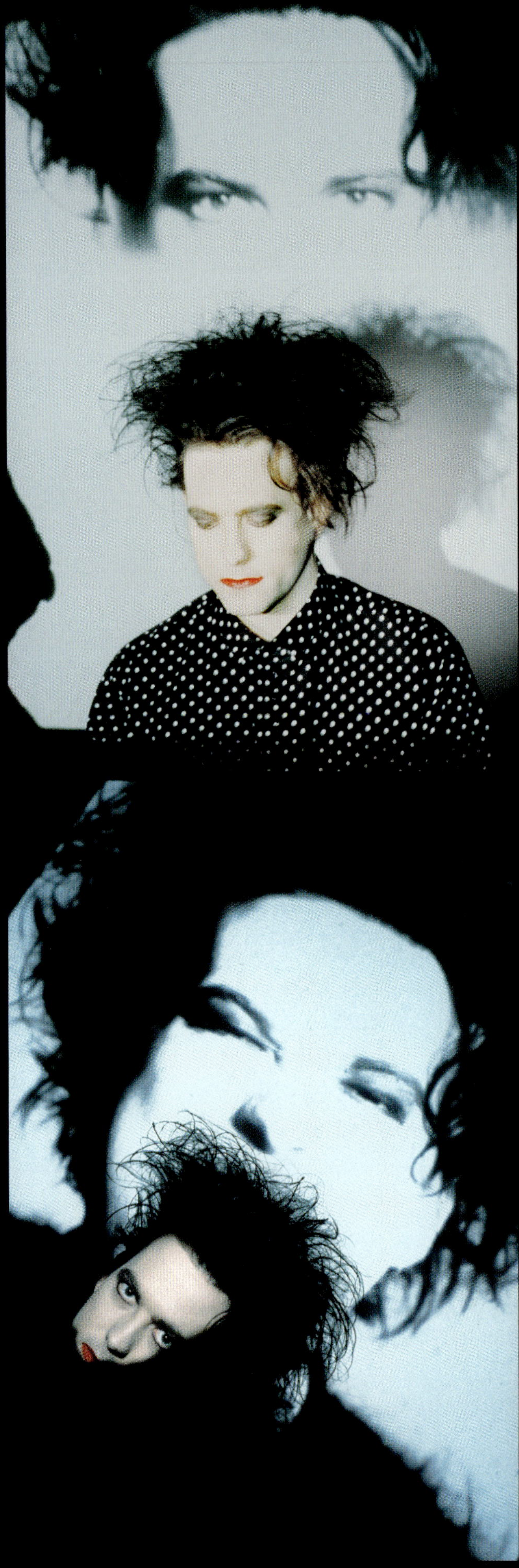

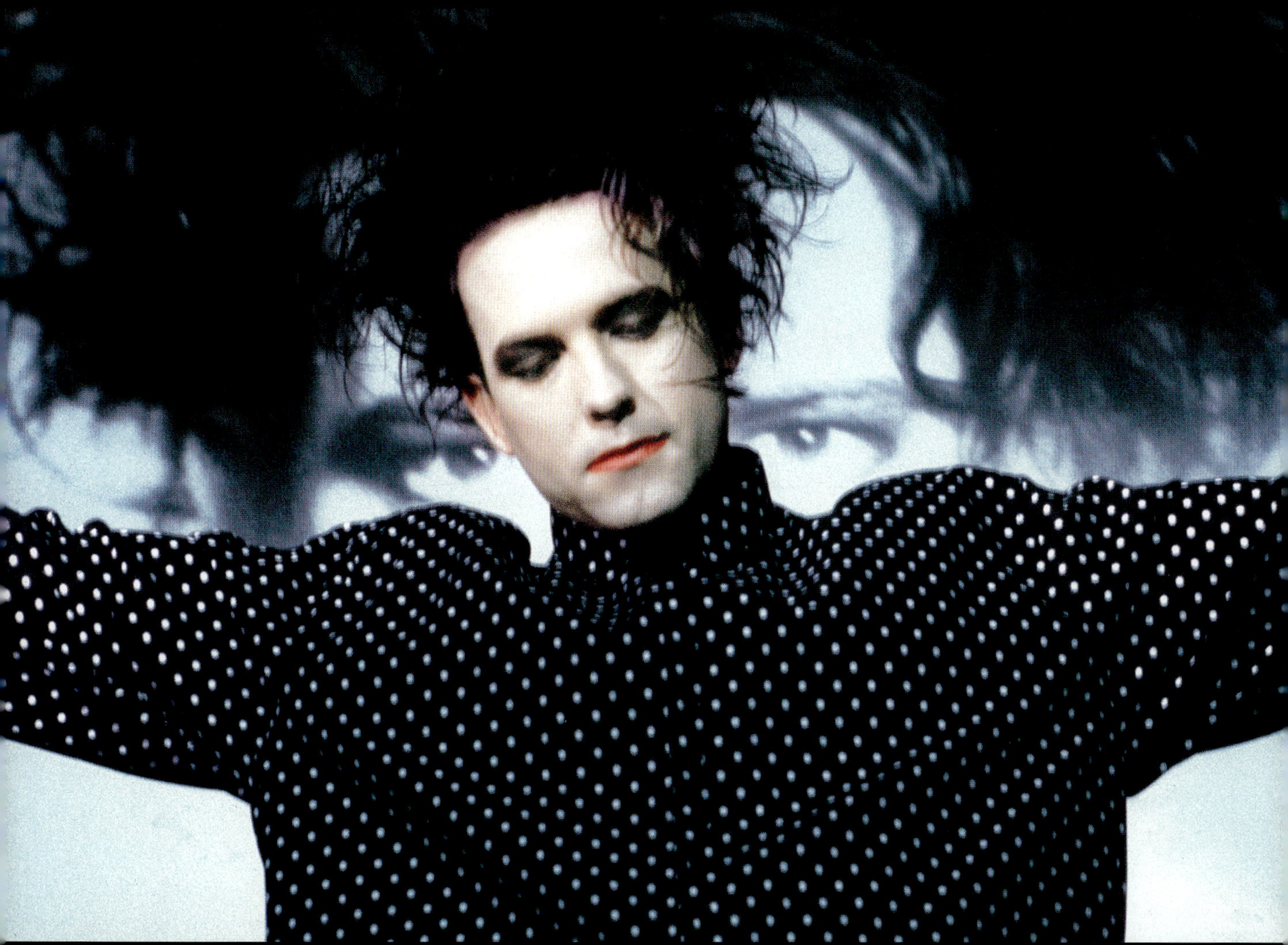

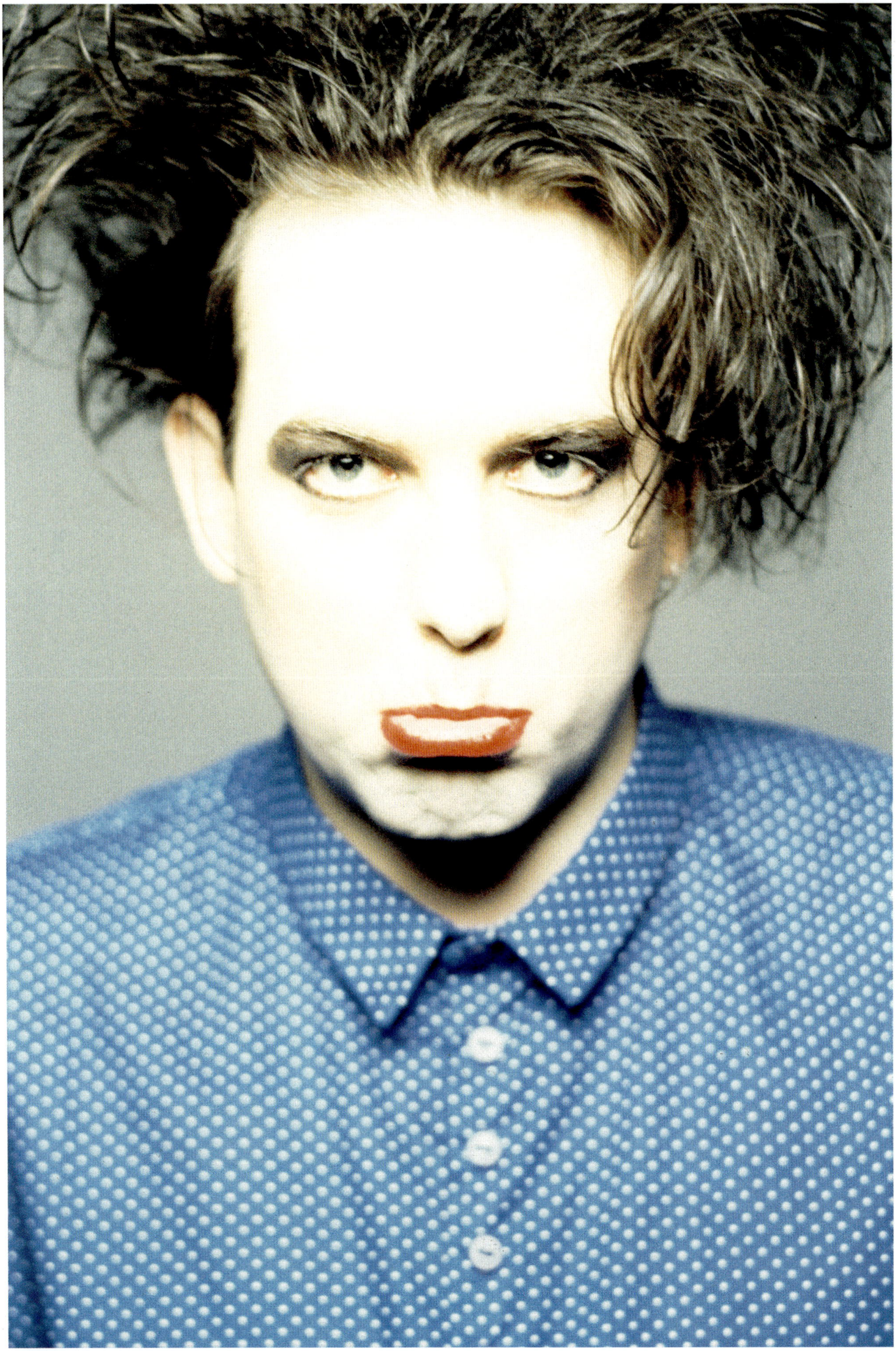

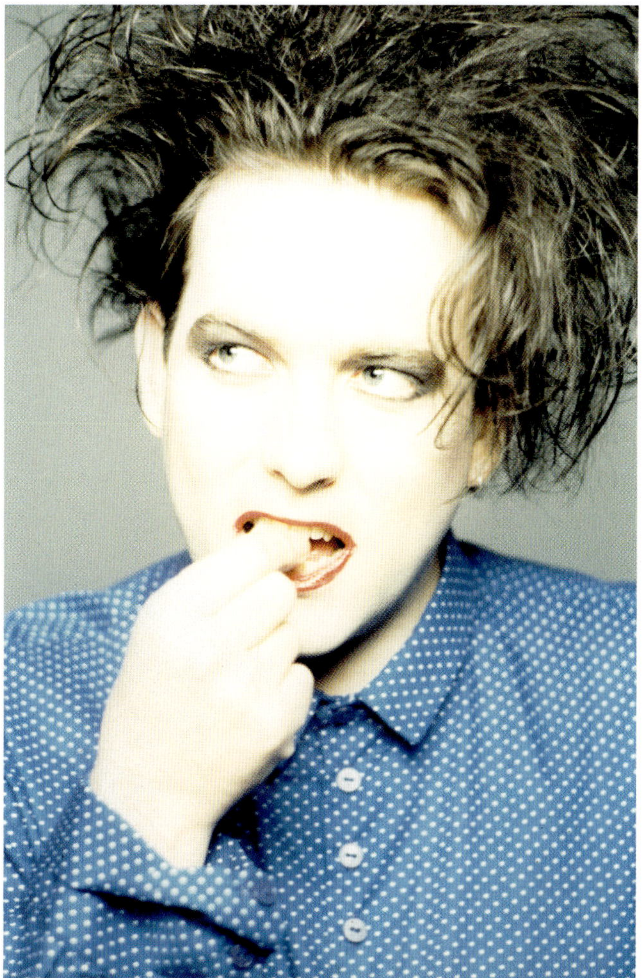

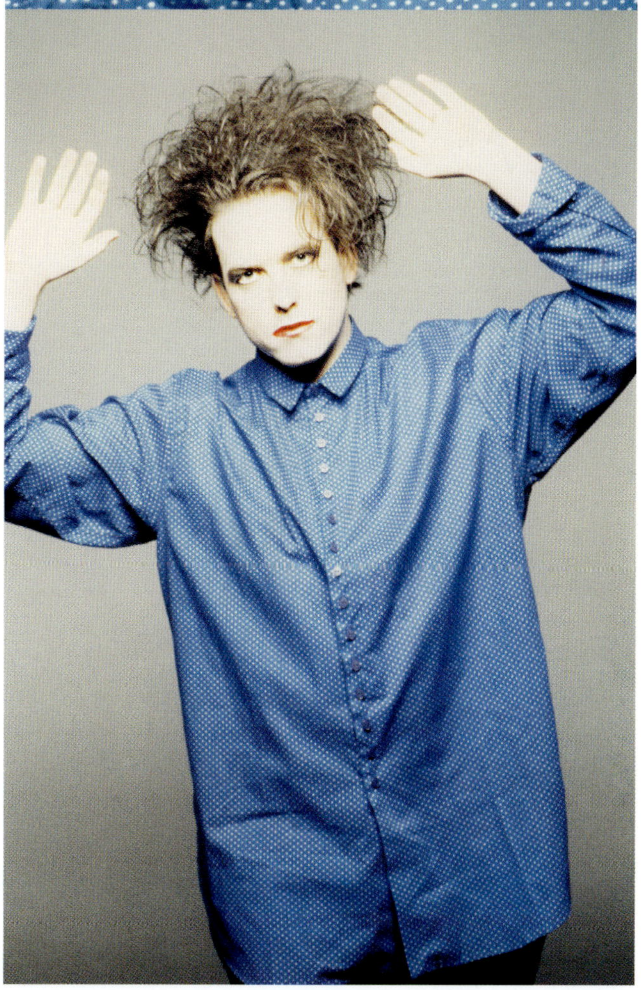

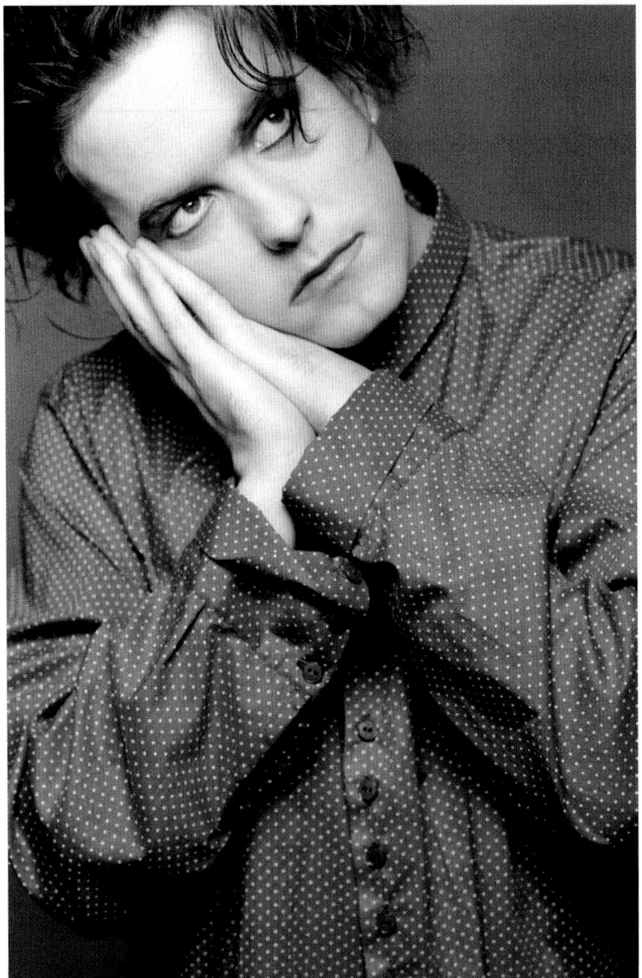

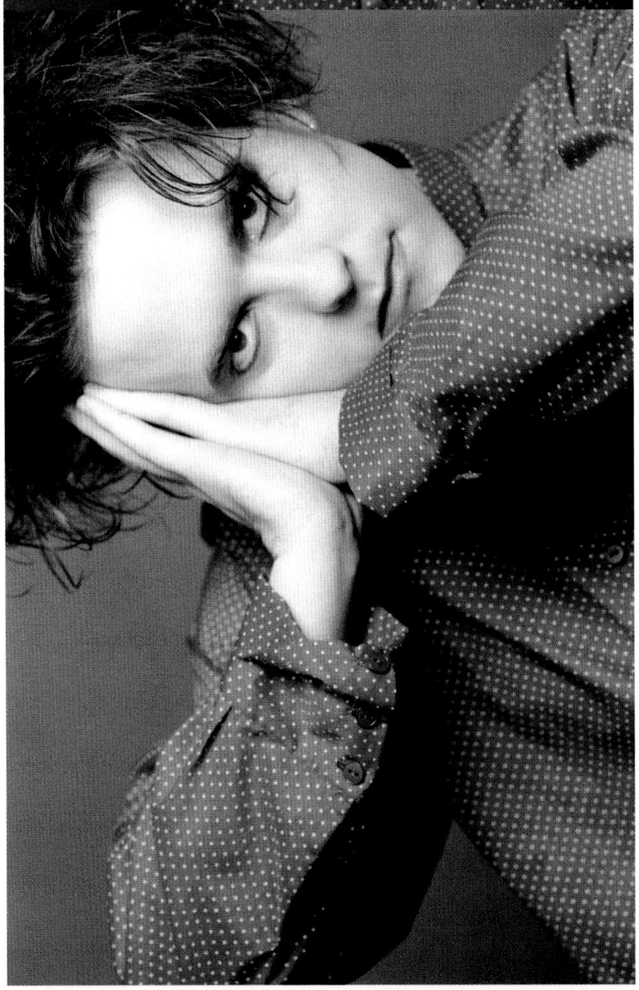

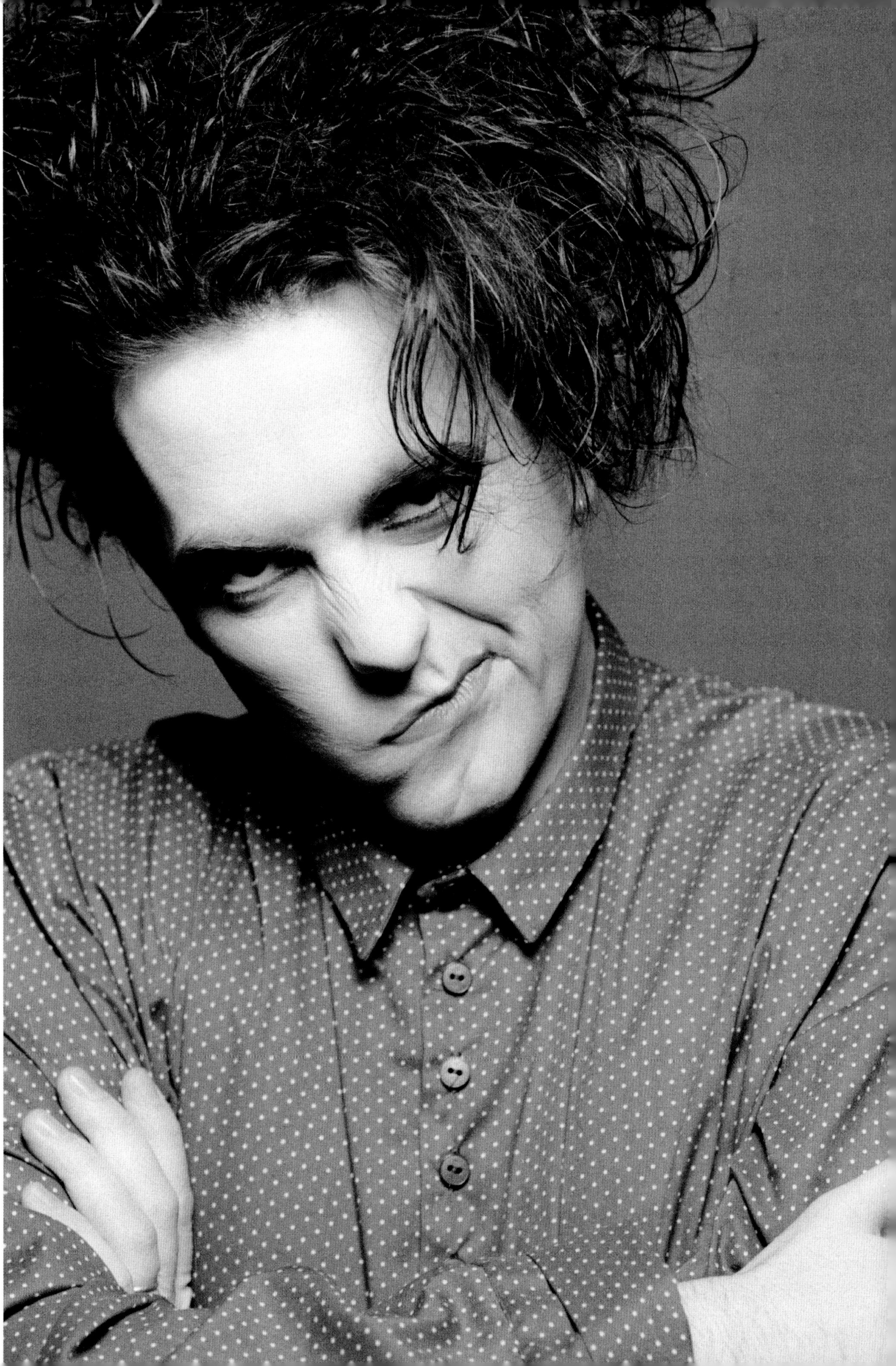

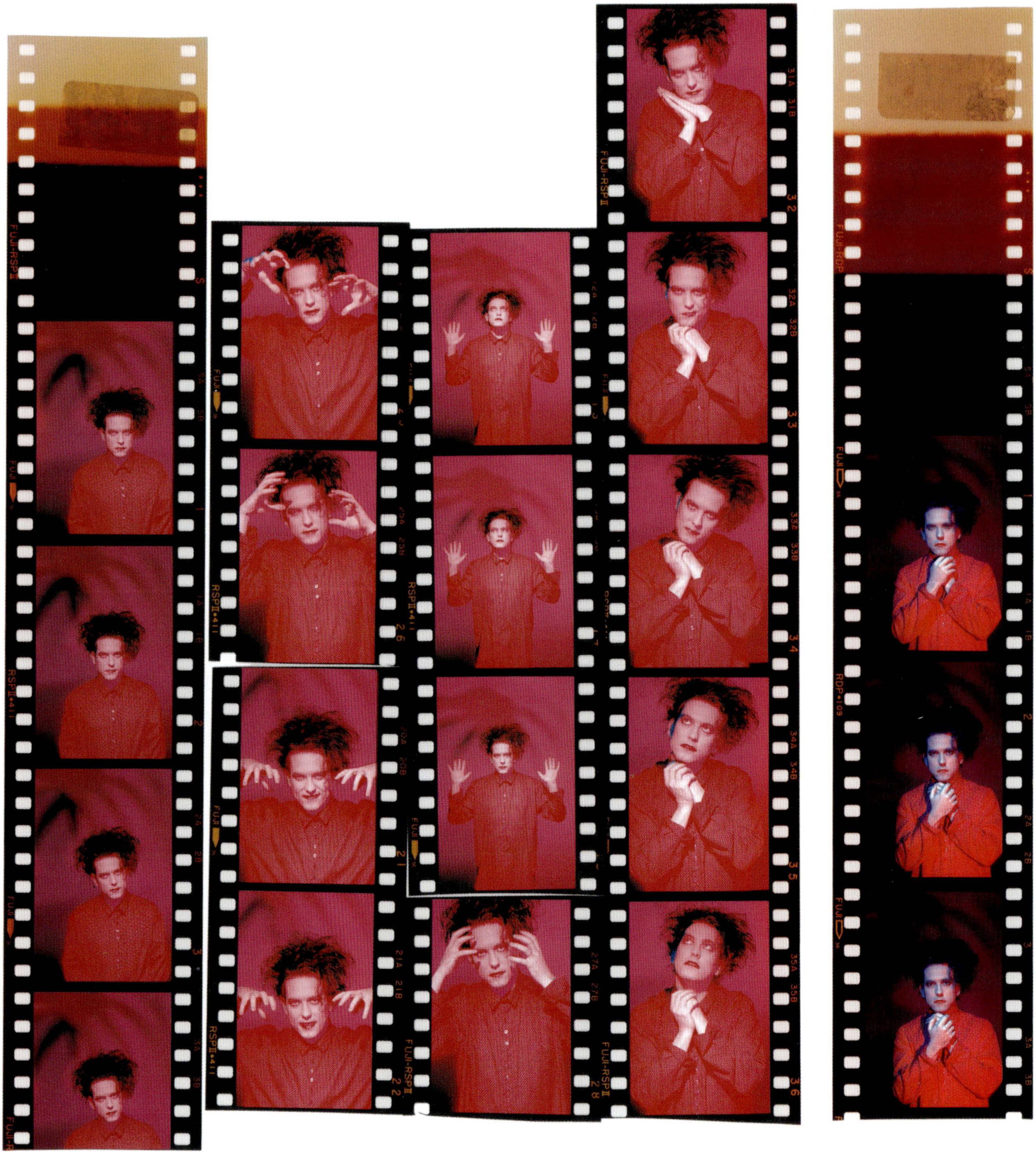

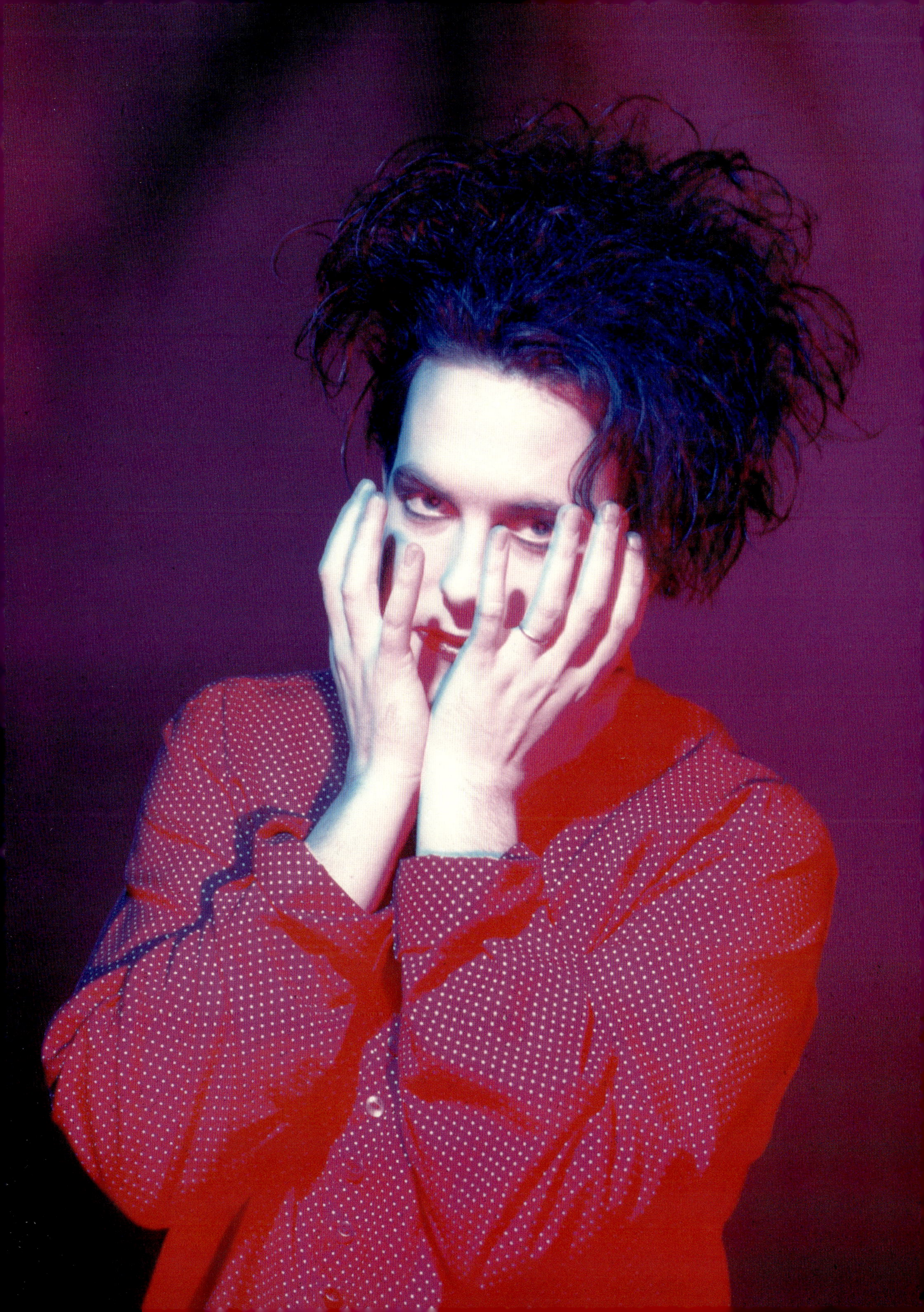

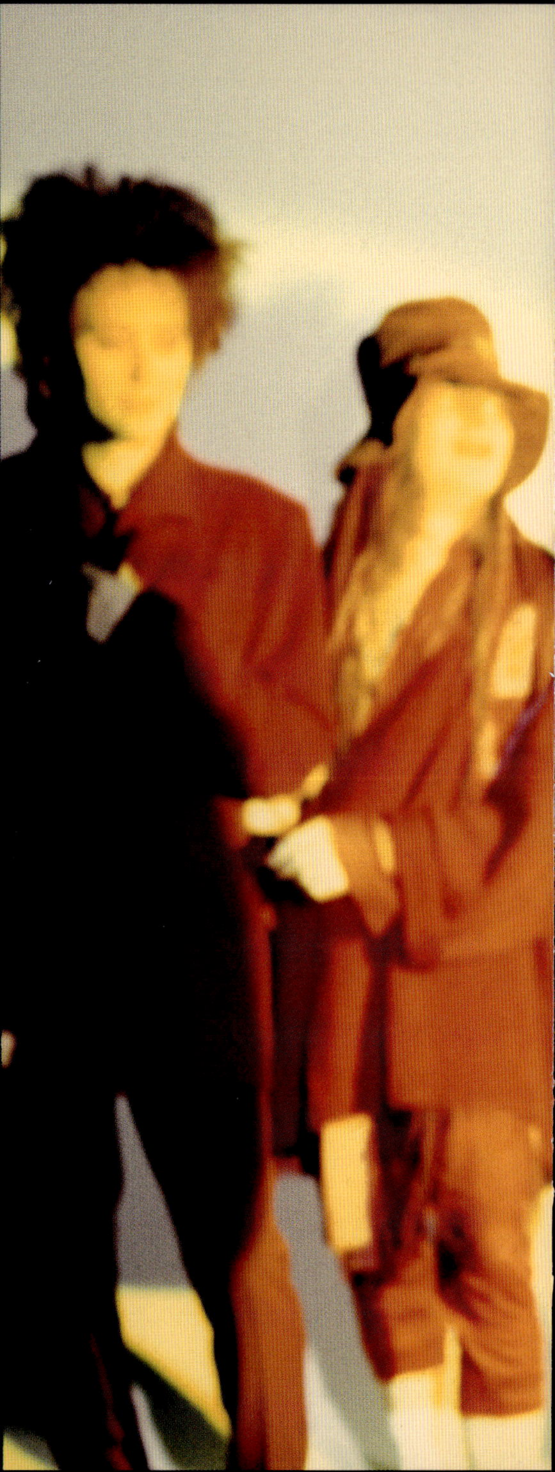

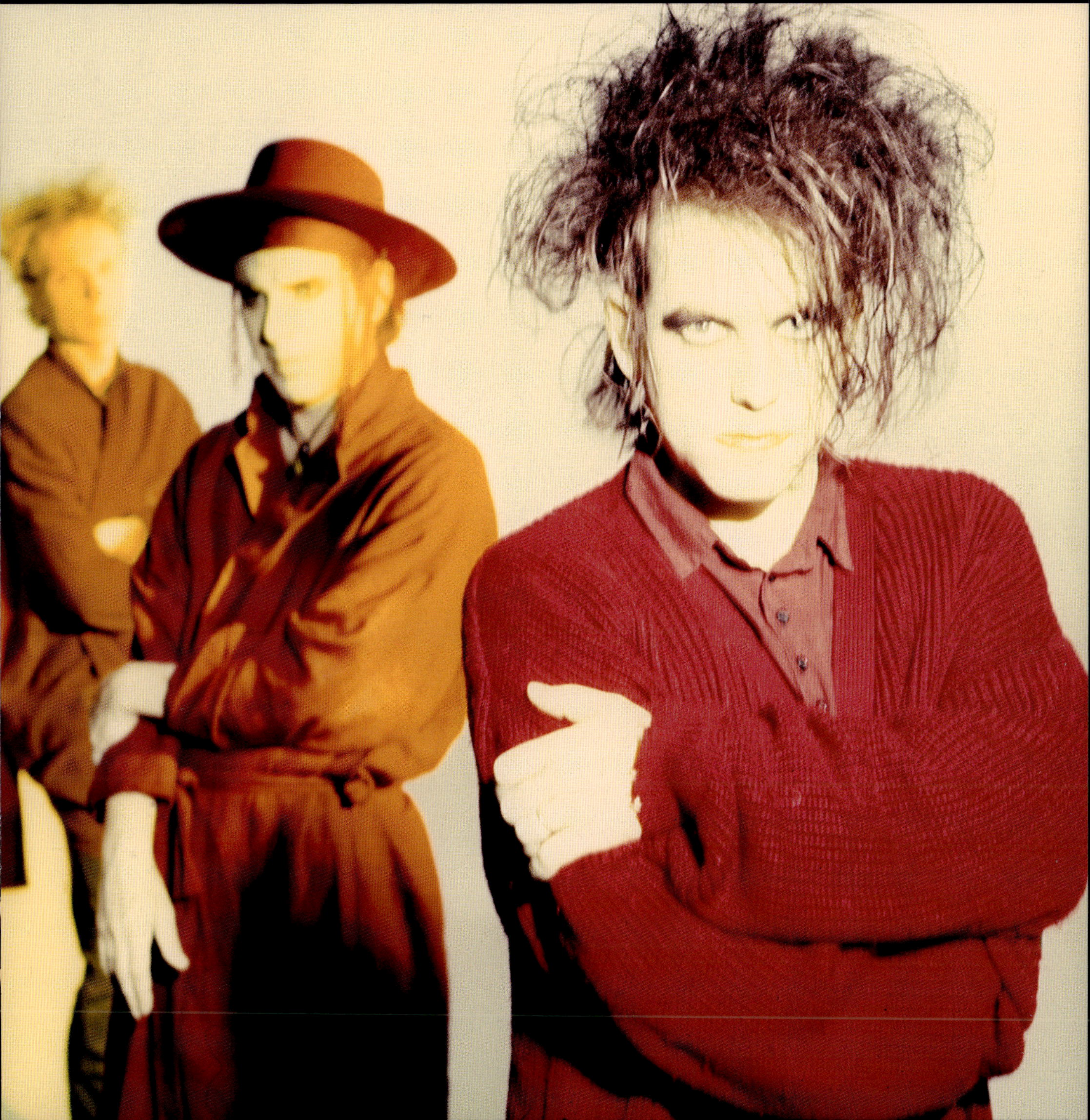

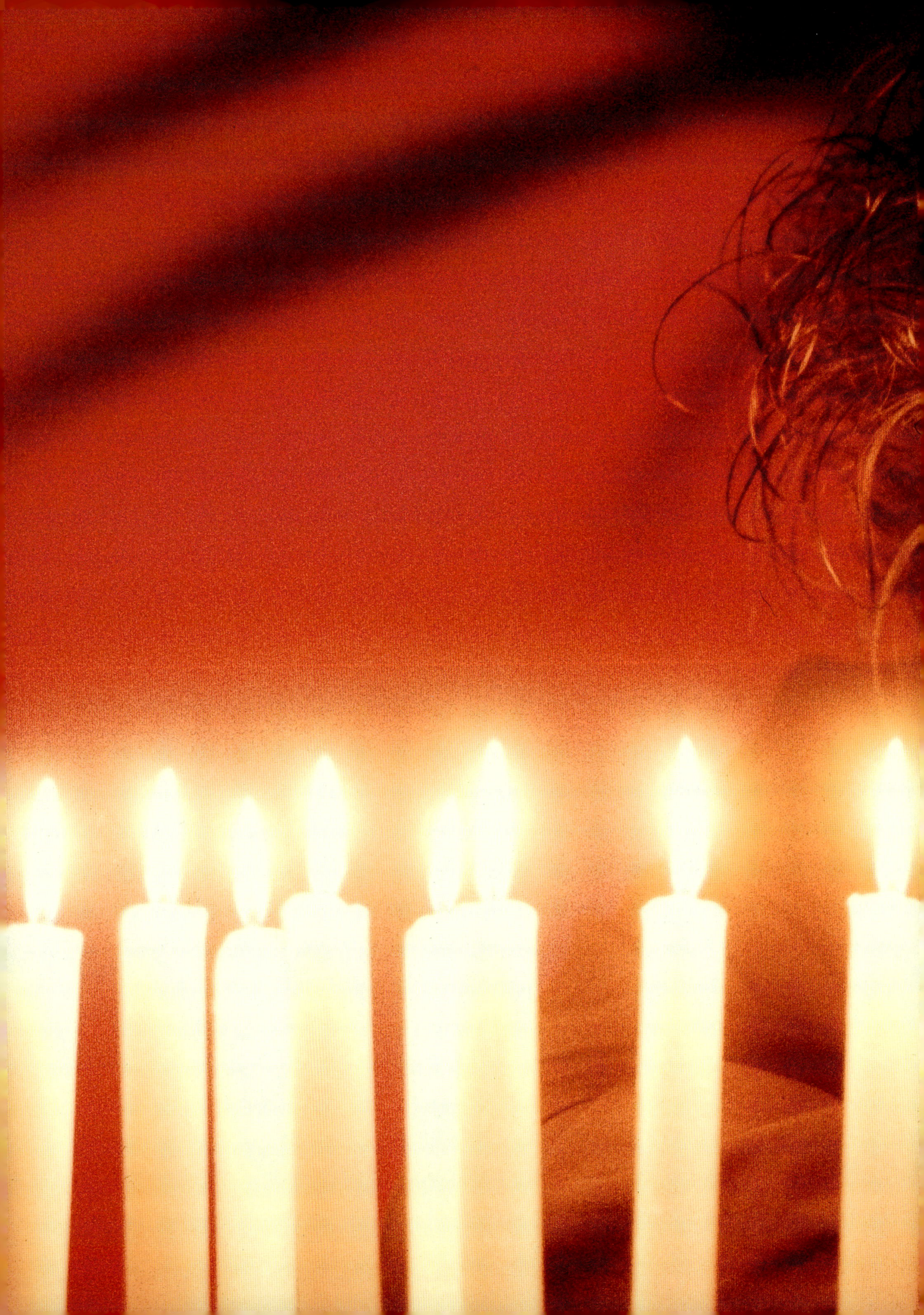

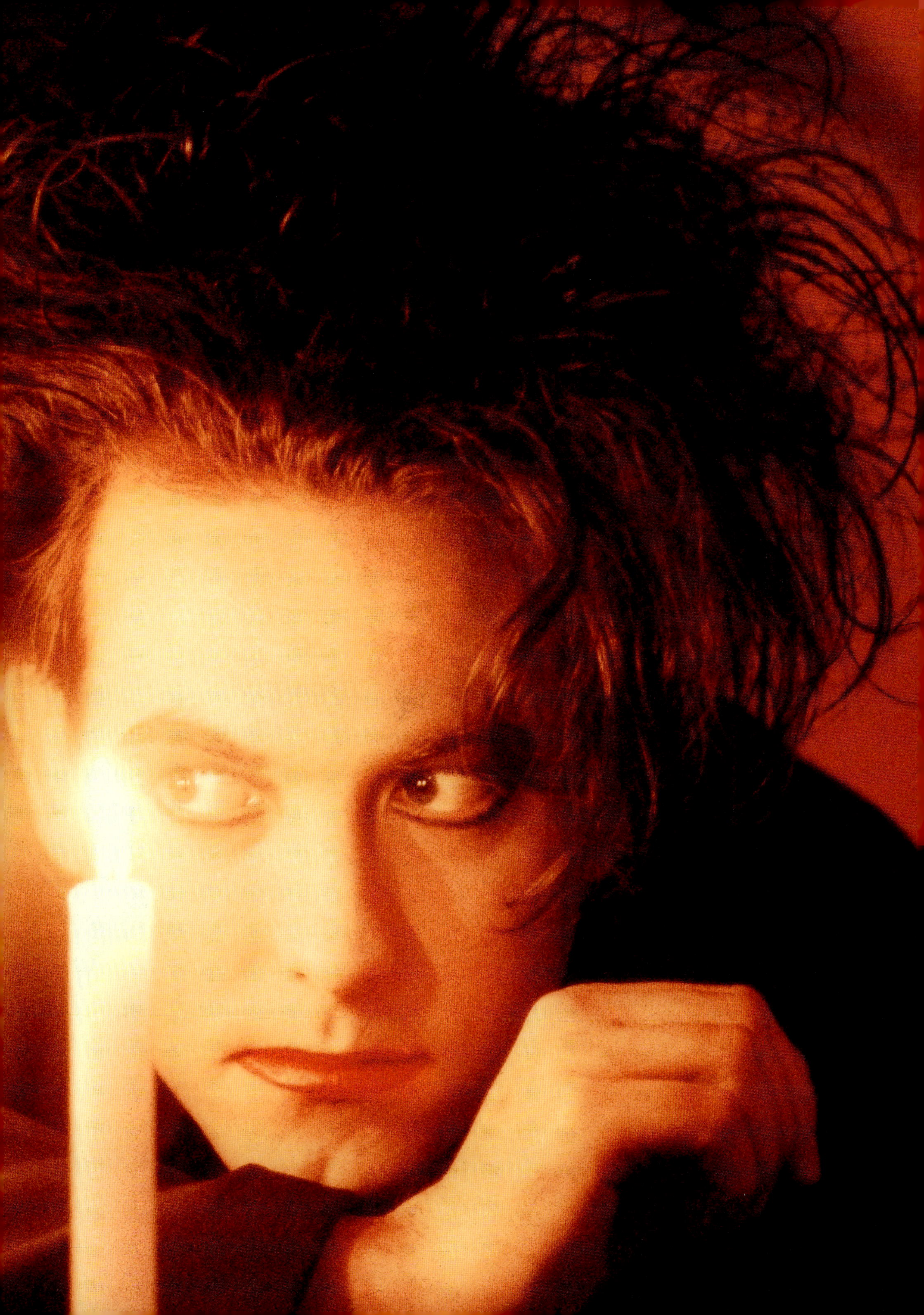

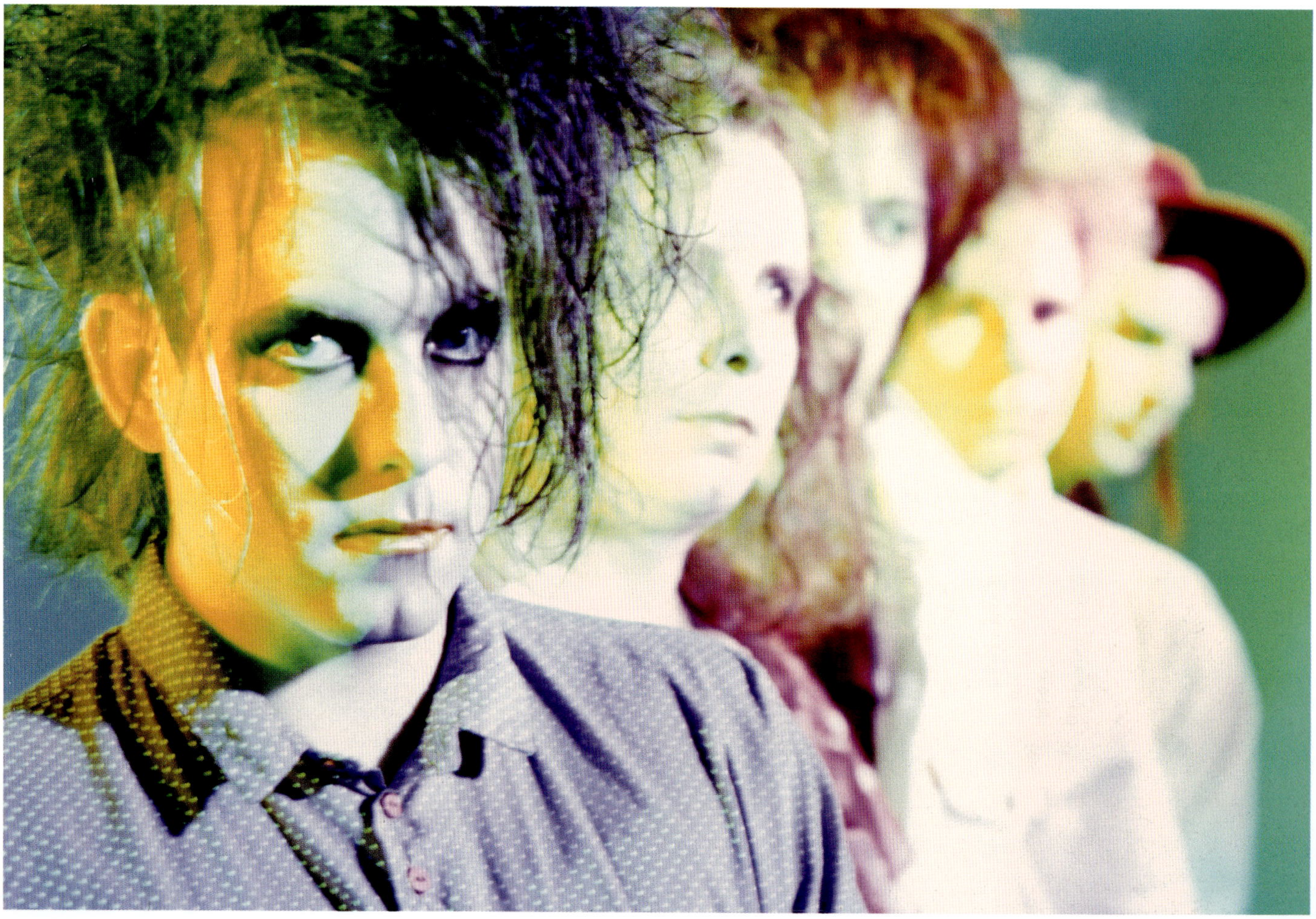

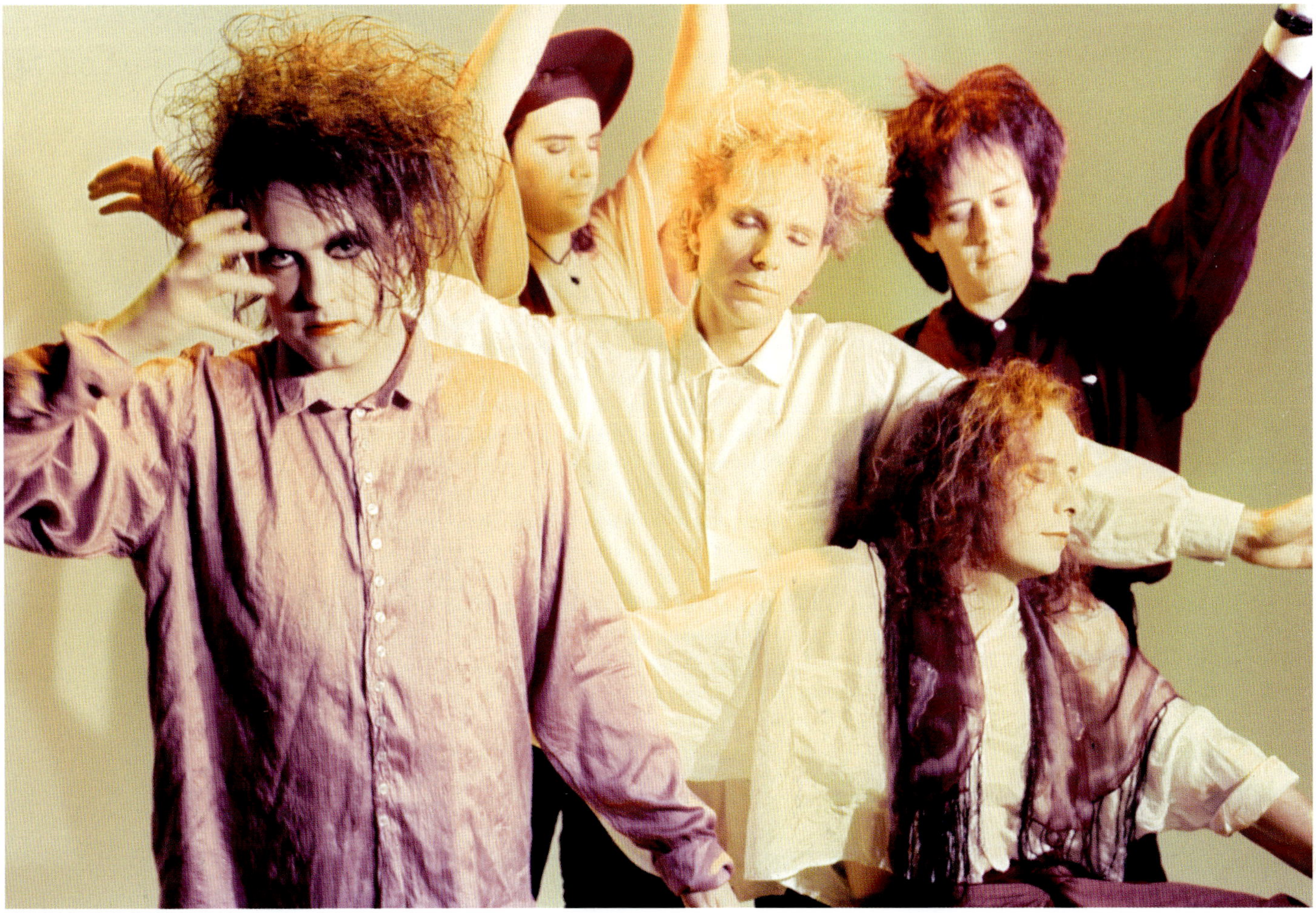

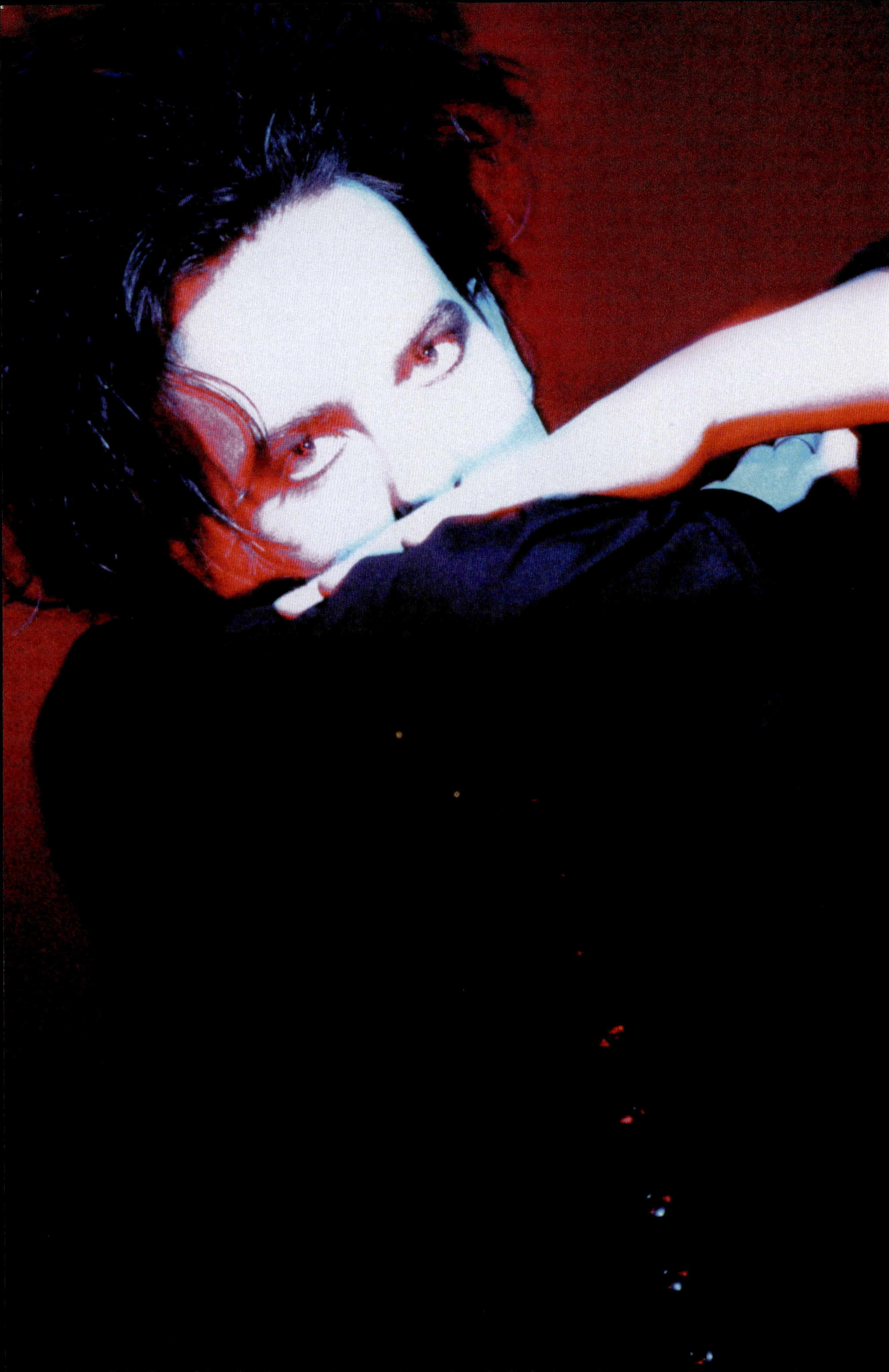

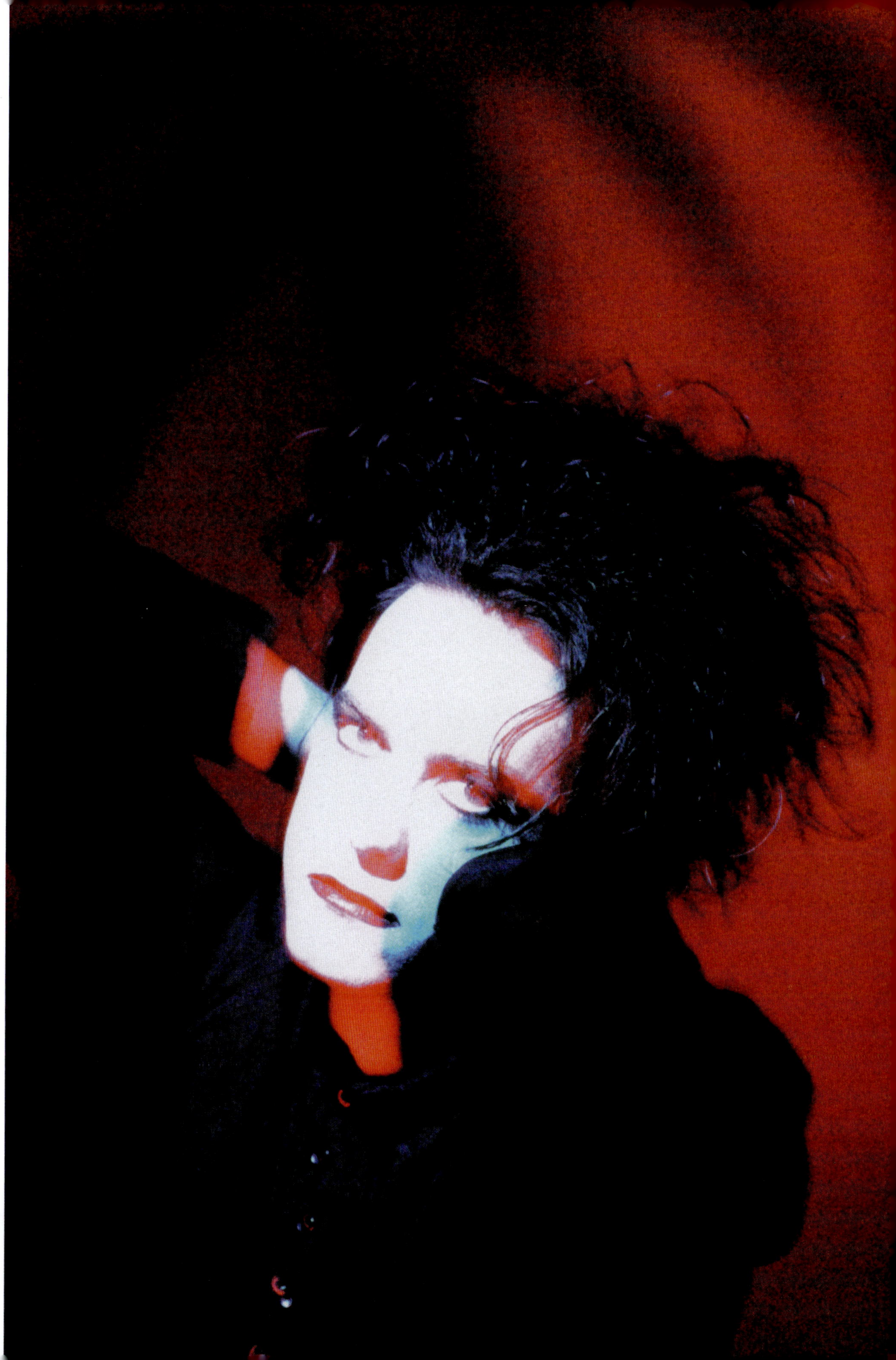

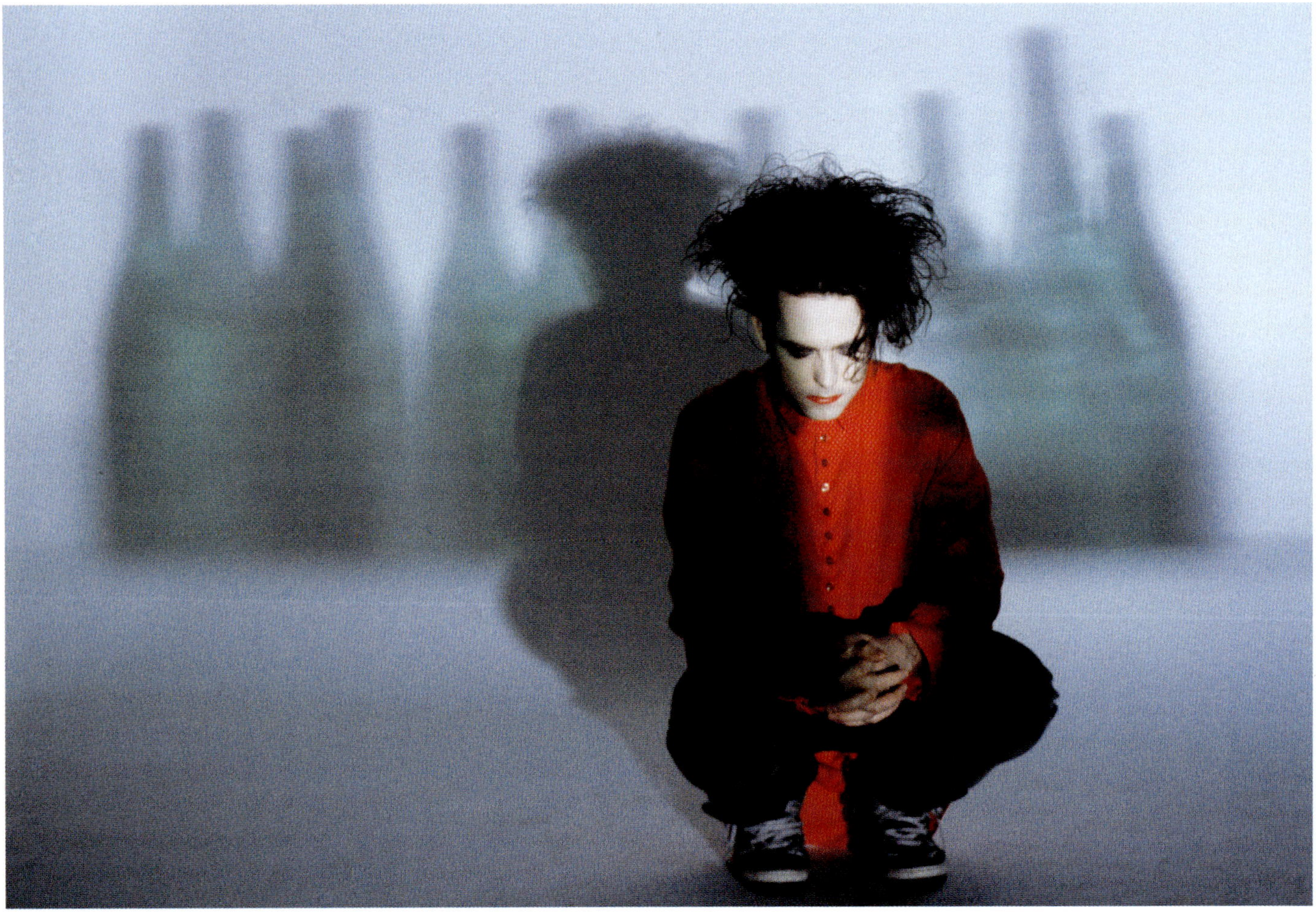

[right] **ROBERT:** AH! TEN GREEN BOTTLES! (WELL… SIX… BUT IF ONE GREEN BOTTLE SHOULD ACCIDENTALLY FALL…) – MAYBE MY FAVOURITE SHOT OF ME BY YOU?

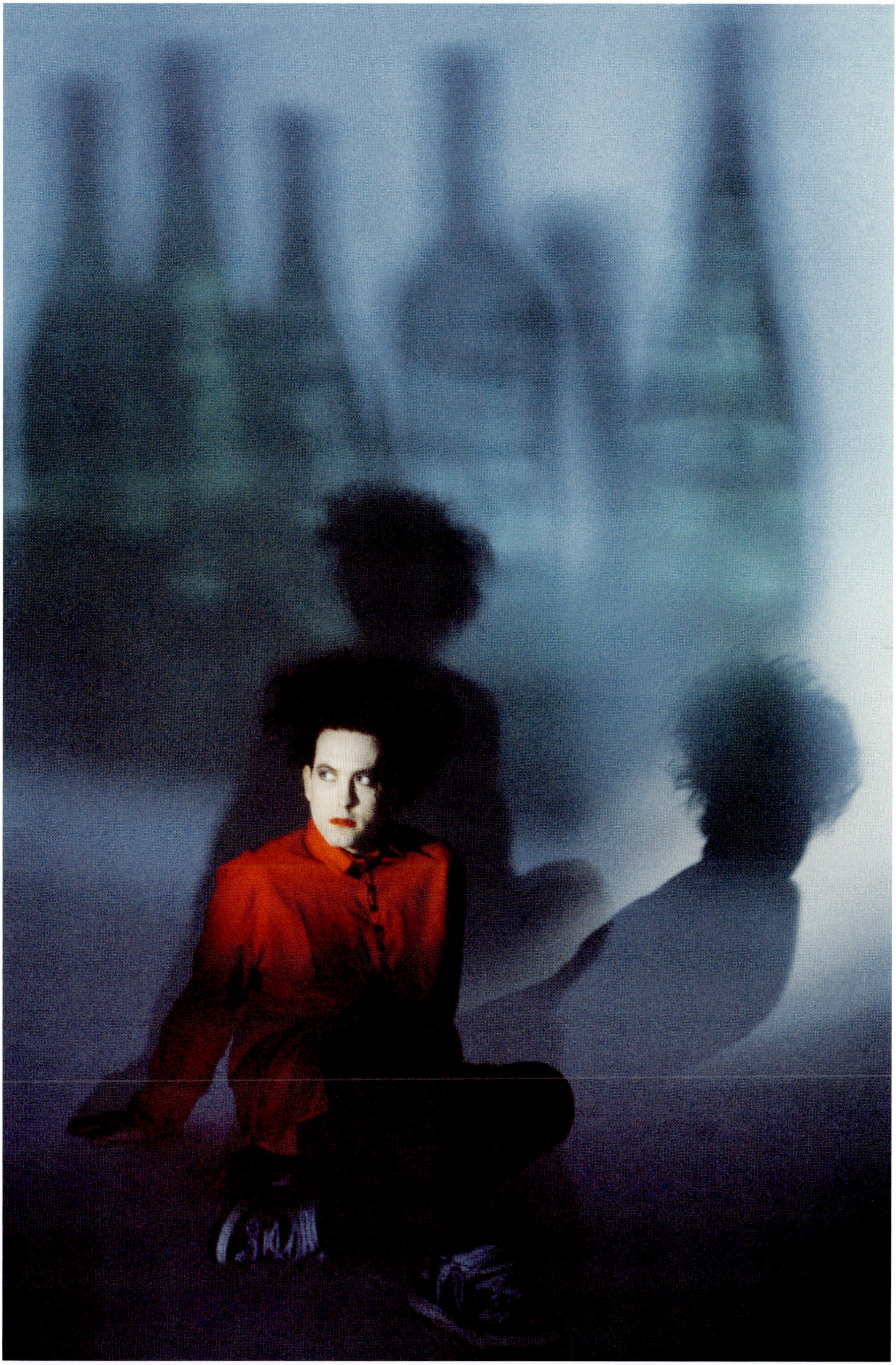

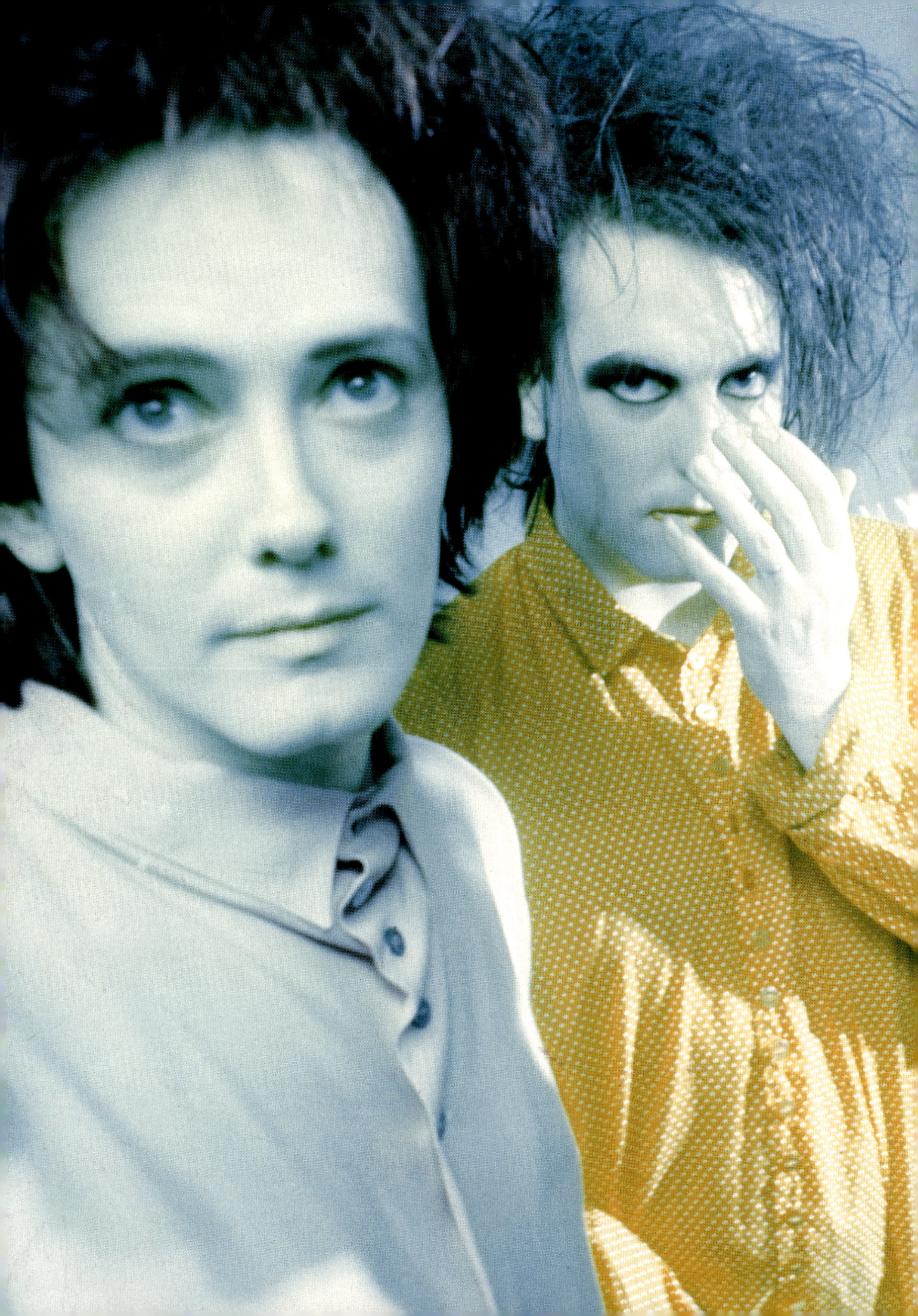

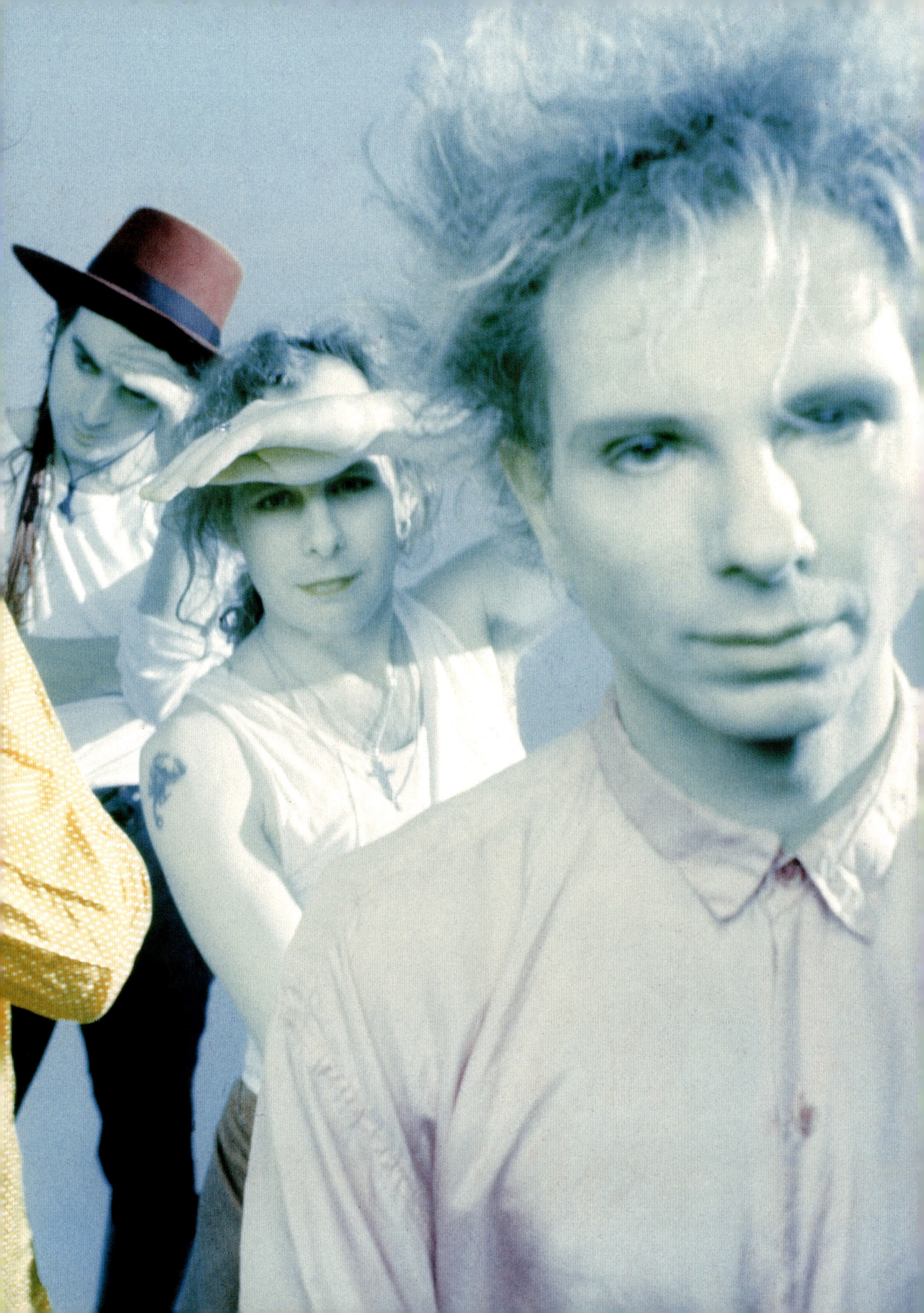

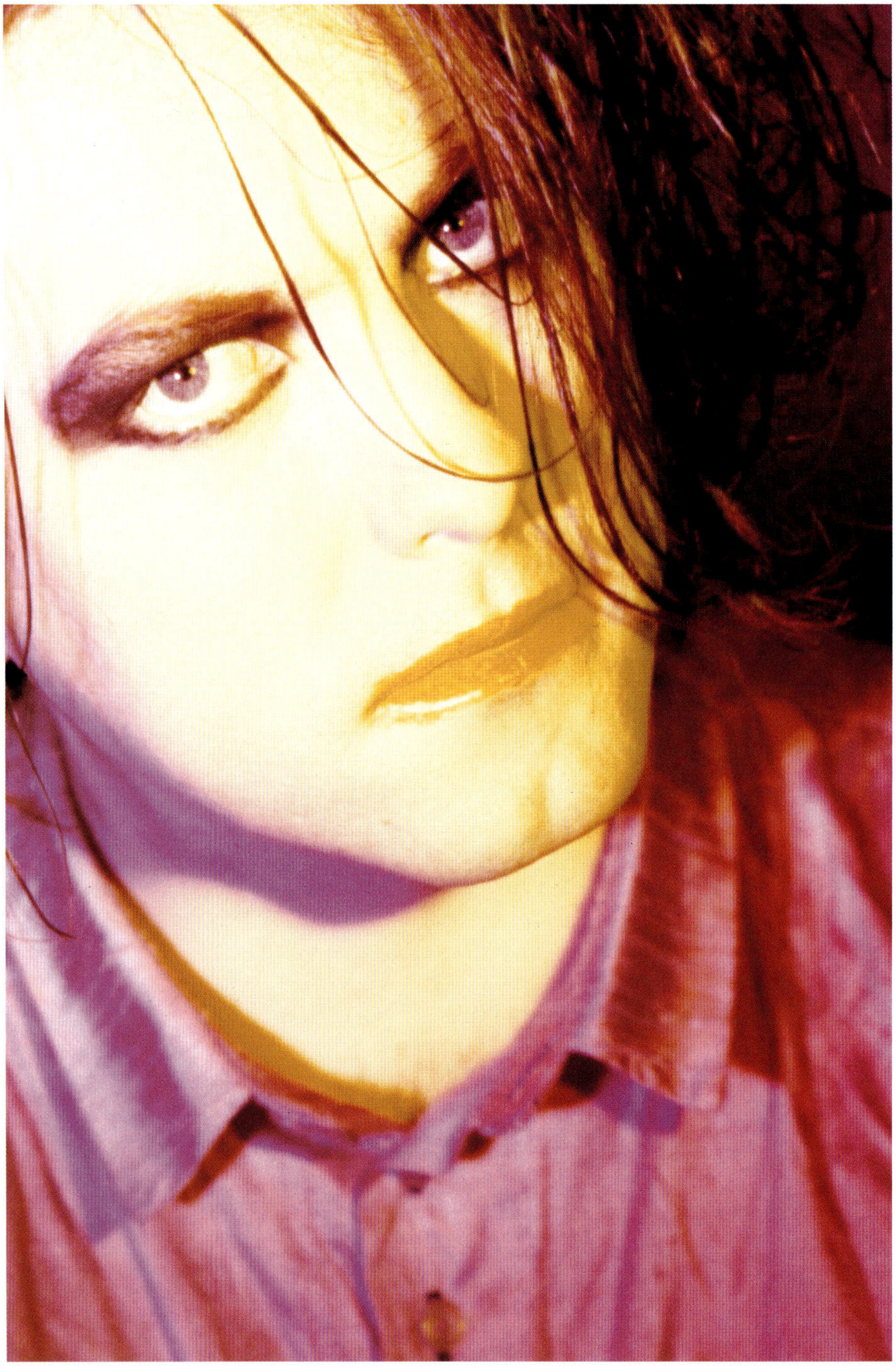

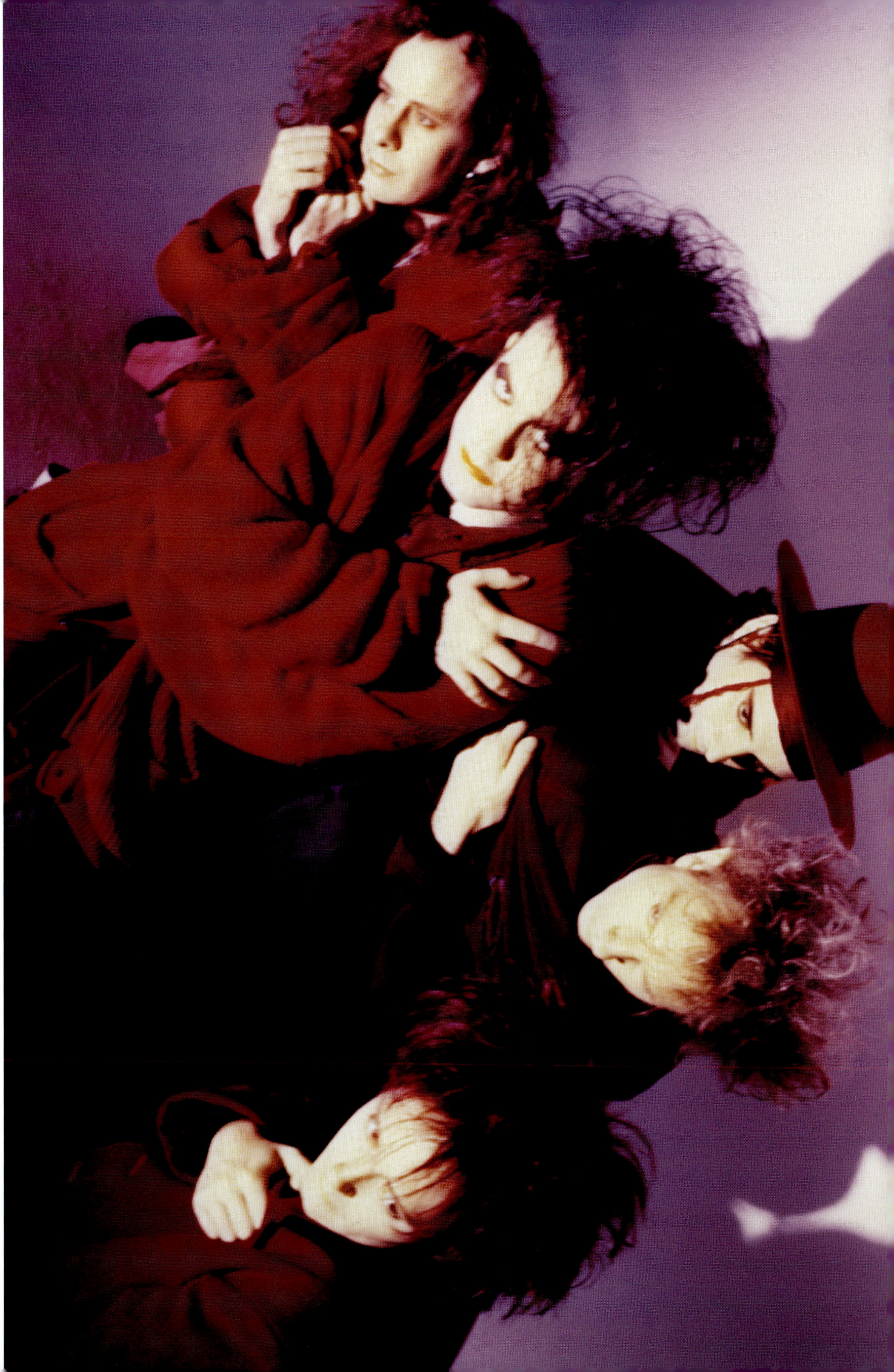

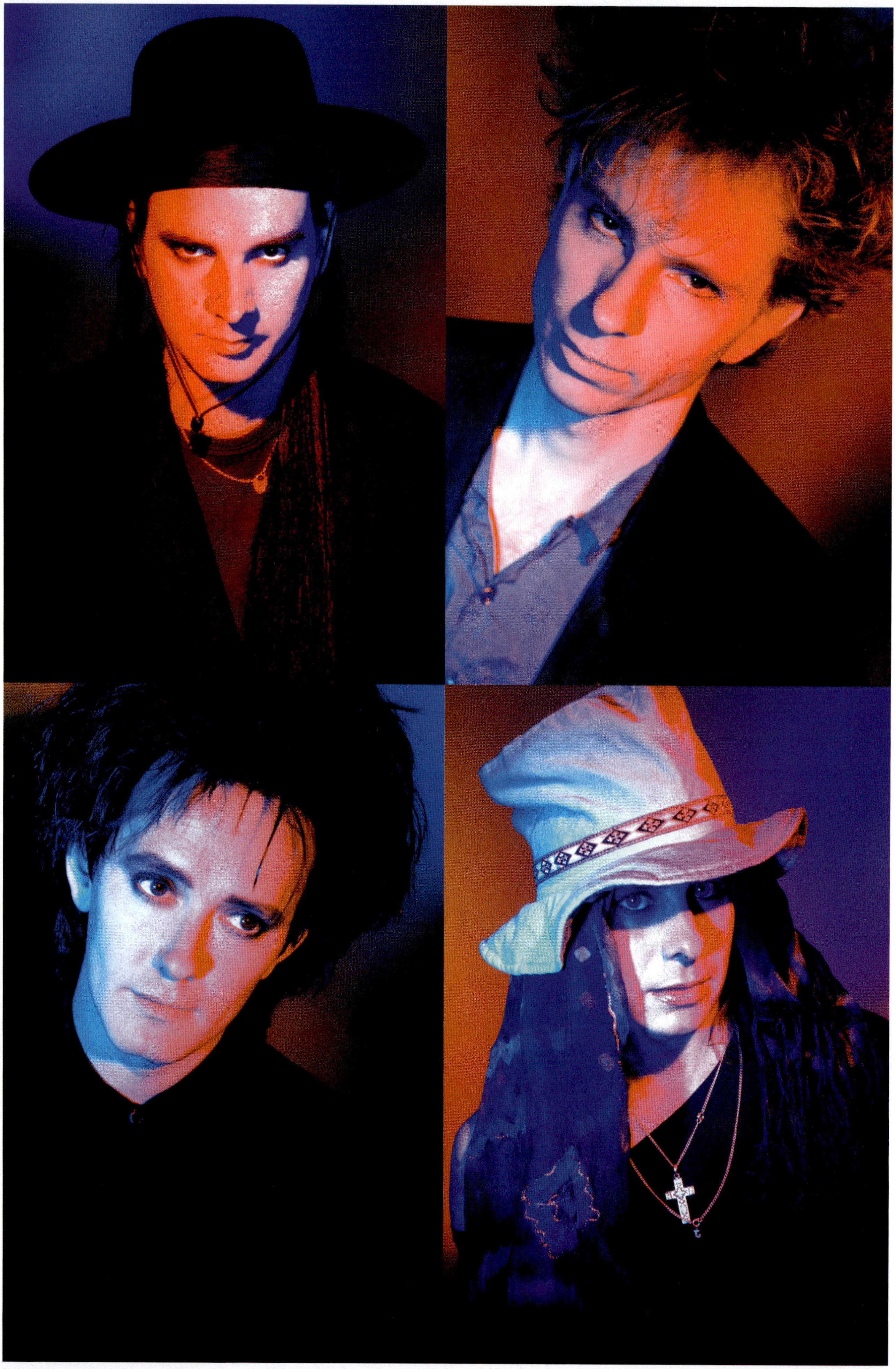

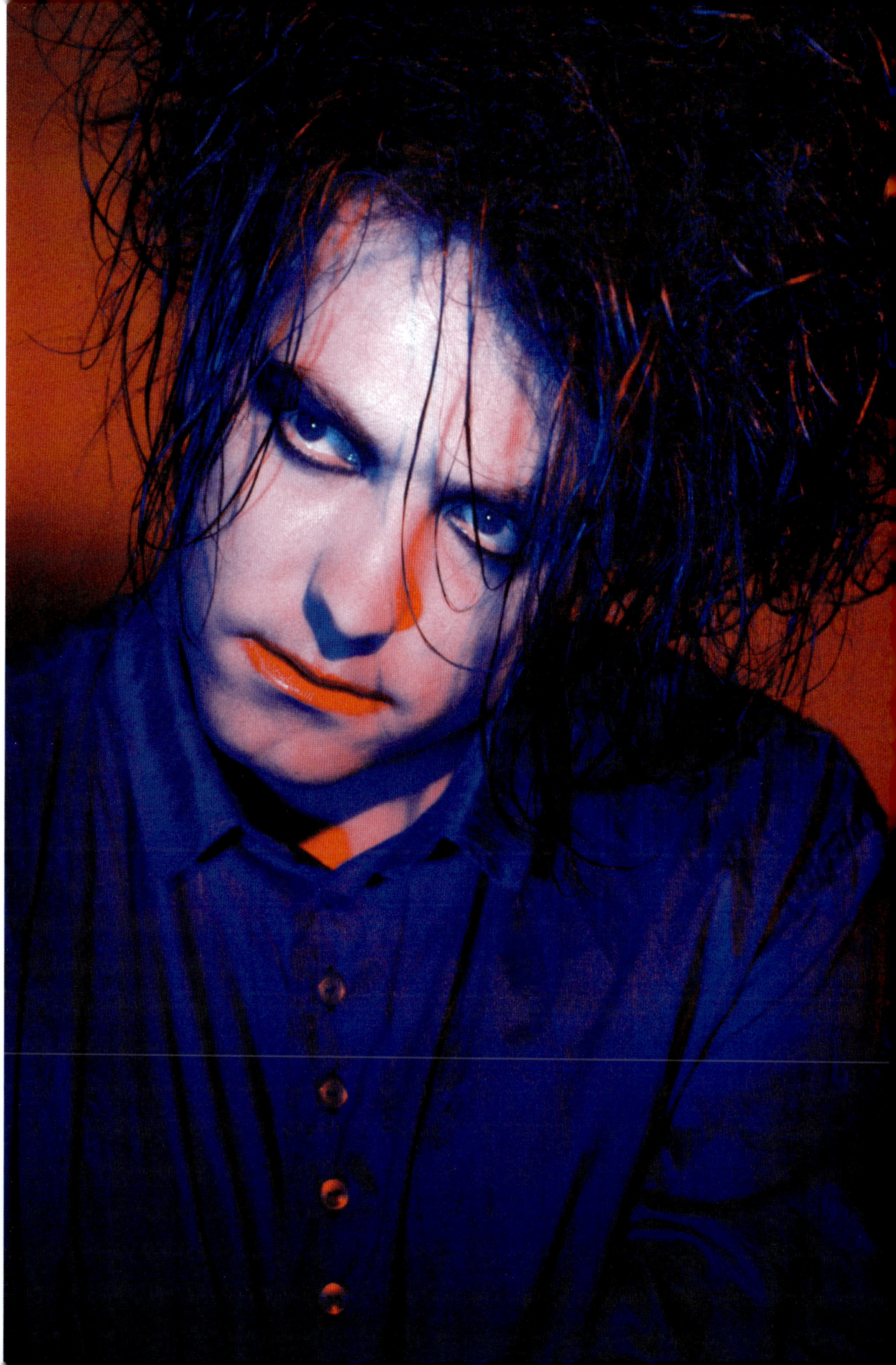

FULHAM STUDIO

'Never Enough' cover session p. 145
(p. 138 to 151)
1990

ROBERT: PHOTOS FOR THE 'NEVER ENOUGH' SINGLE SLEEVE, AS WELL AS SHOTS TO PROMOTE THE *MIXED UP* REMIX ALBUM RELEASE 1990... I AM VERY HAPPY IN MY NEW FAVOURITE SHIRTS – THE SUMMER OF LOVE INDEED!

Paul: I had been commissioned for another session at my studio again. I wracked my brain to come up with something different. I used mirrors, glass and water and a sheet of eight-by-four-foot flexi mirror and a 35mm carousel projector to produce these images to create a certain ambiance. Not being in the digital age, it wasn't a case of manipulating images on a computer afterwards, the pictures are as they were taken!

I took photos of their instruments and projected them with the 35mm carousel onto the wall as a back projection. All shot on the same day with a clever device called the Polaroid Processor. It was an amazing piece of equipment at the time, as it produced instant transparencies.

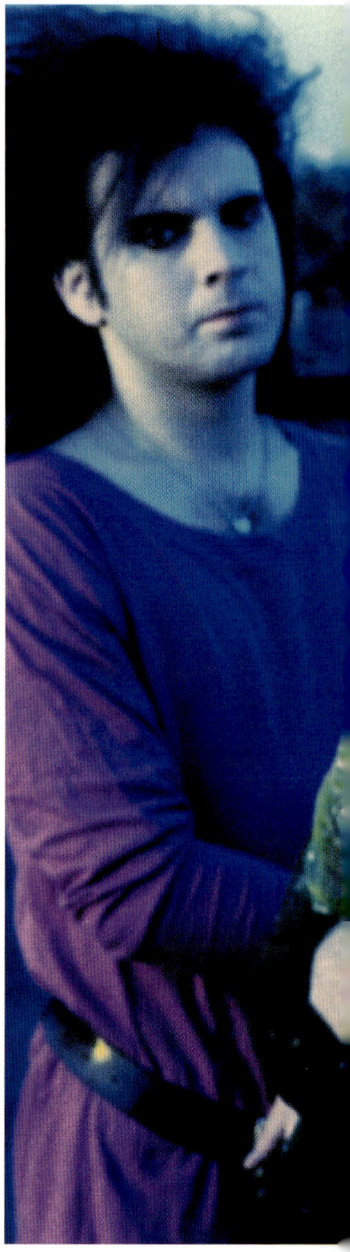

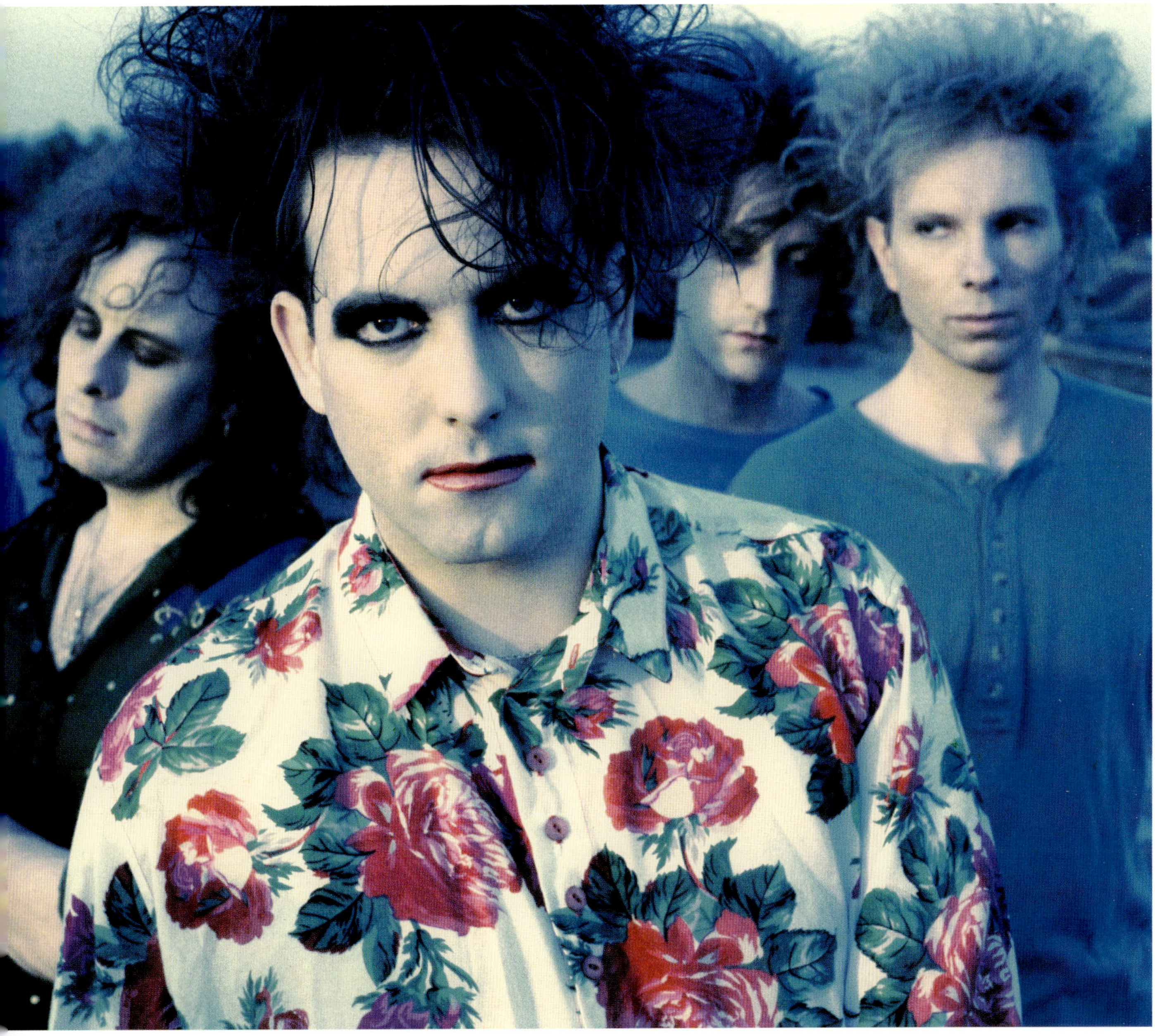

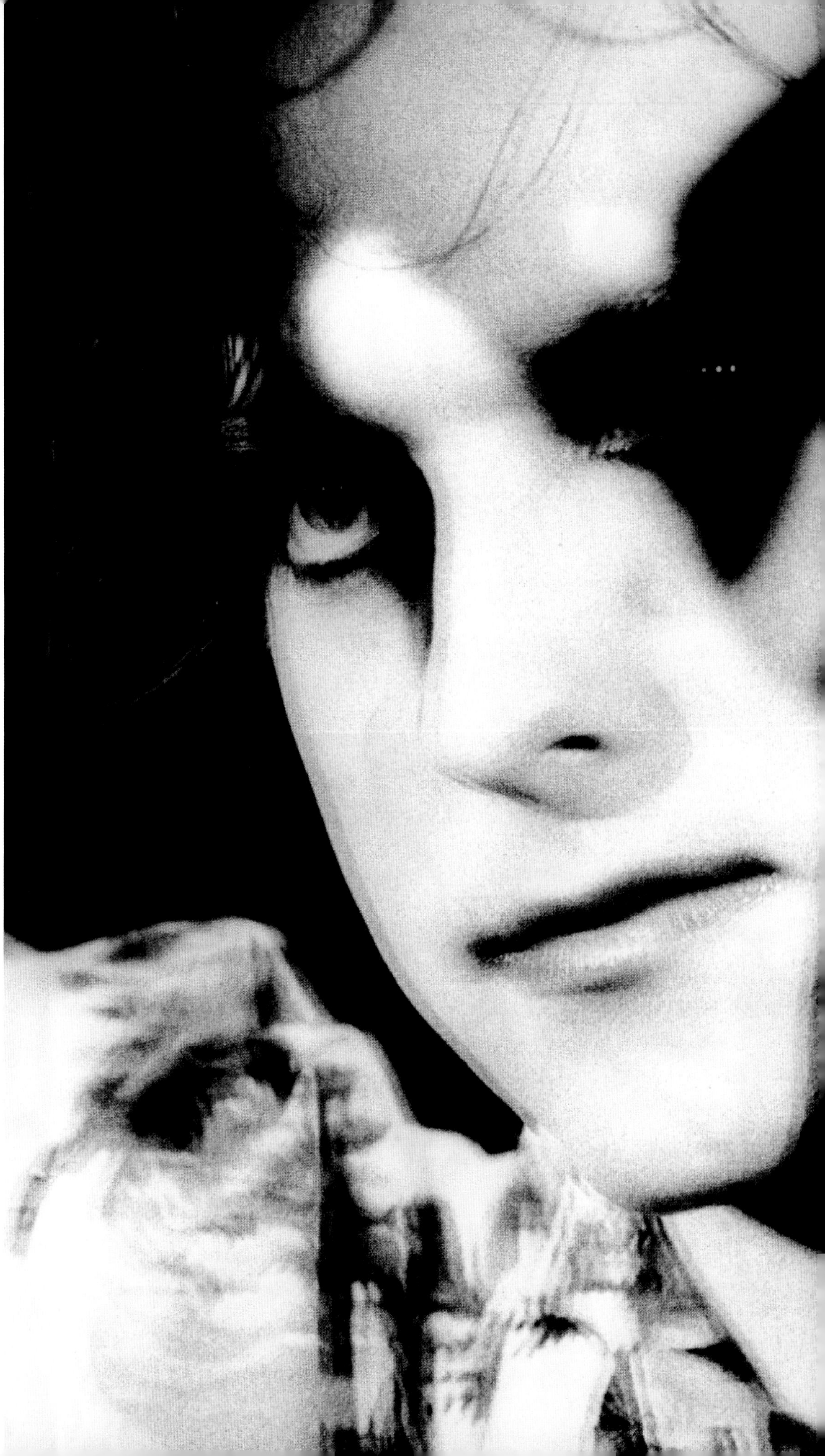

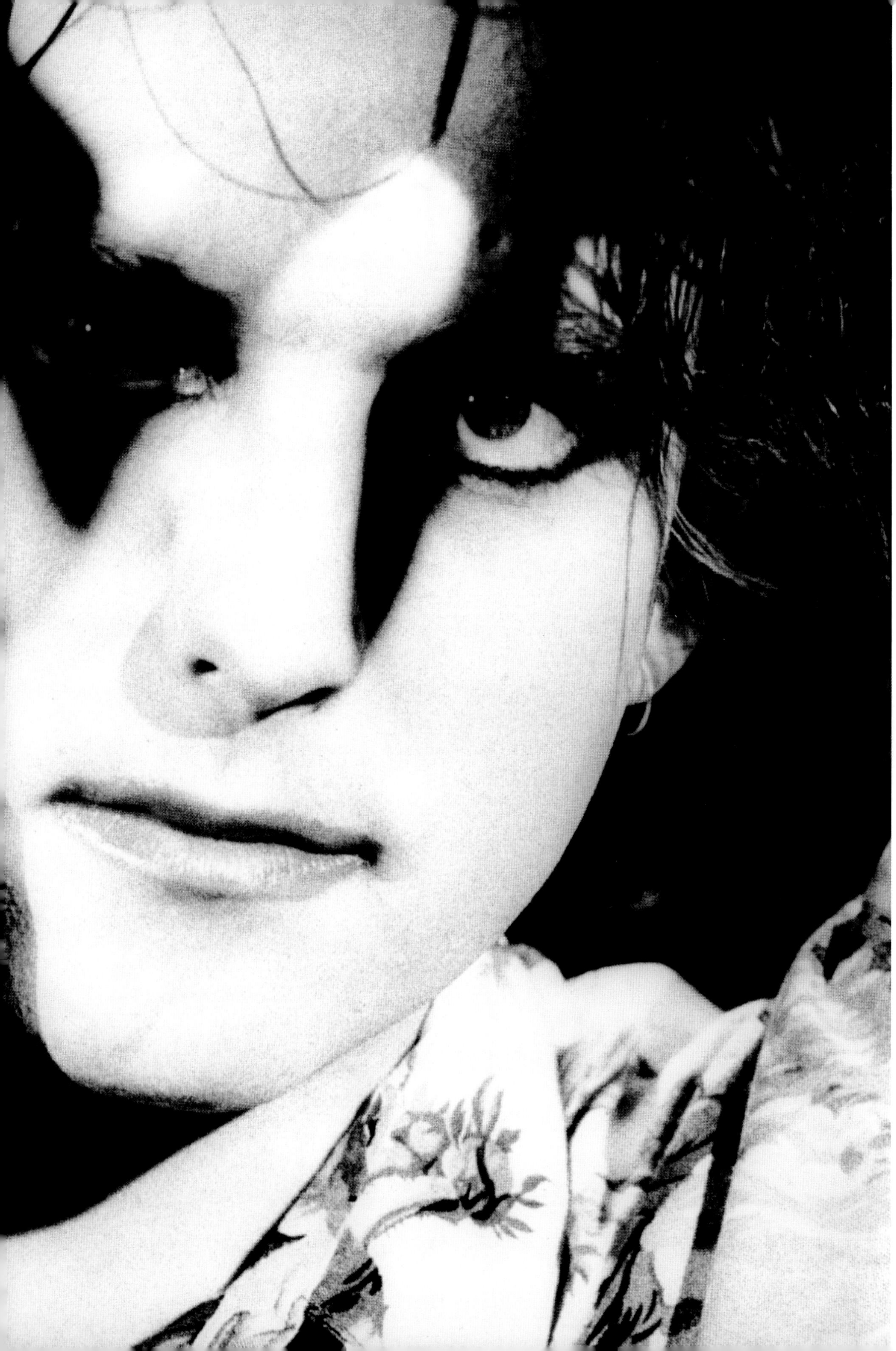

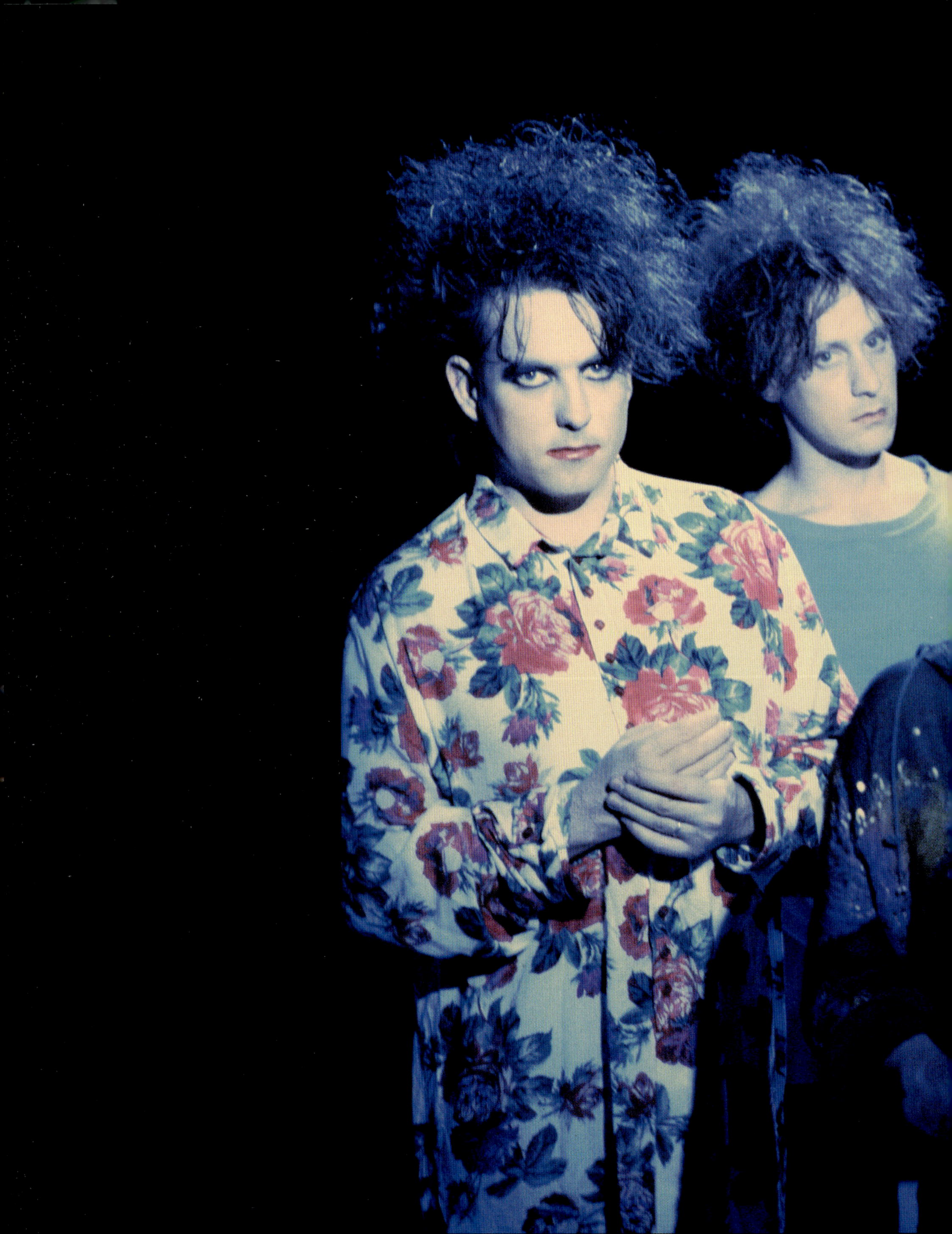

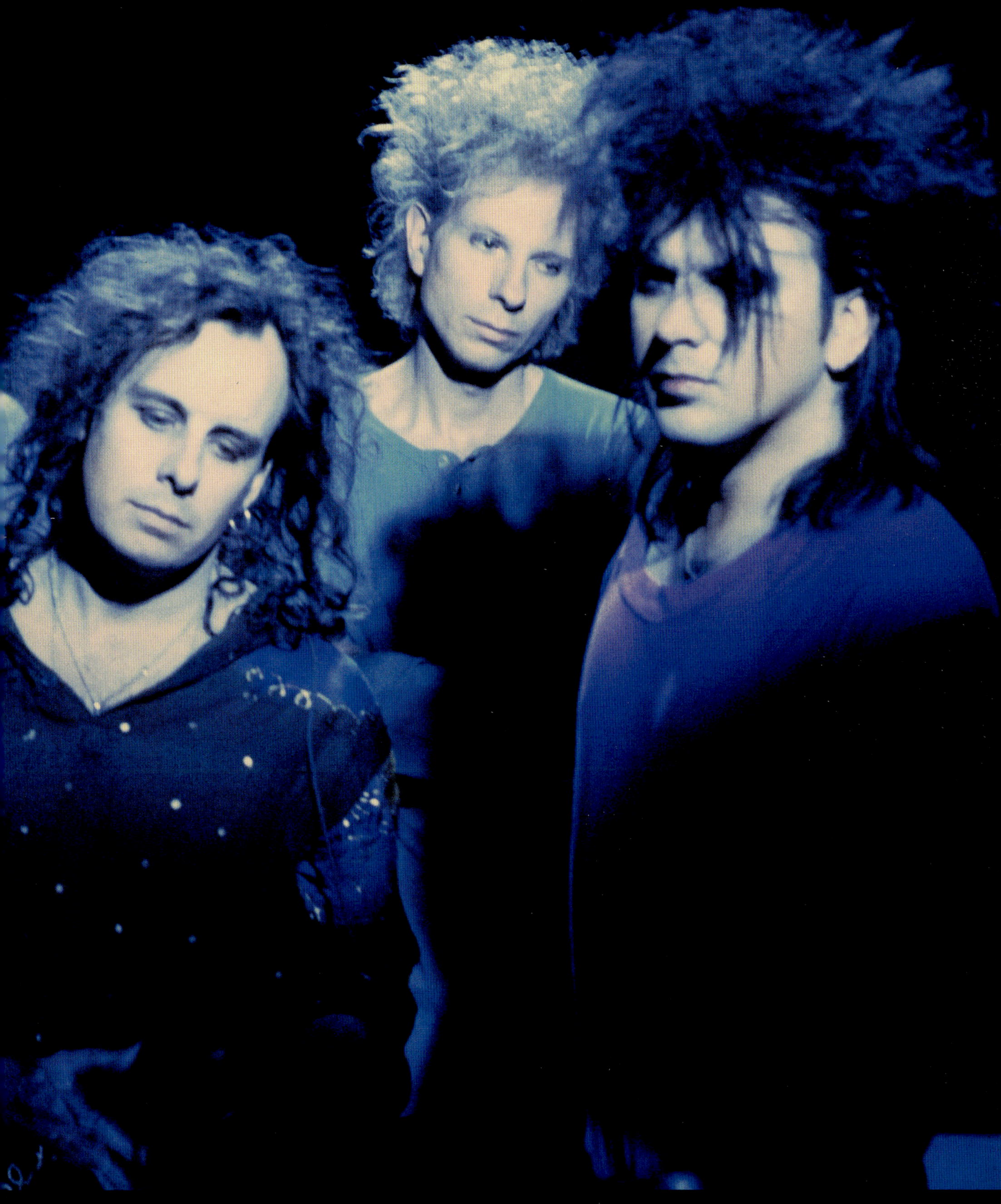

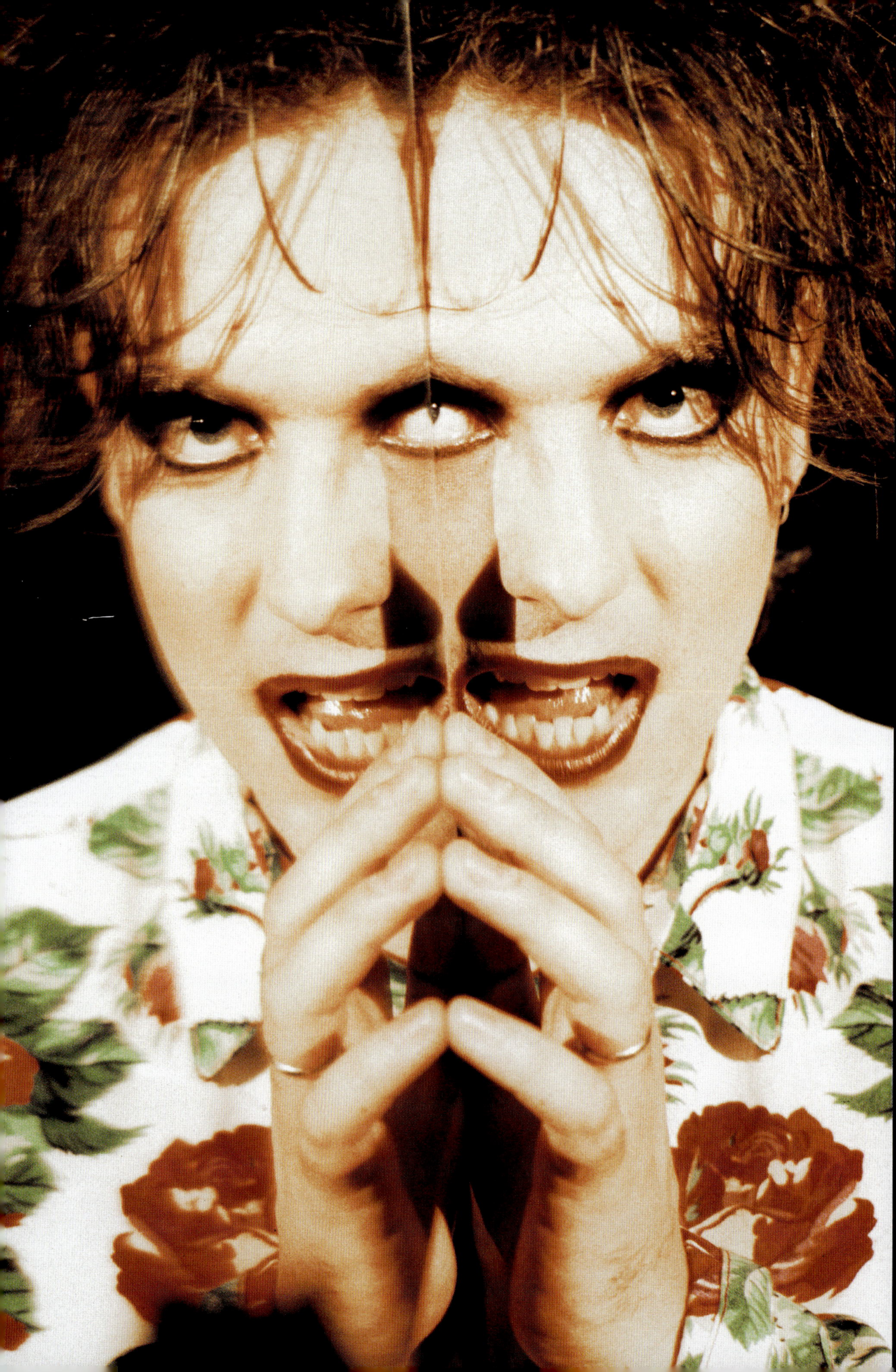

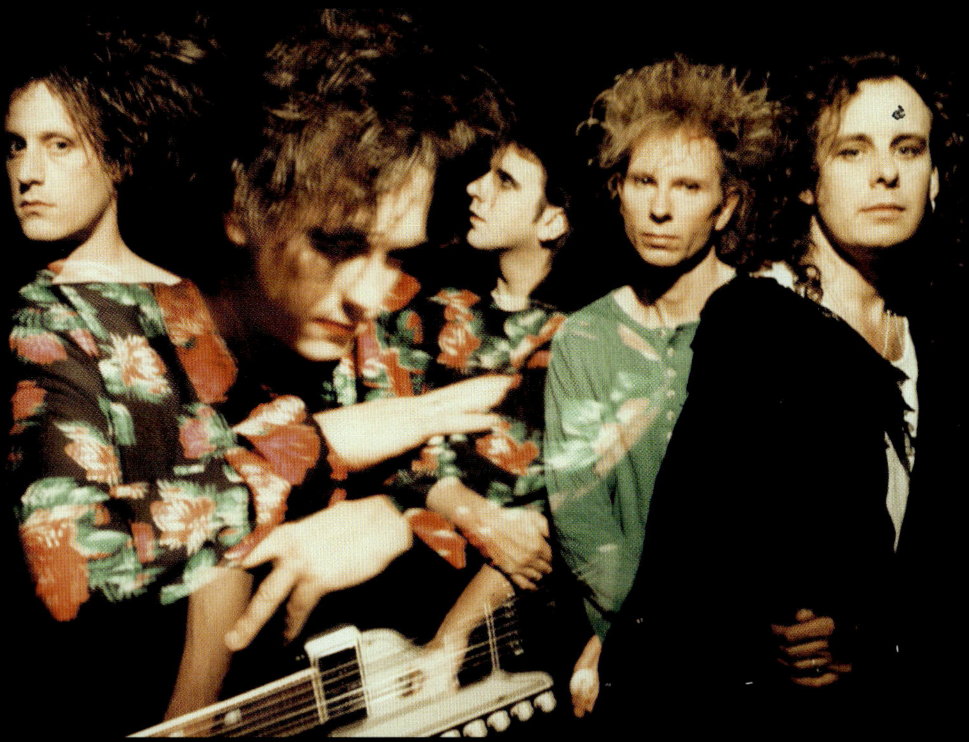

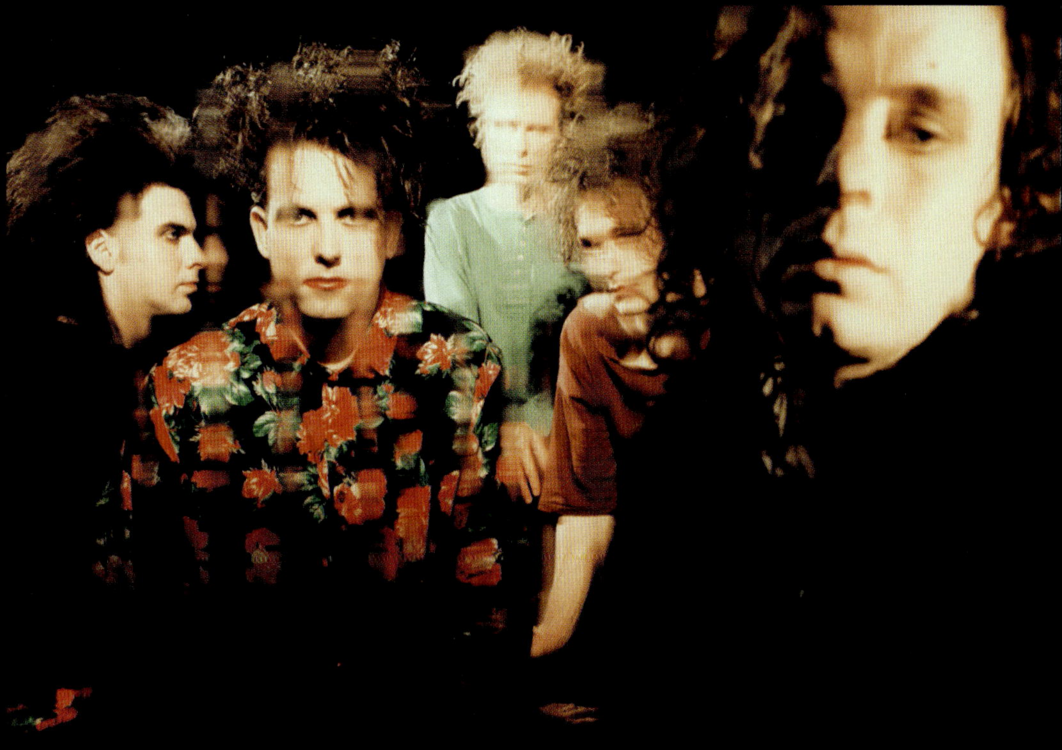

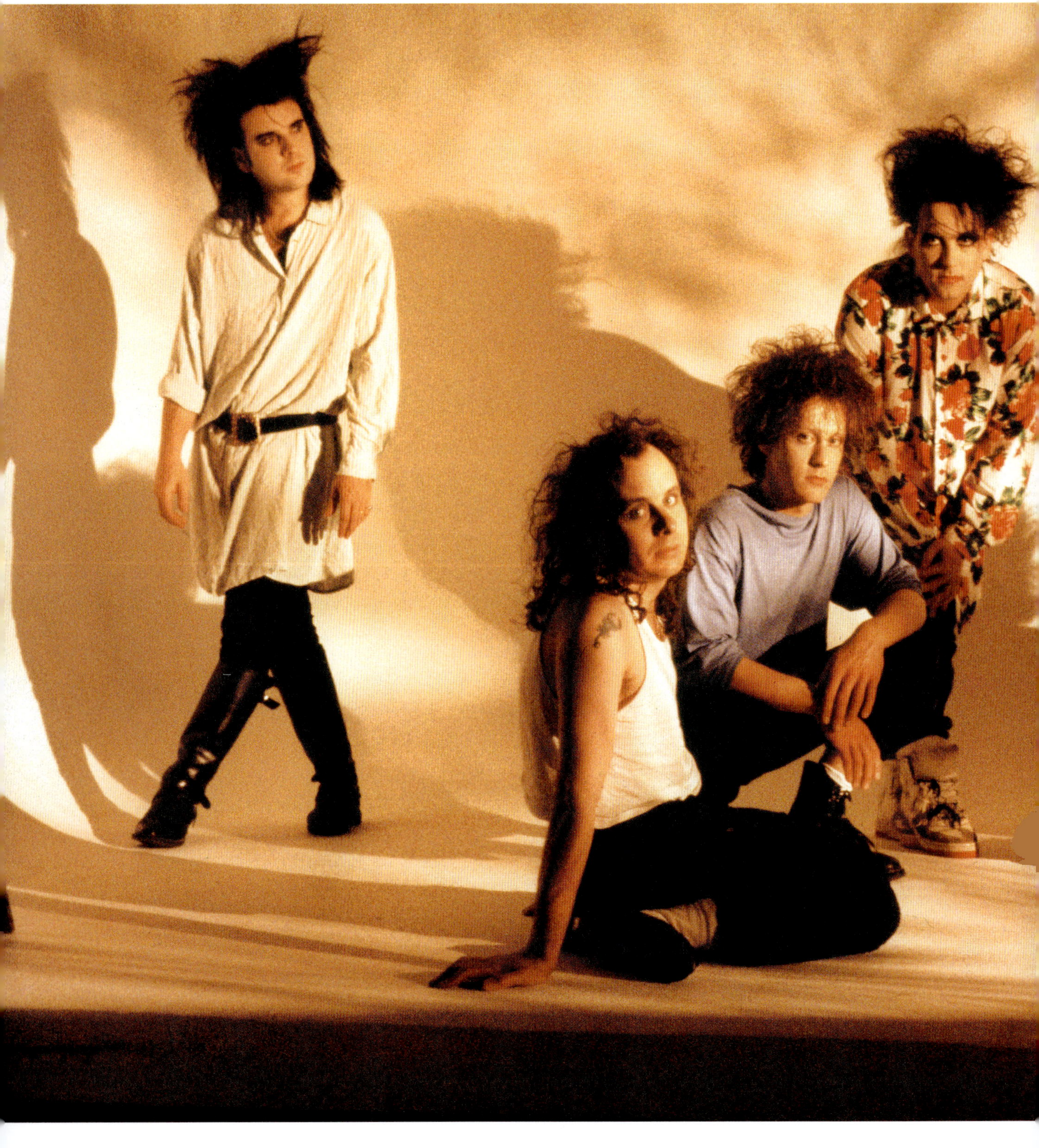

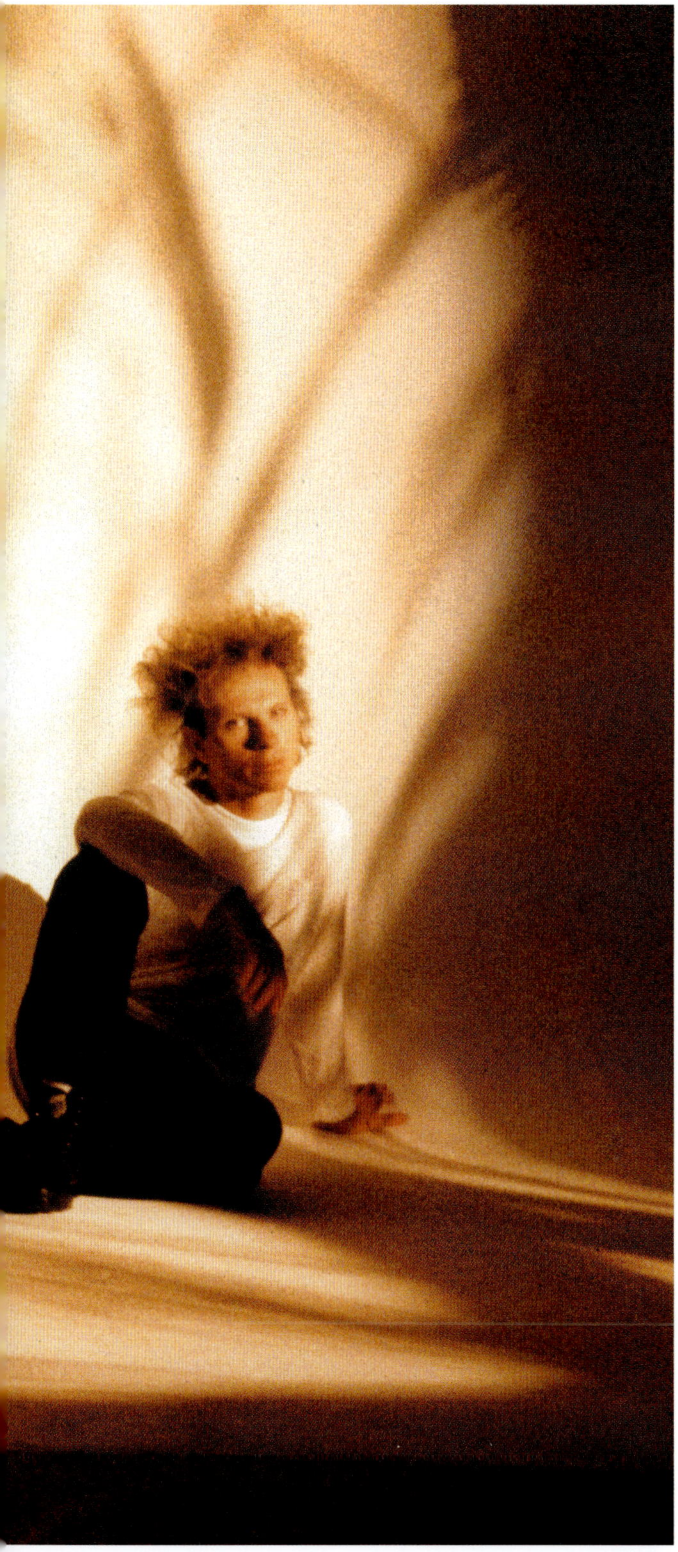

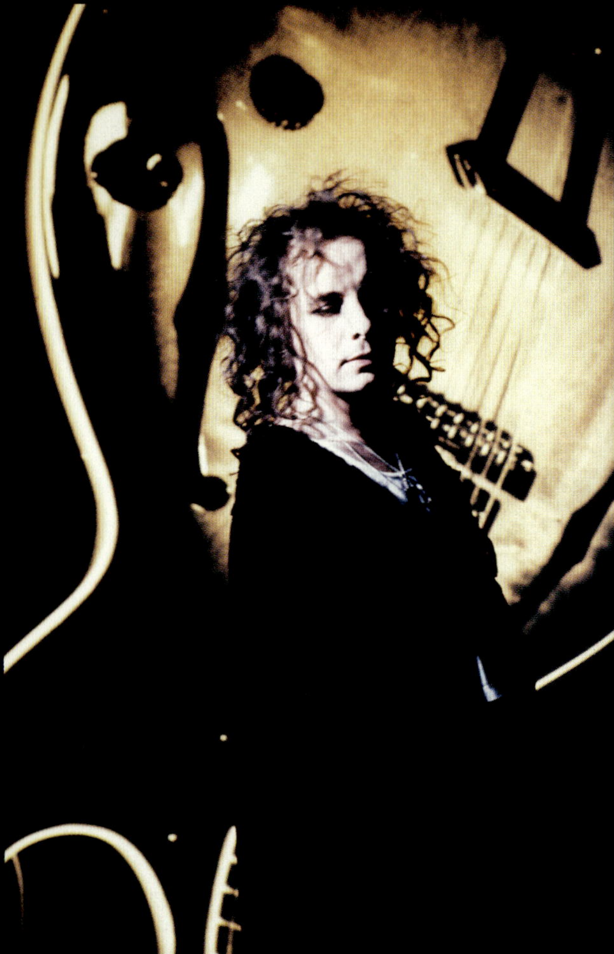
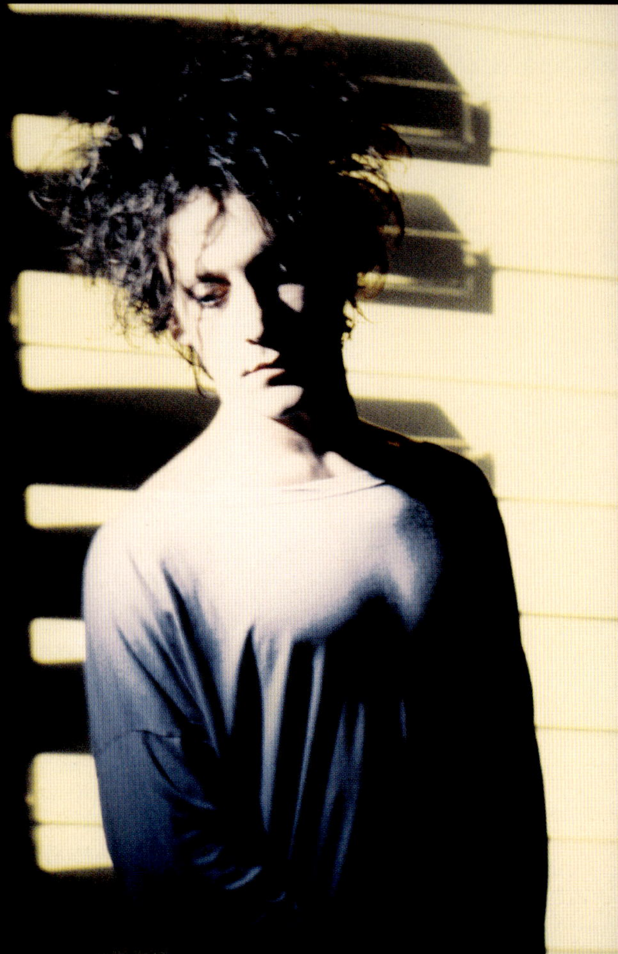
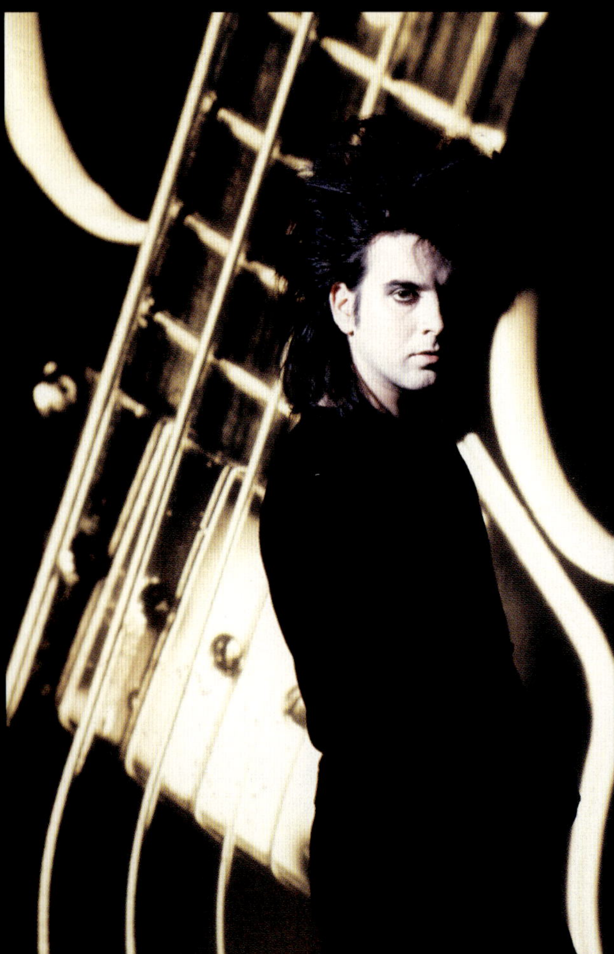
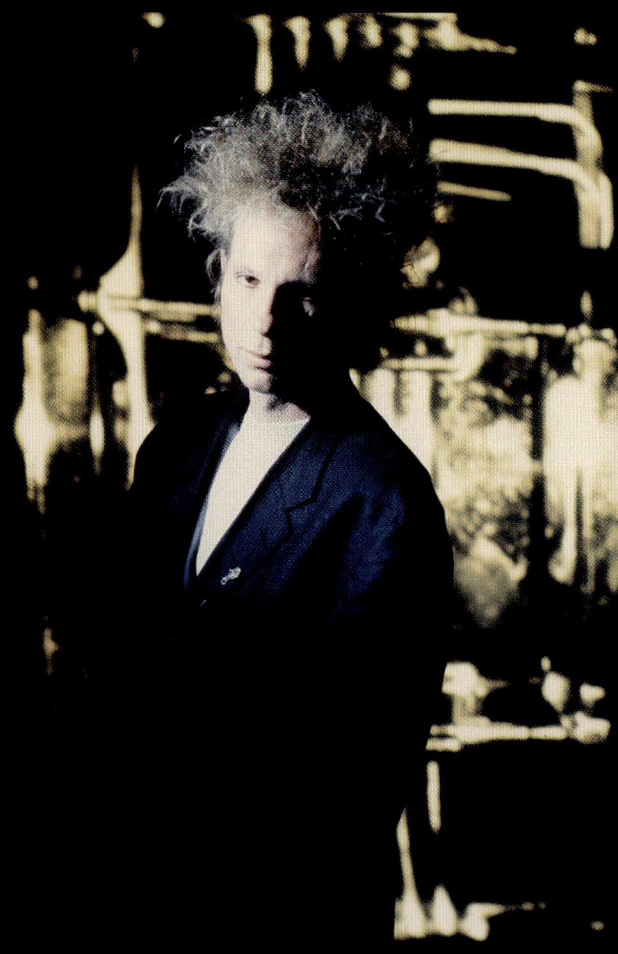

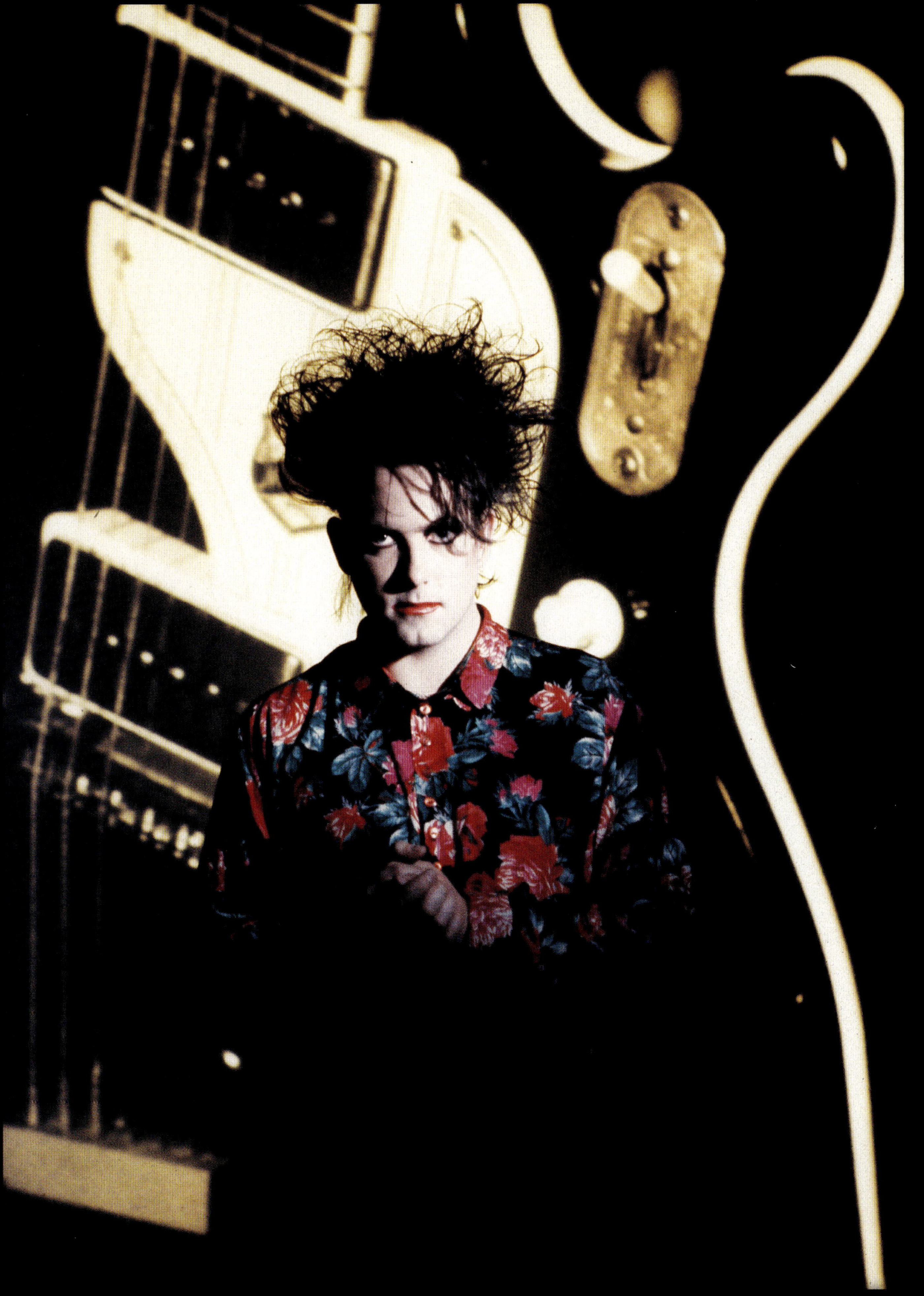

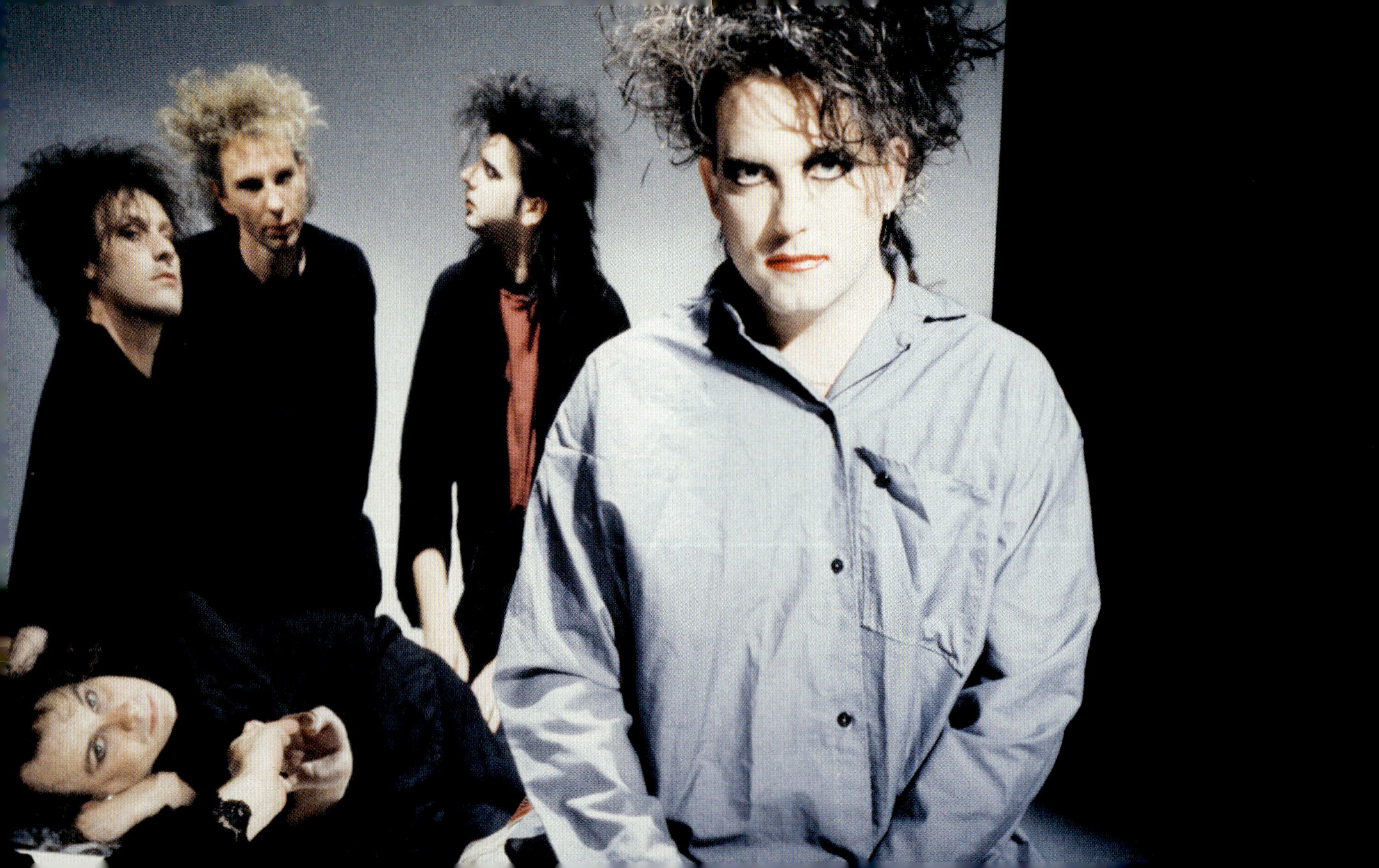

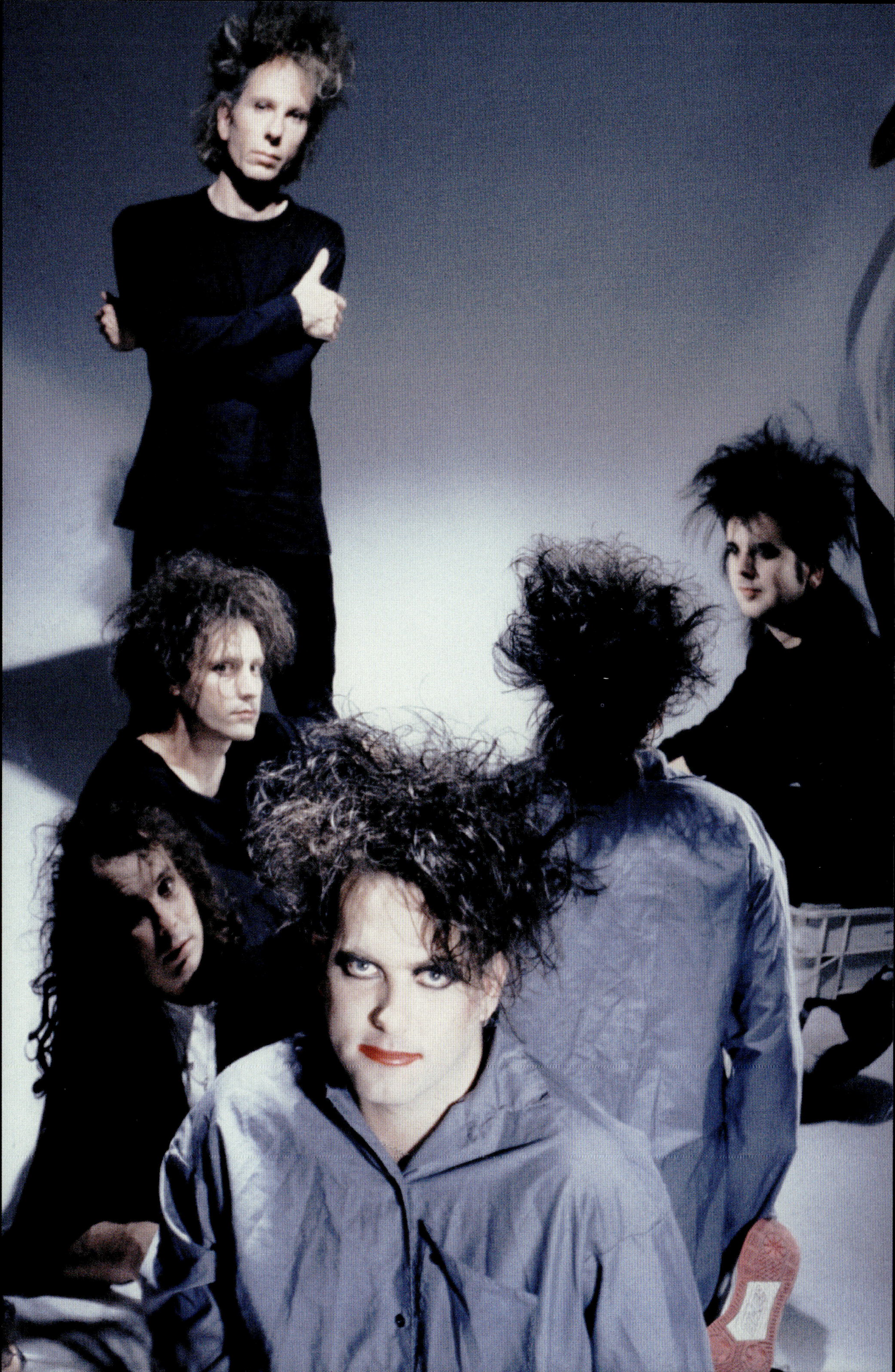

FULHAM STUDIO

[p. 152 to 173]

1991

ROBERT: ANOTHER VERY LONG AND VERY MEMORABLE SESSION – ONE OF THE BEST, I THINK... P162 IS A RARE SHOT OF ME FEEDING THE MANY BIRDS THAT LIVED IN MY HEAD AT THE TIME!

Paul: A two-day shoot for the 1992 calendar and press. First day I had with RS solo and the second day with the whole band. Two very long, tiring days, the first being a bit easier...

The idea of the back drops and big moon prop spilled over into the 'Friday I'm in Love' video p. 160-161.

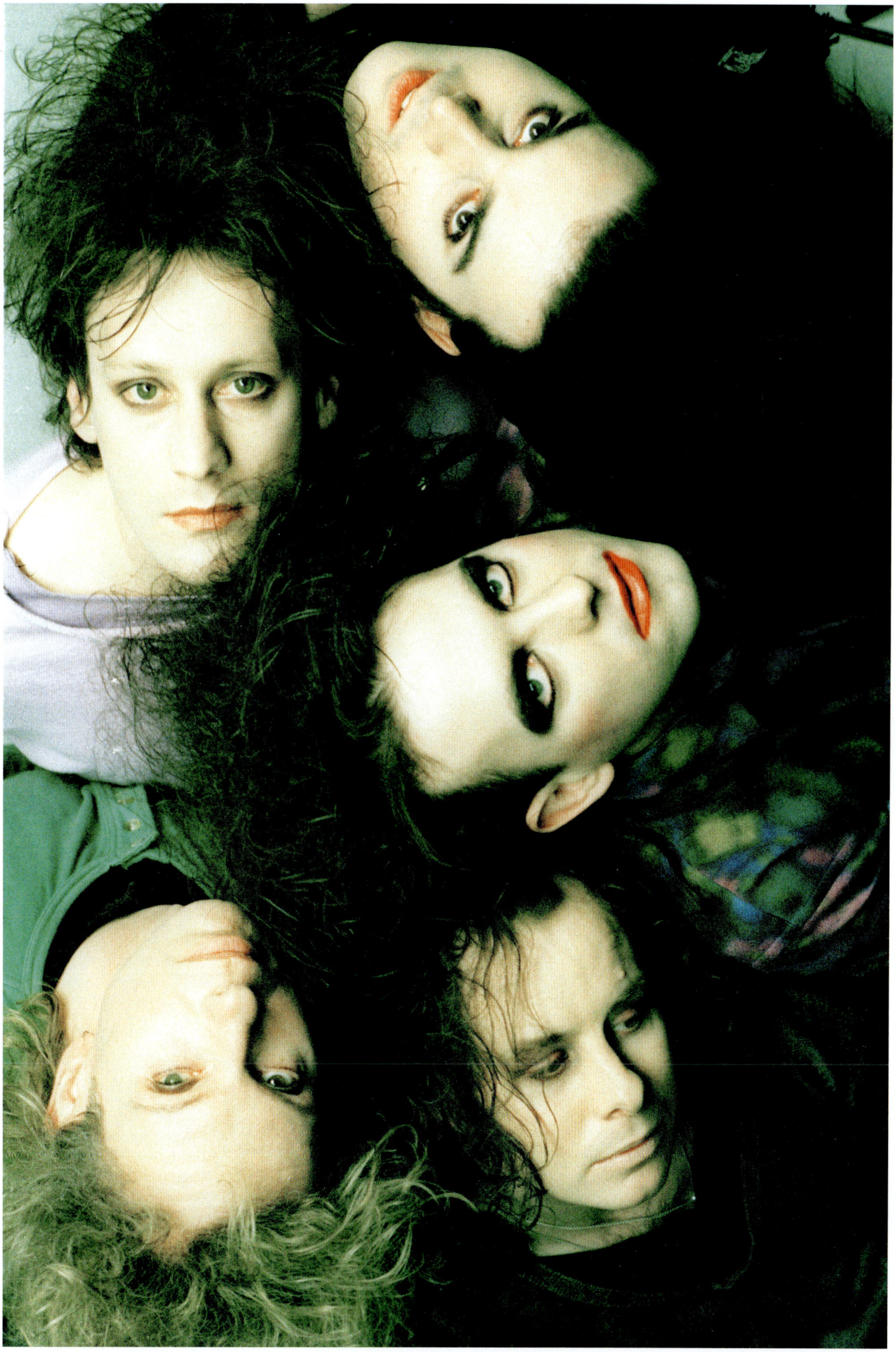

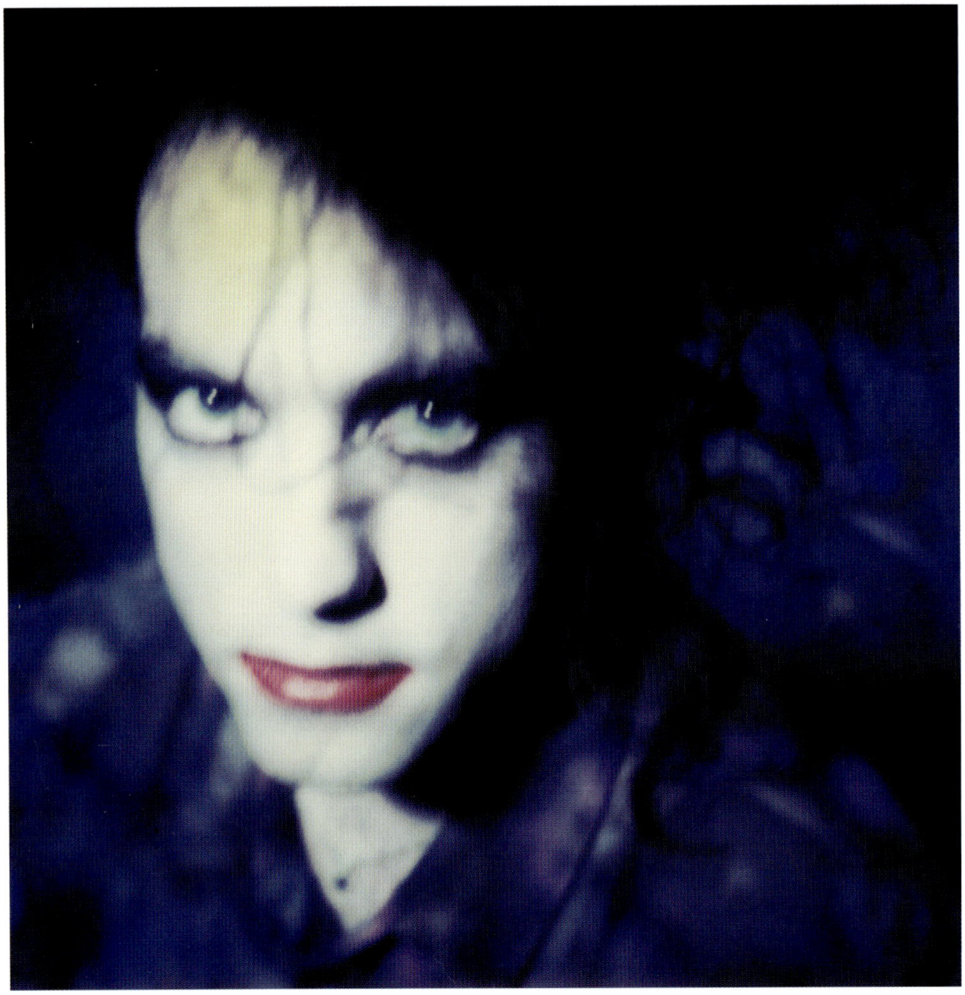

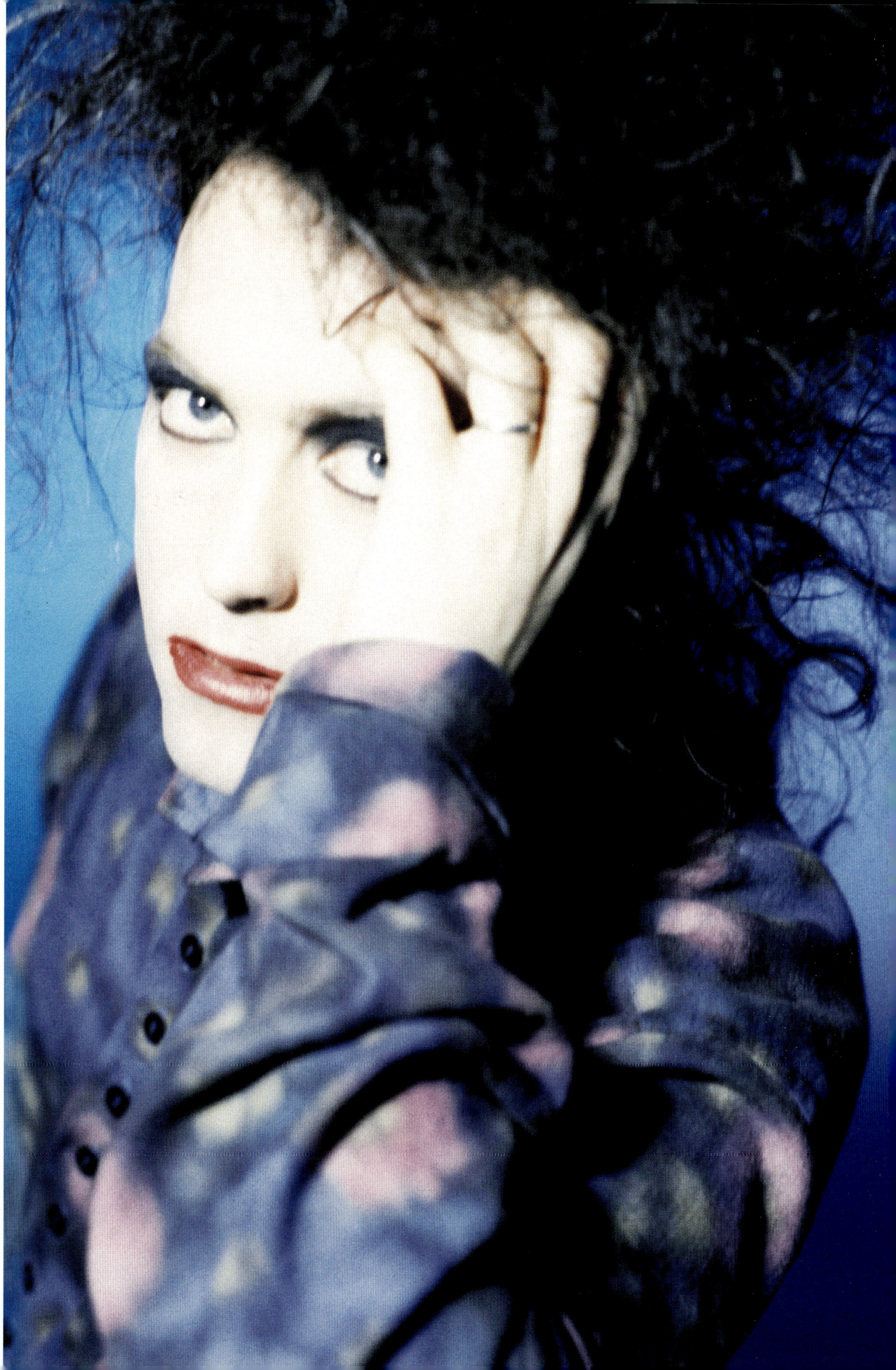

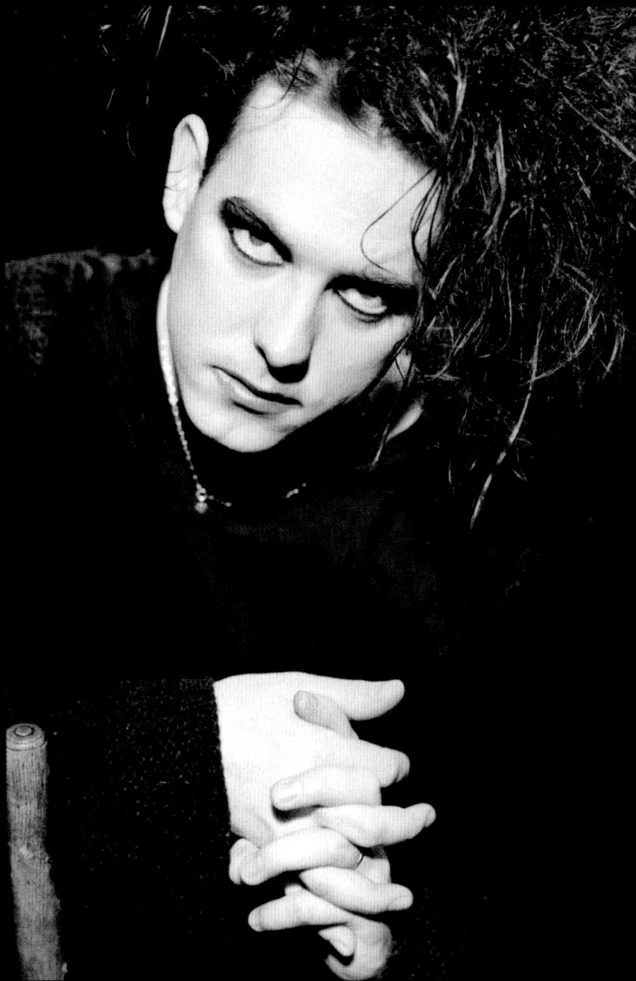

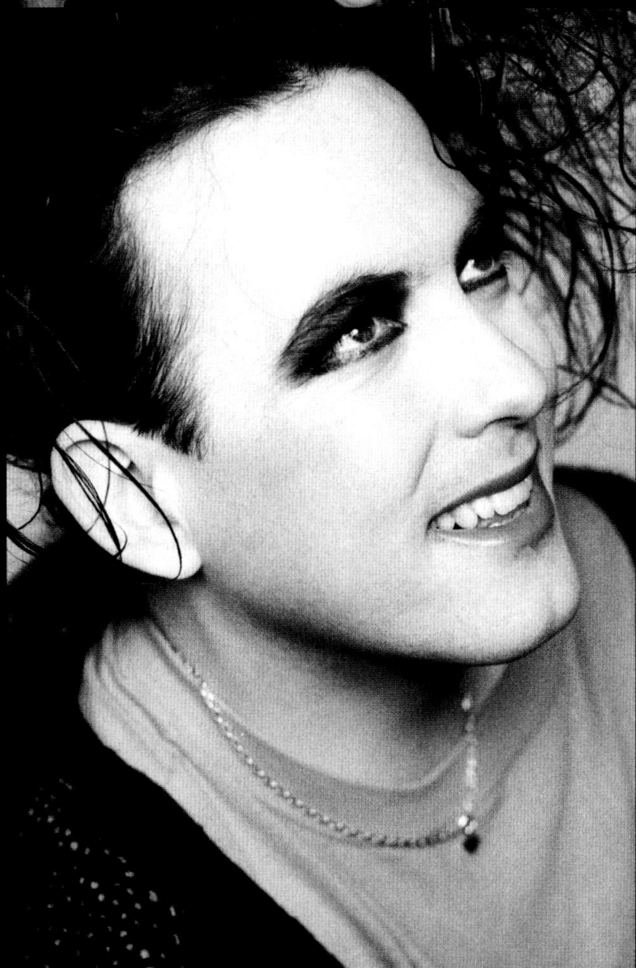

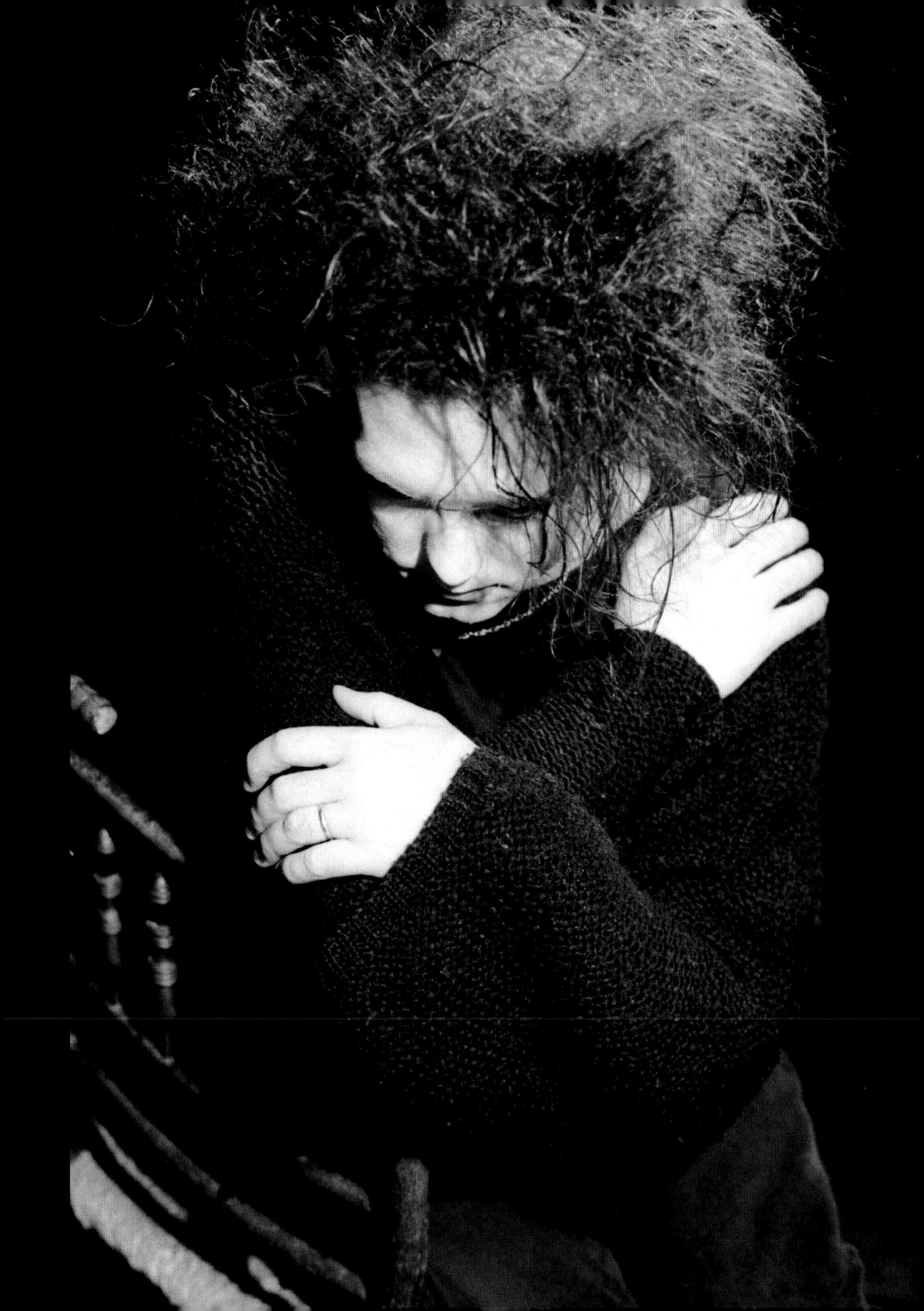

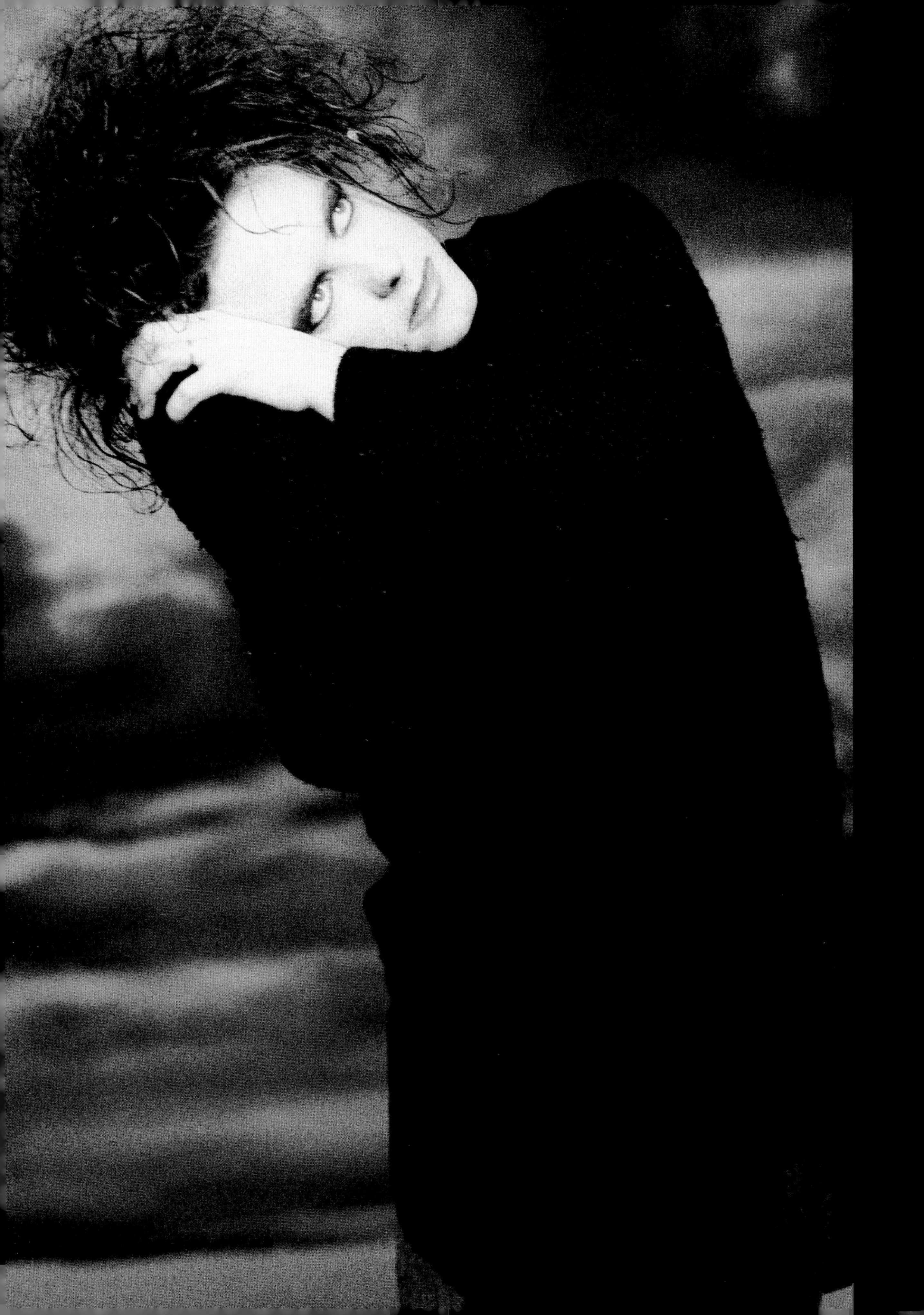

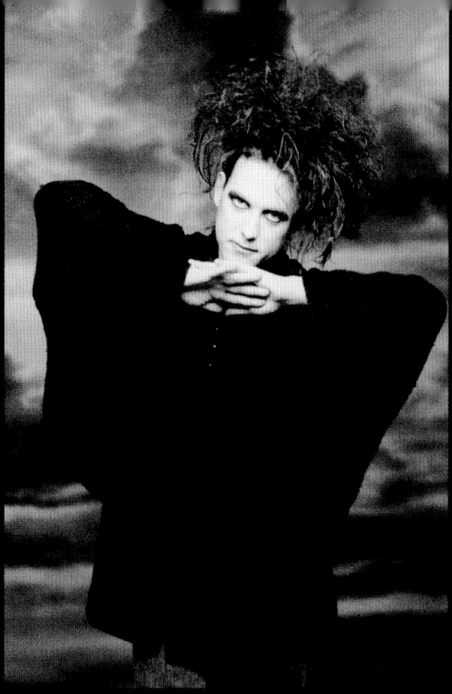
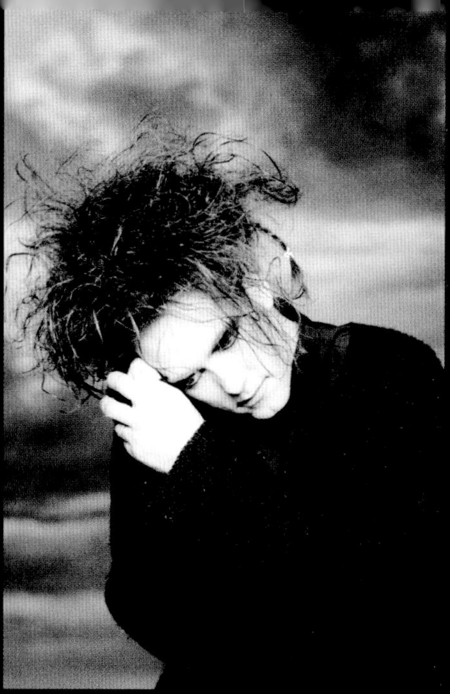
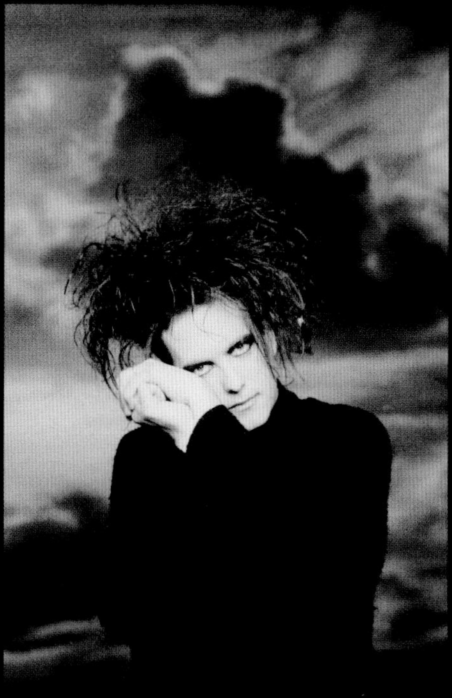
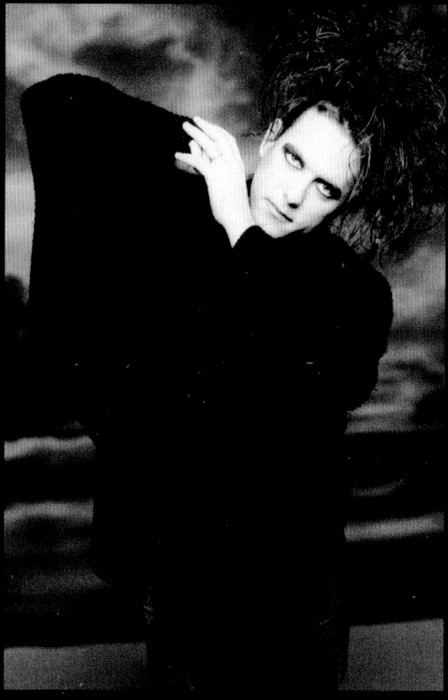

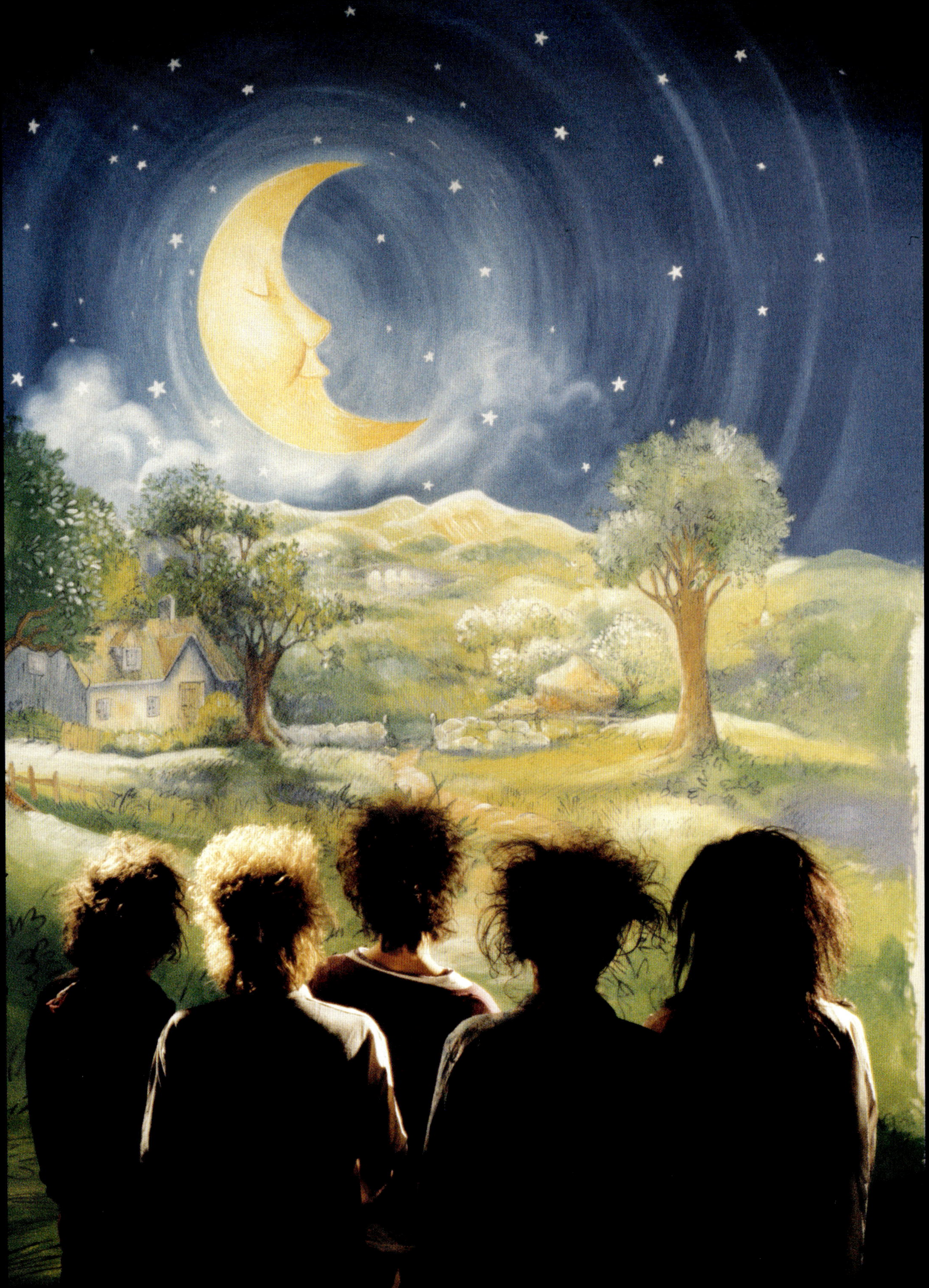

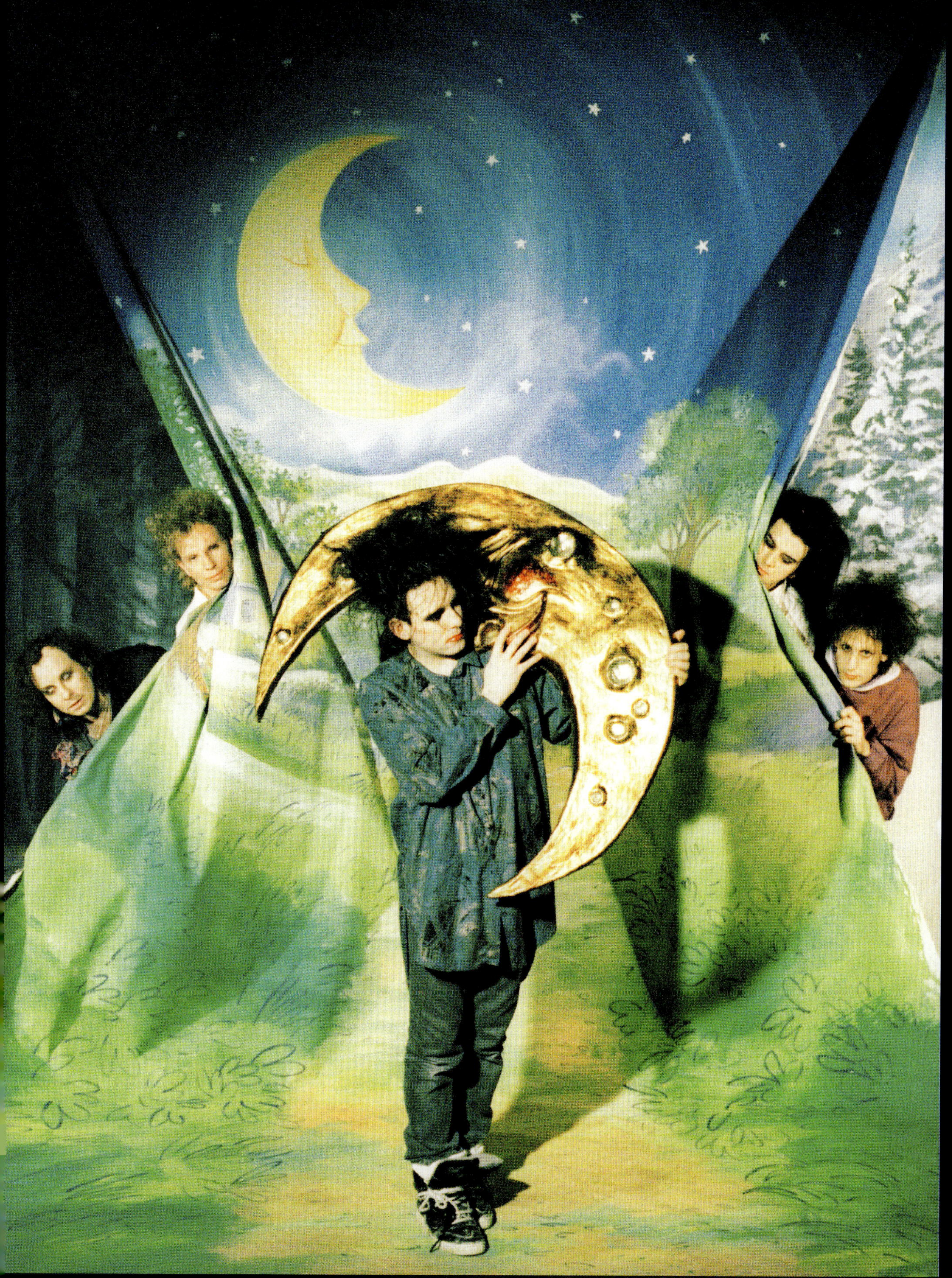

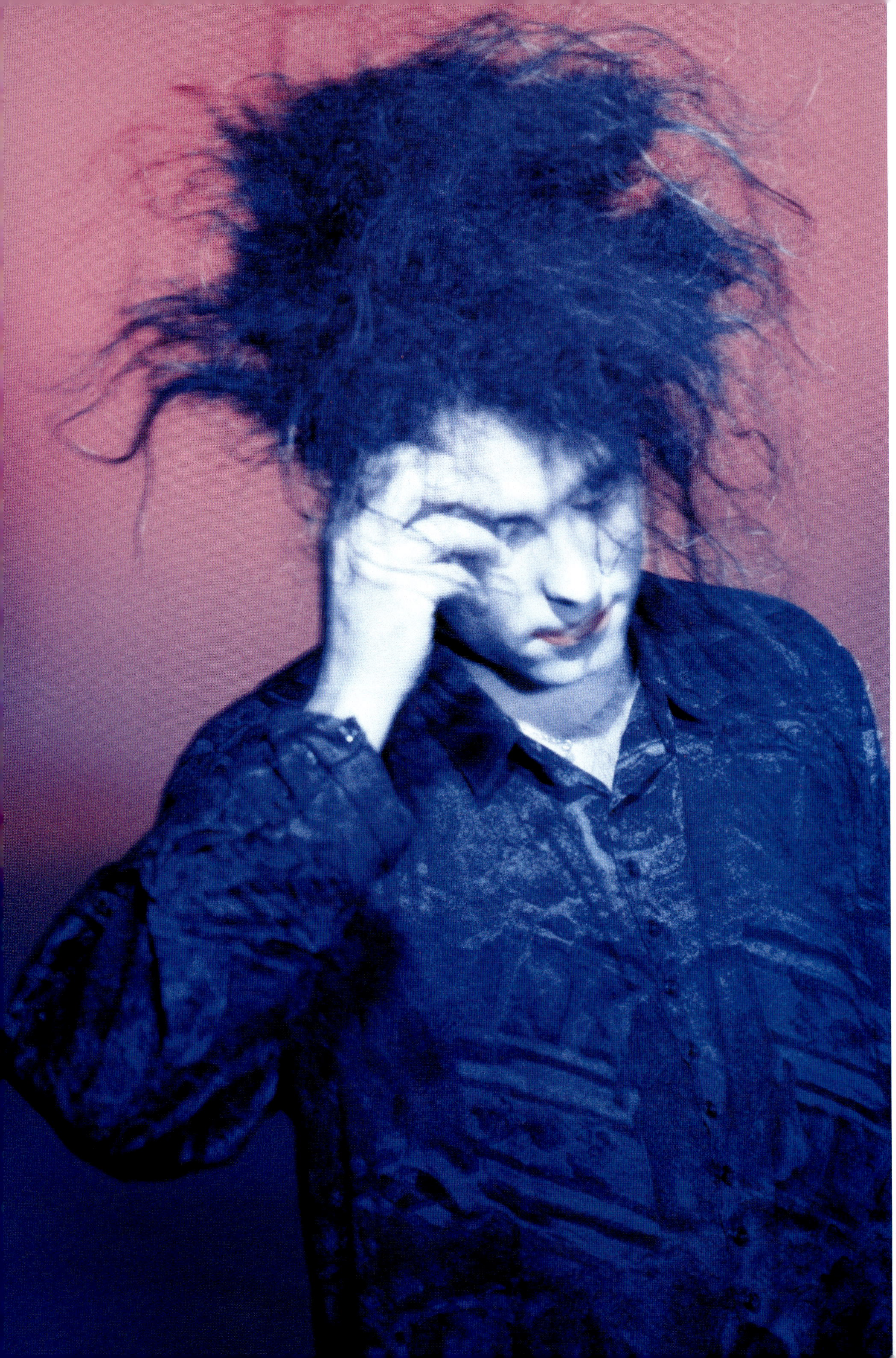

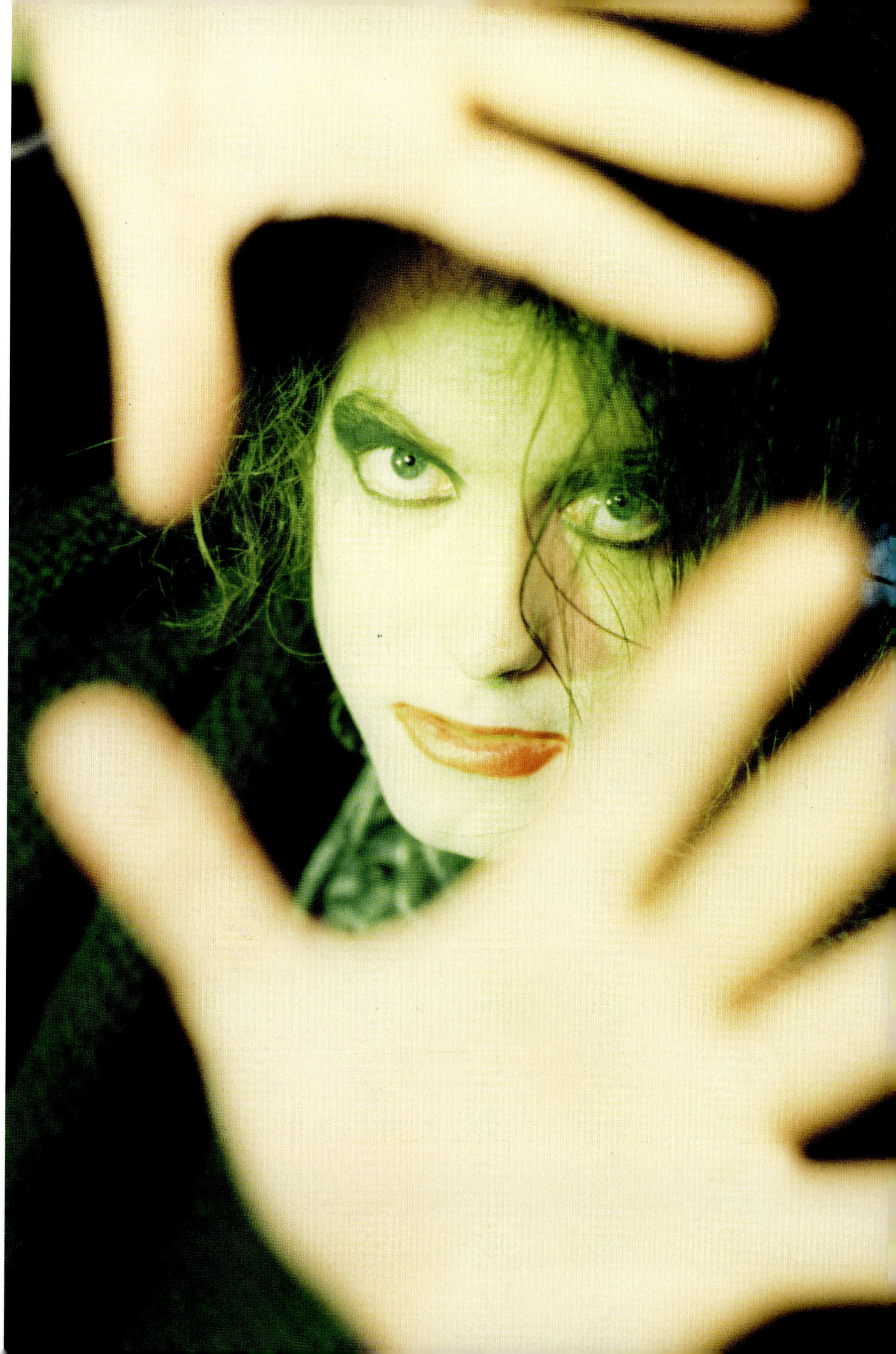

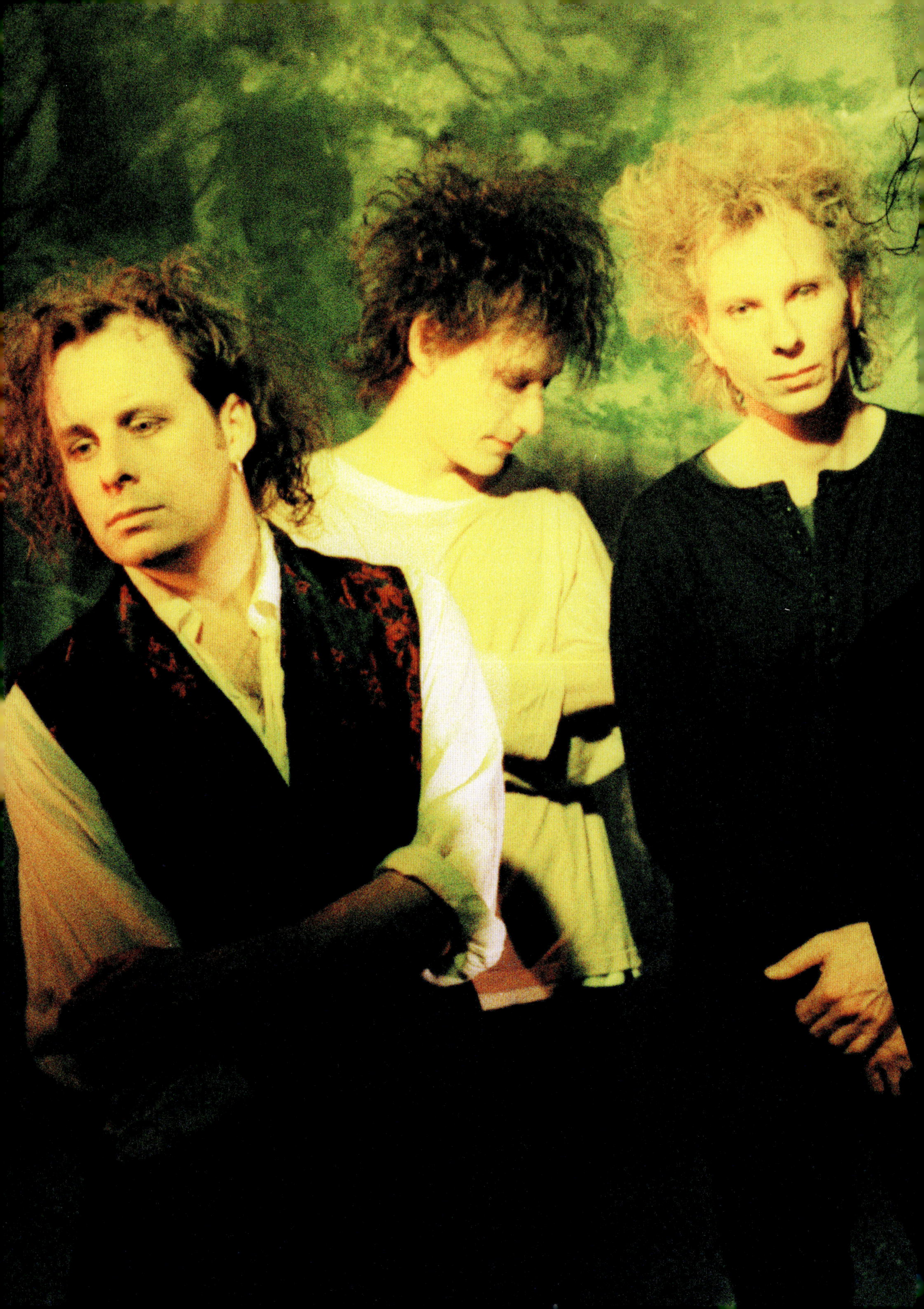

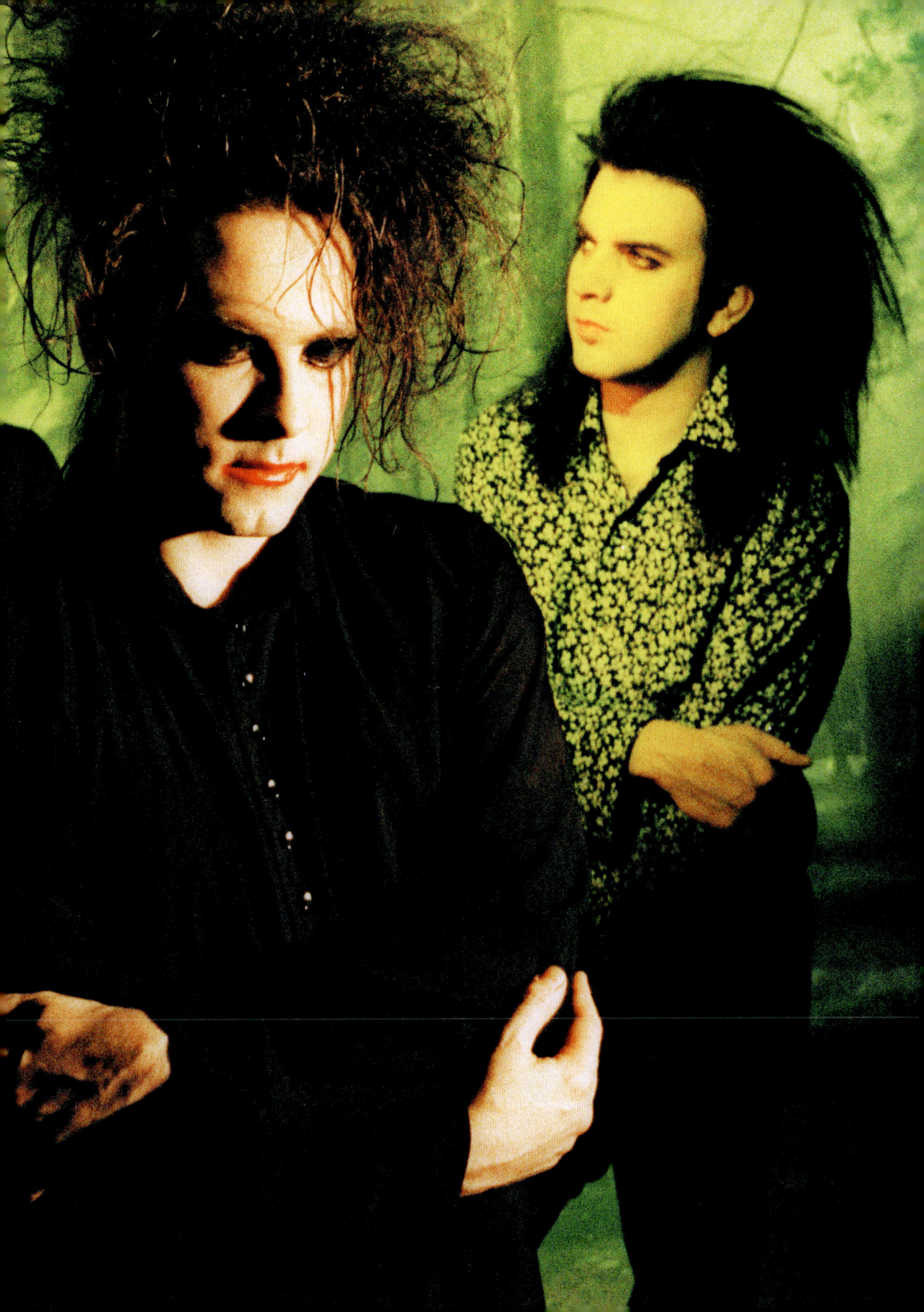

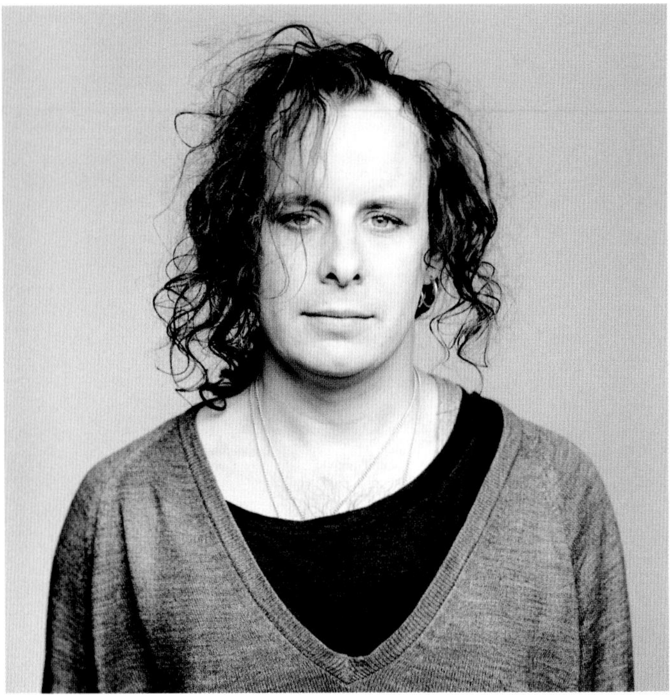
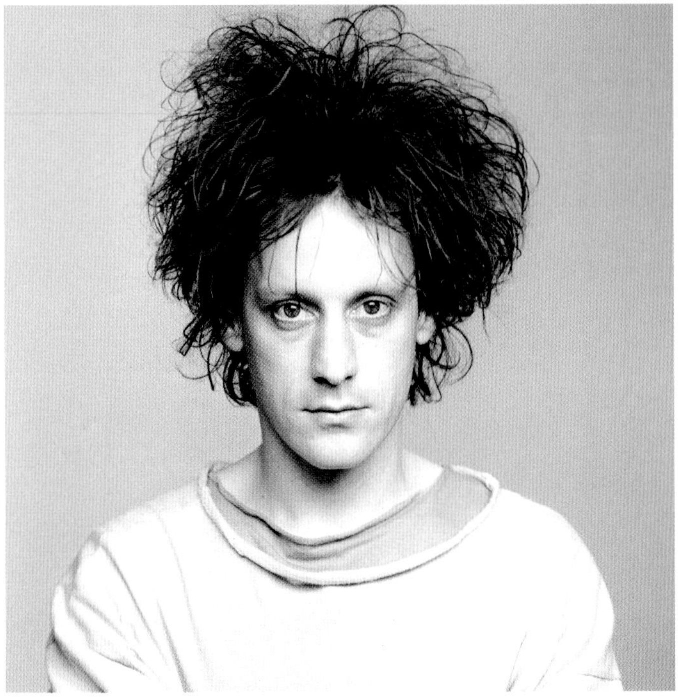
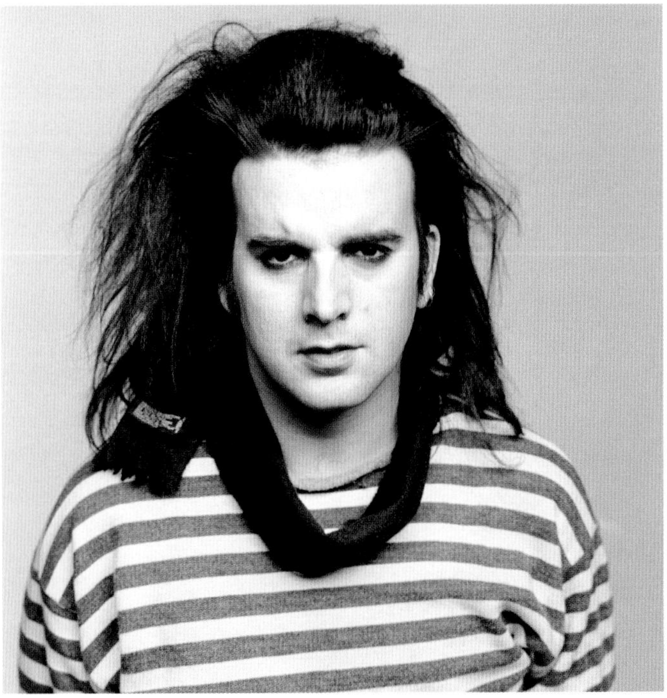
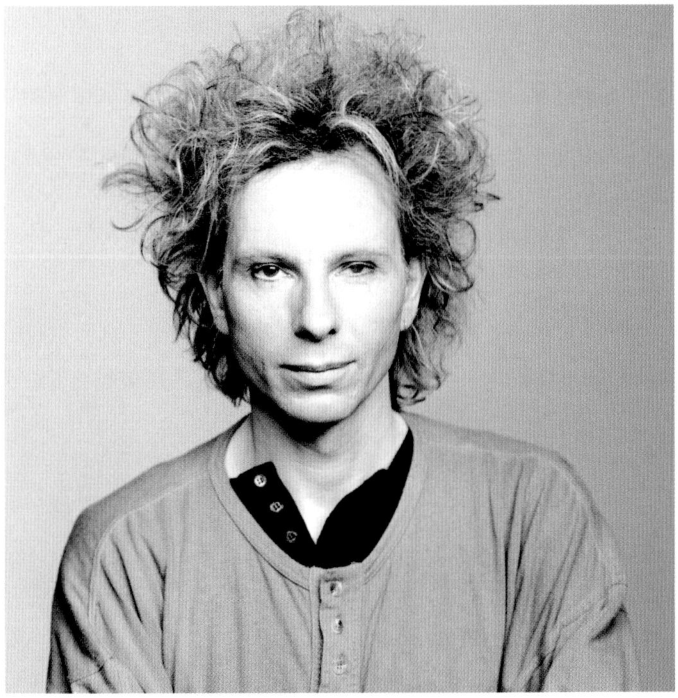

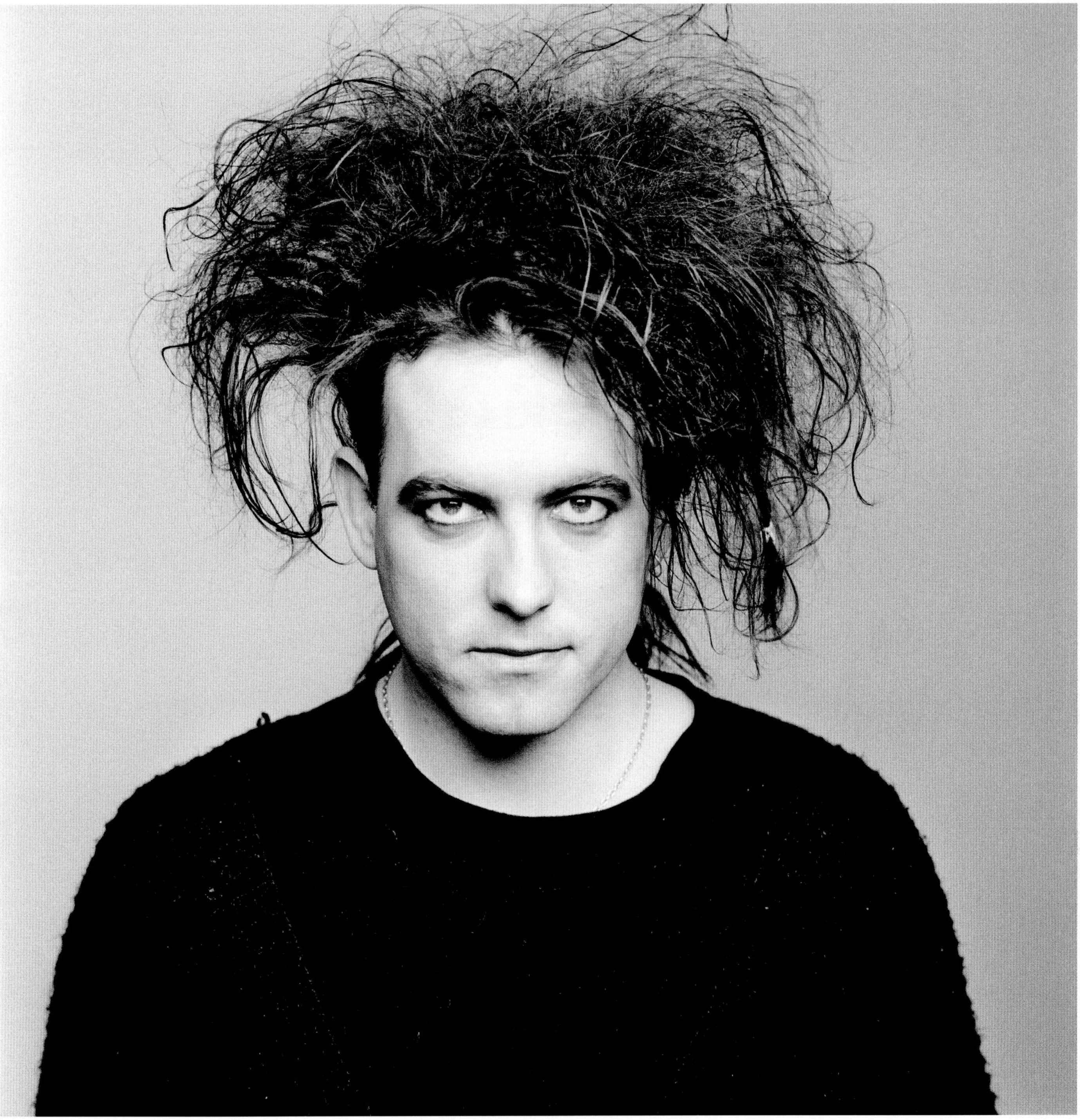

Paul: From the above photo shoot, the band asked for some passport photos, so I obliged. Some of the best mug shots I have taken!

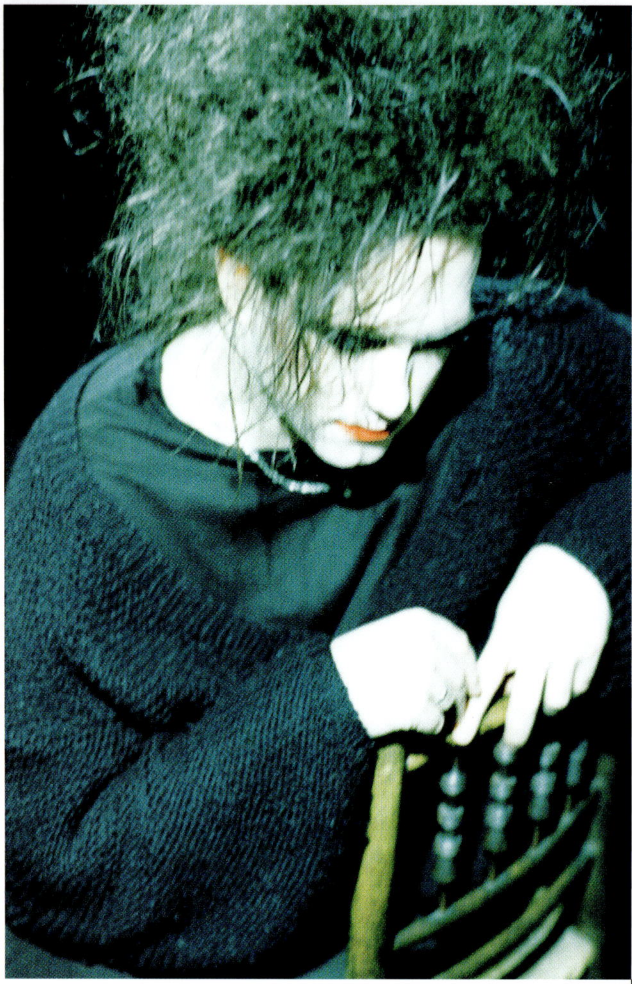

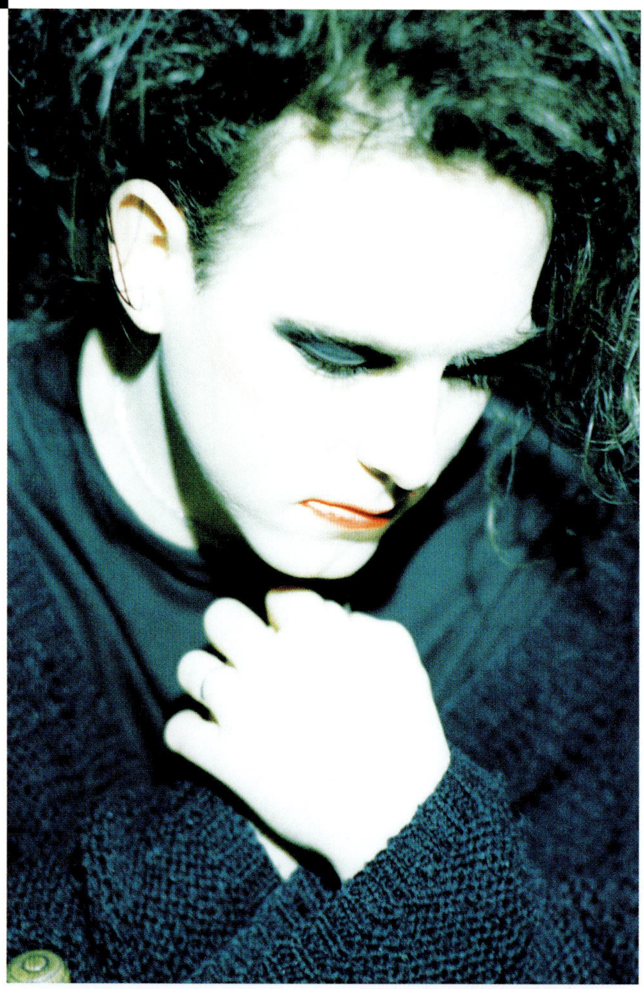

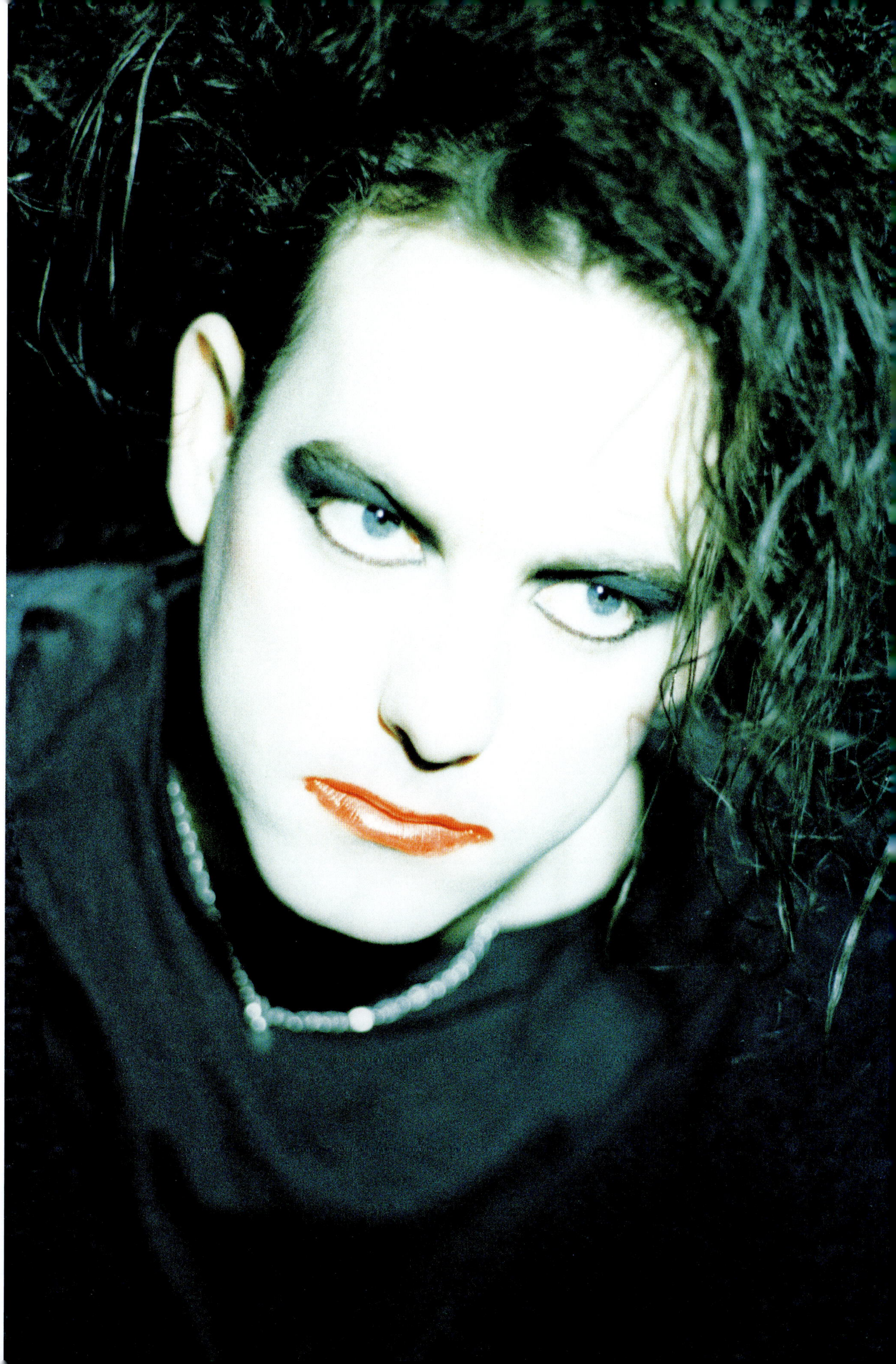

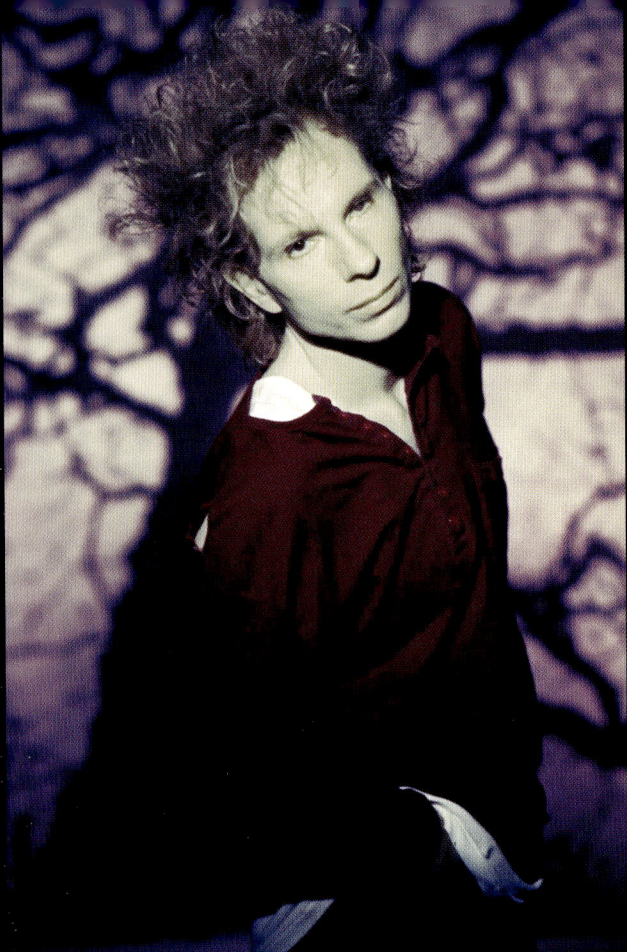
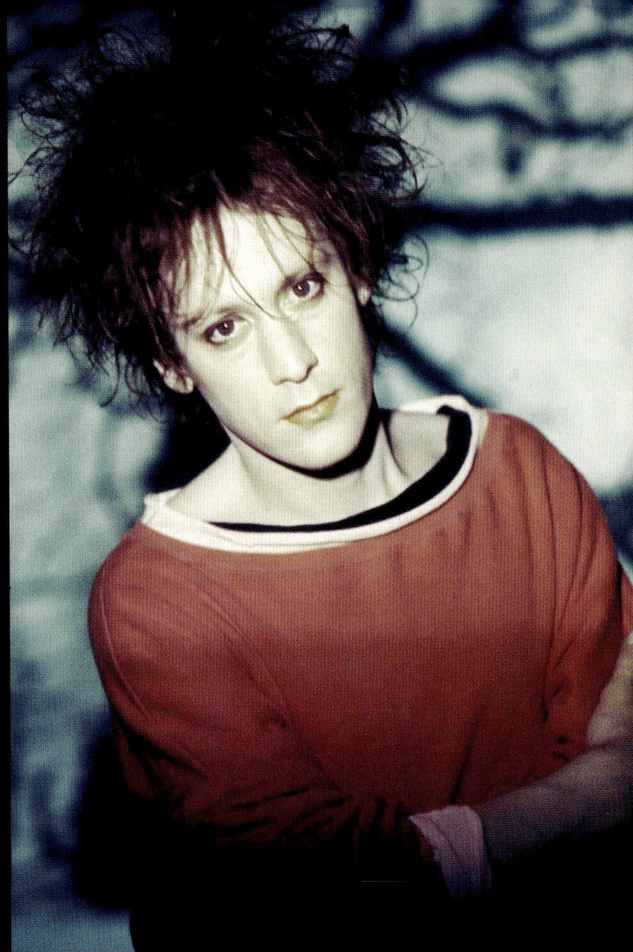
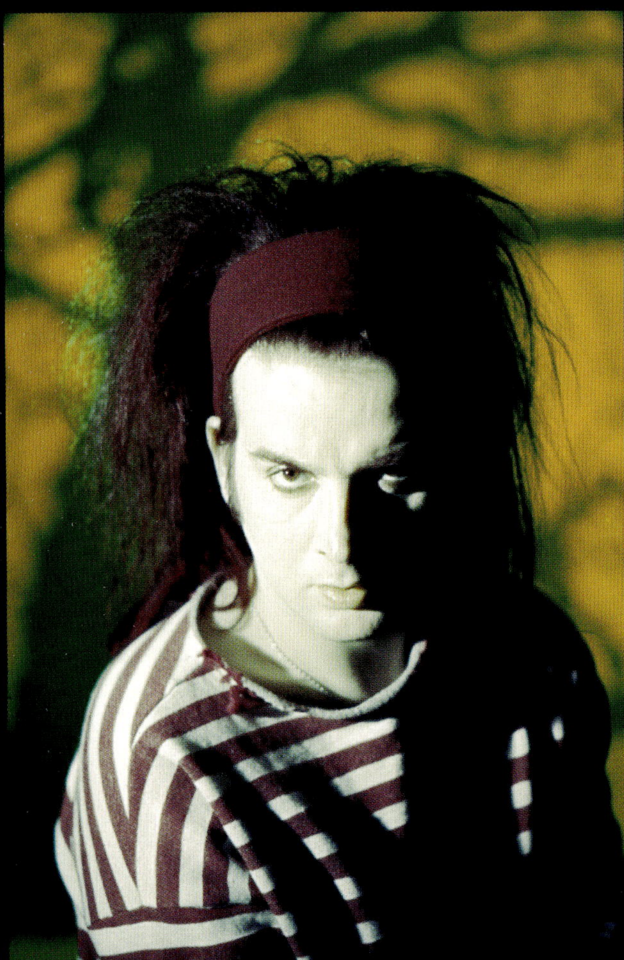
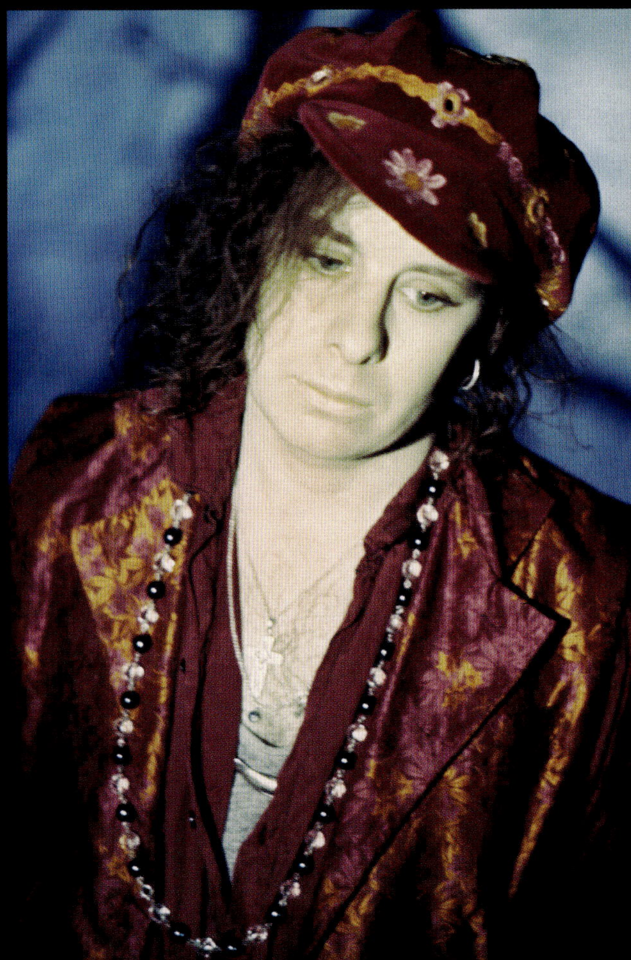

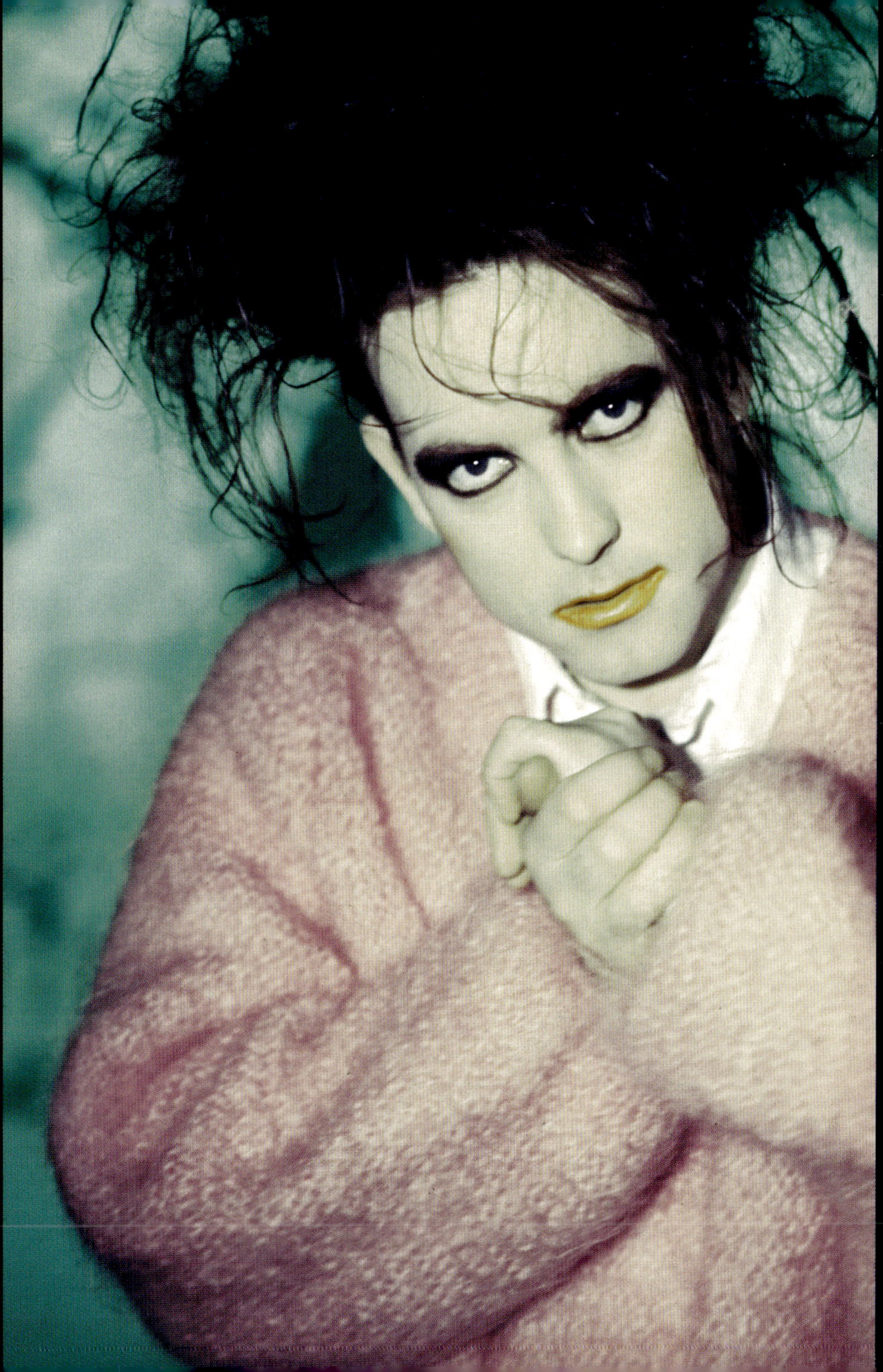

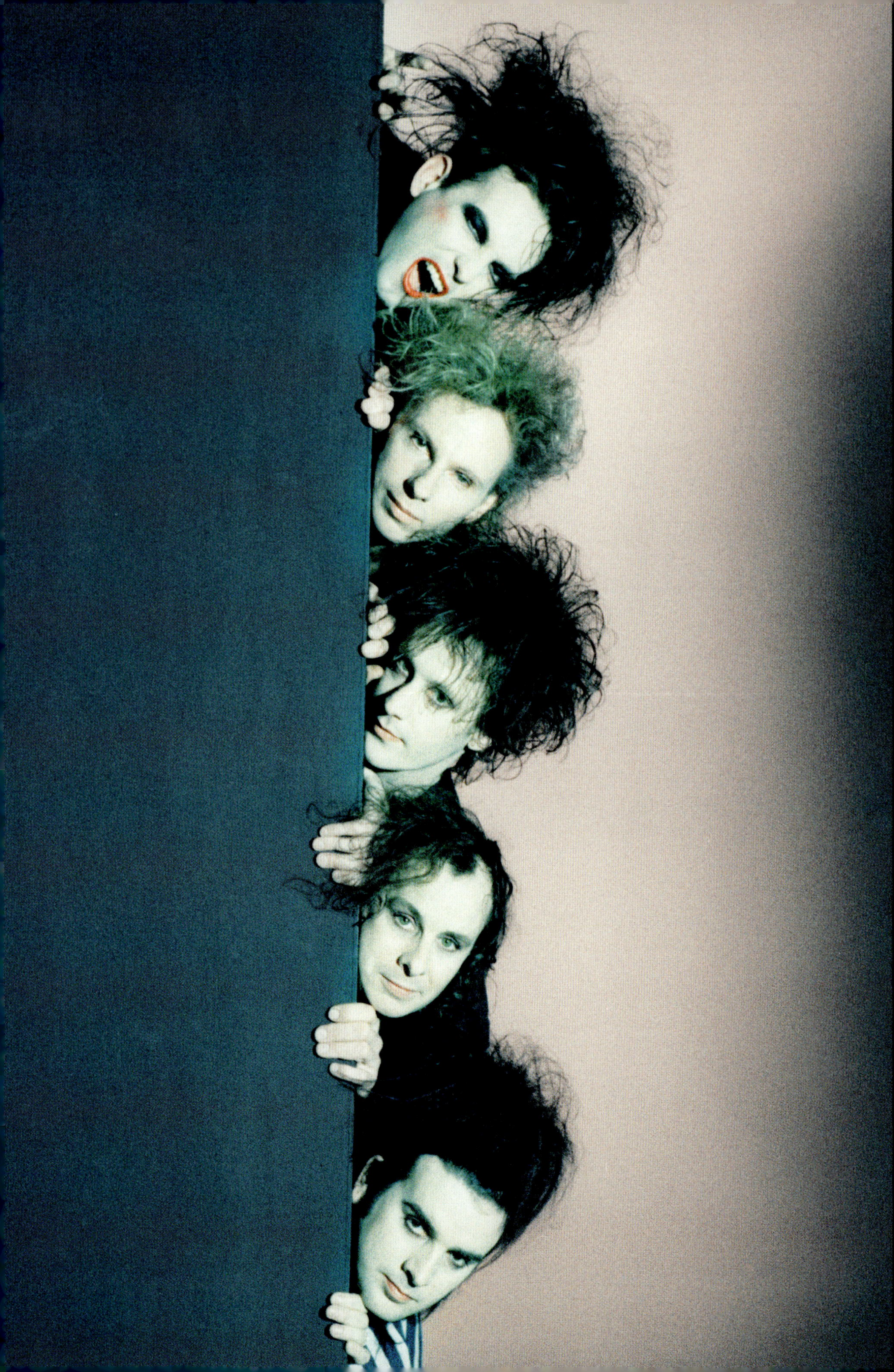

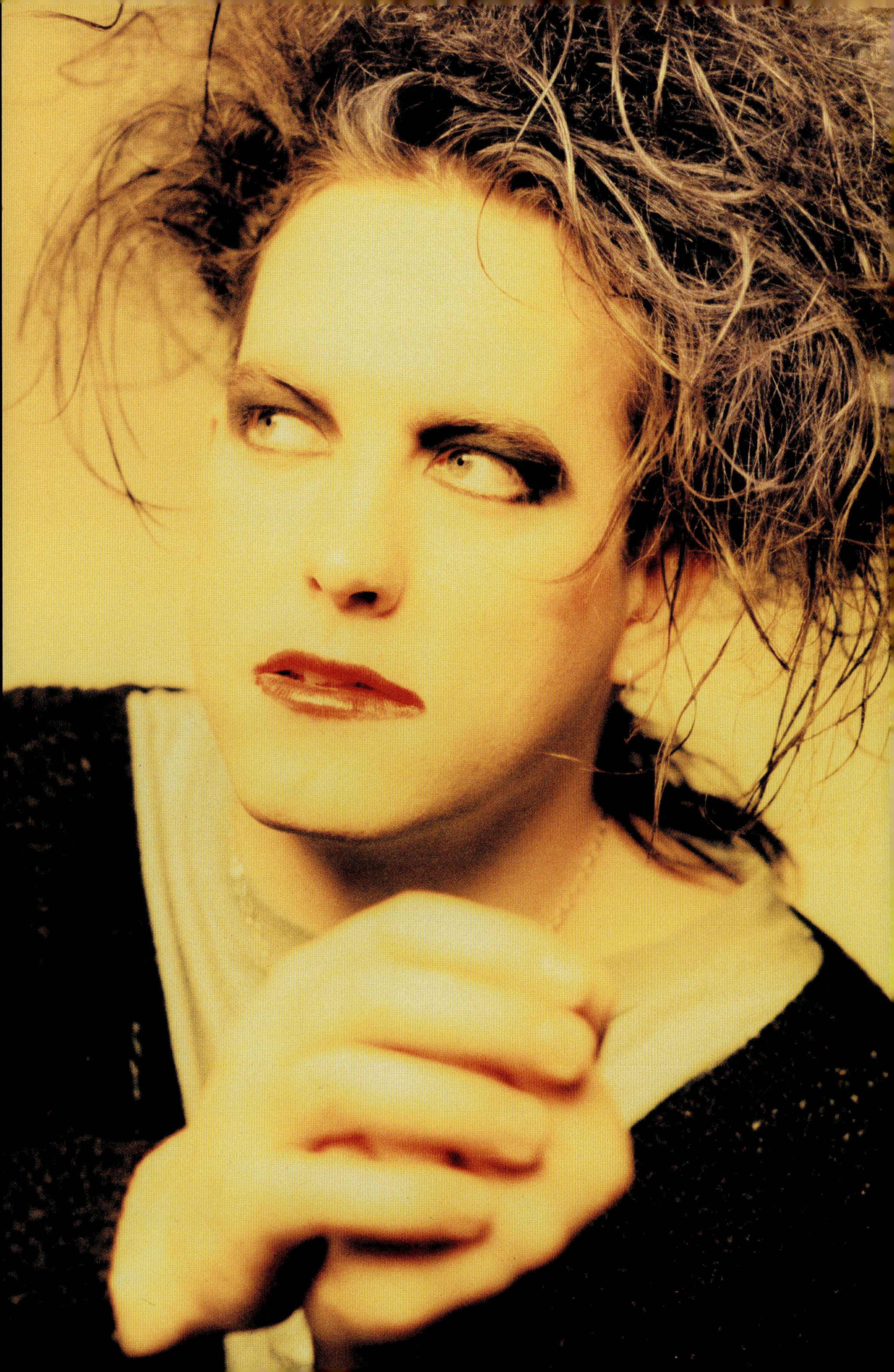

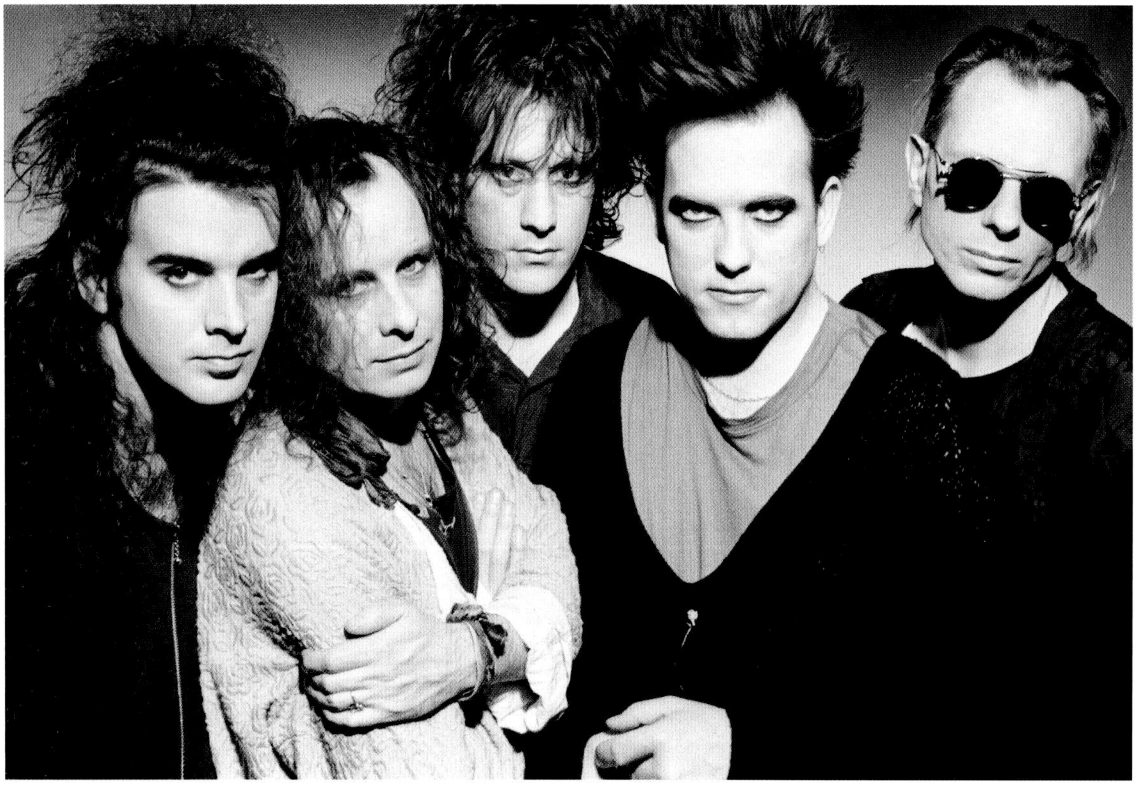

CALENDAR SHOOT
for the 1993 calendar
(p. 174 to 181)
1992

ROBERT: OH NO! THE BIRDS ARE GONE!

Paul: Also Press and cover of *Select Magazine.*

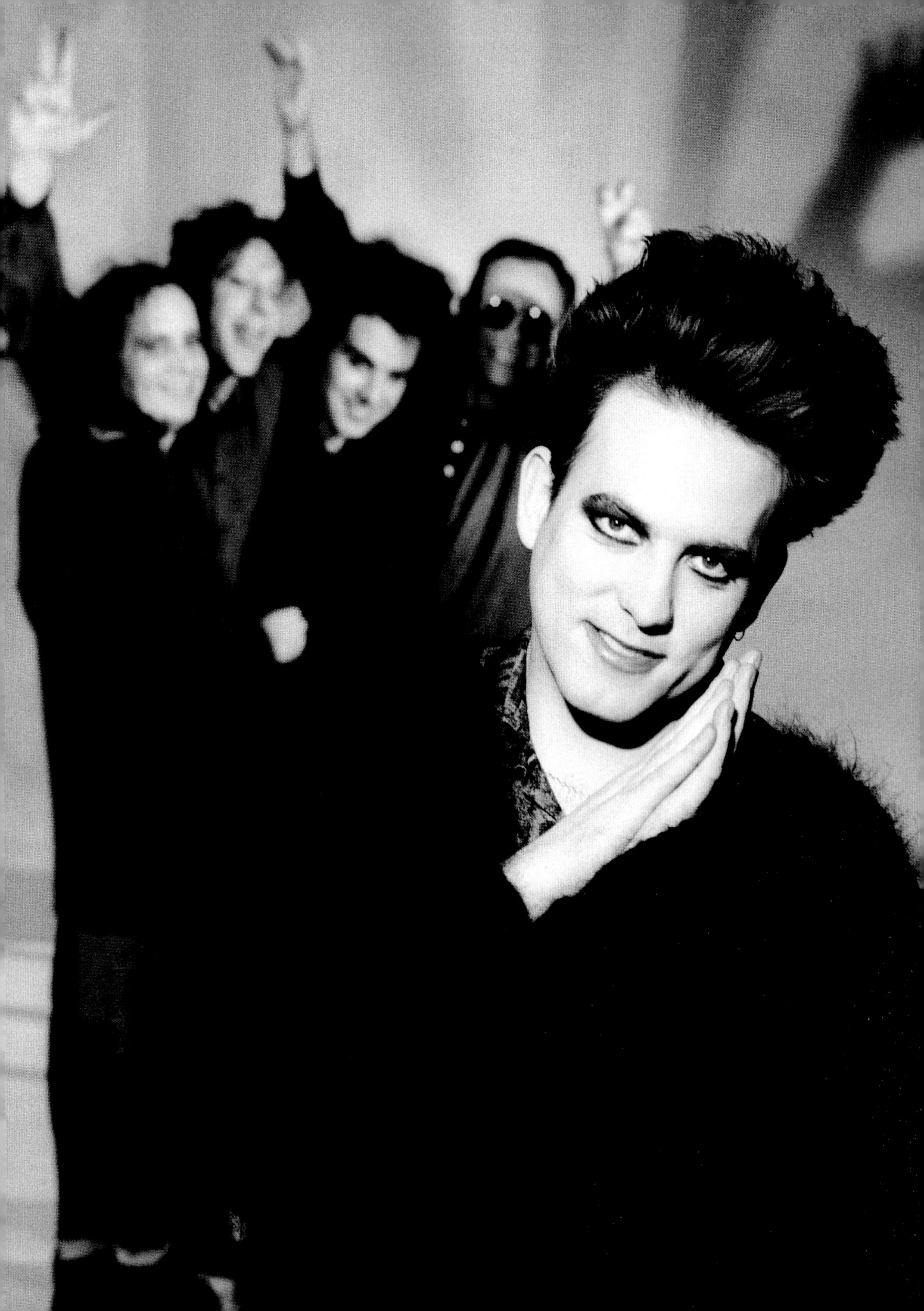

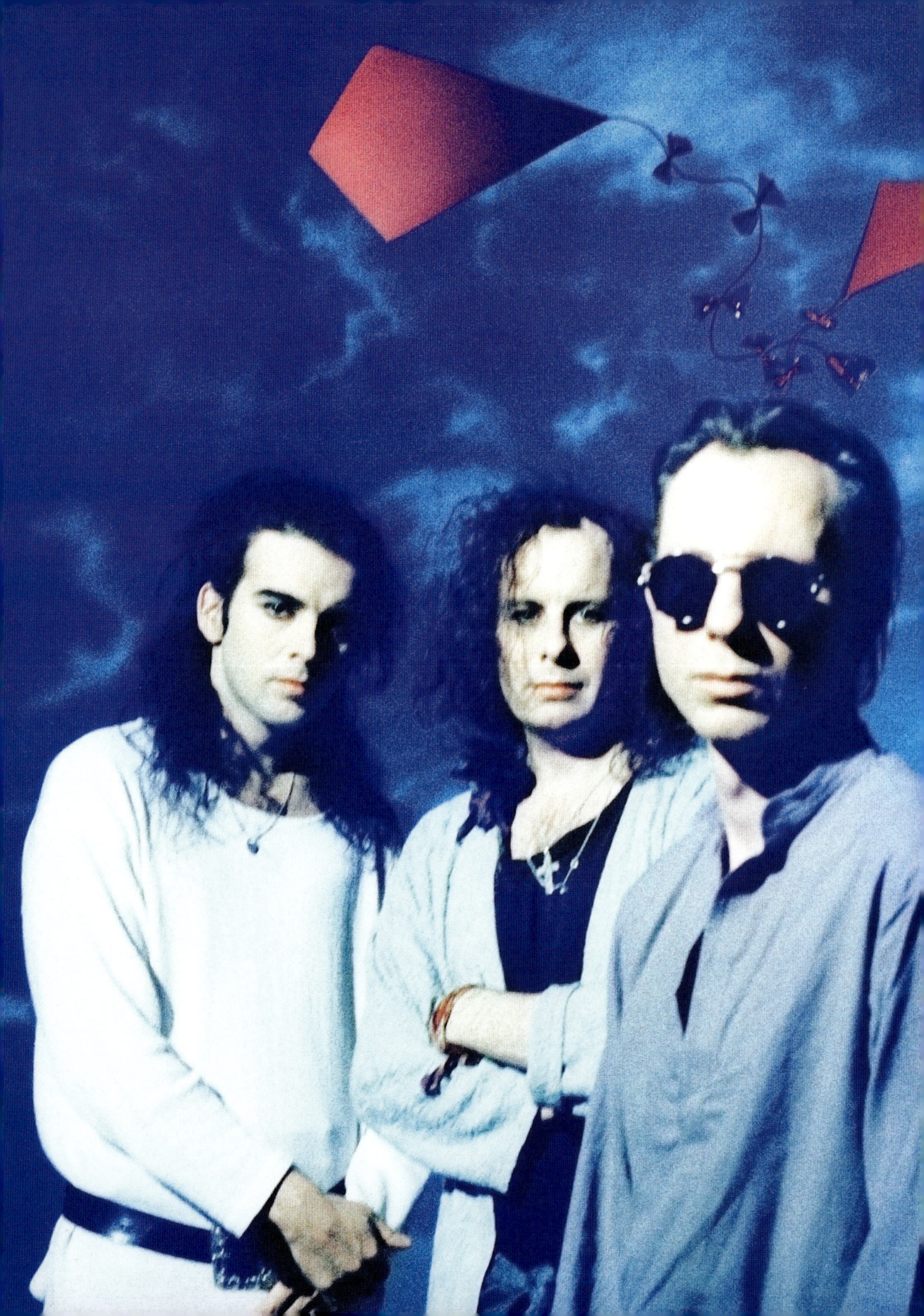

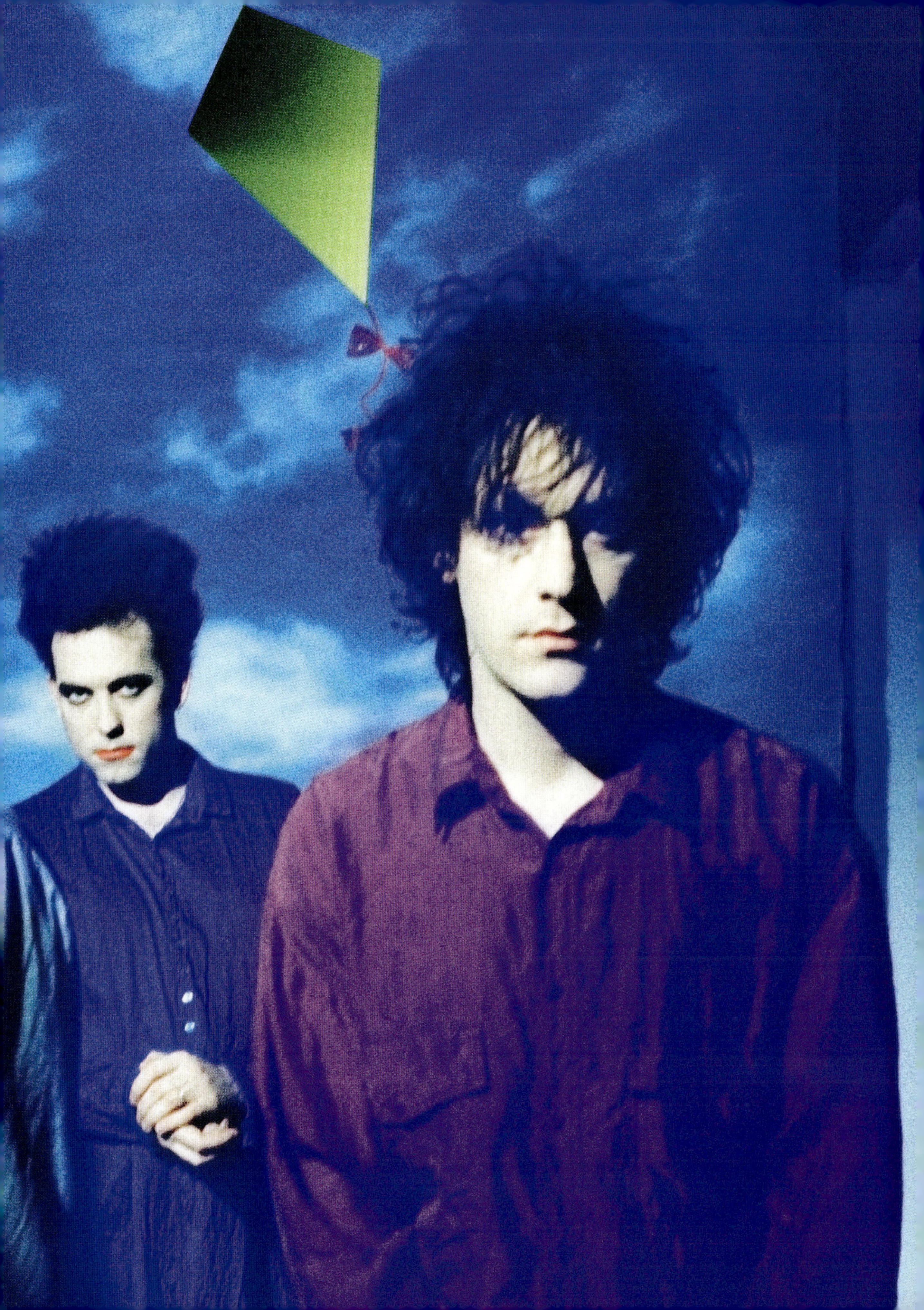

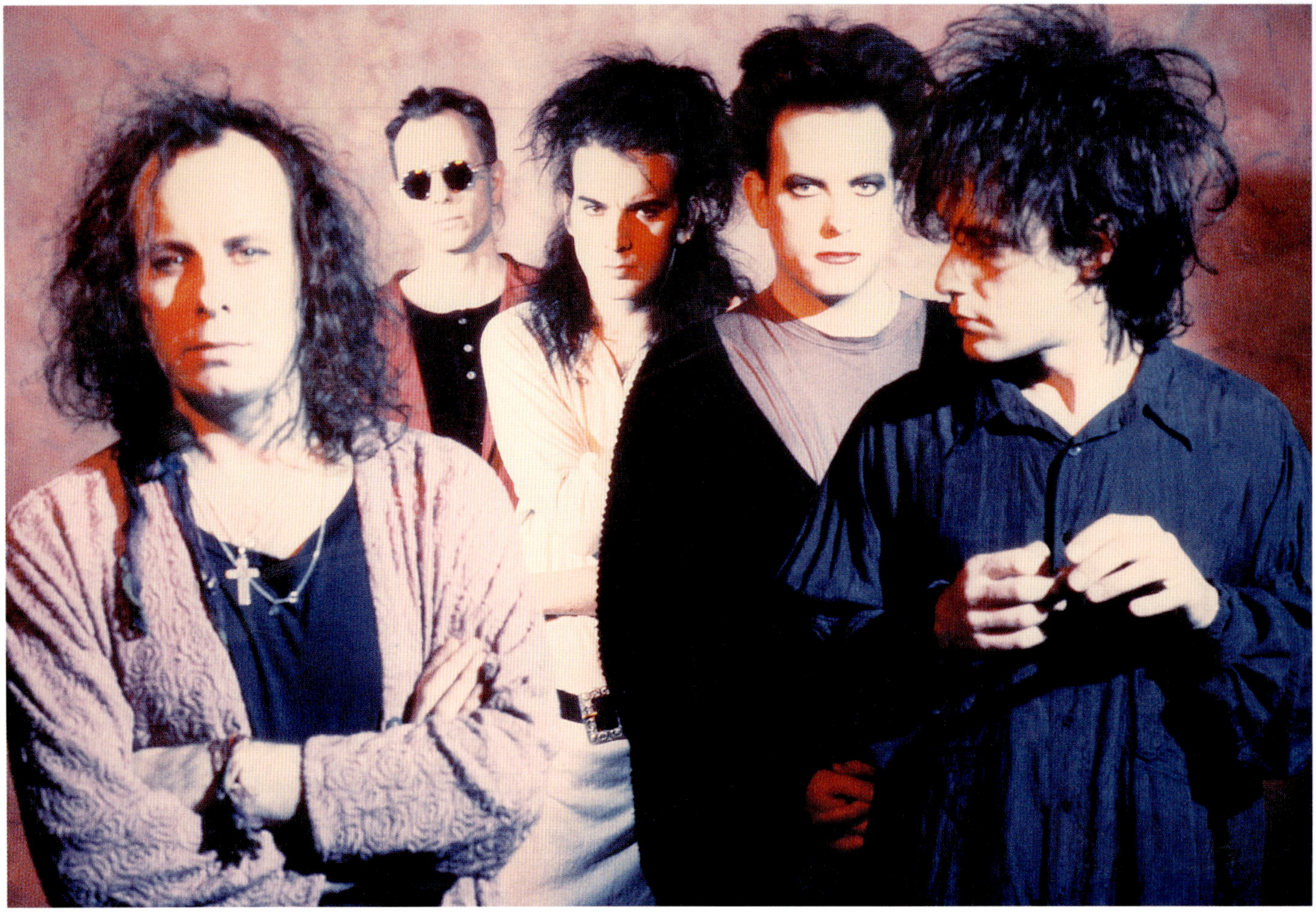

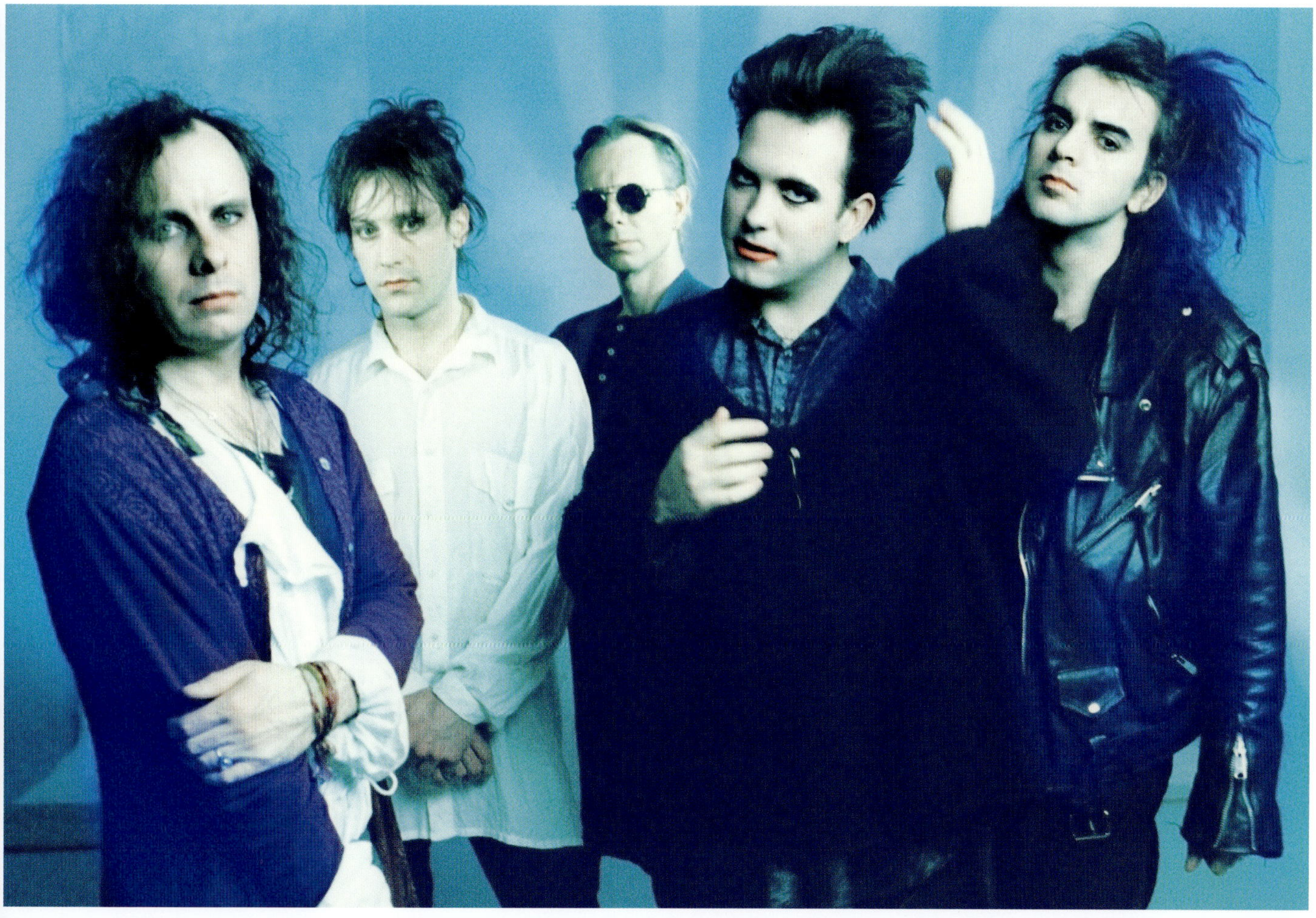

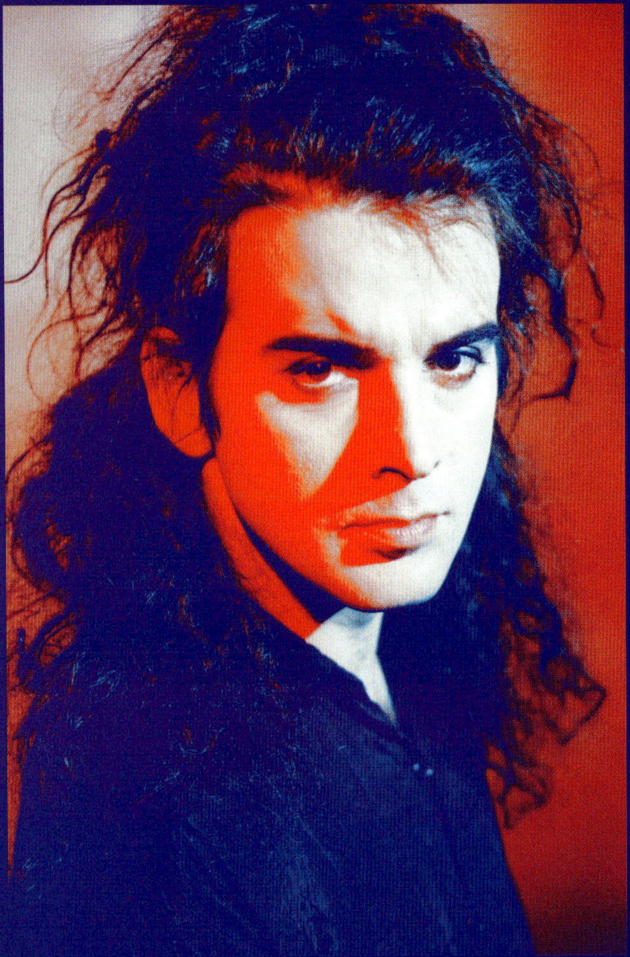
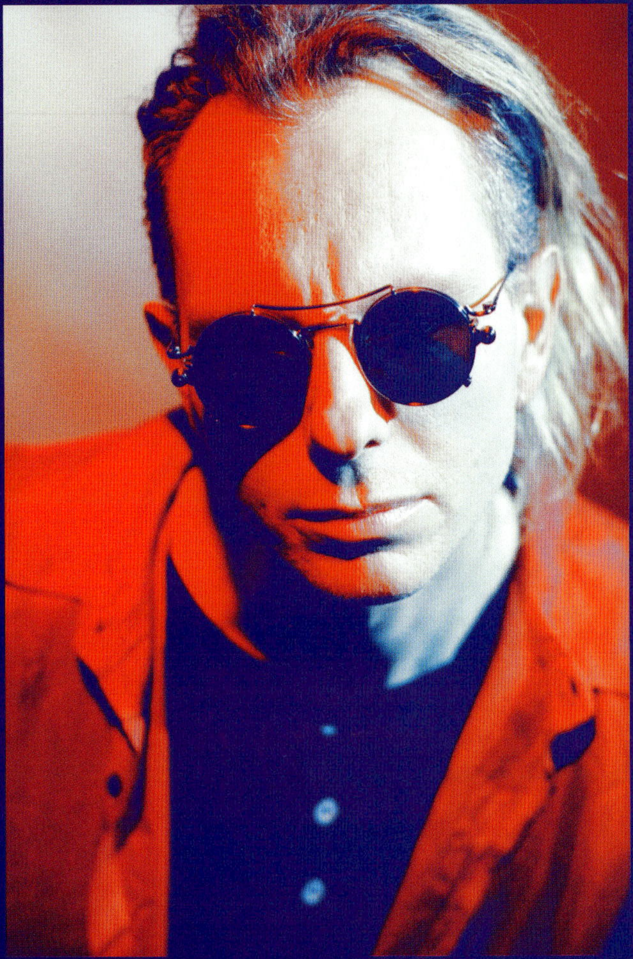
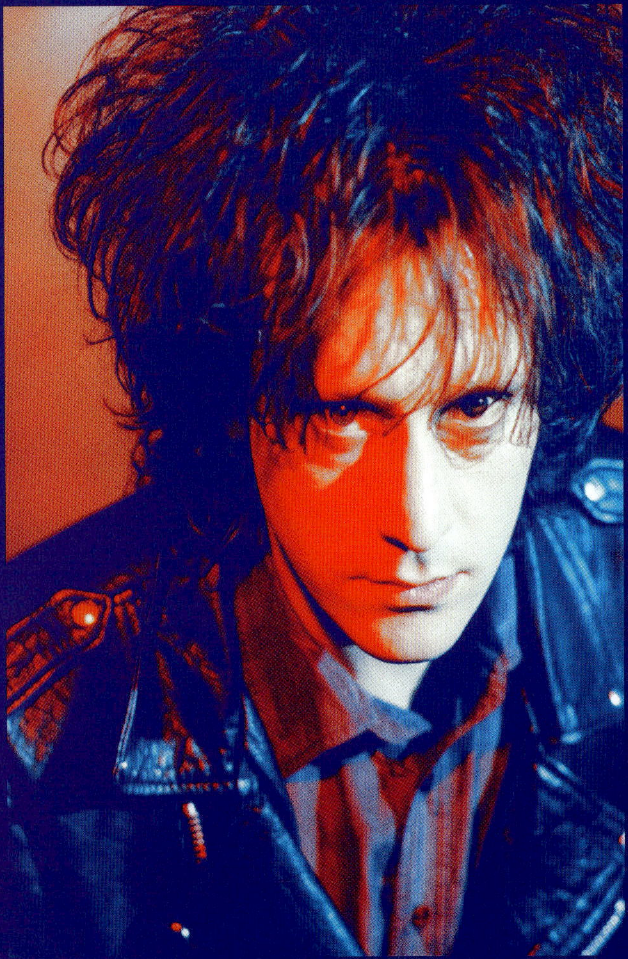
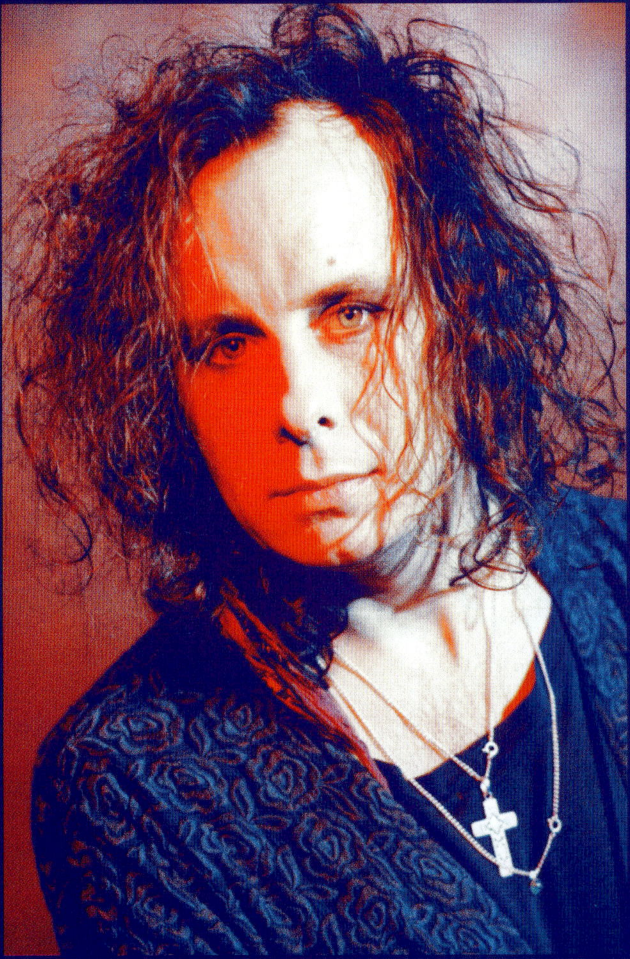

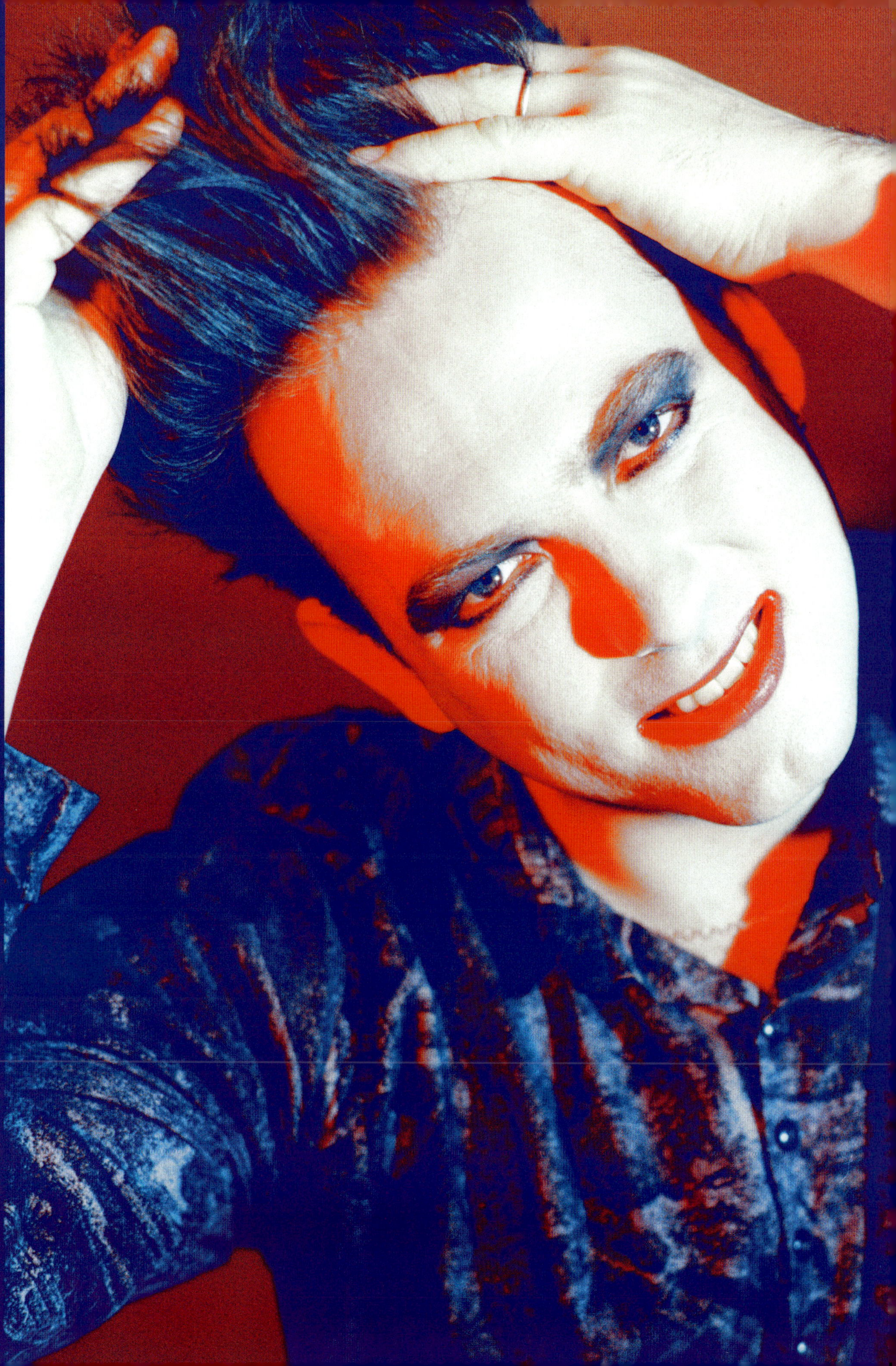

RECORDING STUDIO

Sussex

[p. 182 to 189]

1993

ROBERT: WE ARE NOW A QUARTET AGAIN, AND WOULD SOON BE A TRIO… GETTING OUR HEADS TOGETHER IN THE COUNTRY DIDN'T REALLY WORK OUT! THIS WAS A PRETTY WEIRD PERIOD OF THE BAND, A LOT OF UNCERTAINTY… IF NOTHING ELSE, THIS SESSION PROVED THE OLD ADAGE 'WEARING LEATHER JACKETS DOTH NOT A BAND MAKE'… I DO LIKE THE SOFA SHOTS THOUGH!

Paul: Fiction Records, through RS, commissioned me to do some press pictures as there was a new line up. This was another one of those sessions where I turned up not knowing what to expect! The band were demoing new songs. I used the surrounding grounds to the best advantage, given that they weren't very exciting. Inside had slightly more interesting features. I have an aversion to green in photographs, so ended up shooting a lot more in black-and-white than colour. Through cross processing the film, I created images which gave vivid colours (no

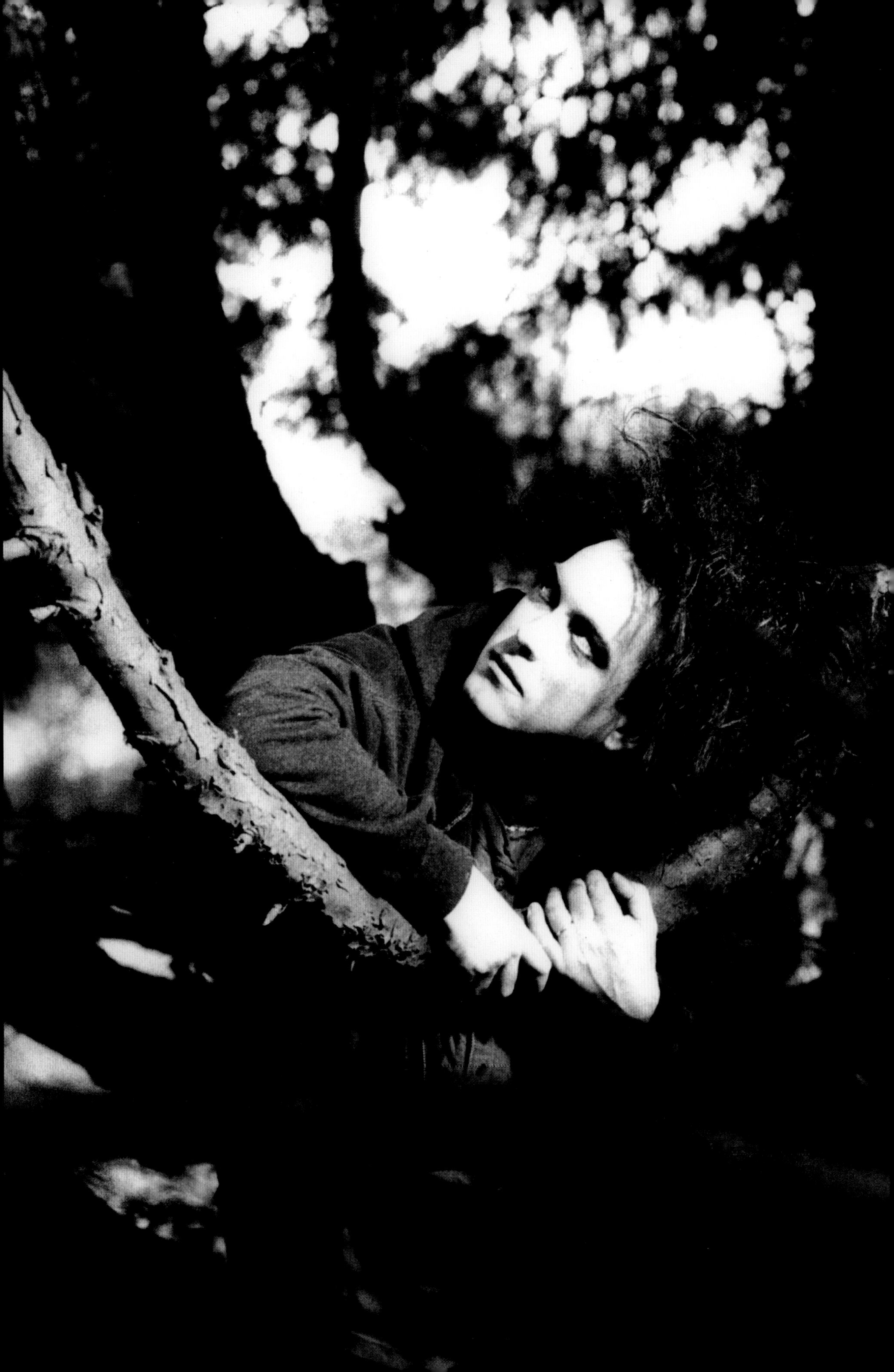

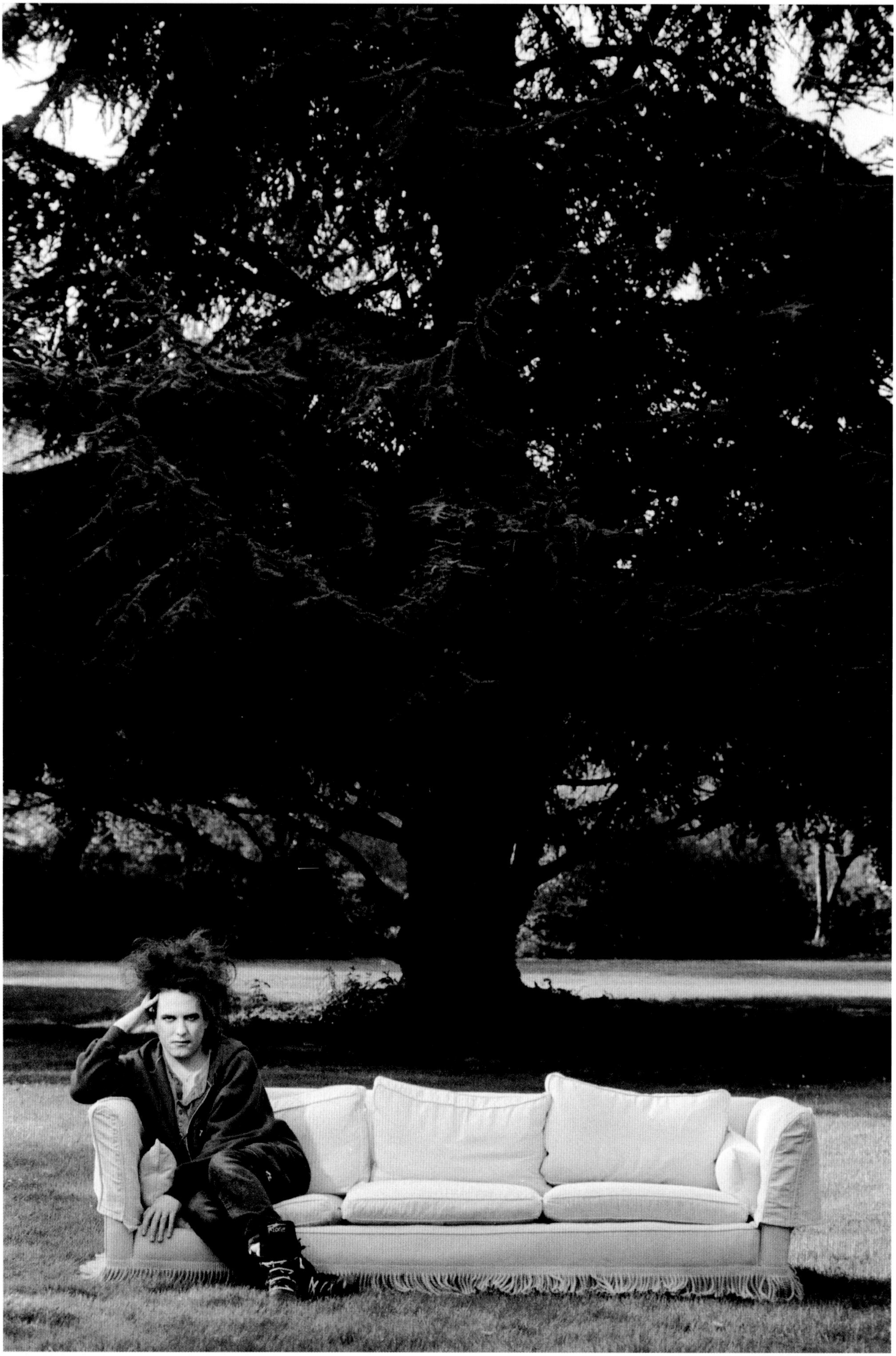

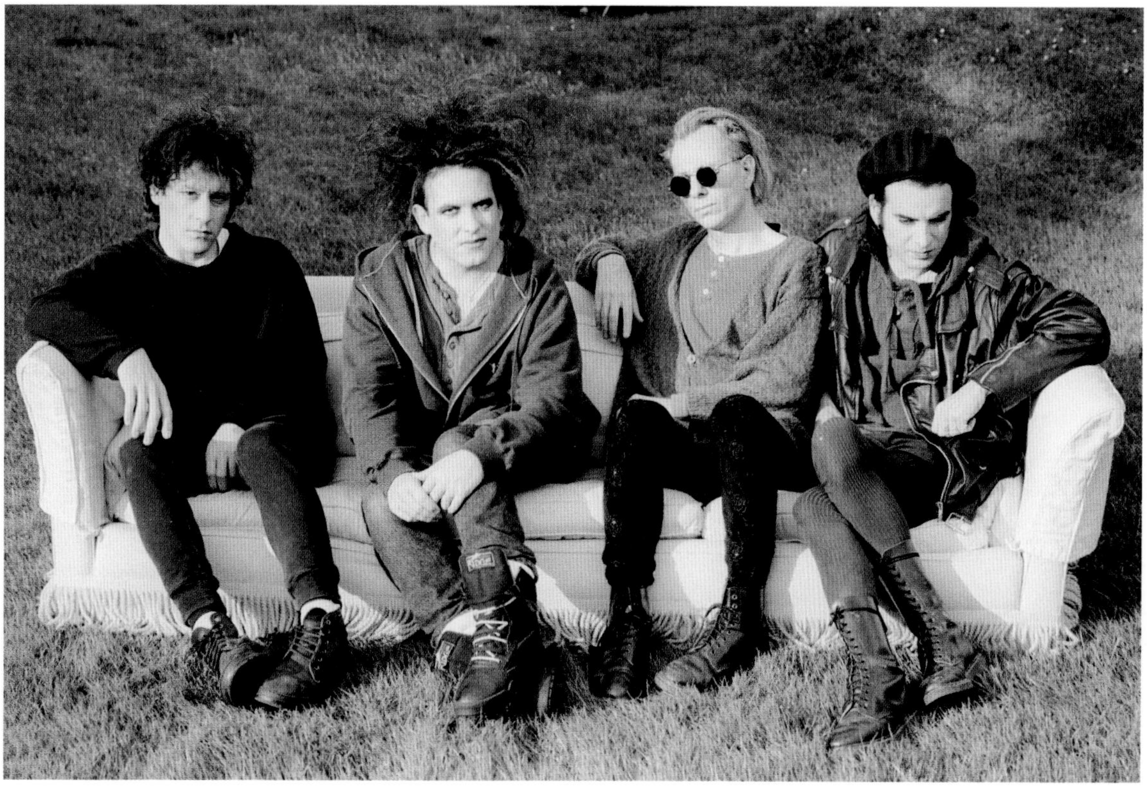

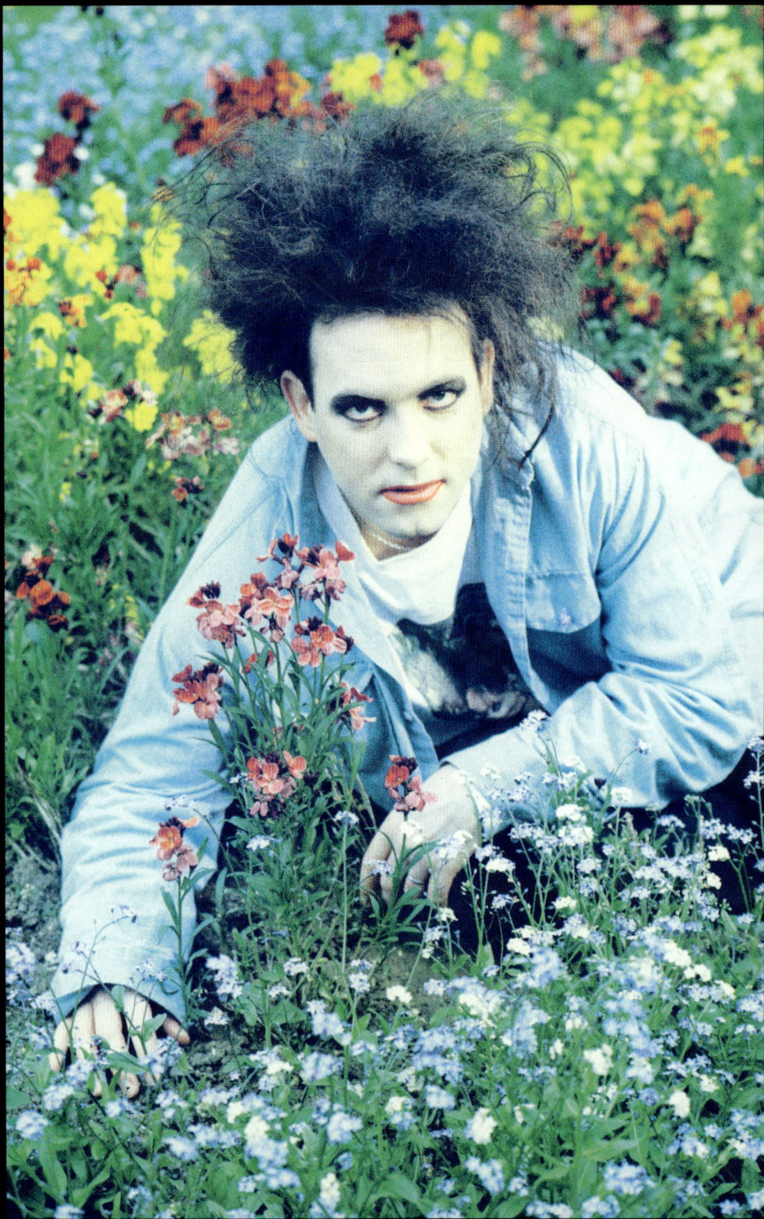

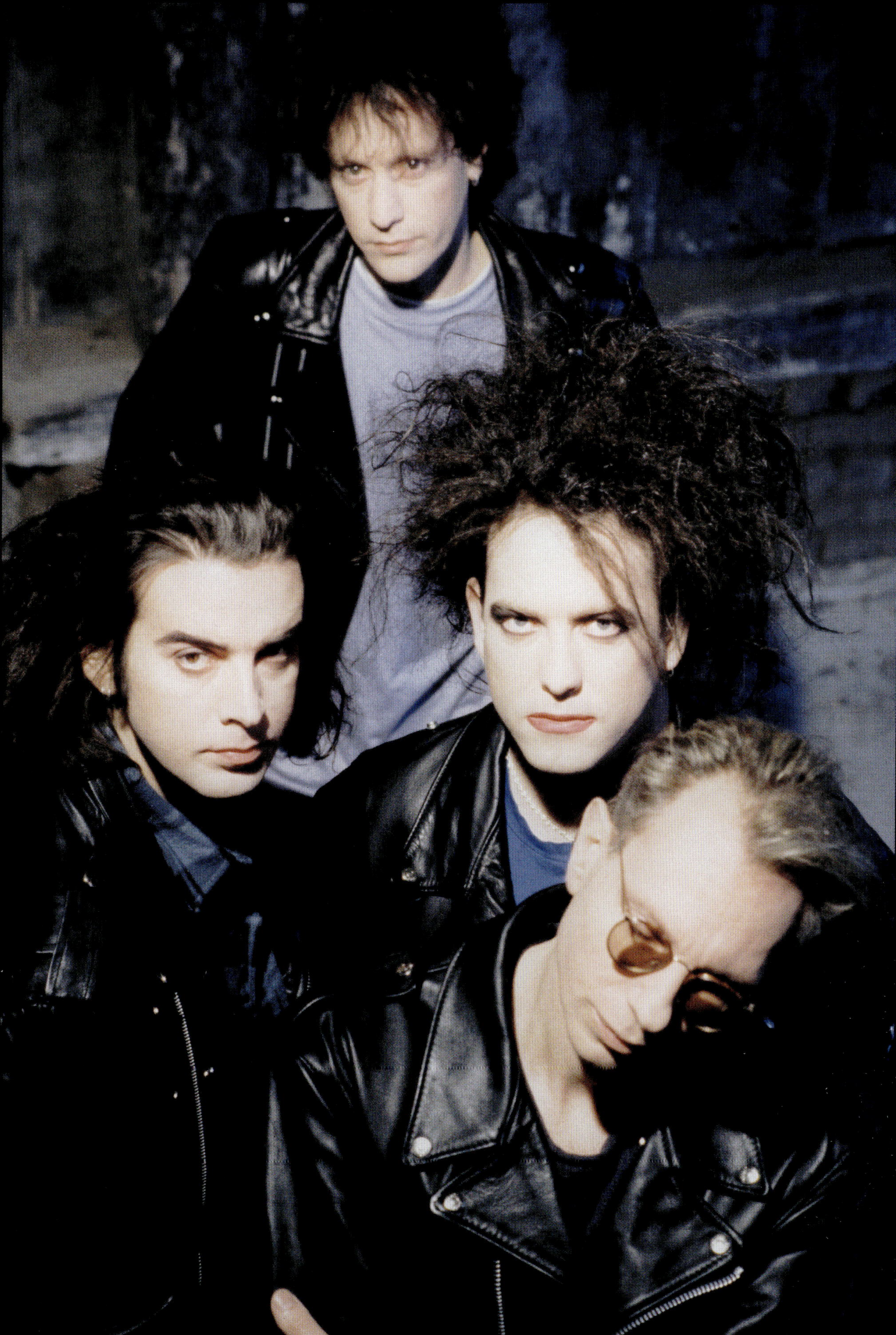

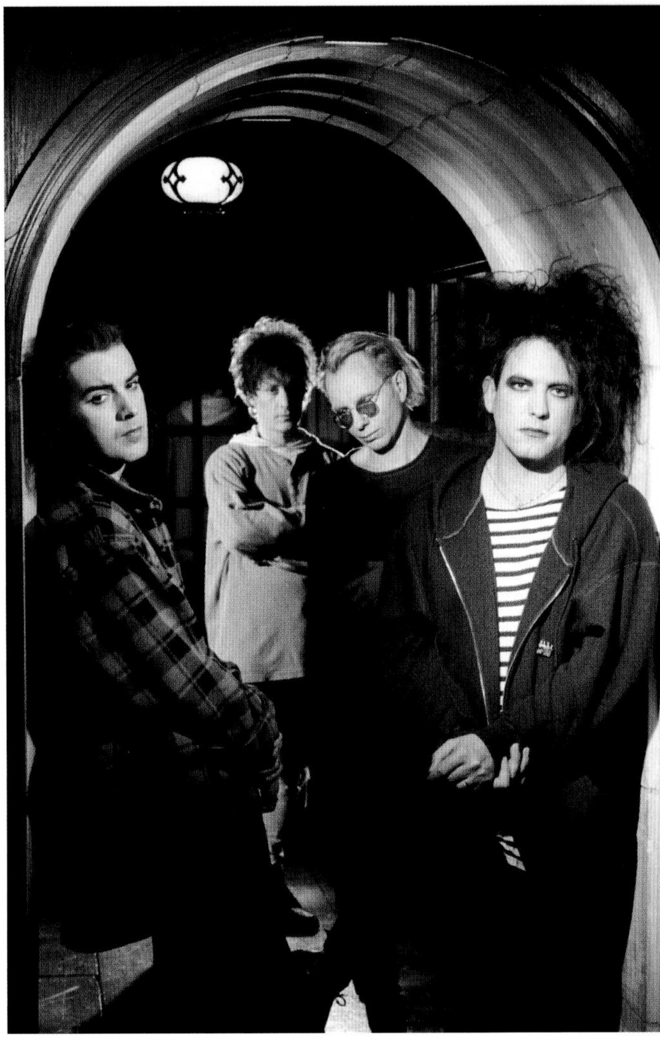

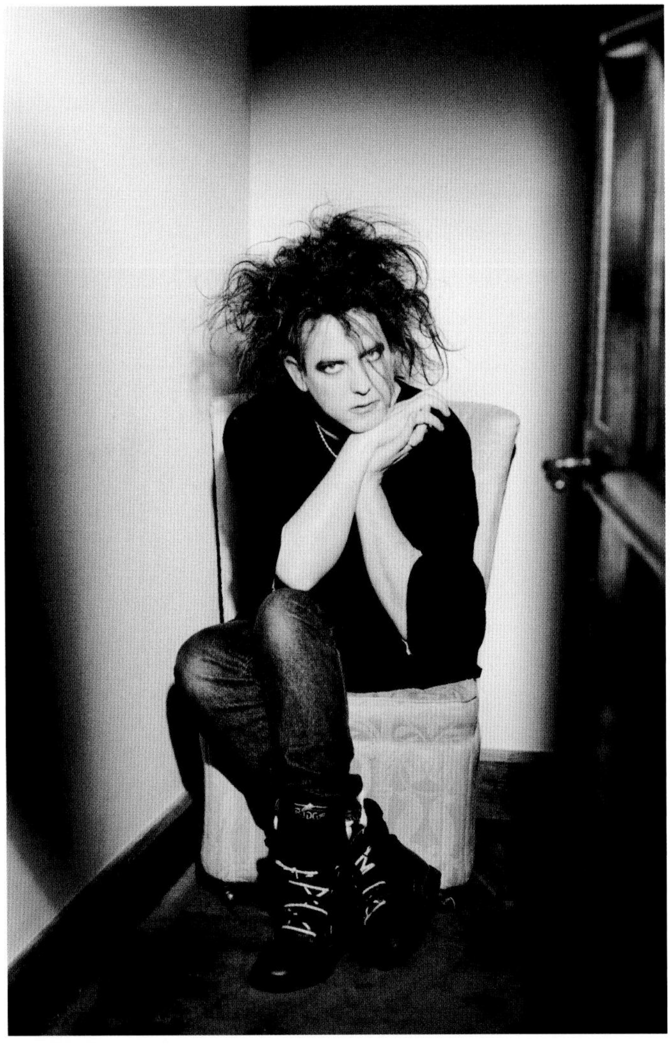

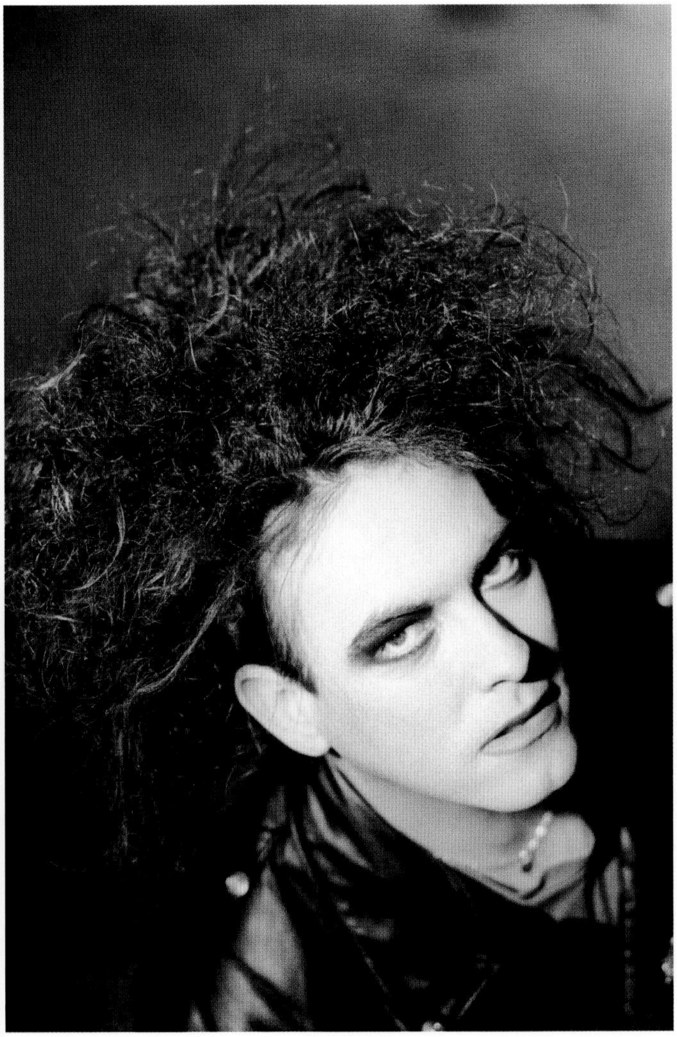

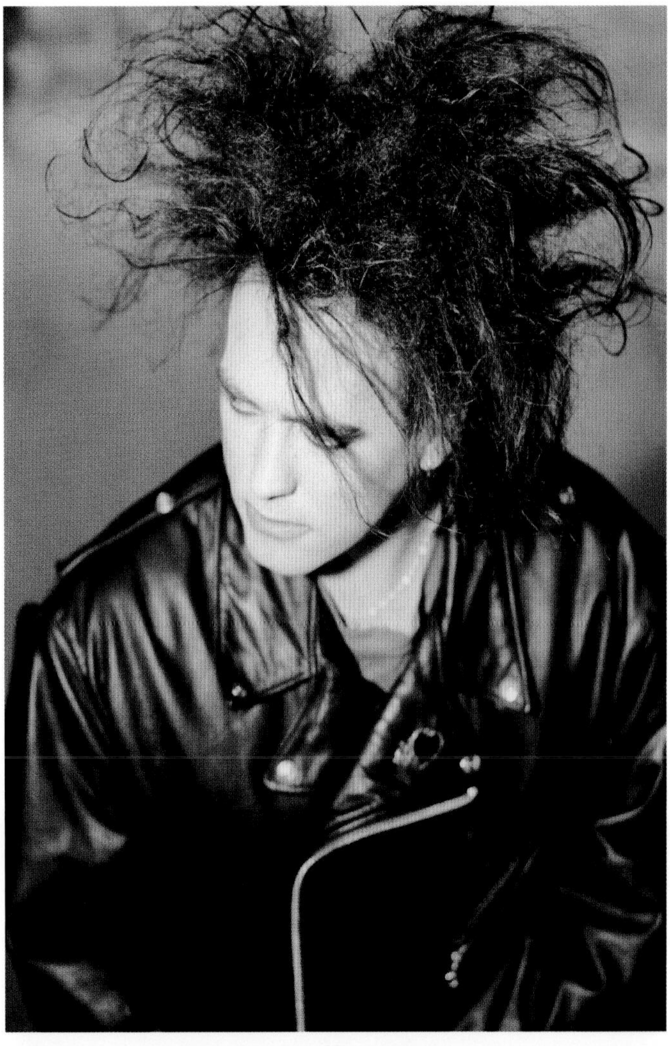

ST CATHERINE'S COURT
Bath
(p. 190 to 201)
1995

ROBERT: BORIS IS NOW GONE... JASON HAS REPLACED HIM... AND ROGER IS BACK ON KEYS. THIS WAS A PRETTY CHAOTIC CALENDAR SHOOT AS I REMEMBER – WE ALWAYS HAD A LOT OF FUN AT ST CATHERINE'S... TOO MUCH FUN PERHAPS?!!

Paul: My first time at St Catherine's Court in Bath. This

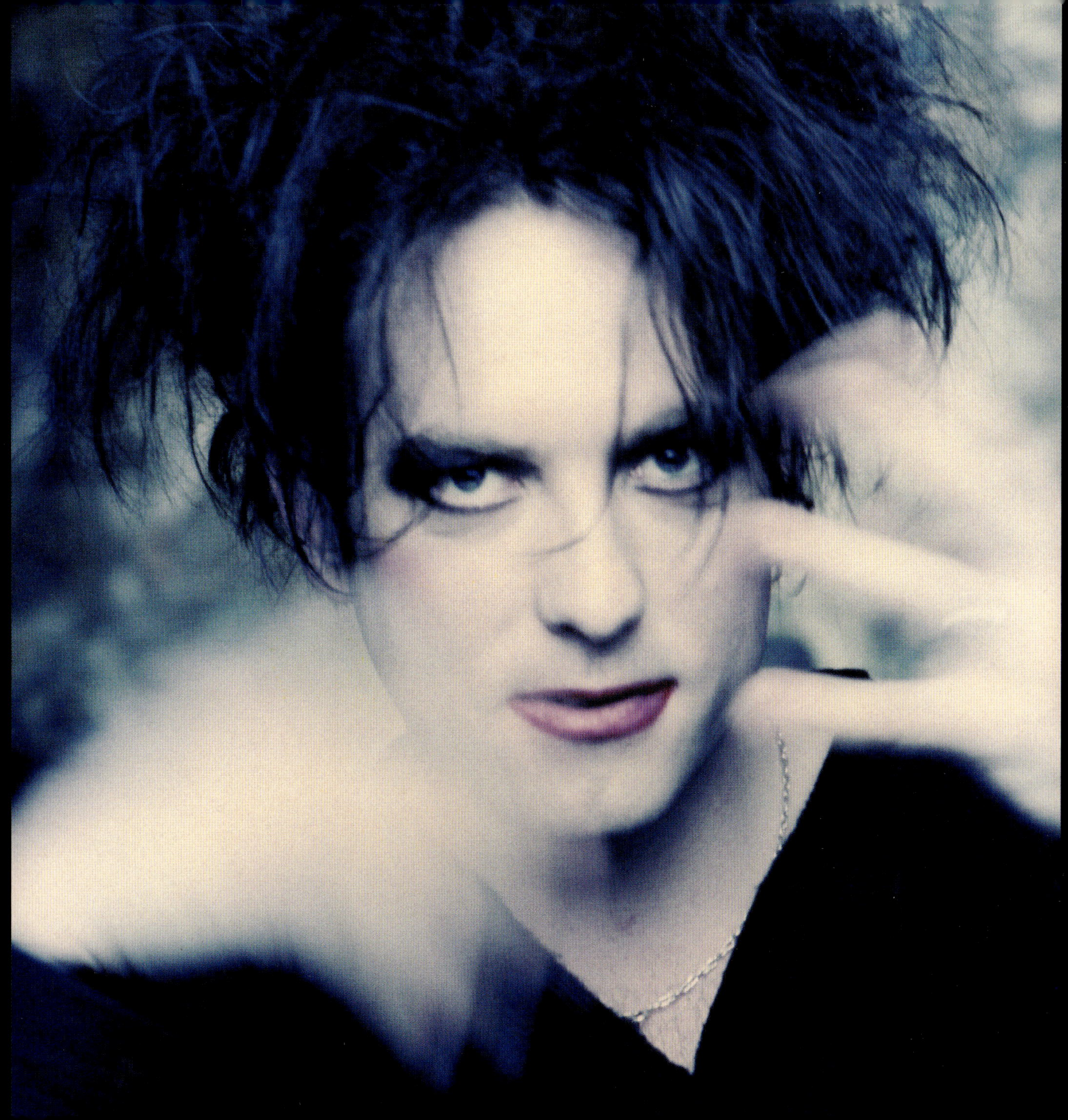

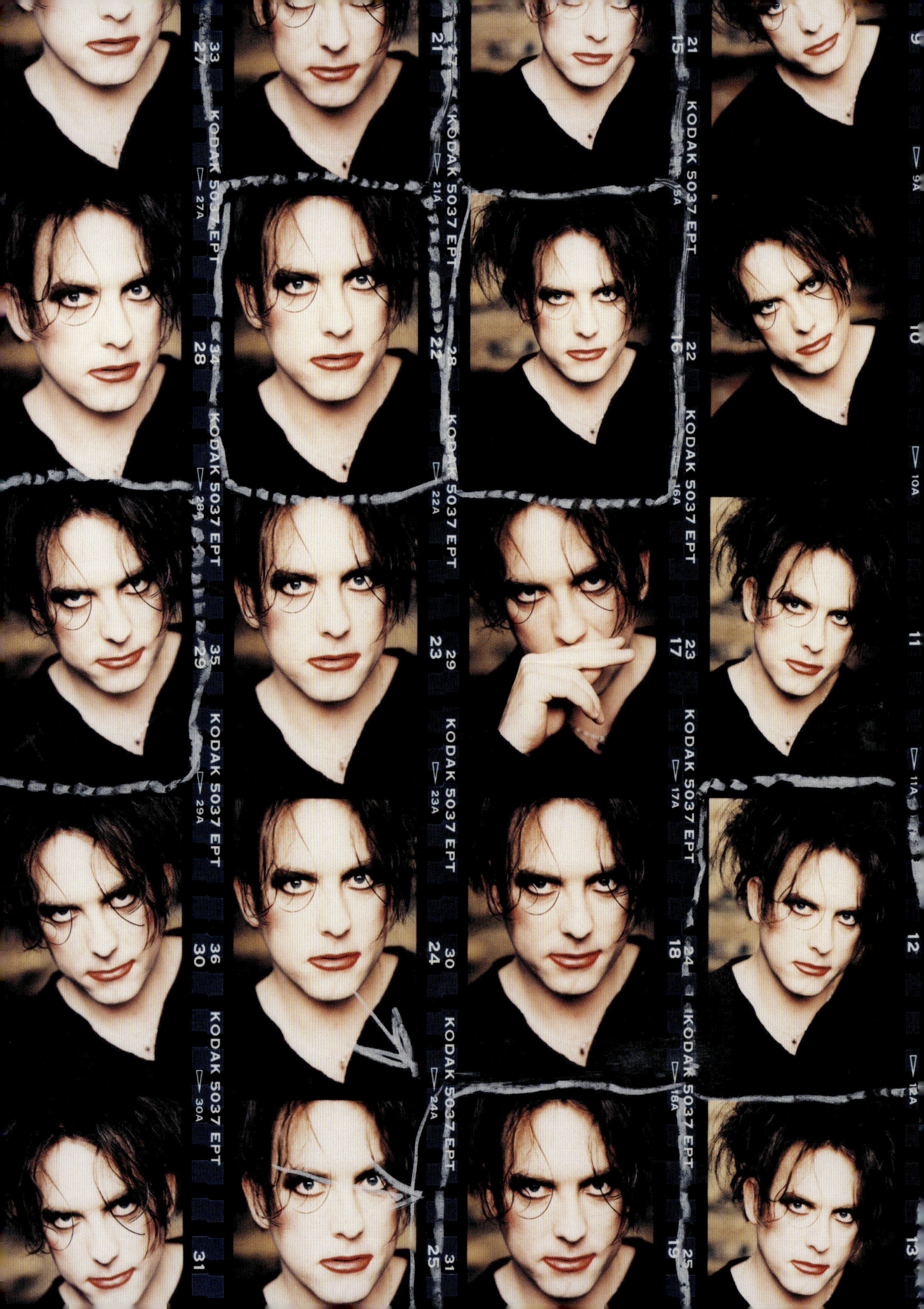
KODAK 5037 EPT

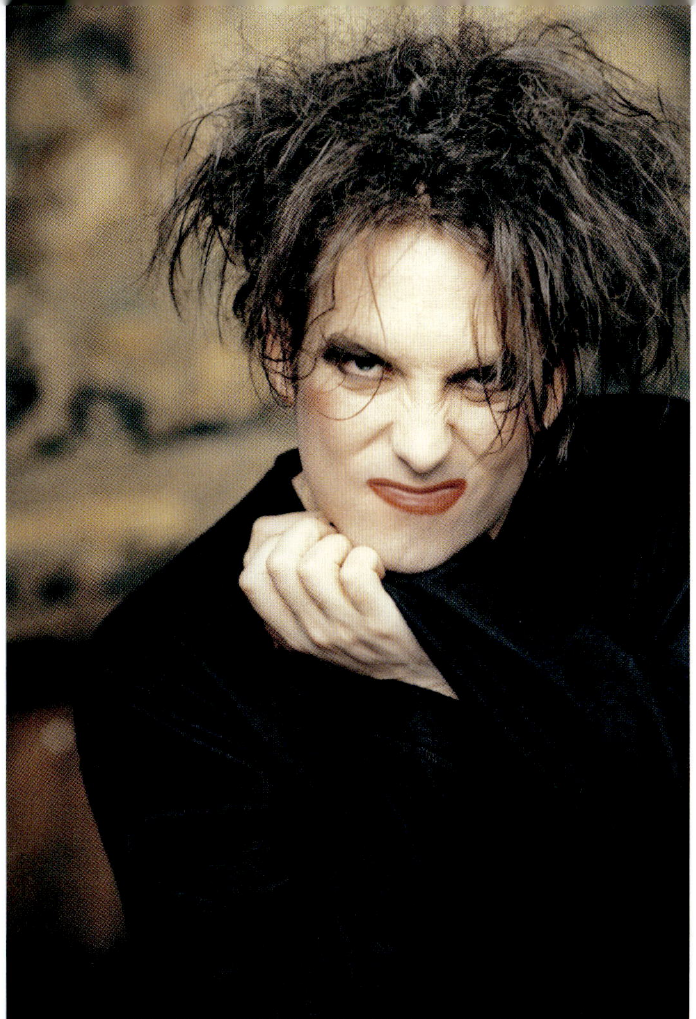
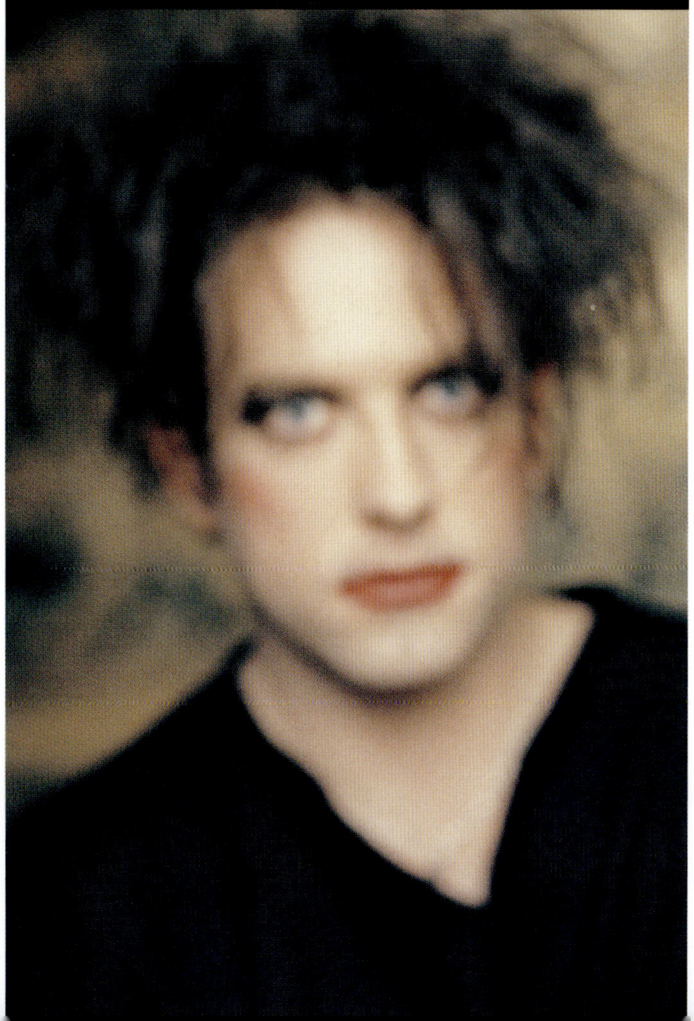

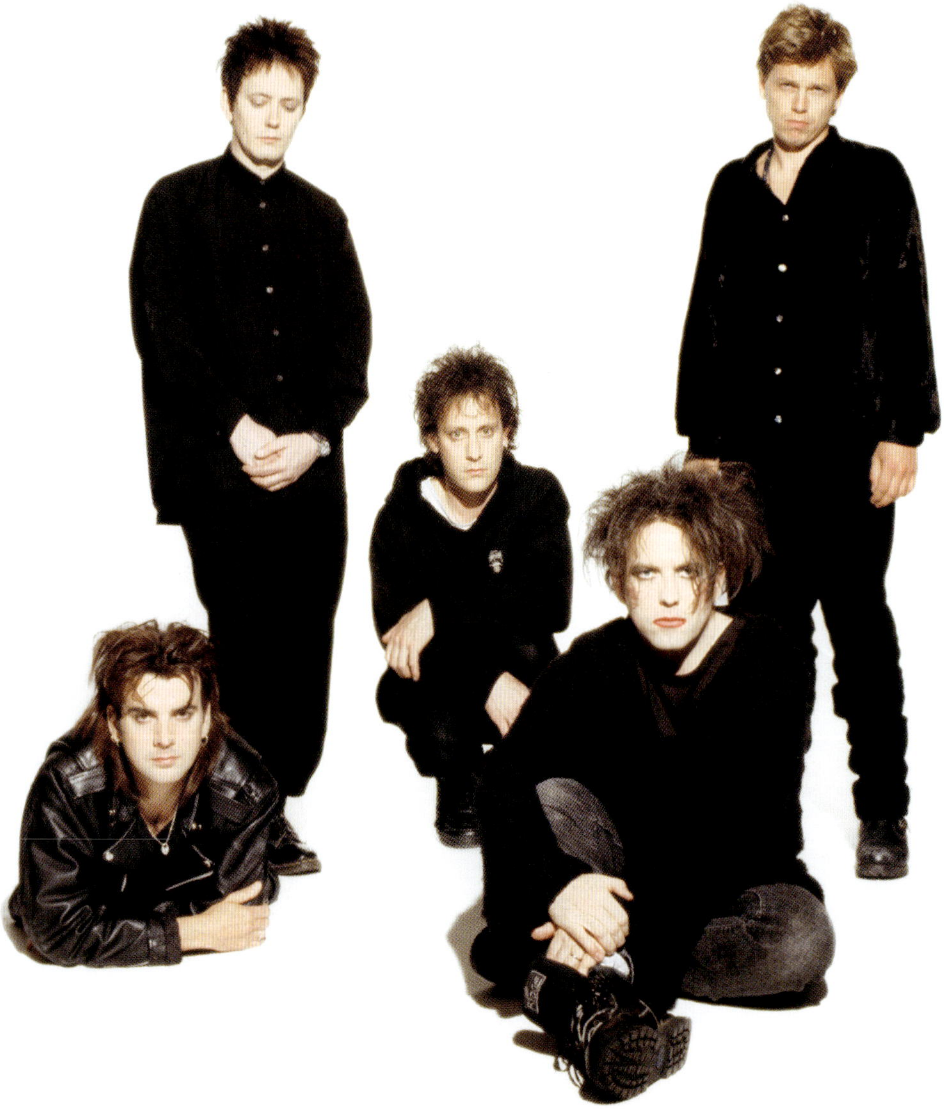

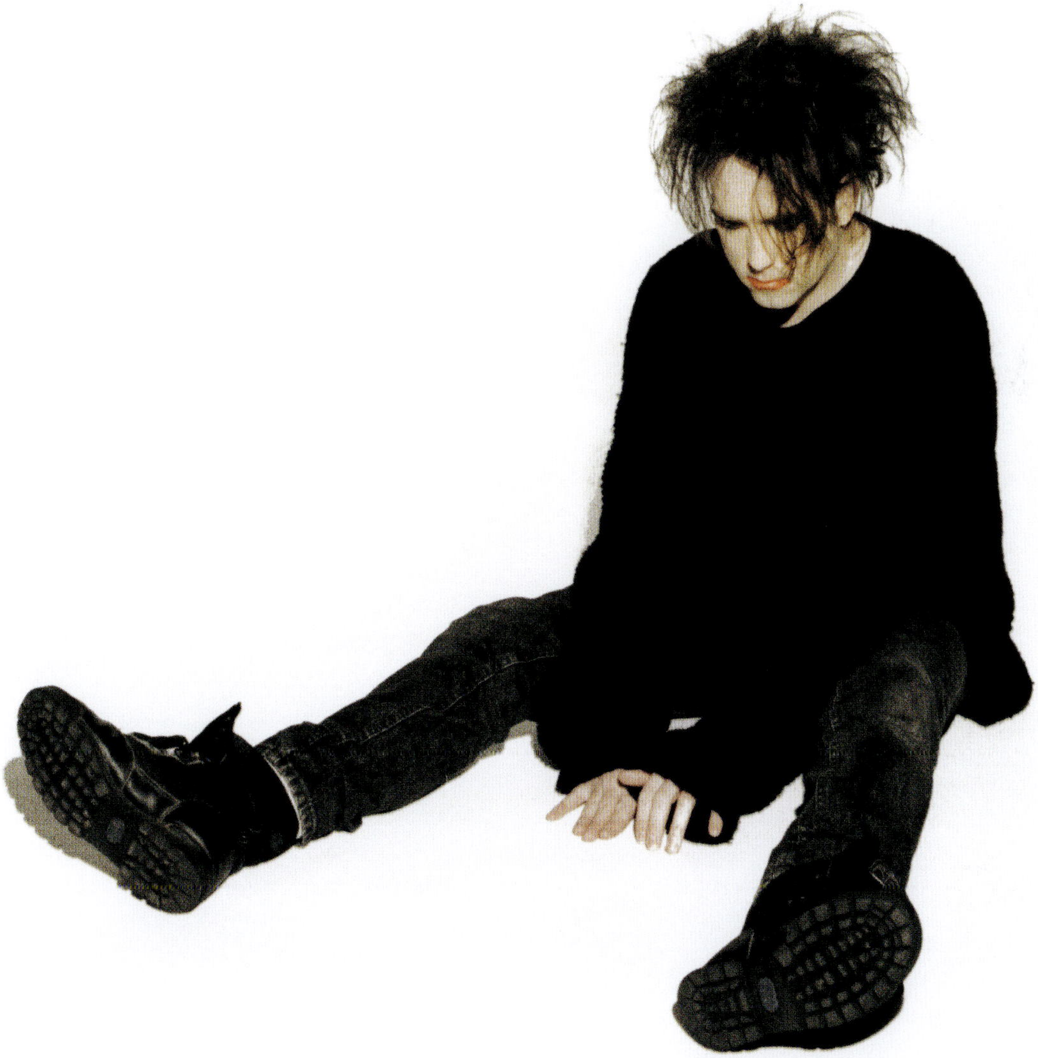

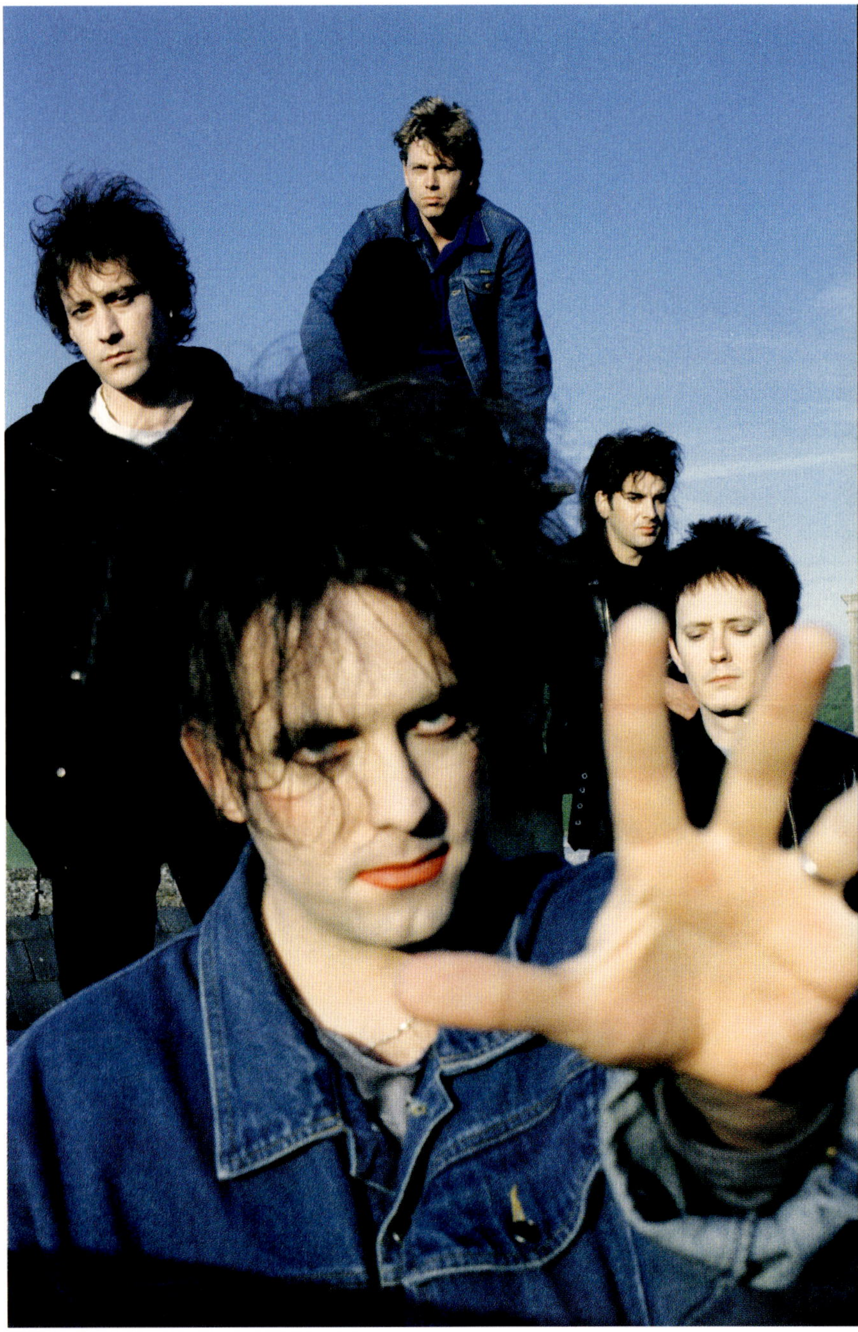

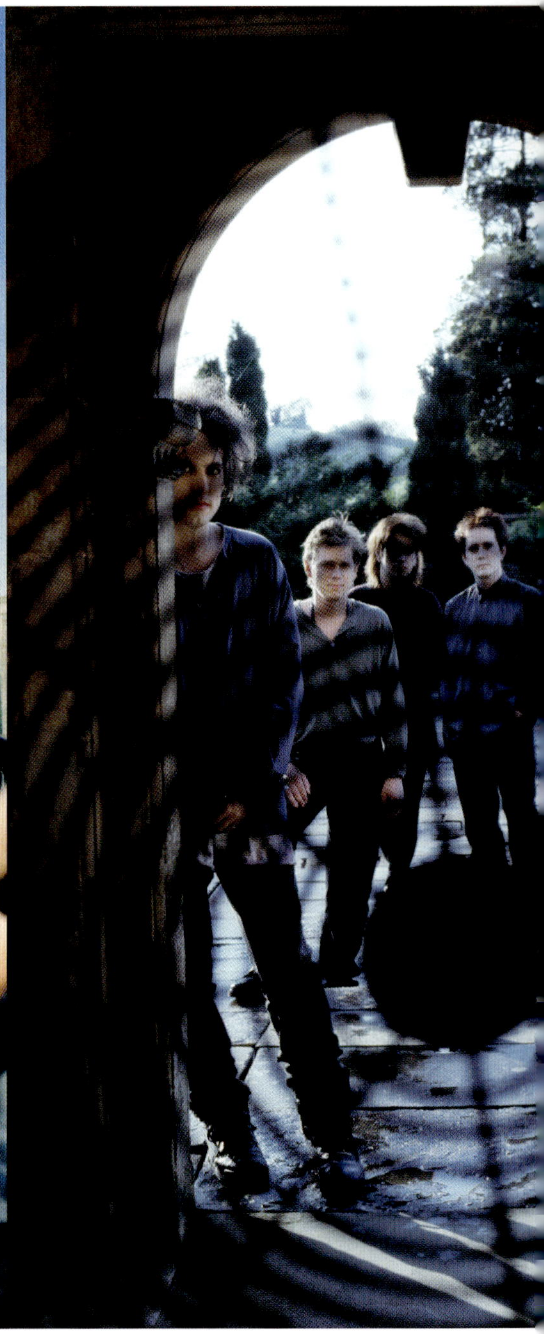

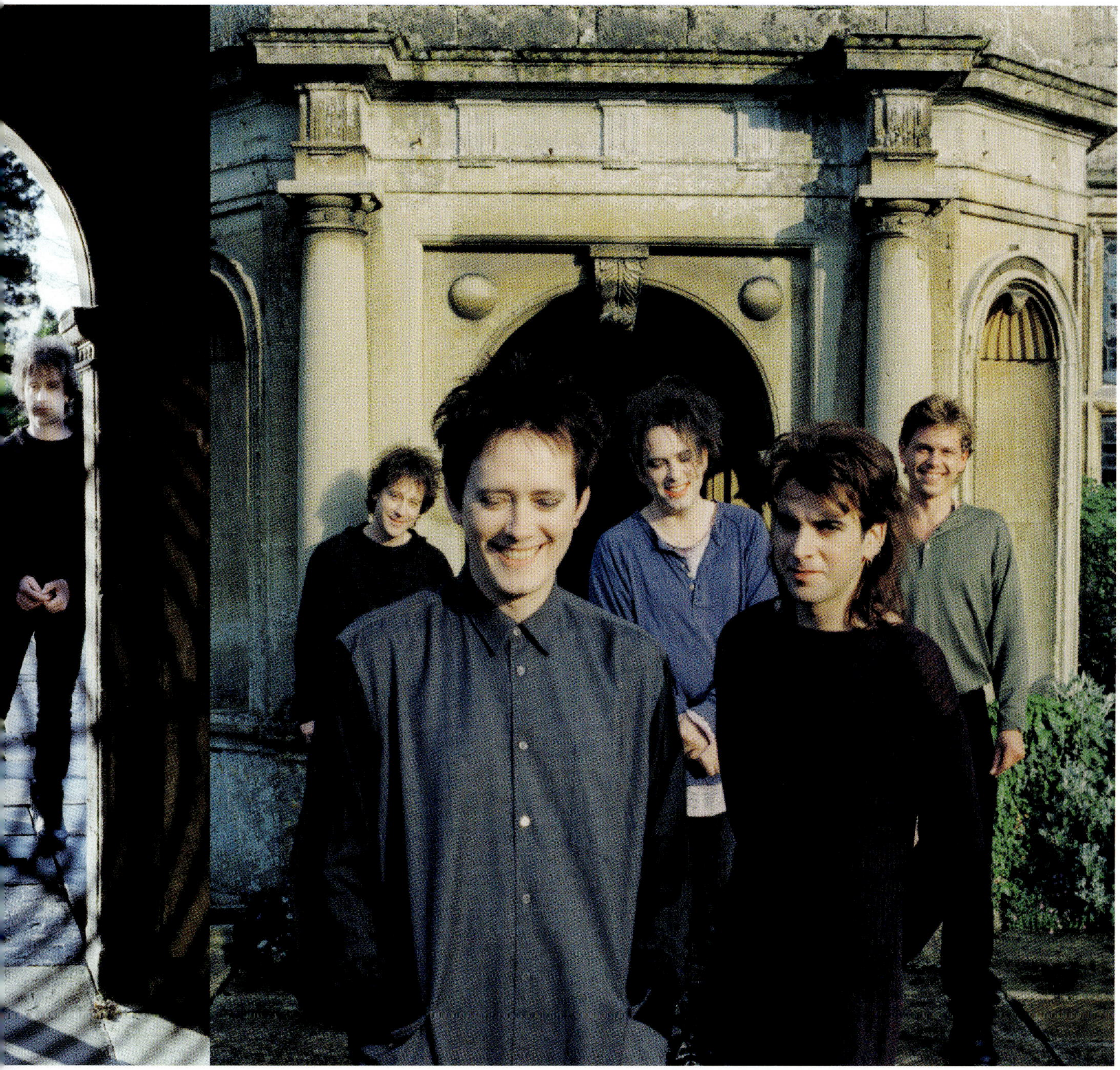

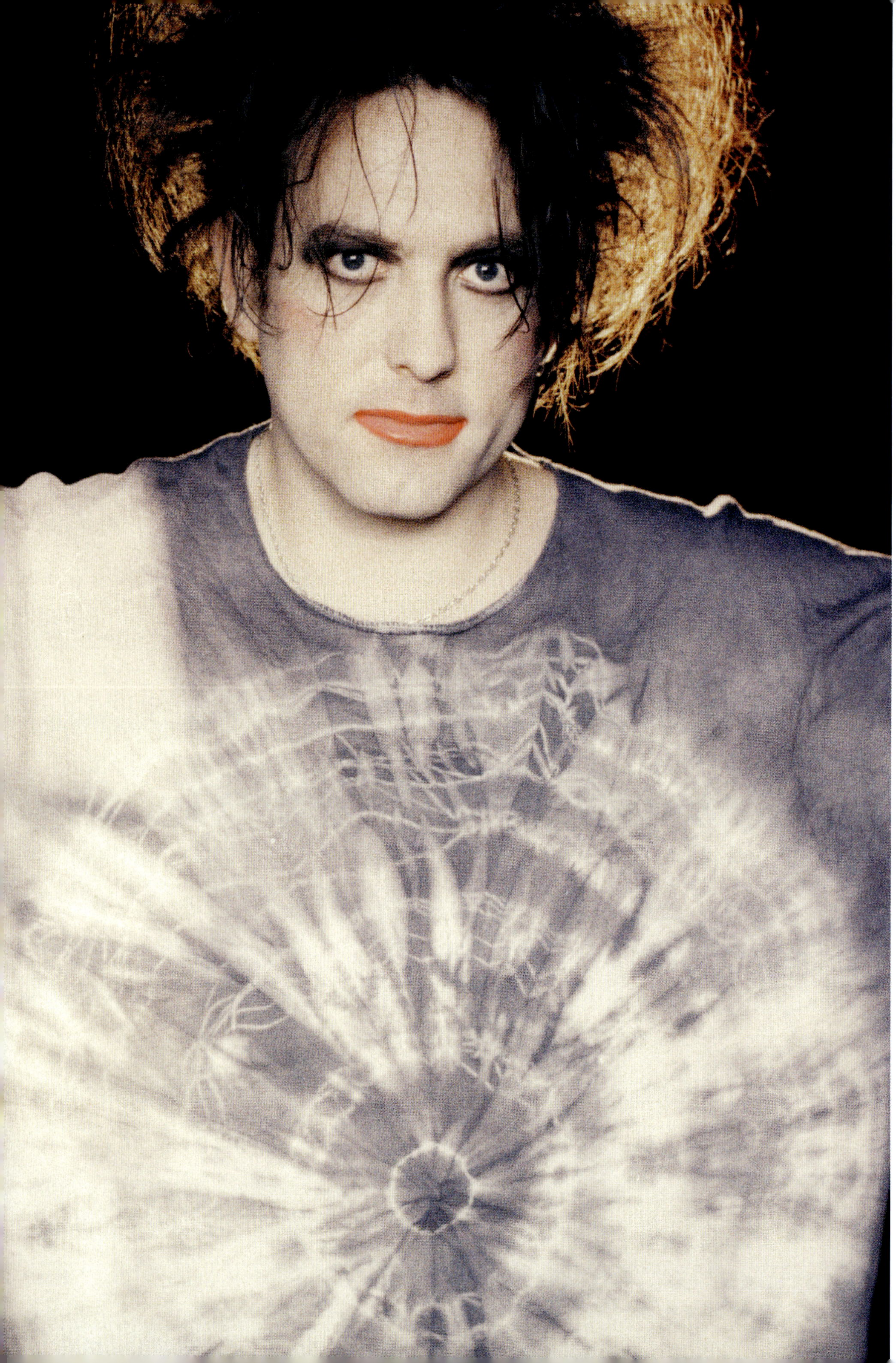

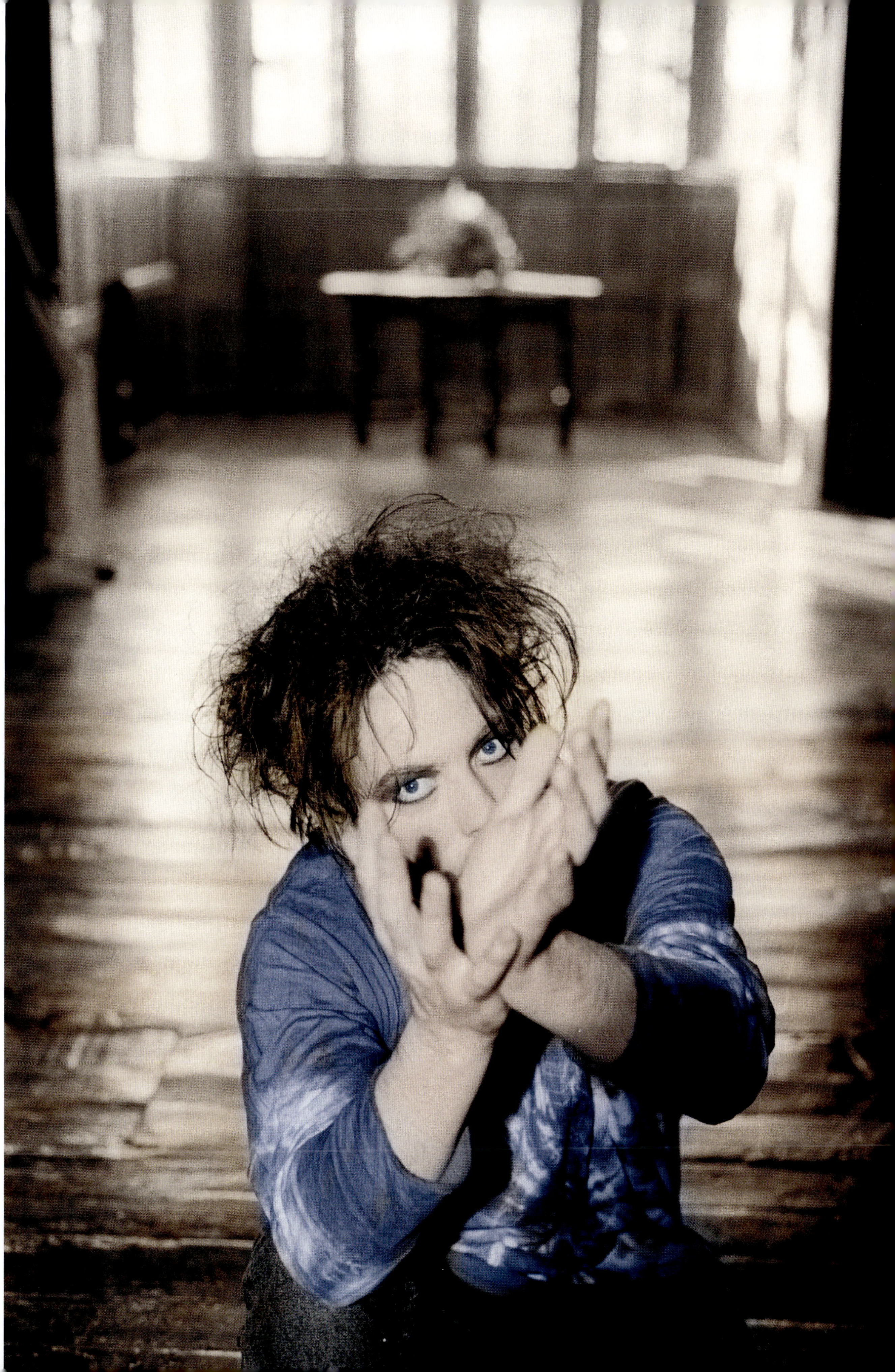

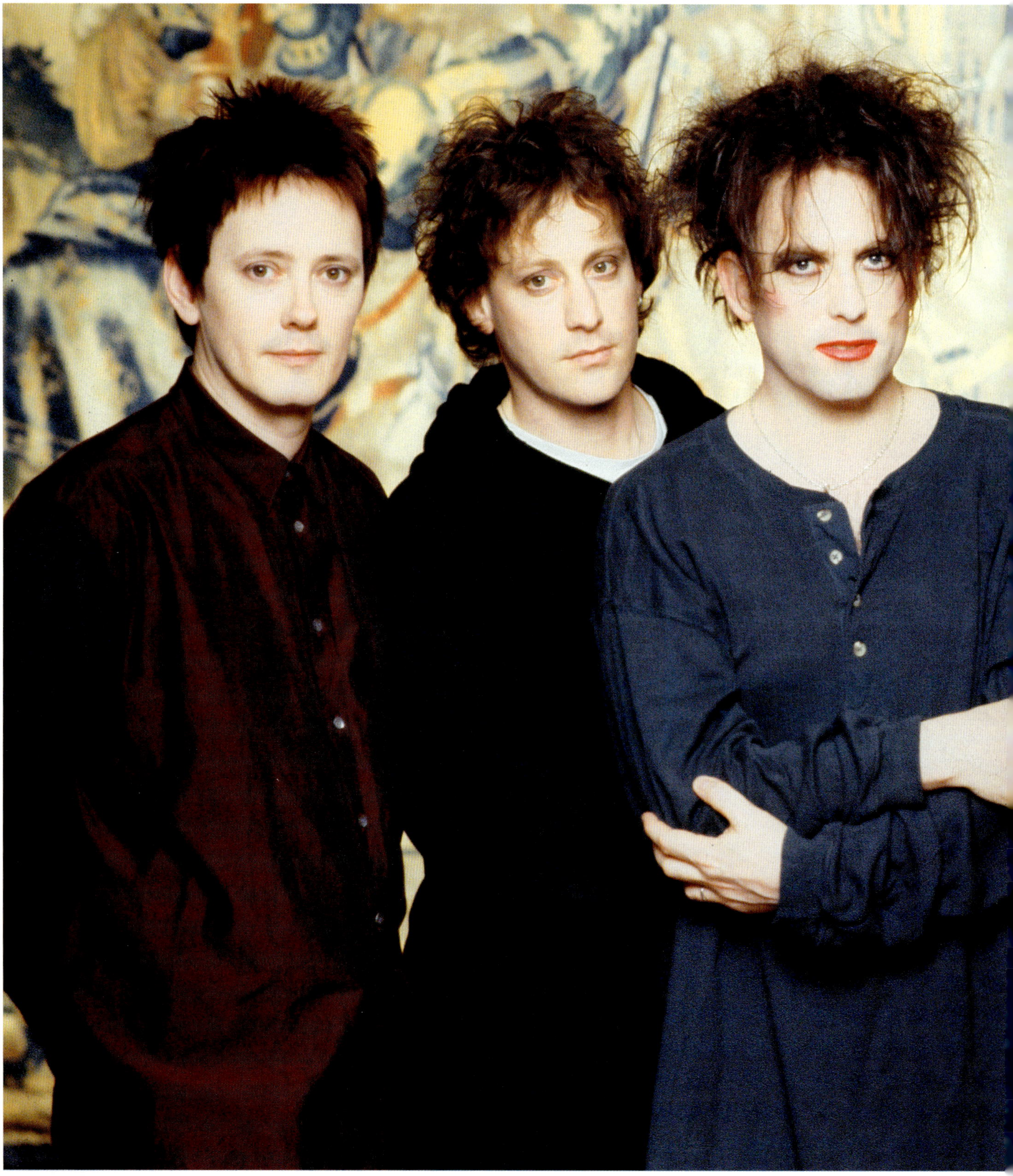

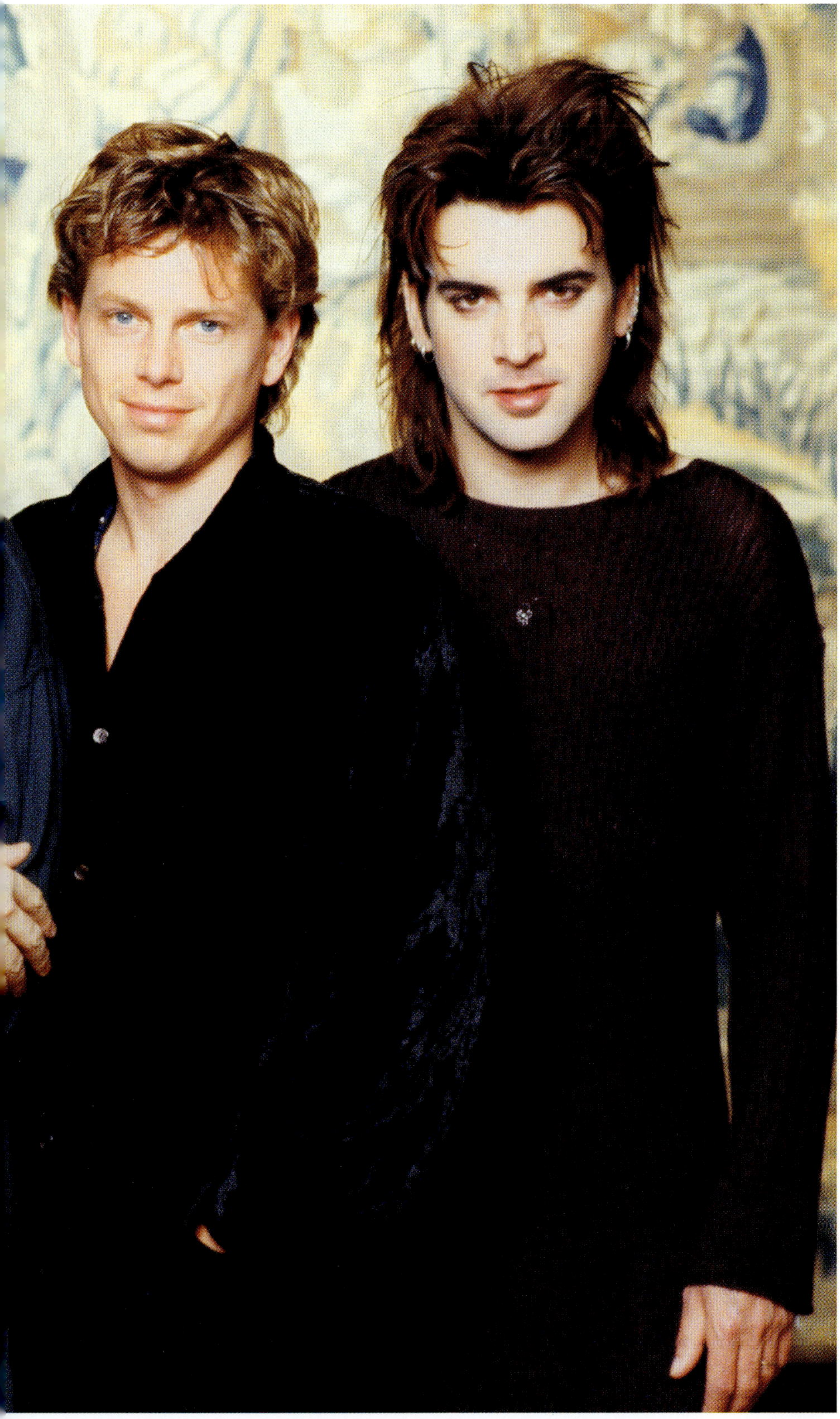

ST CATHERINE'S COURT

Bath

[p.202 to 217]

1996

ROBERT: ANOTHER ST CATHERINE'S SHOOT – I THINK WE WERE THERE FOR DECADES! – THIS TIME FOR *WILD MOOD SWINGS* ALBUM PROMOTION. I REALLY LOVED THIS SESSION – VERY UNUSUALLY, I THINK WE ALL DID – PARTICULARLY THE FISH-EYE STUFF... NOT SO SURE ABOUT THE YELLOW CAR BLANKET THOUGH?

Paul: Back at St Catherine's Court, knowing what to expect this time. We talked about the images for the *Wild Mood Swings* album. Robert had various props that we used in the shoot. Our twist on this session was to use a fish-eye lens to distort the images, which worked really well. I always looked forward to shoots with the band as we always created interesting and quirky images to match the great music.

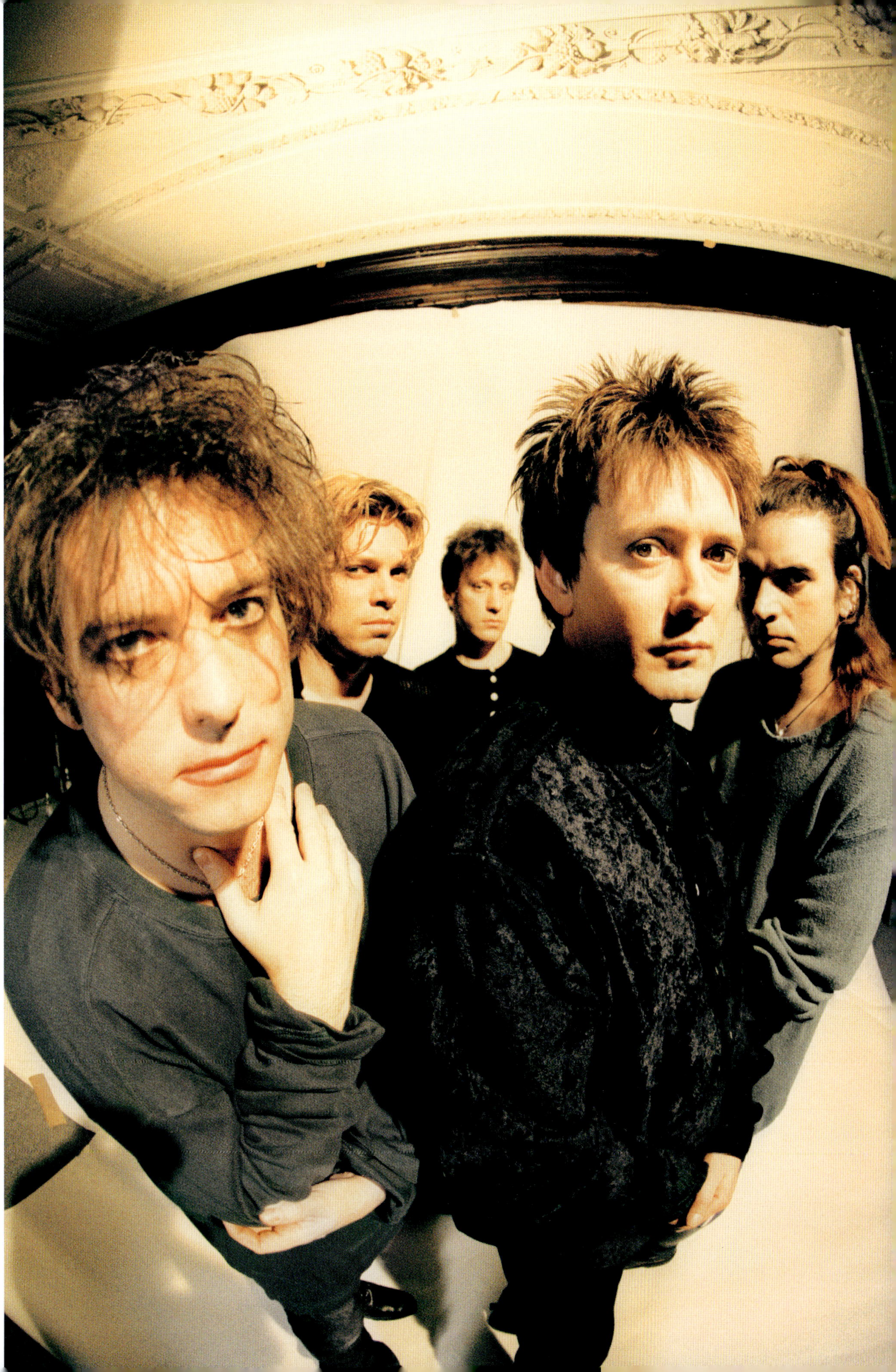

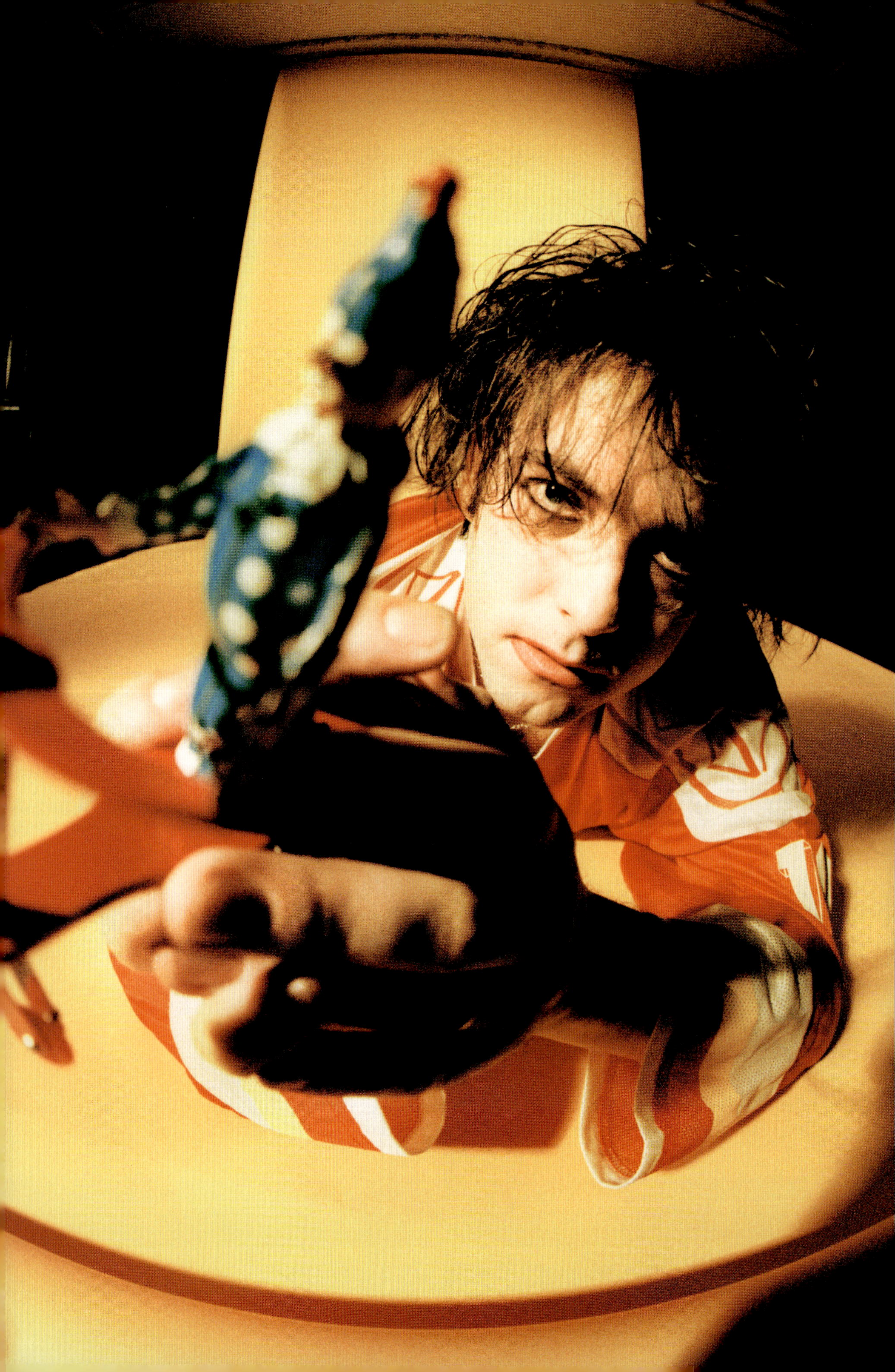

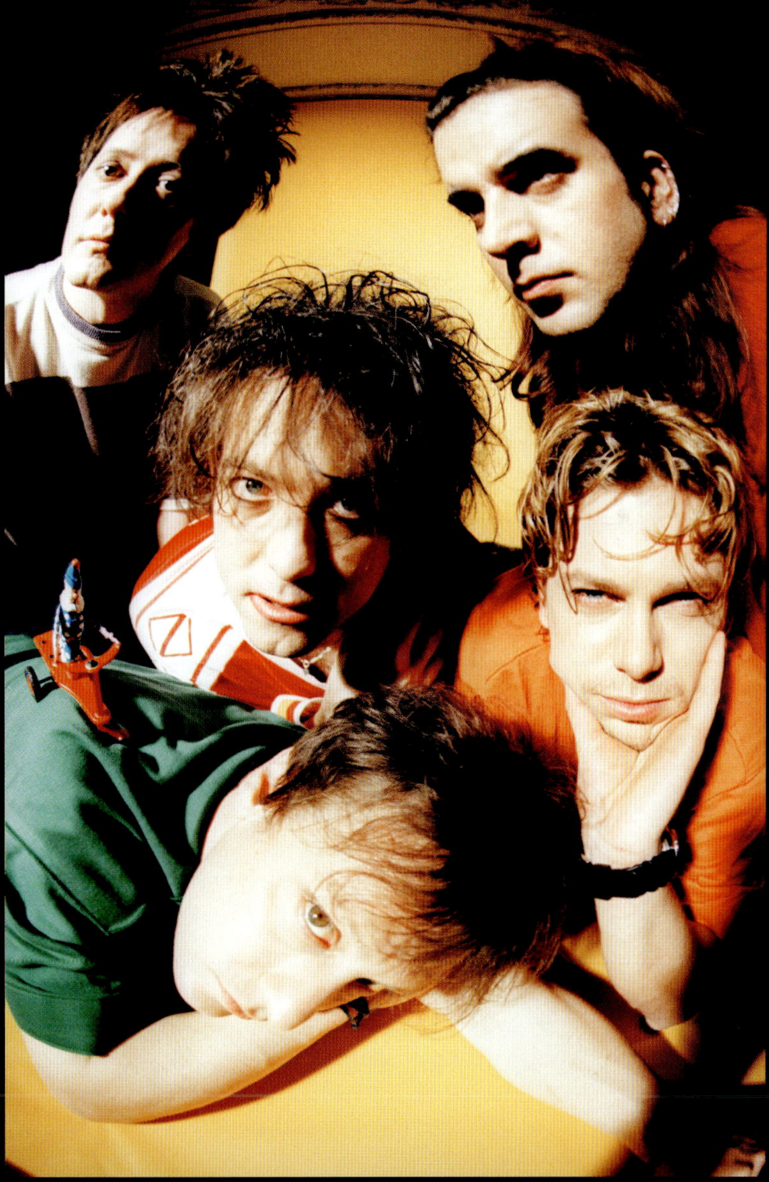

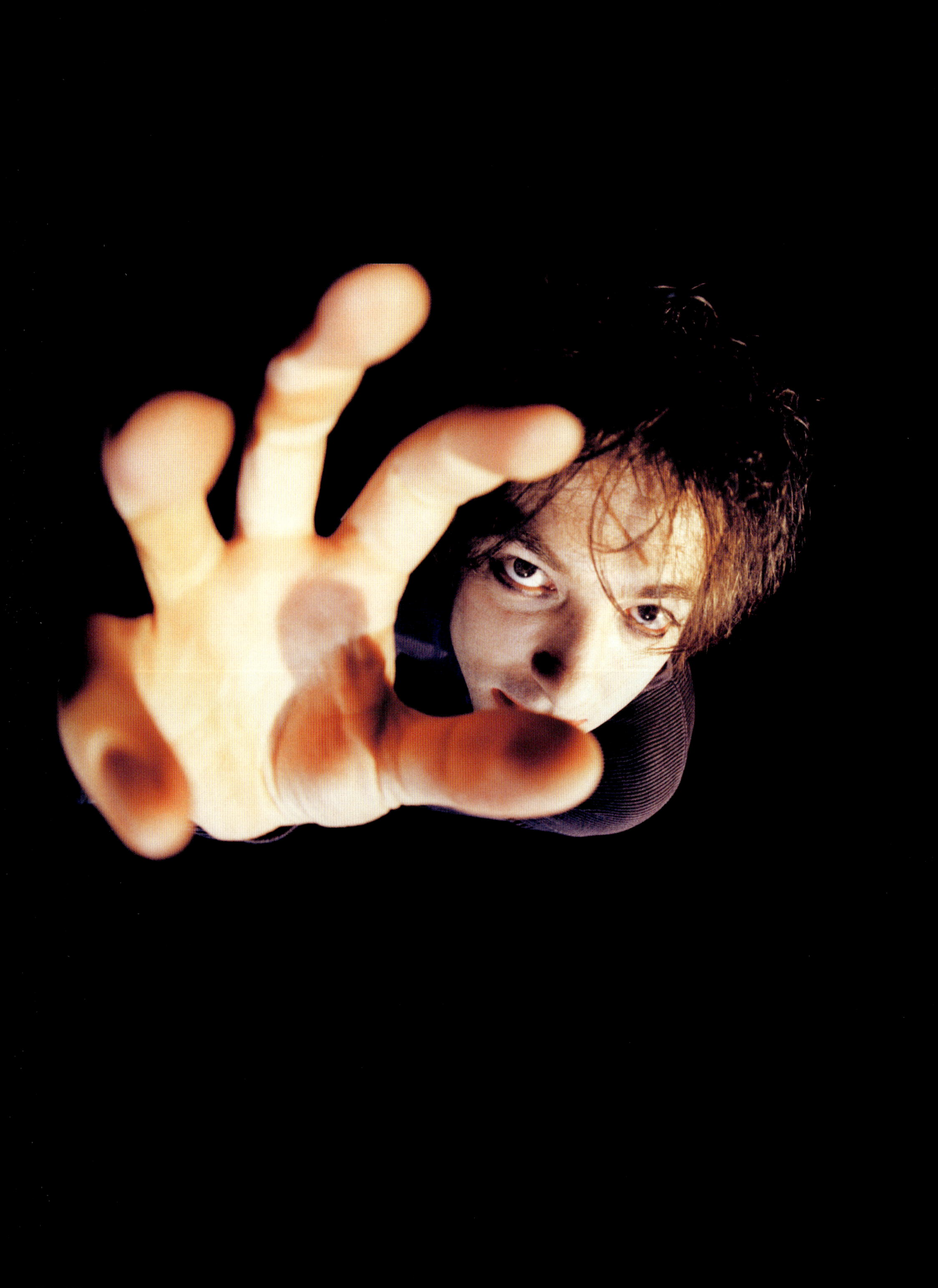

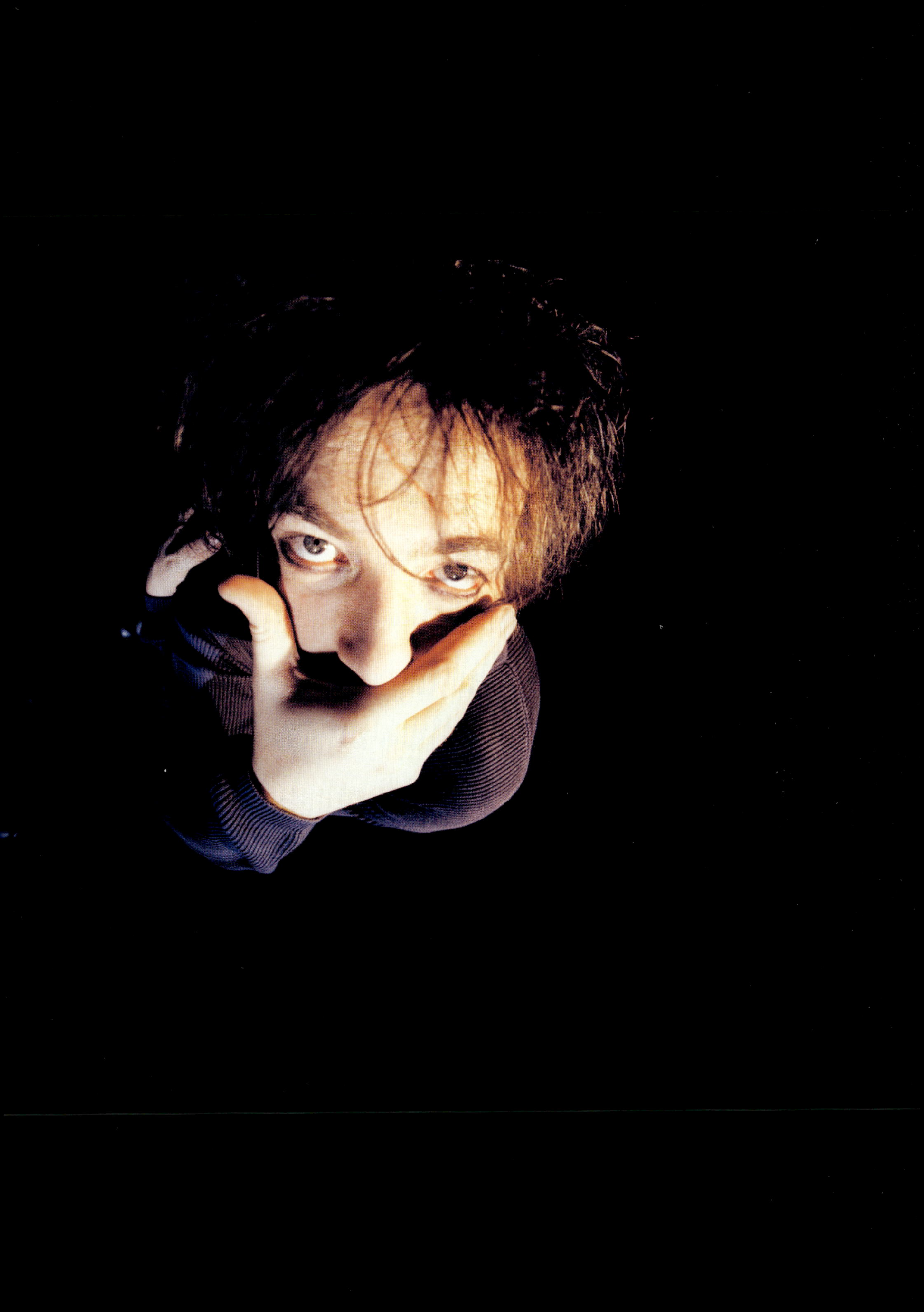

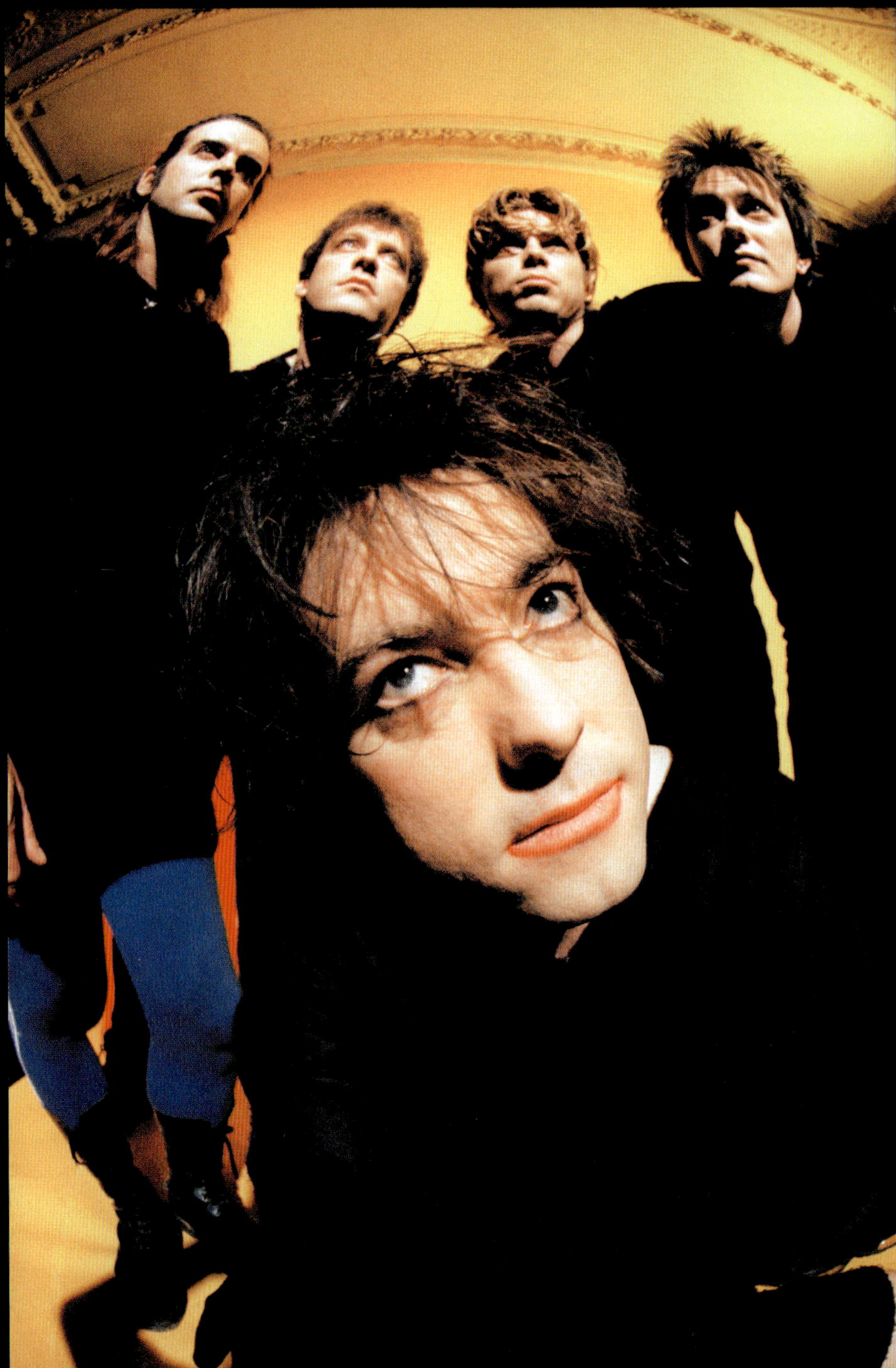

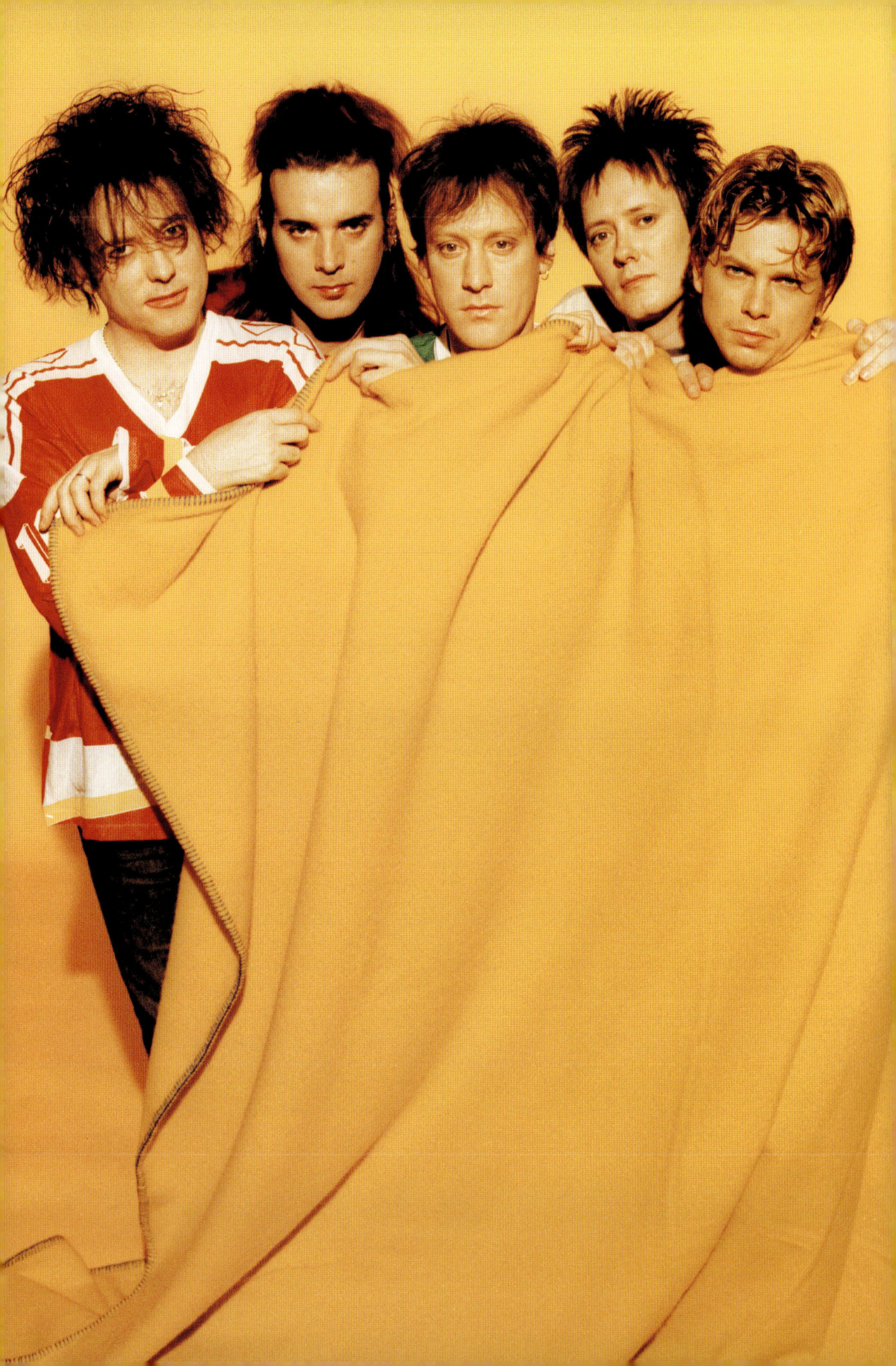

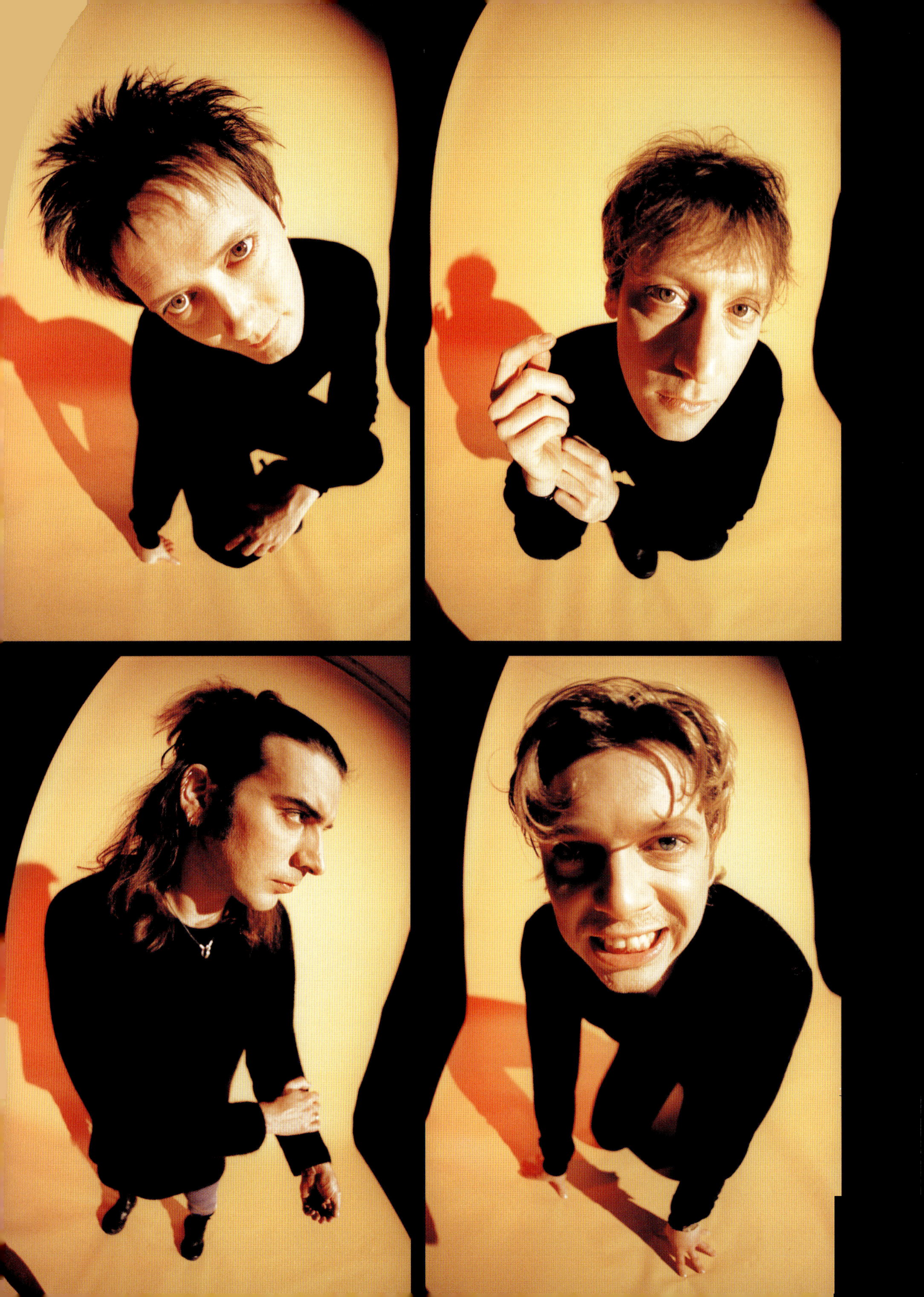

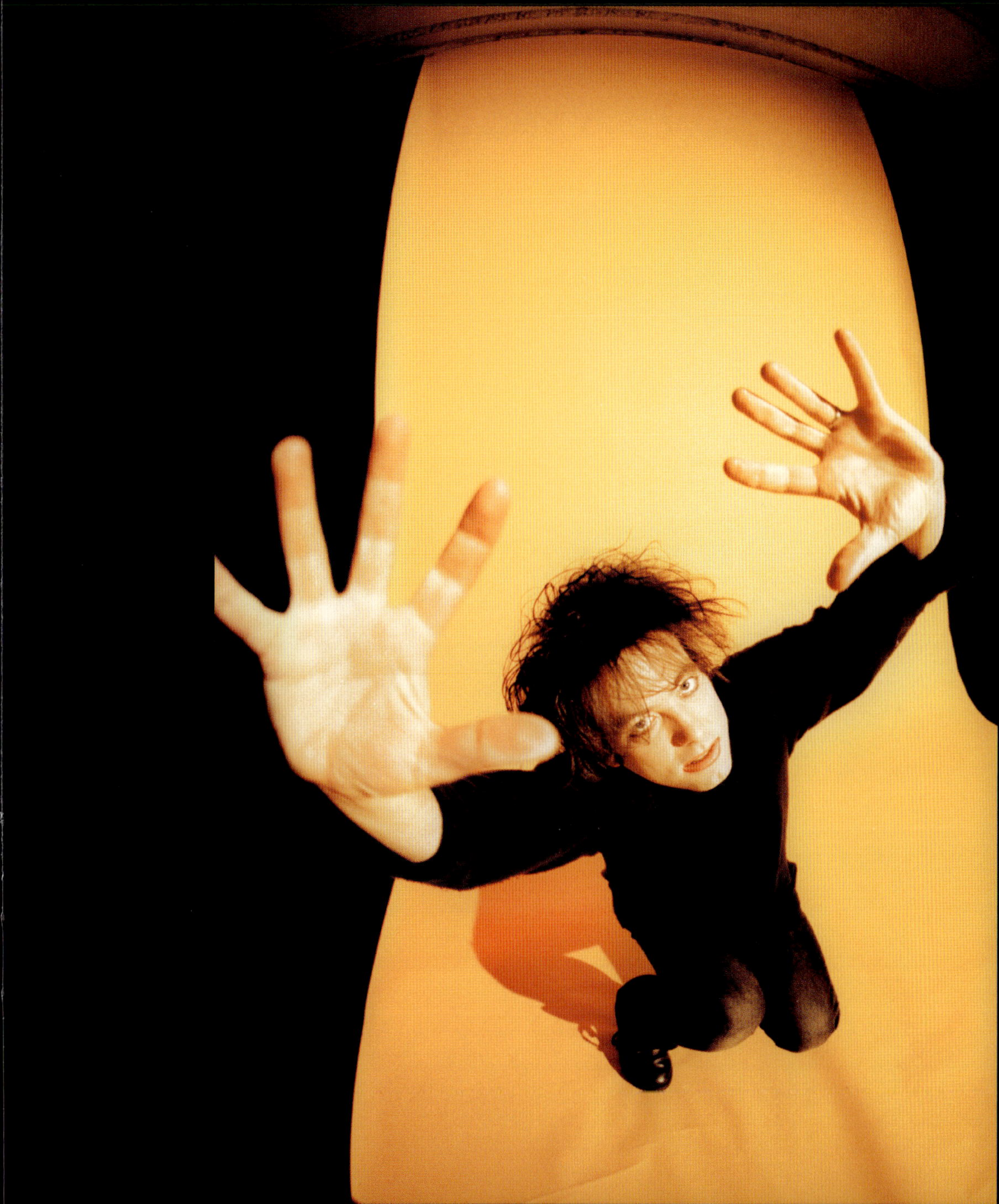

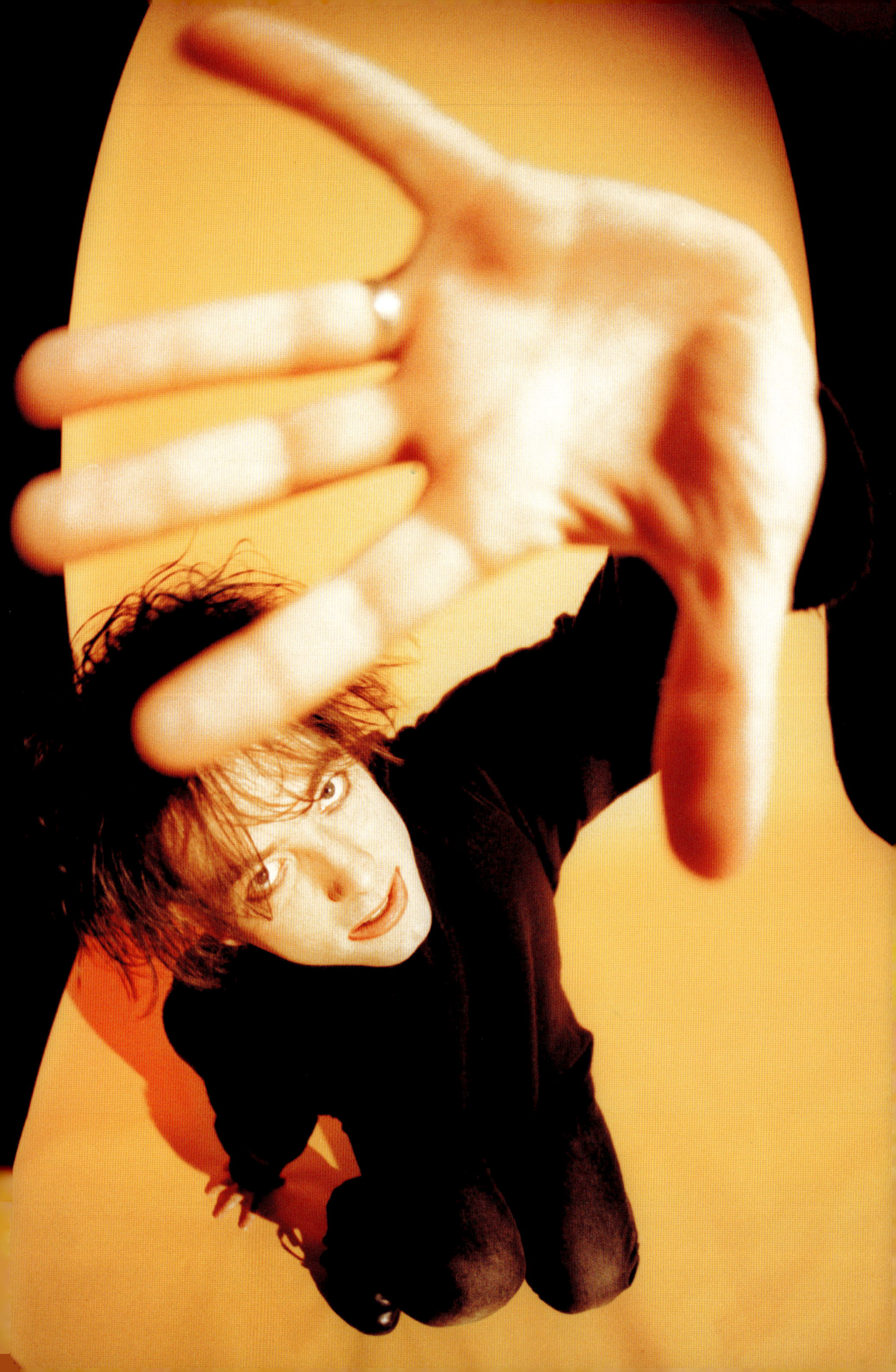

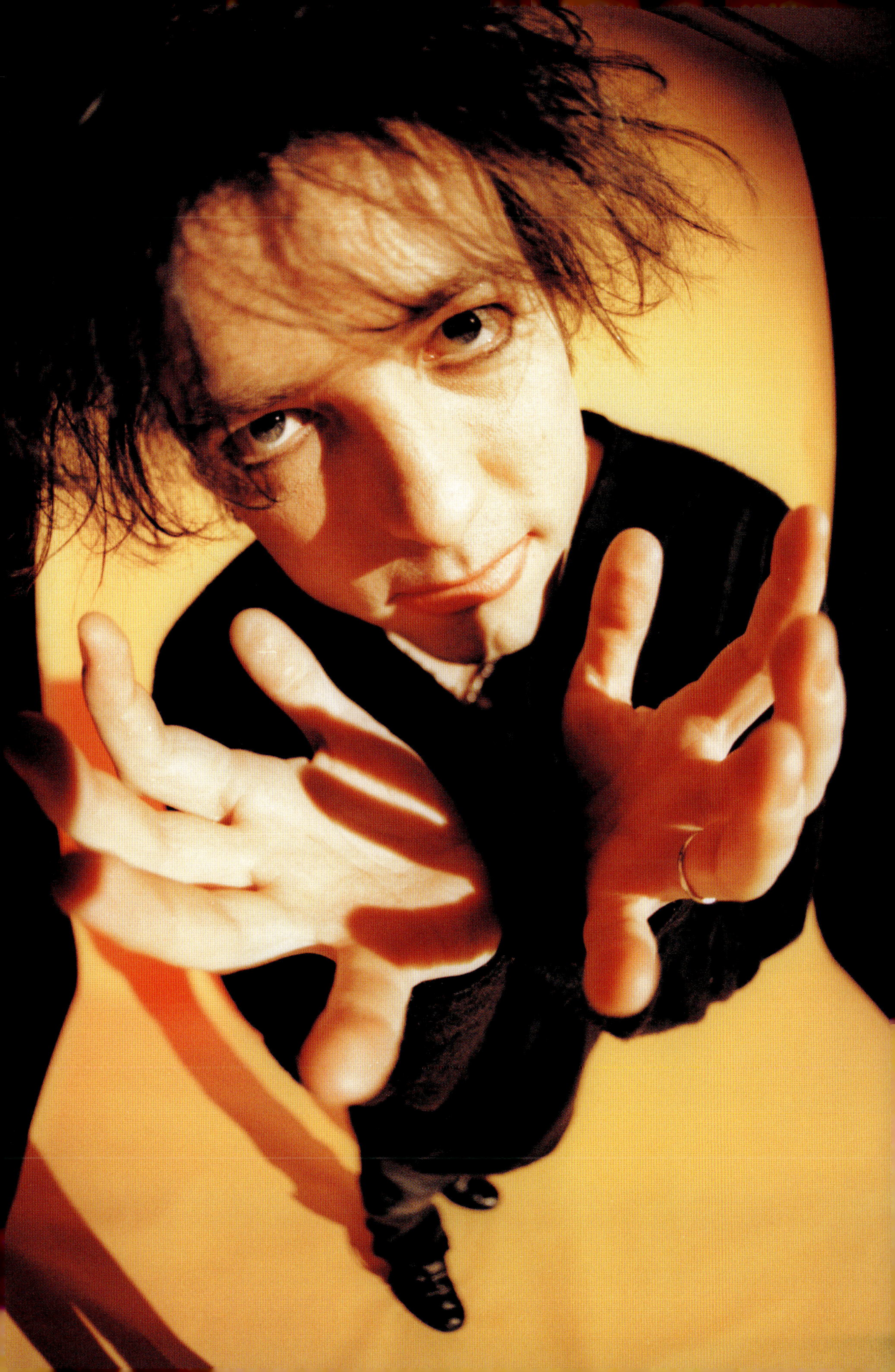

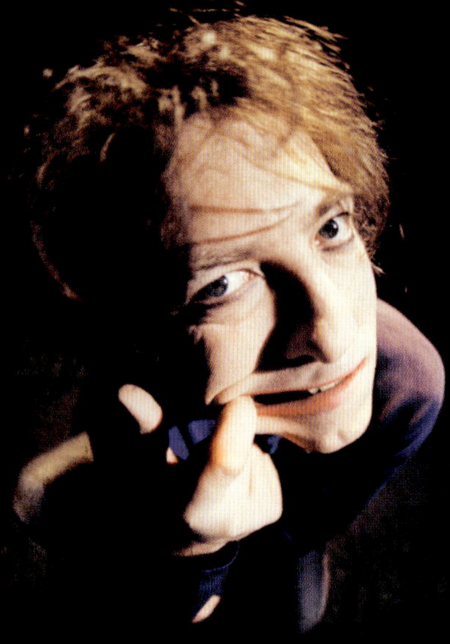
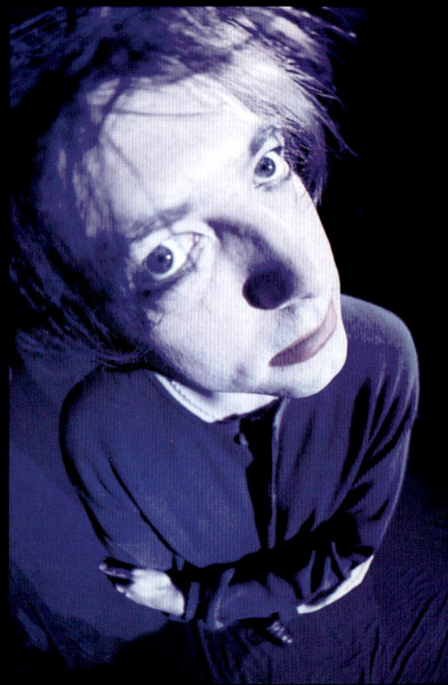
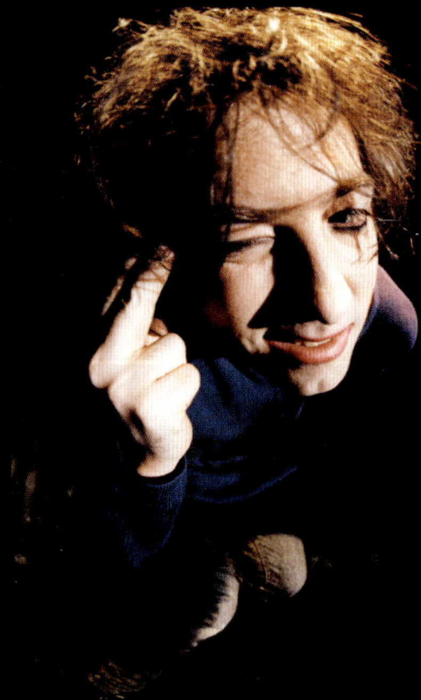
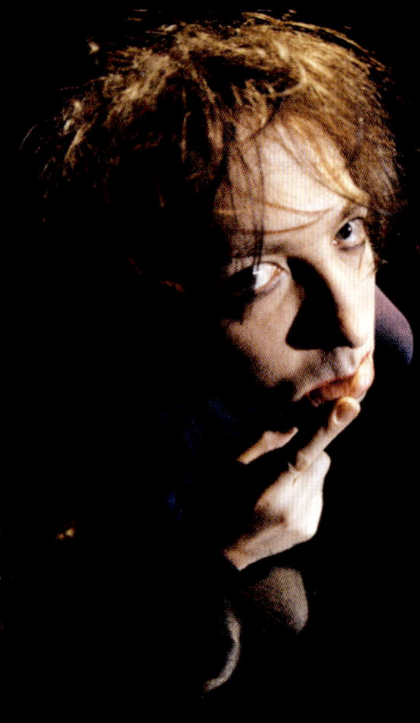
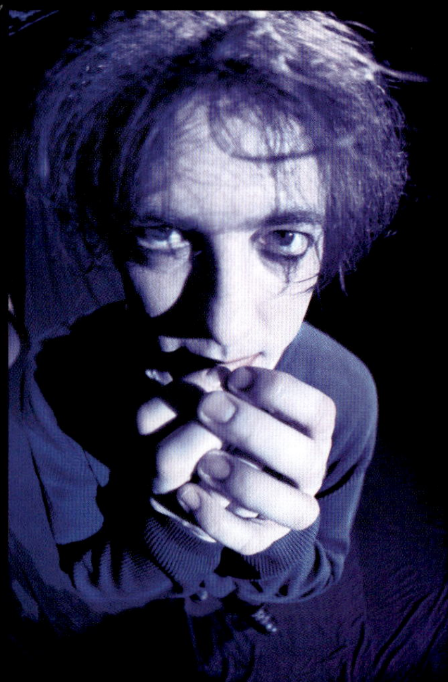

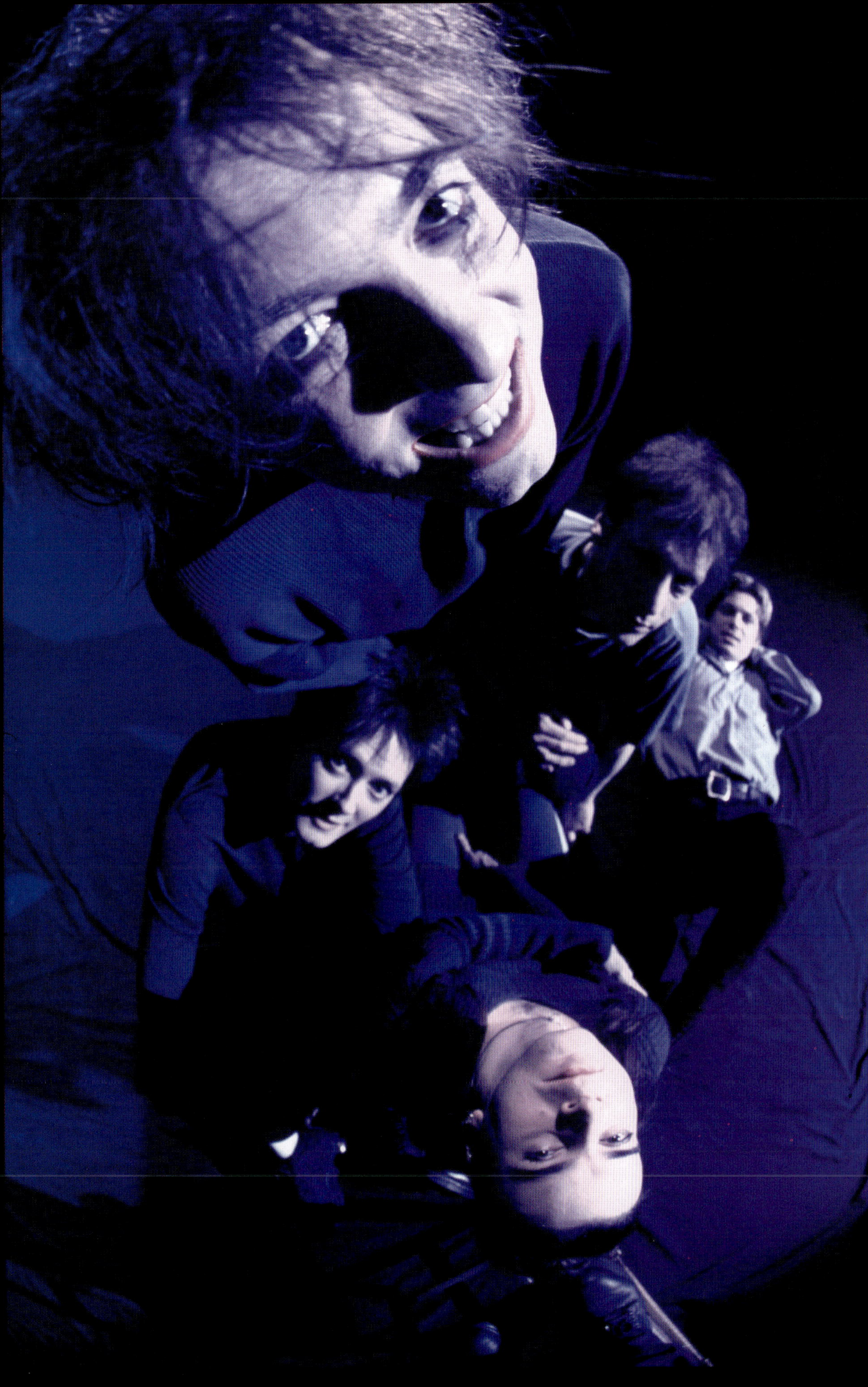

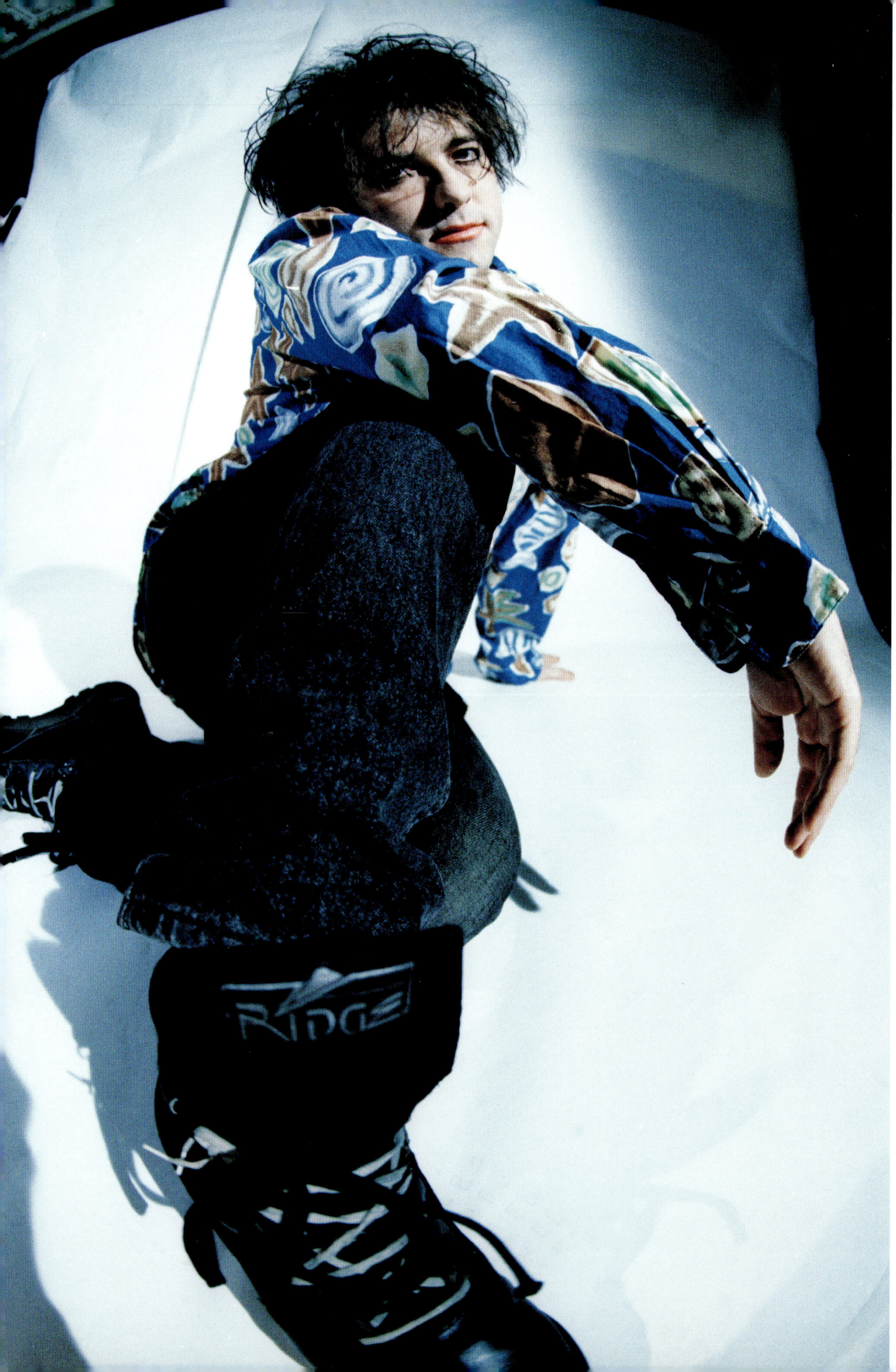

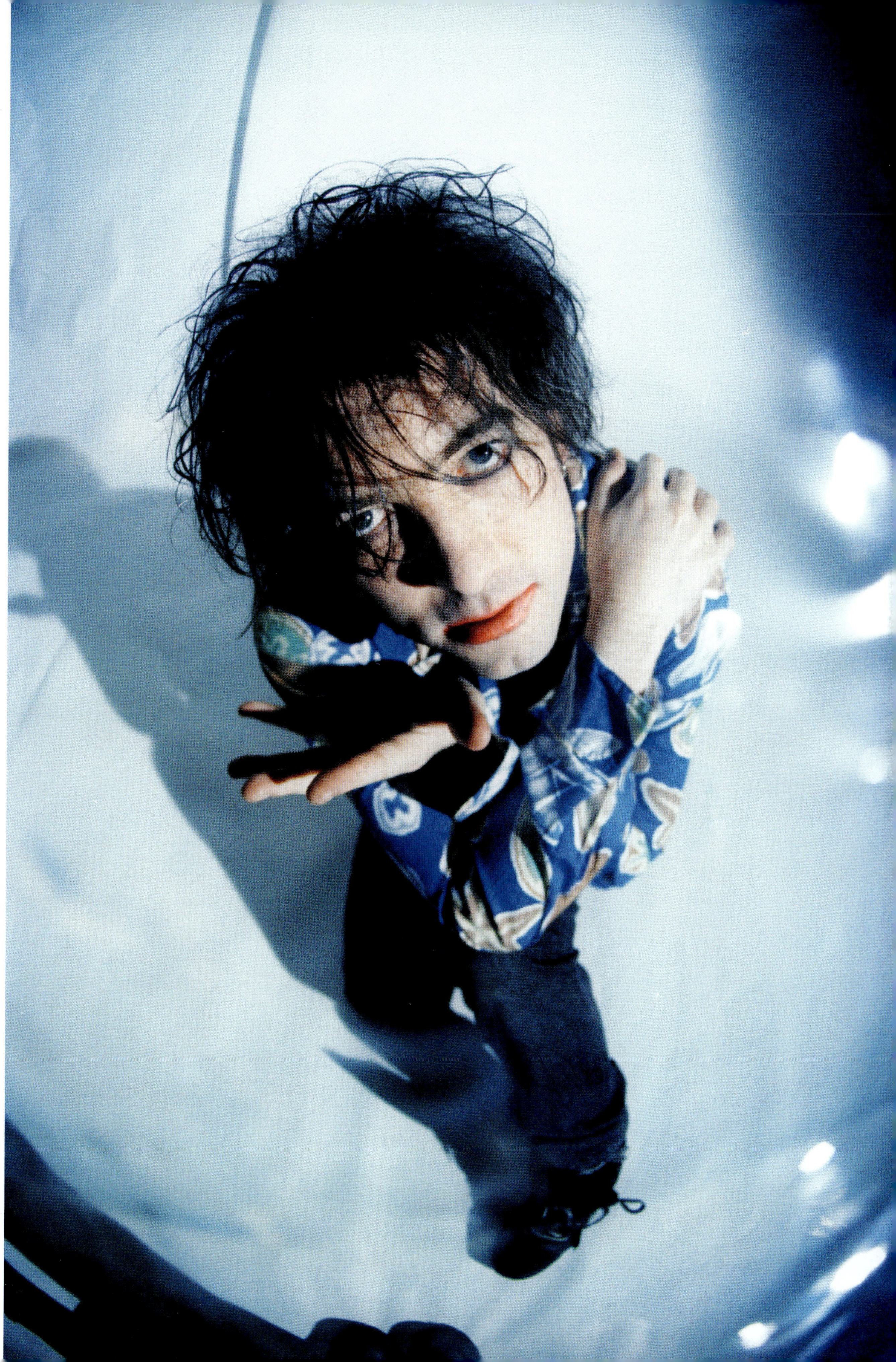

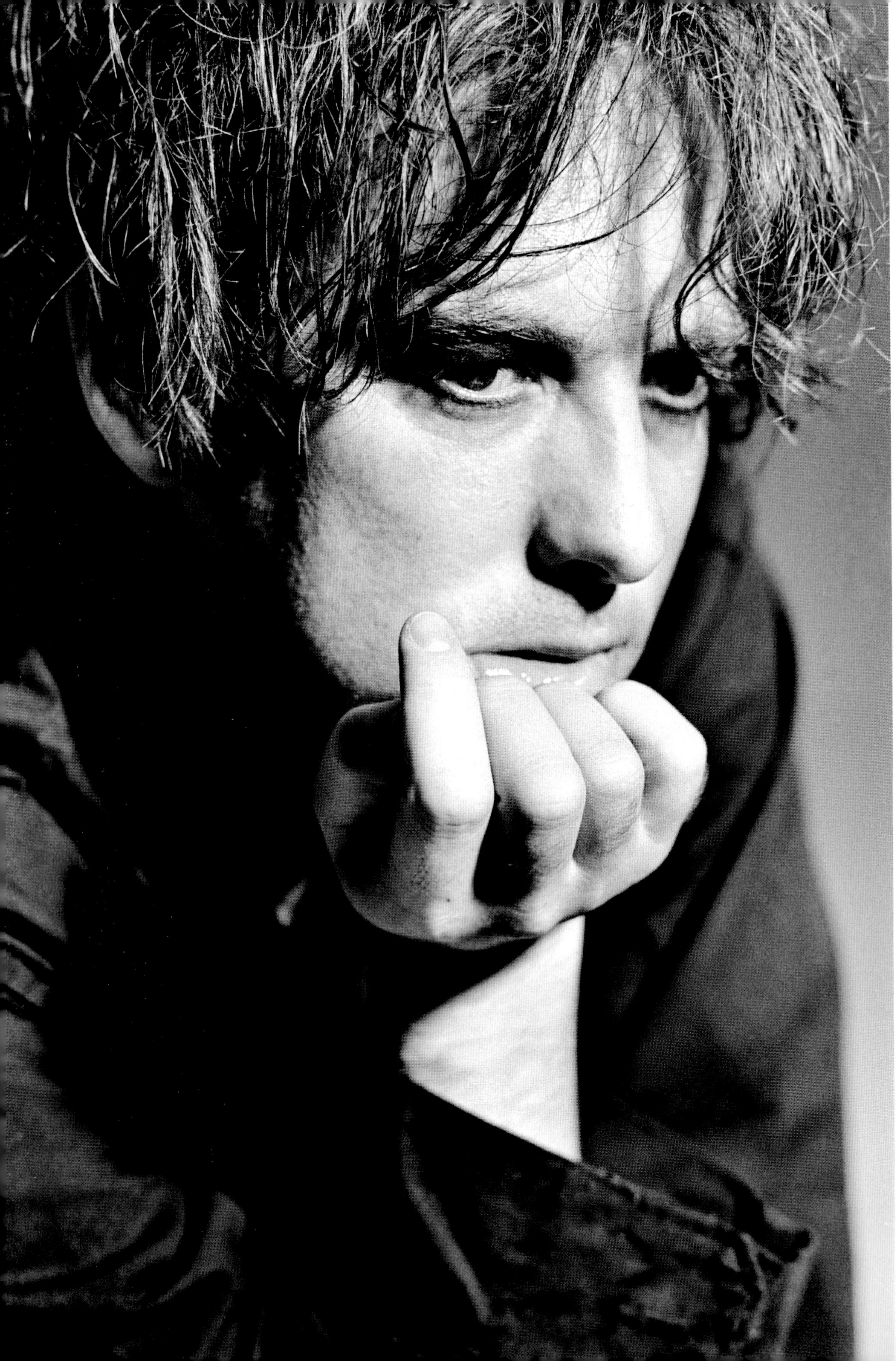

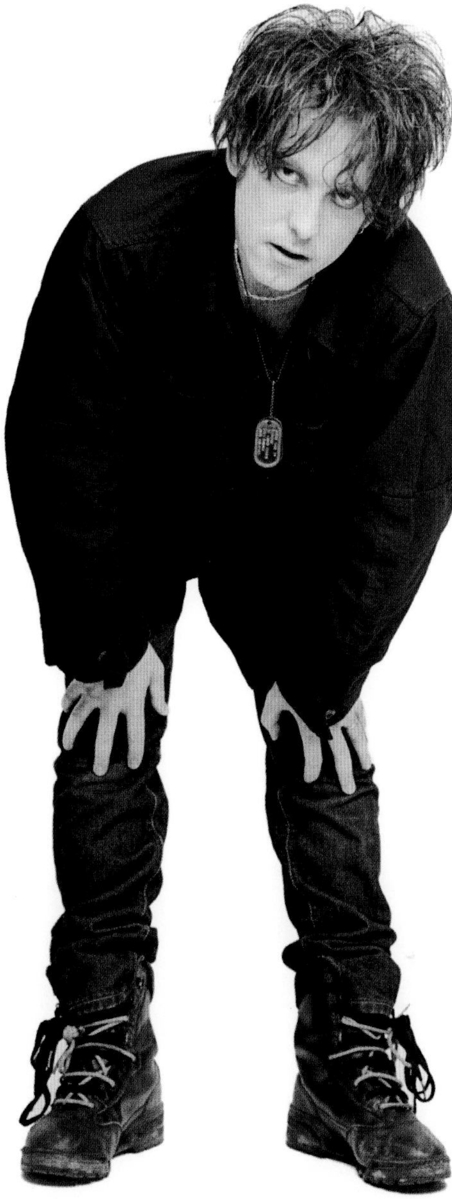

FULHAM STUDIO

[p.218 to 239]

1997

ROBERT: THIS SESSION WAS TO PROMOTE THE 'WRONG NUMBER' SINGLE AND *GALORE* SINGLES COLLECTION ALBUM 1997… LIME GREEN, LIME GREEN AND TANGERINE…

Paul: This was a solo session; nothing against the band, but always a lot easier! We both had lots of inspiration. Towards the end of the session, I managed to get Robert to career around the studio, which ended up as some of my favourite pictures.

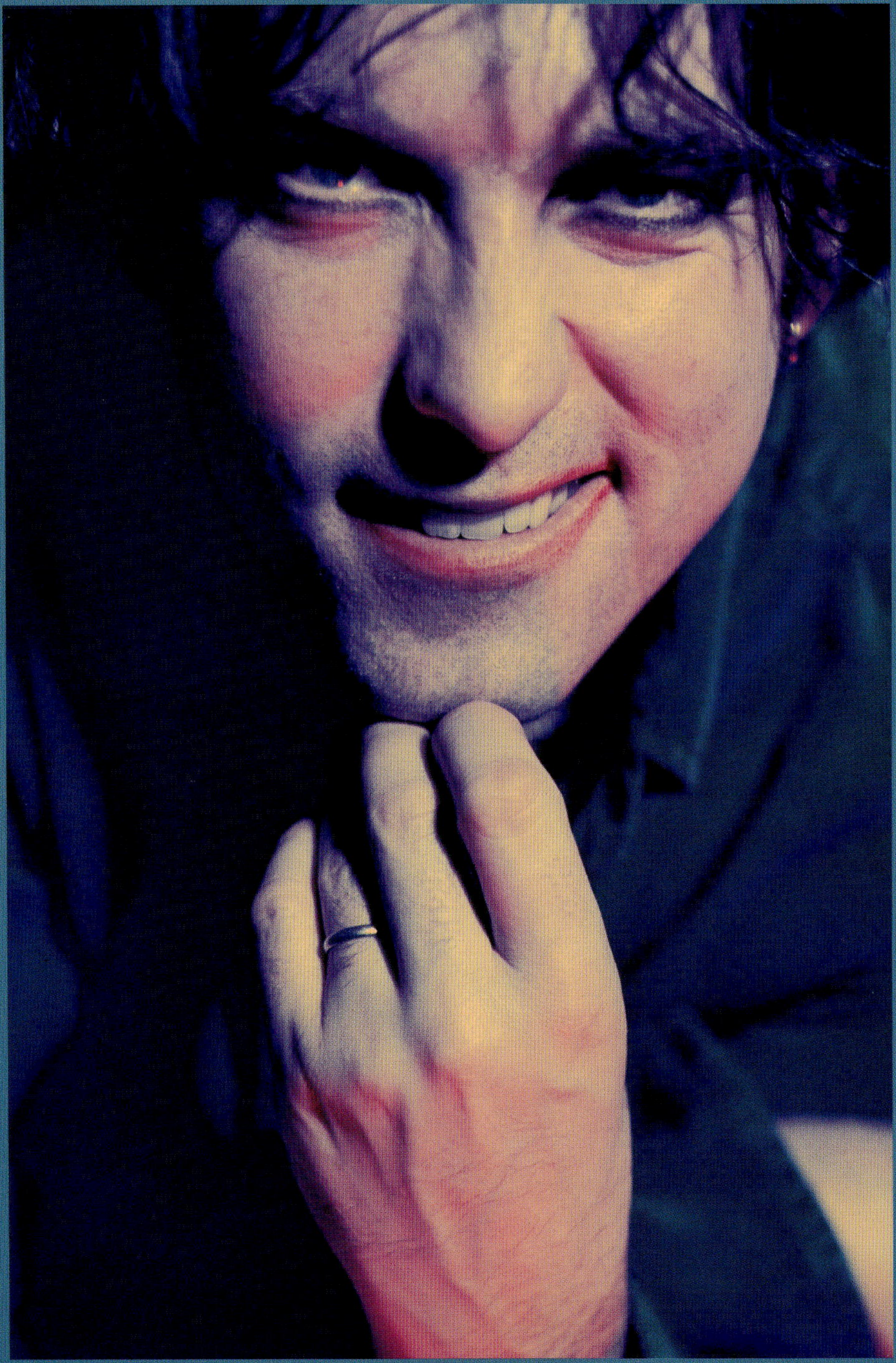

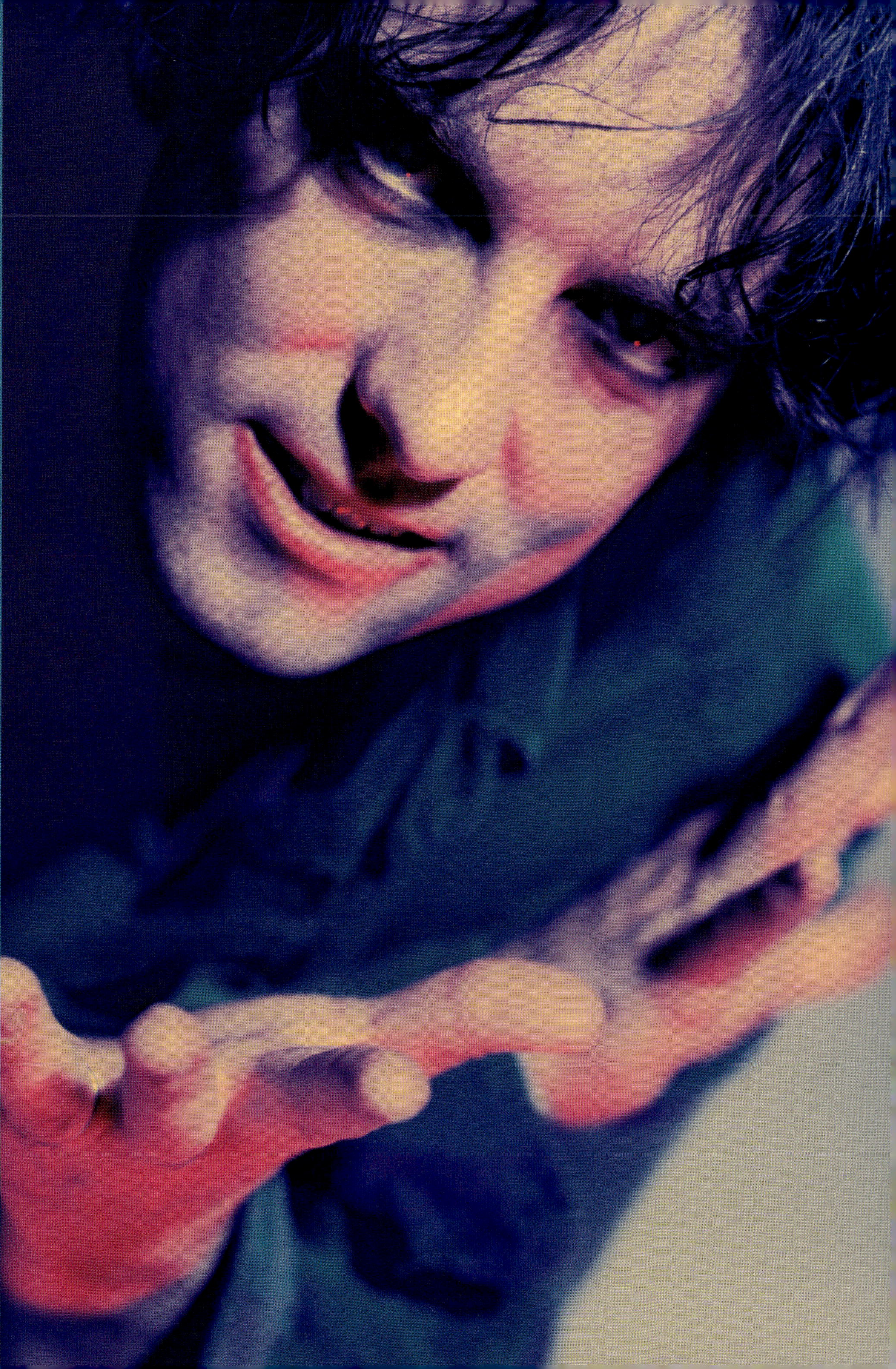

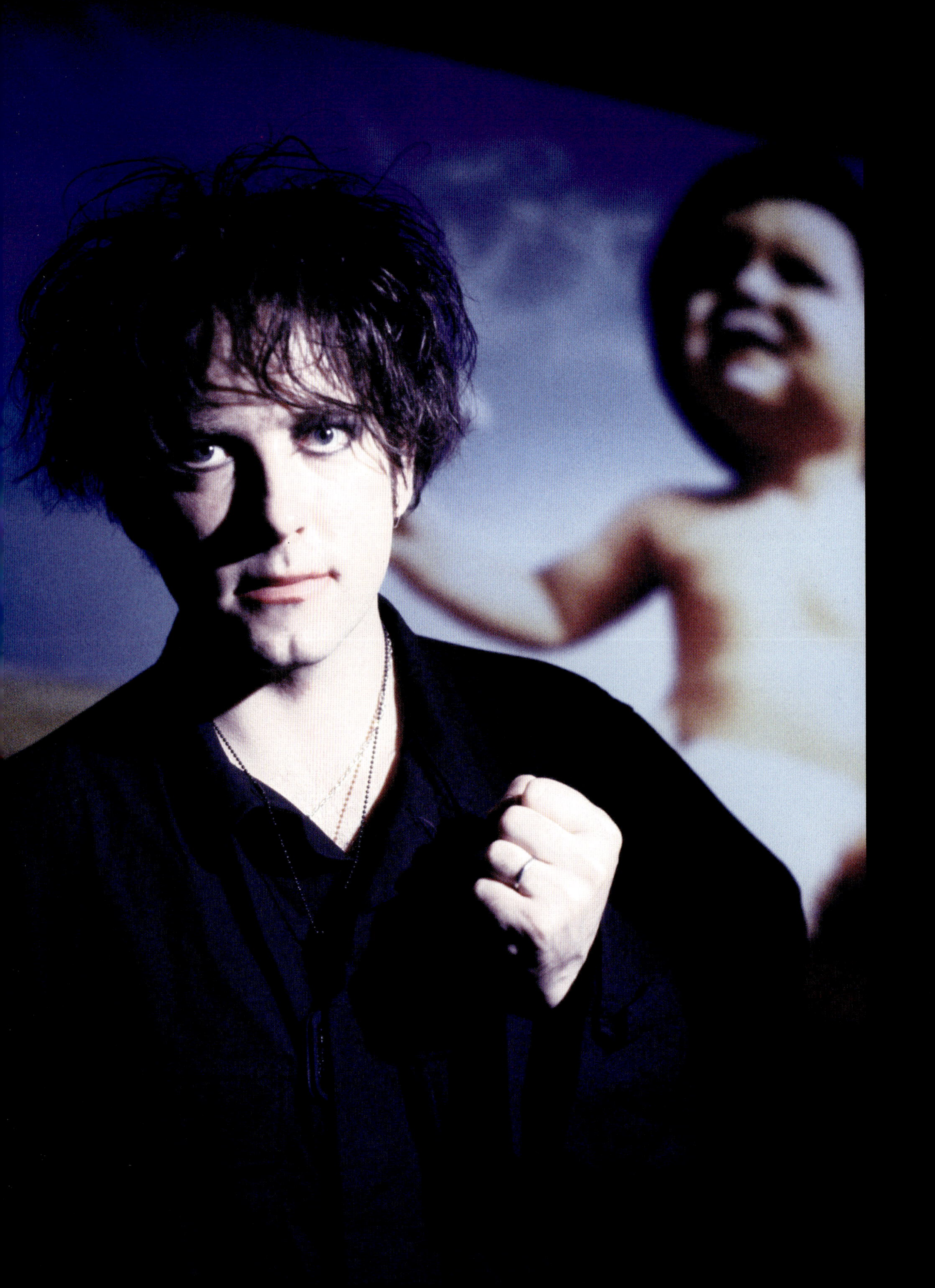

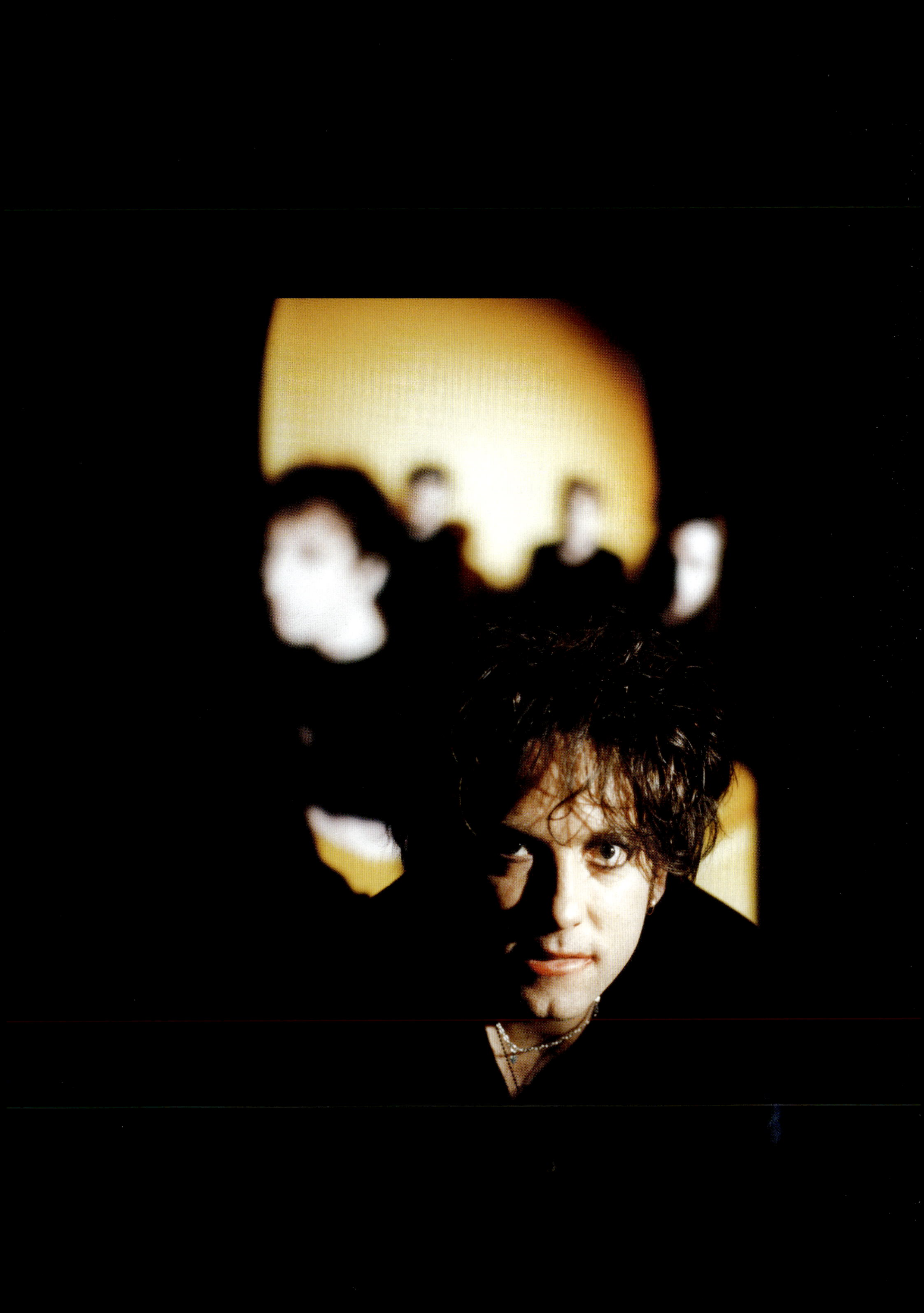

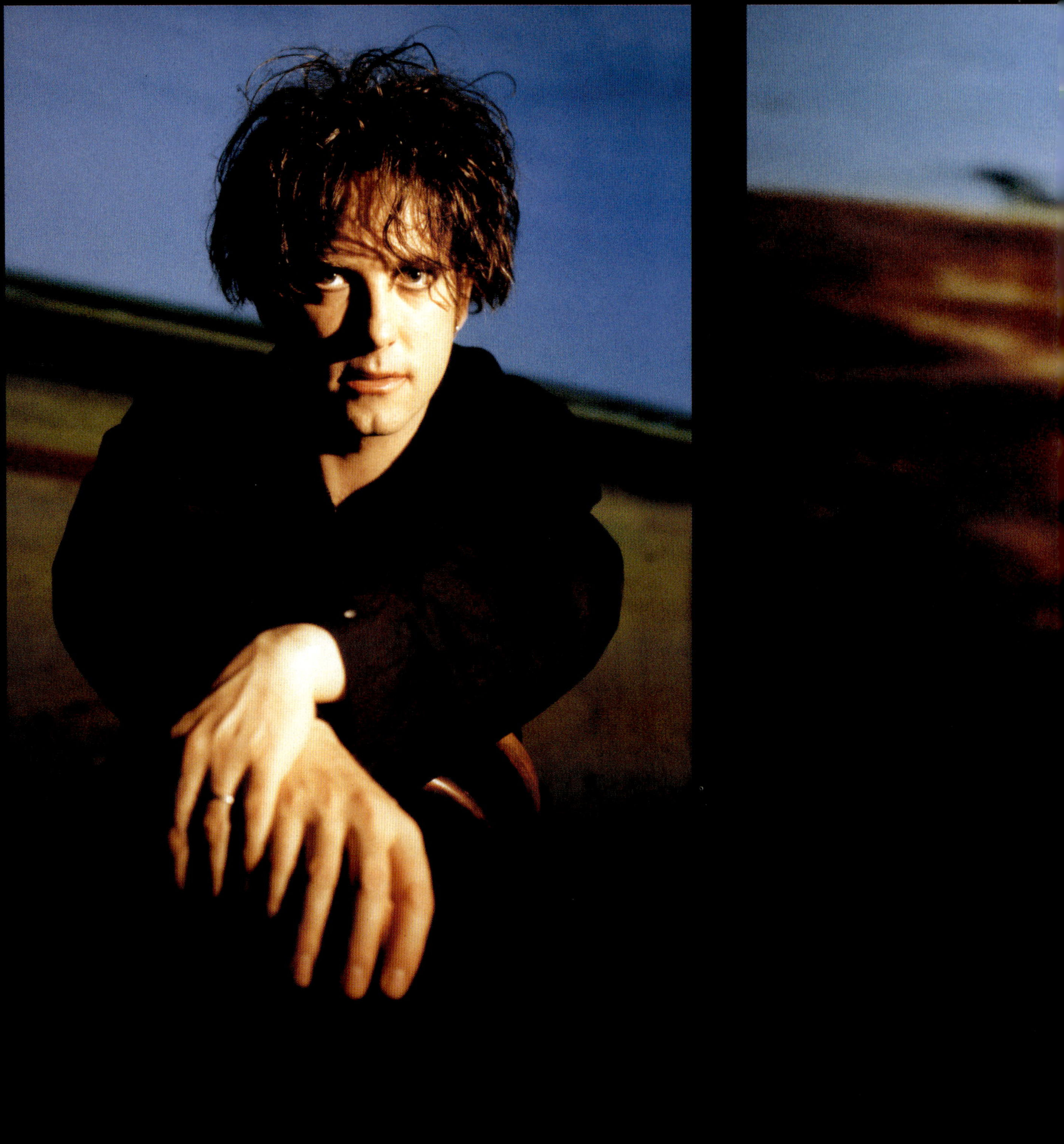

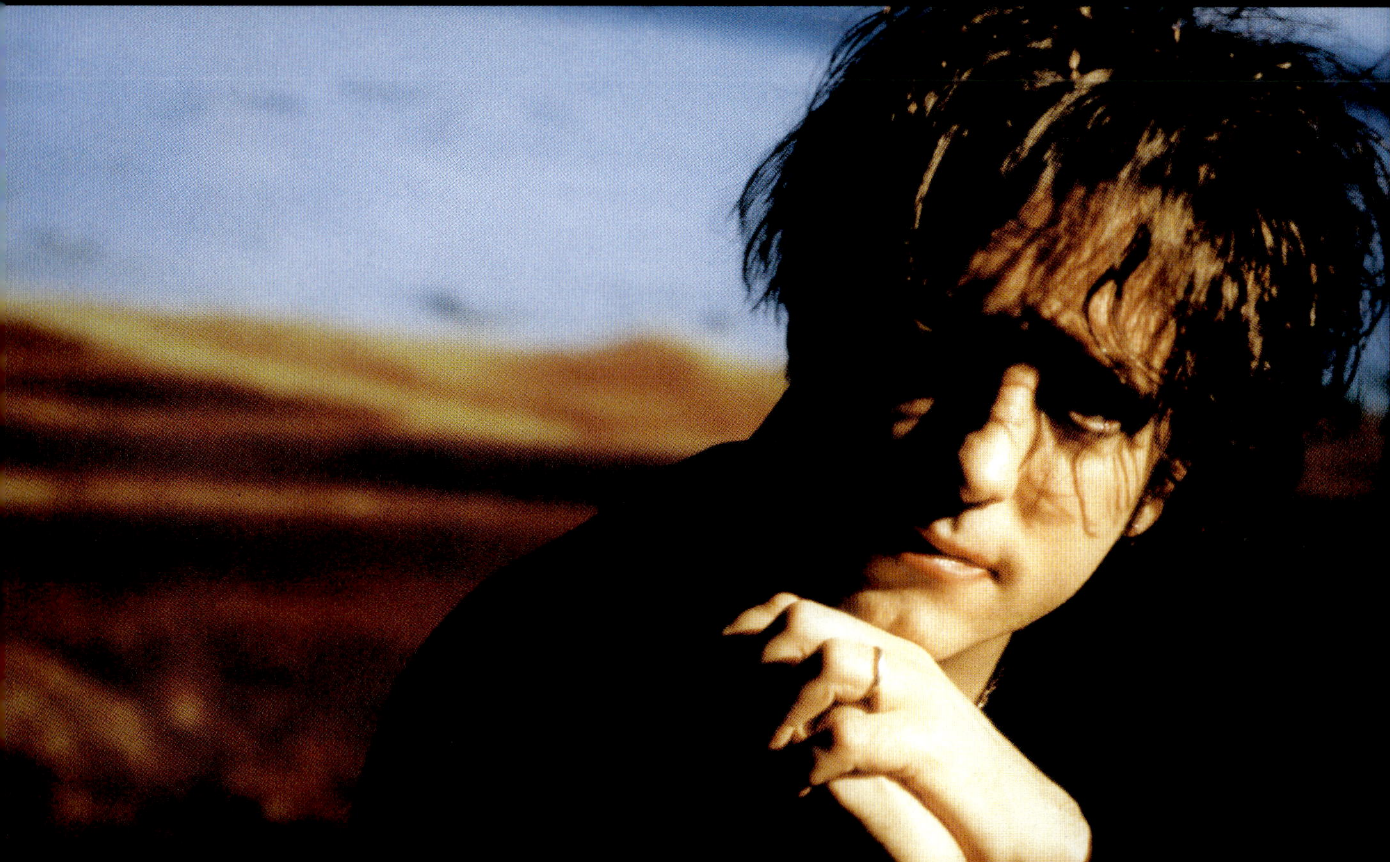

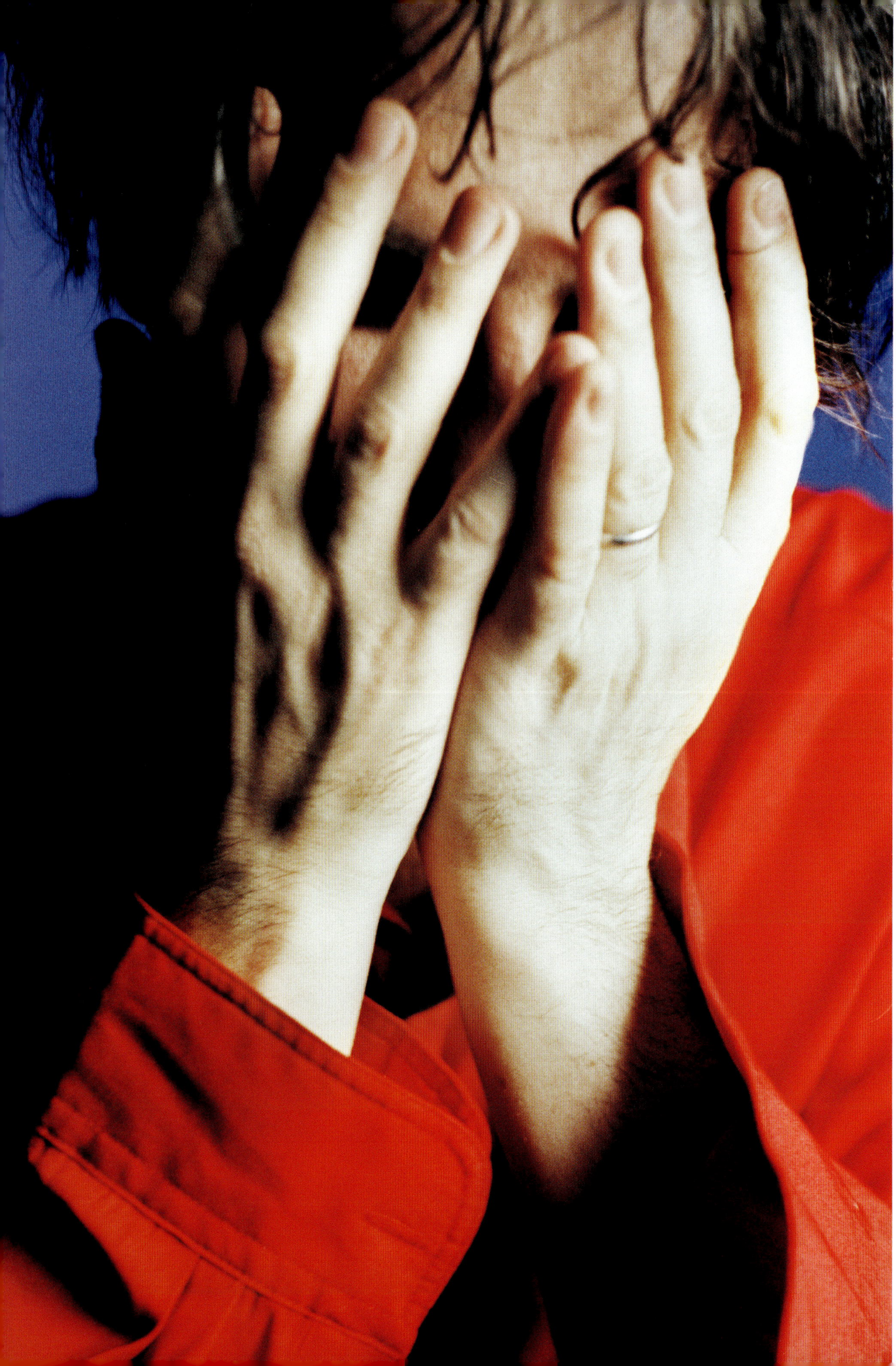

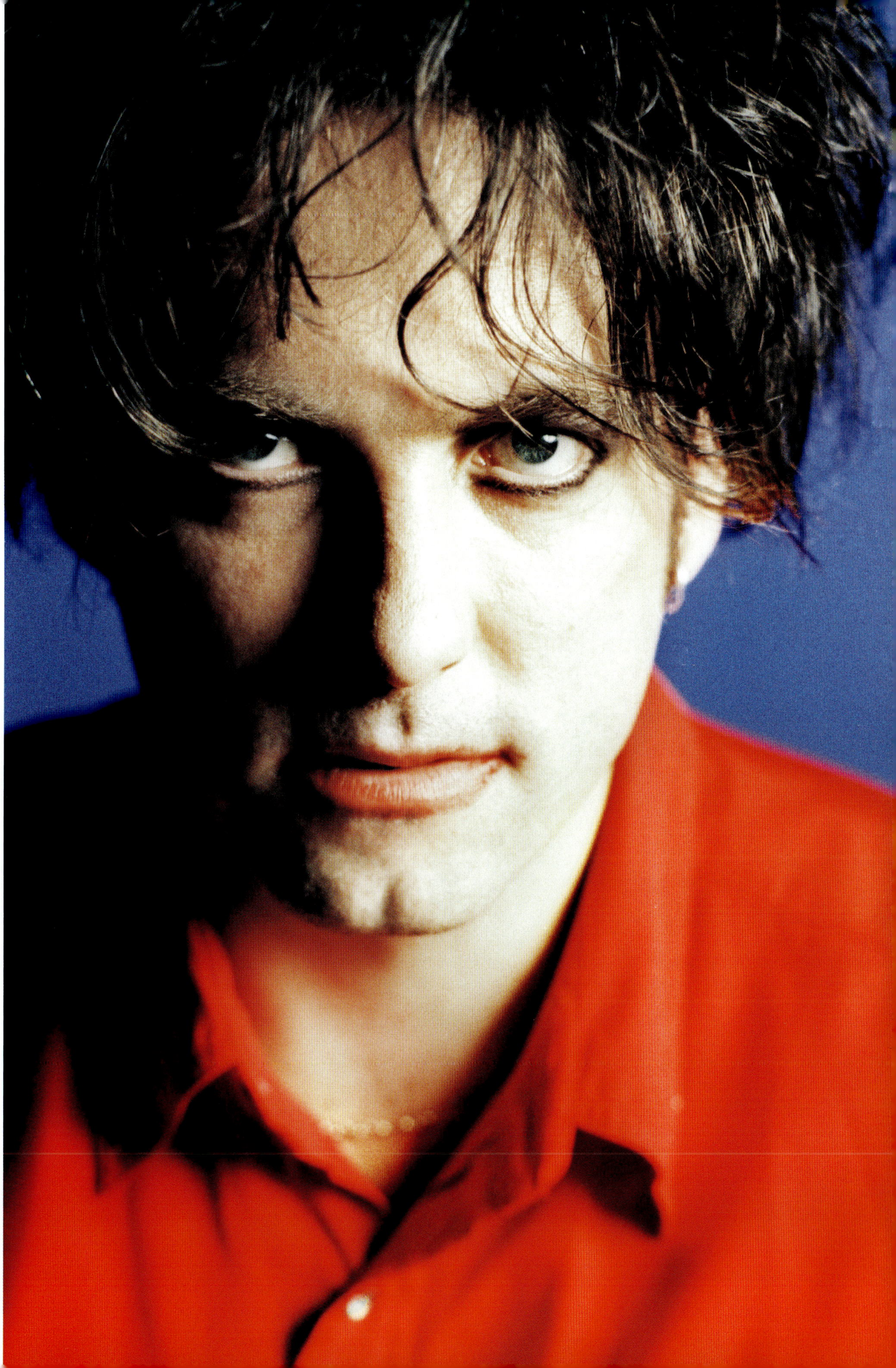

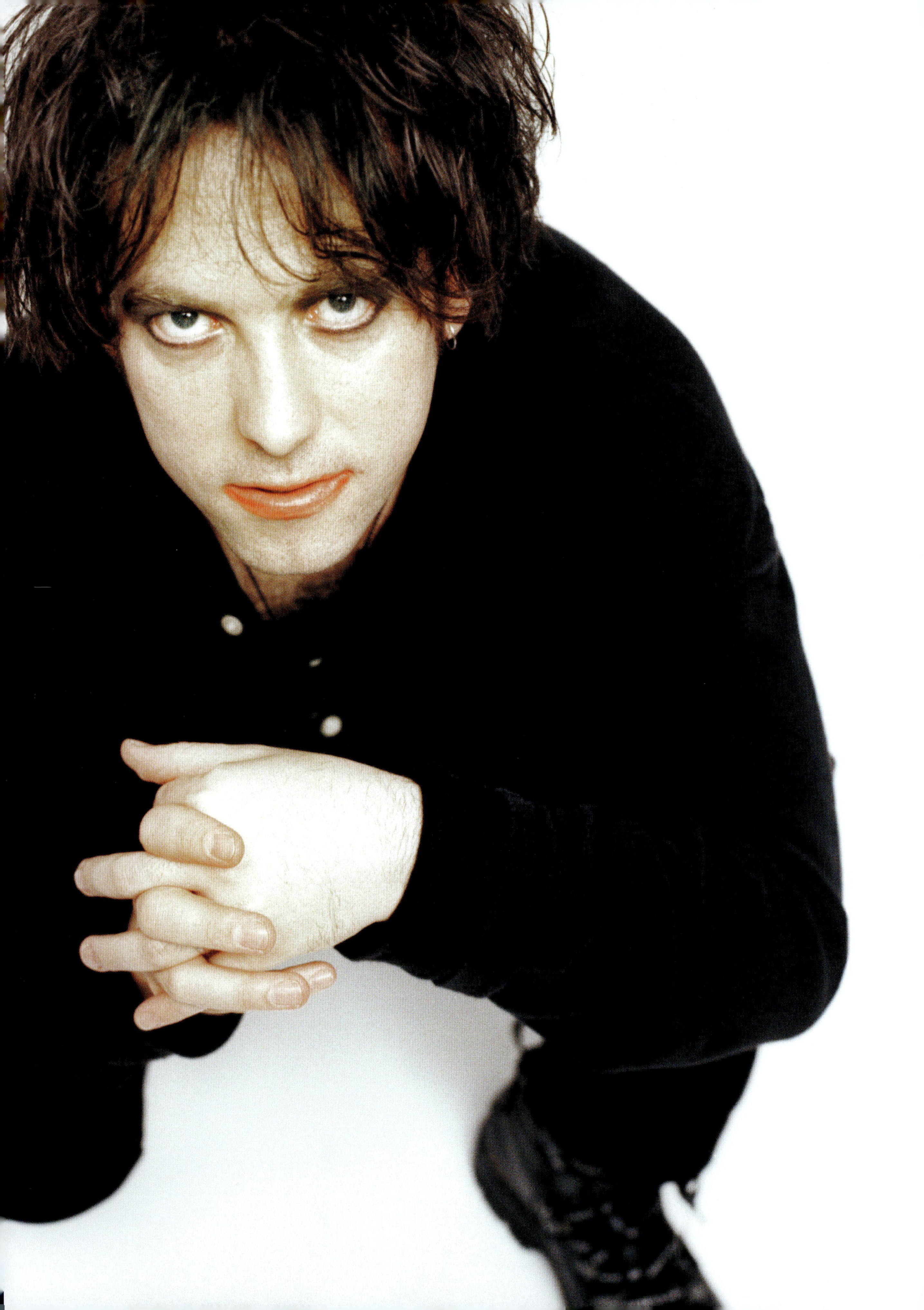

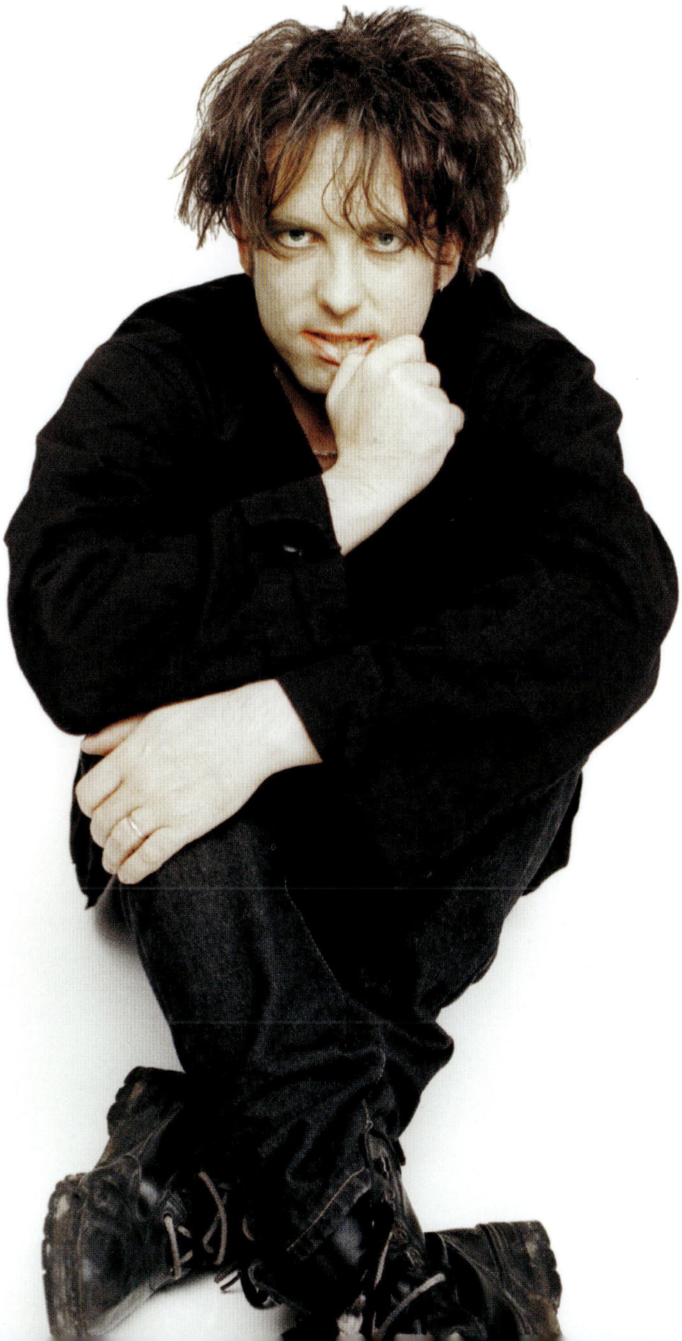

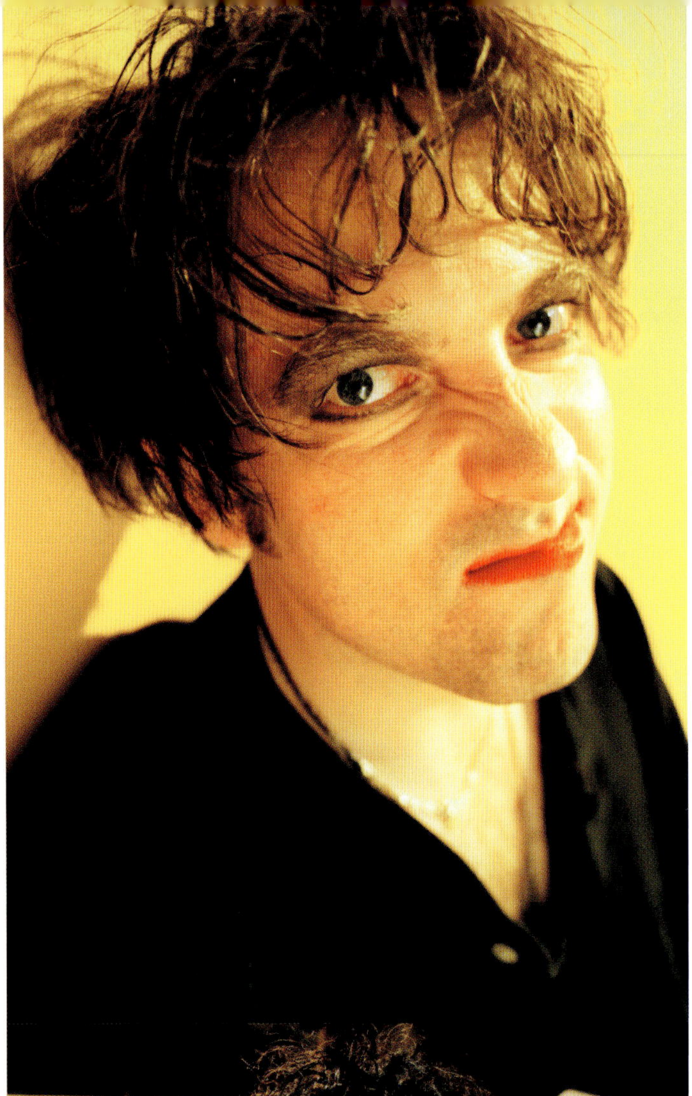

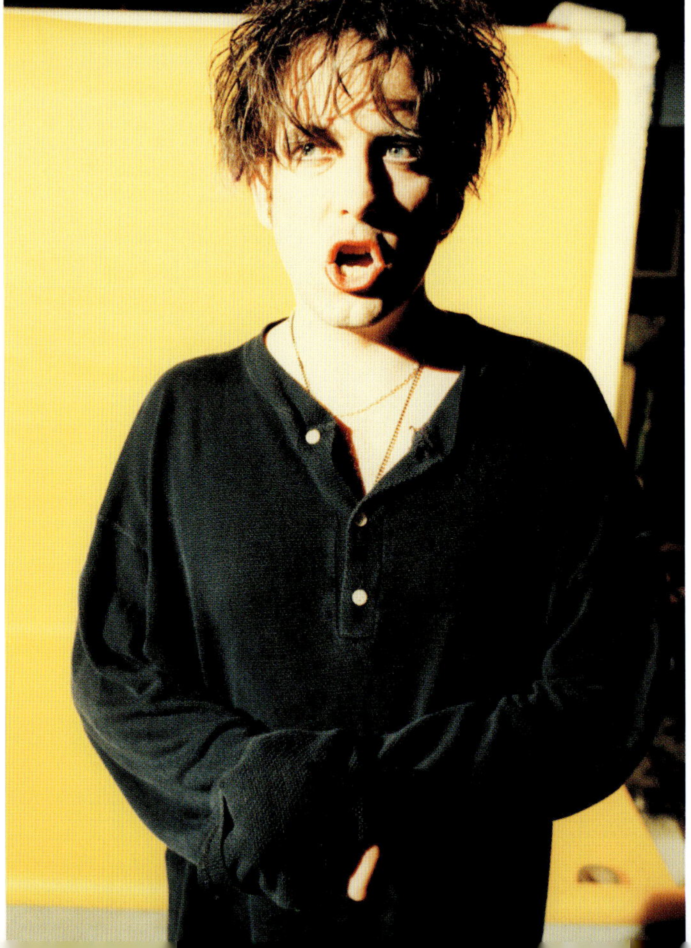

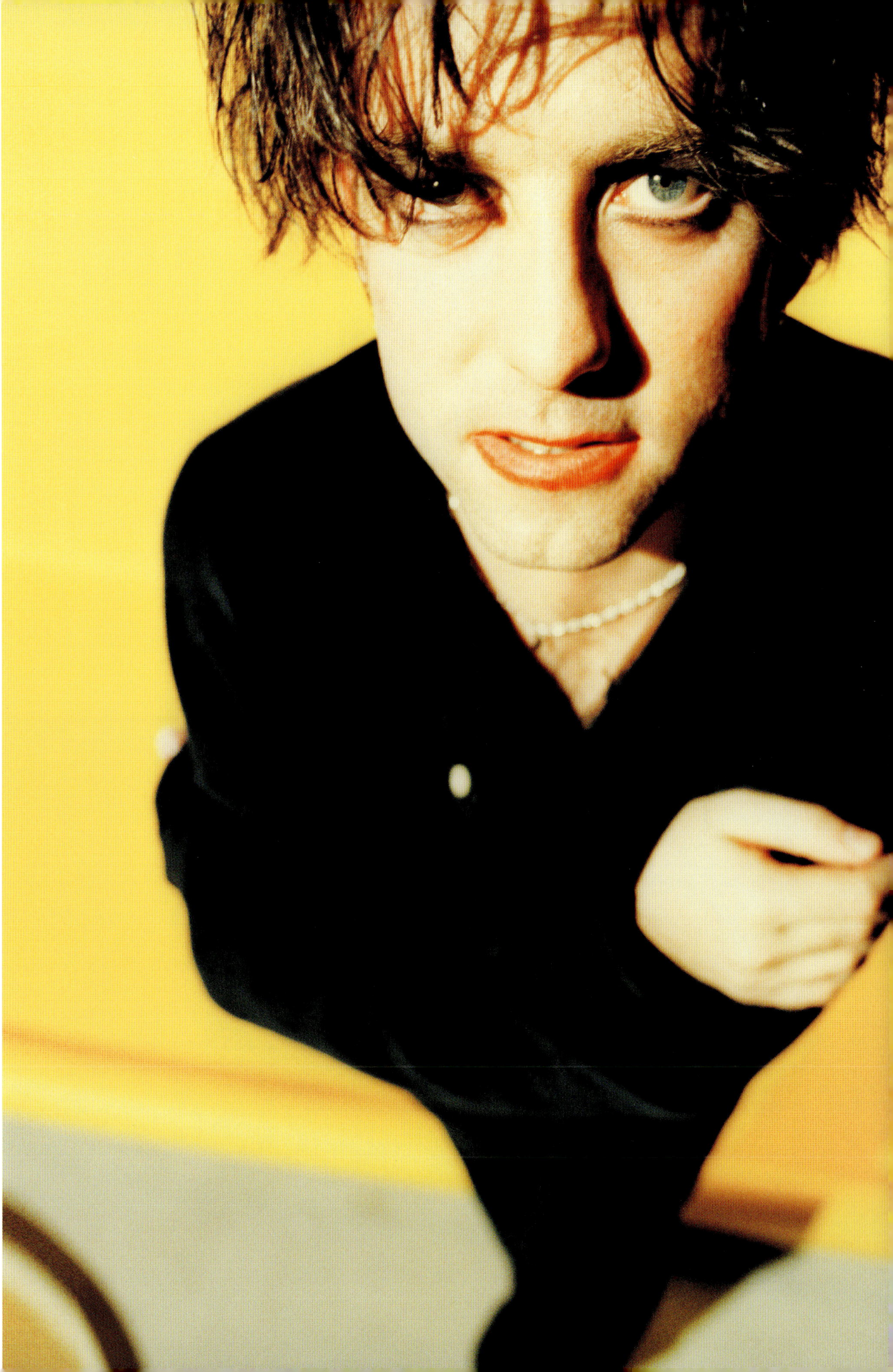

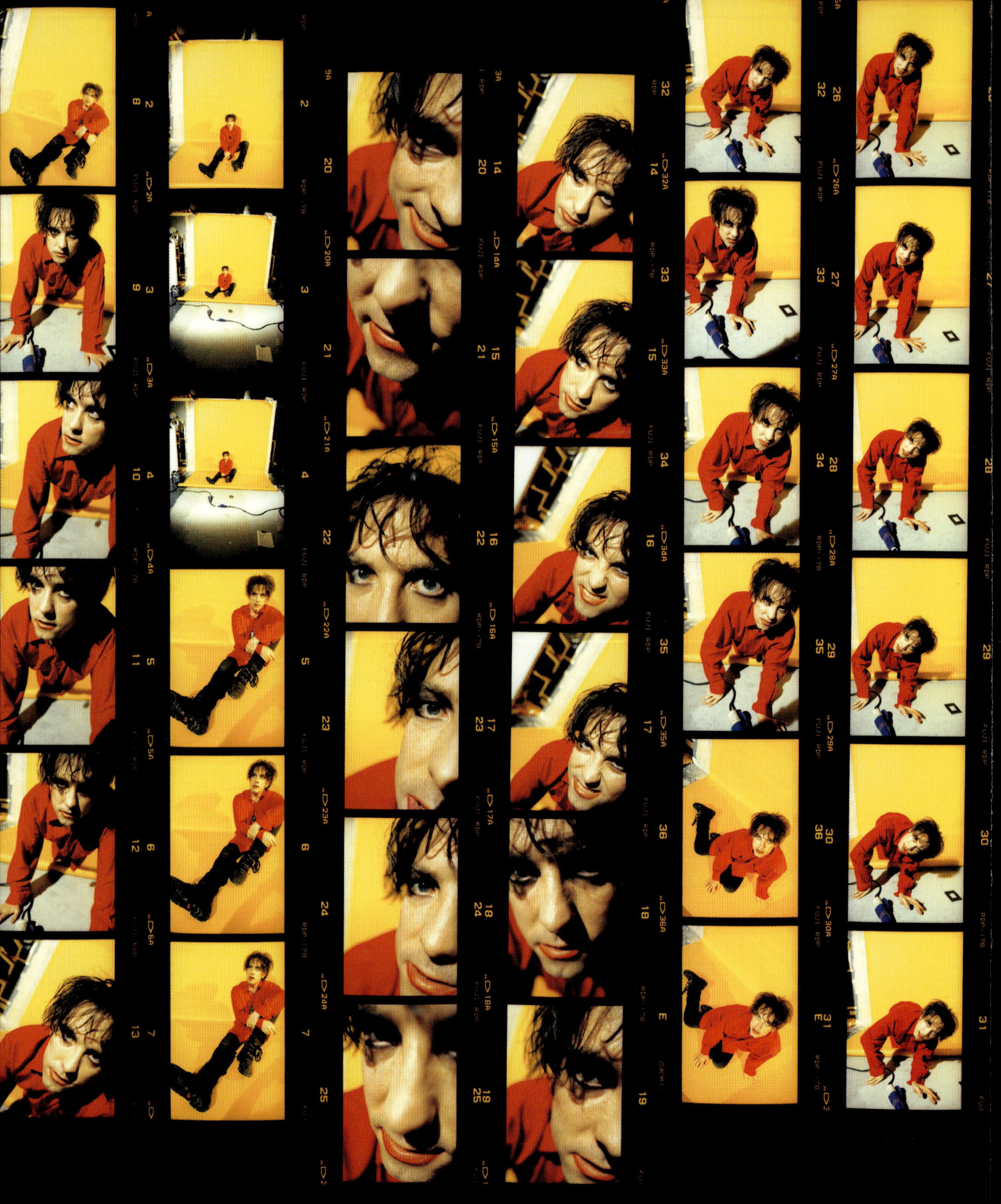

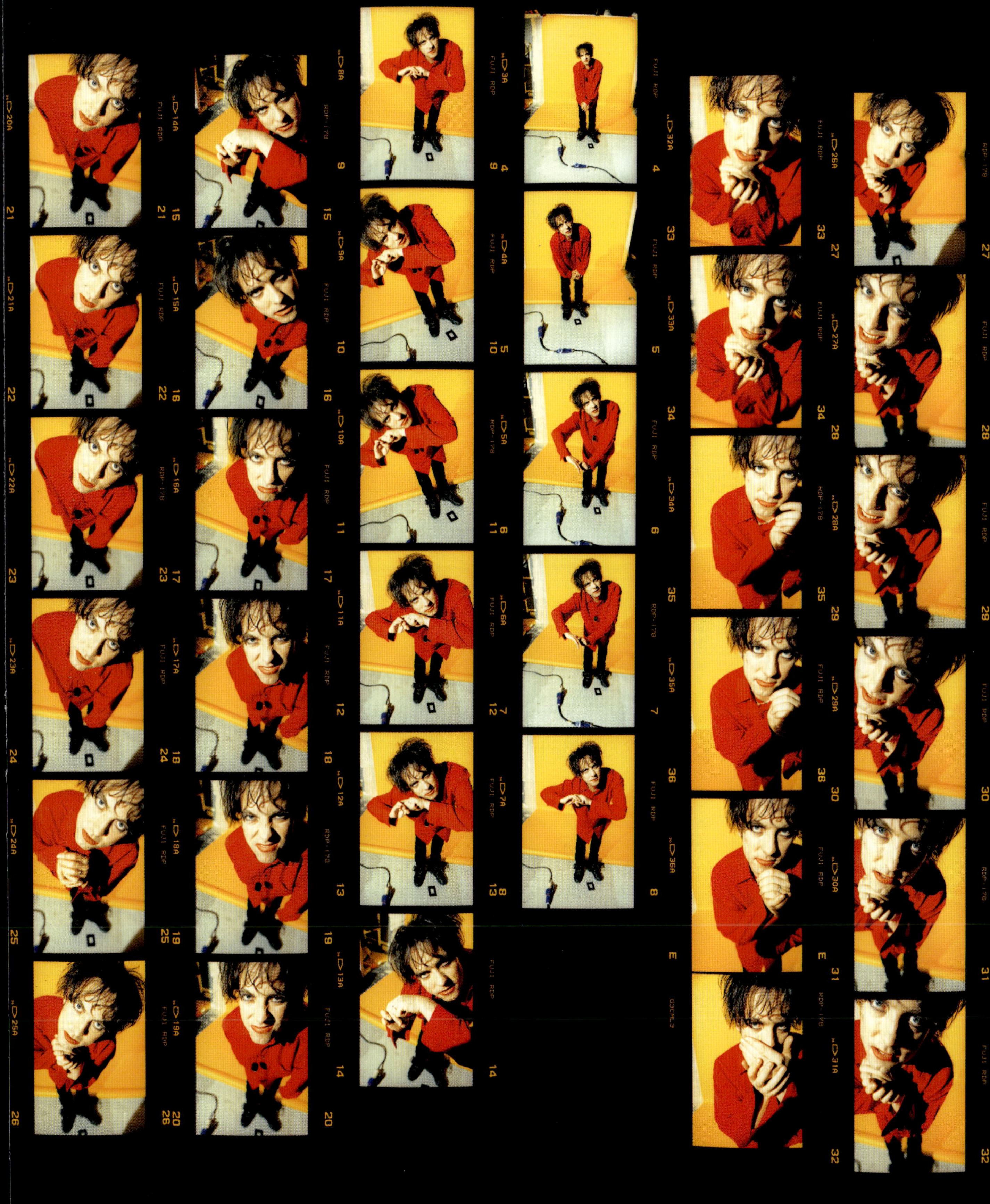

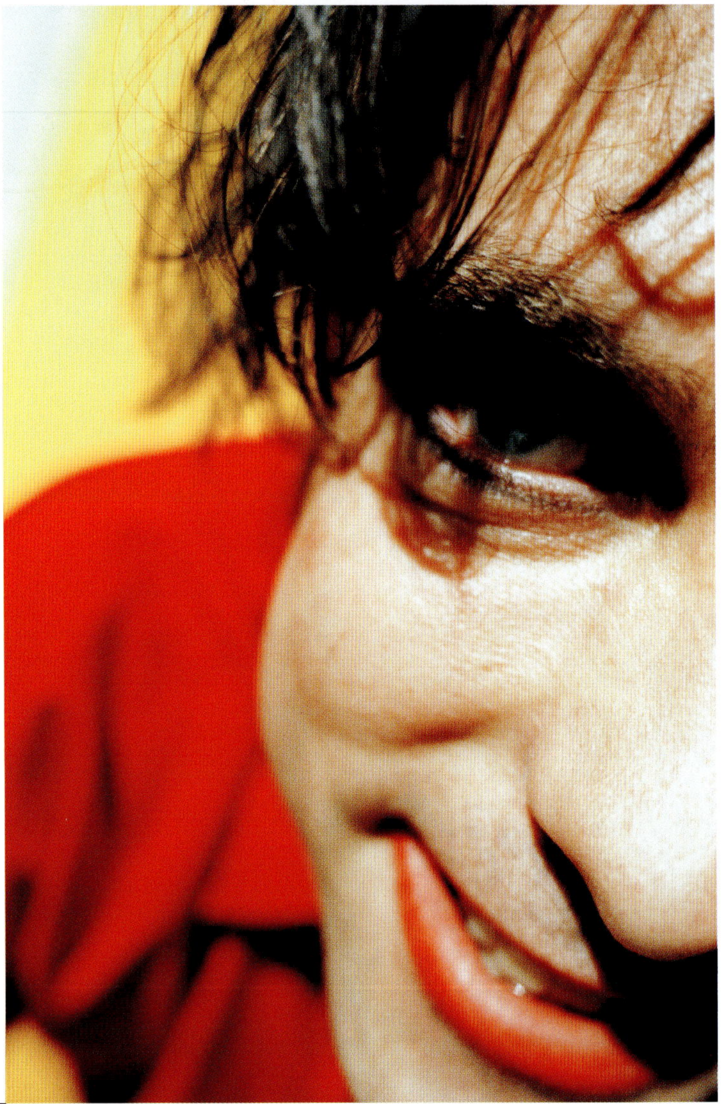
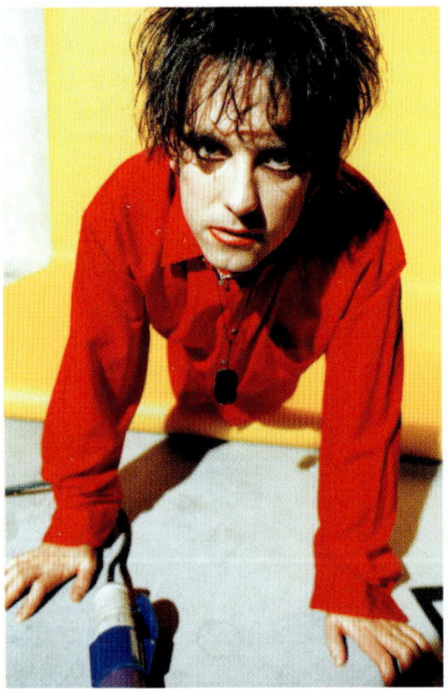
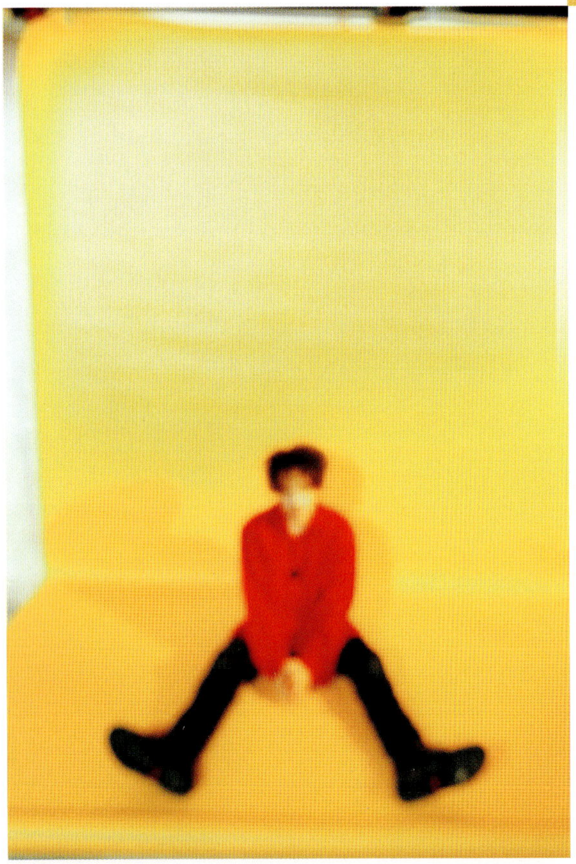
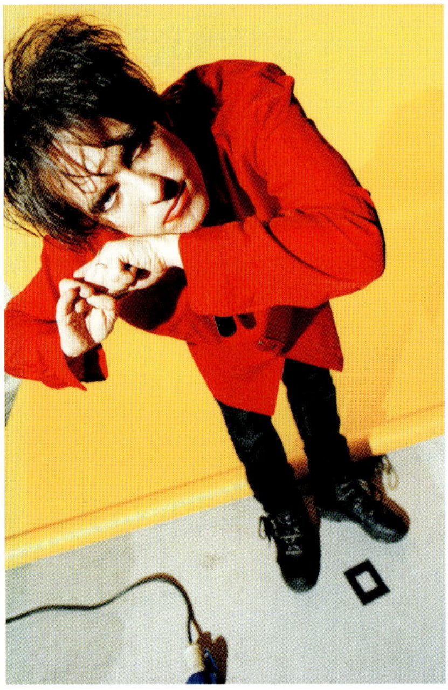

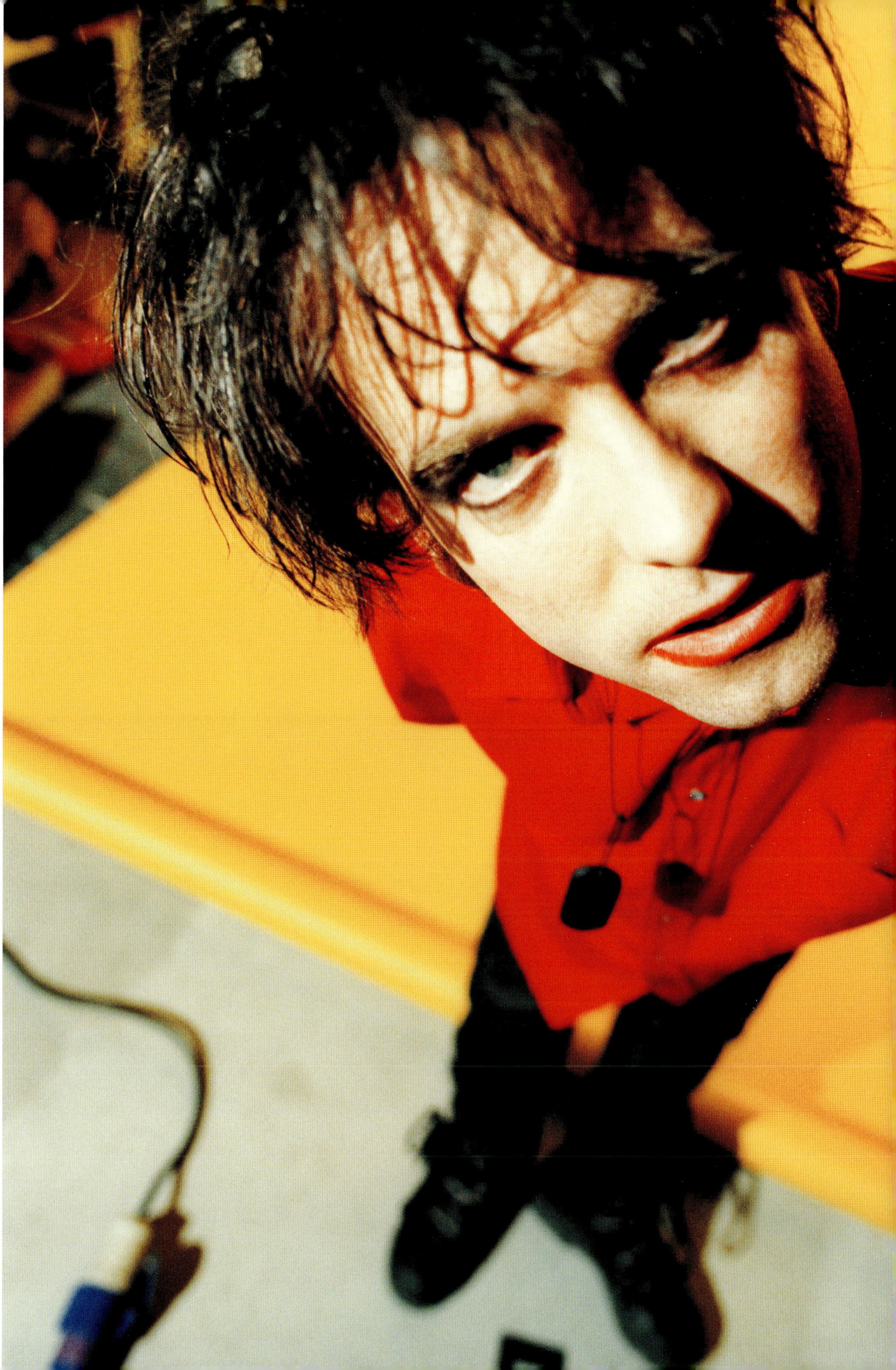

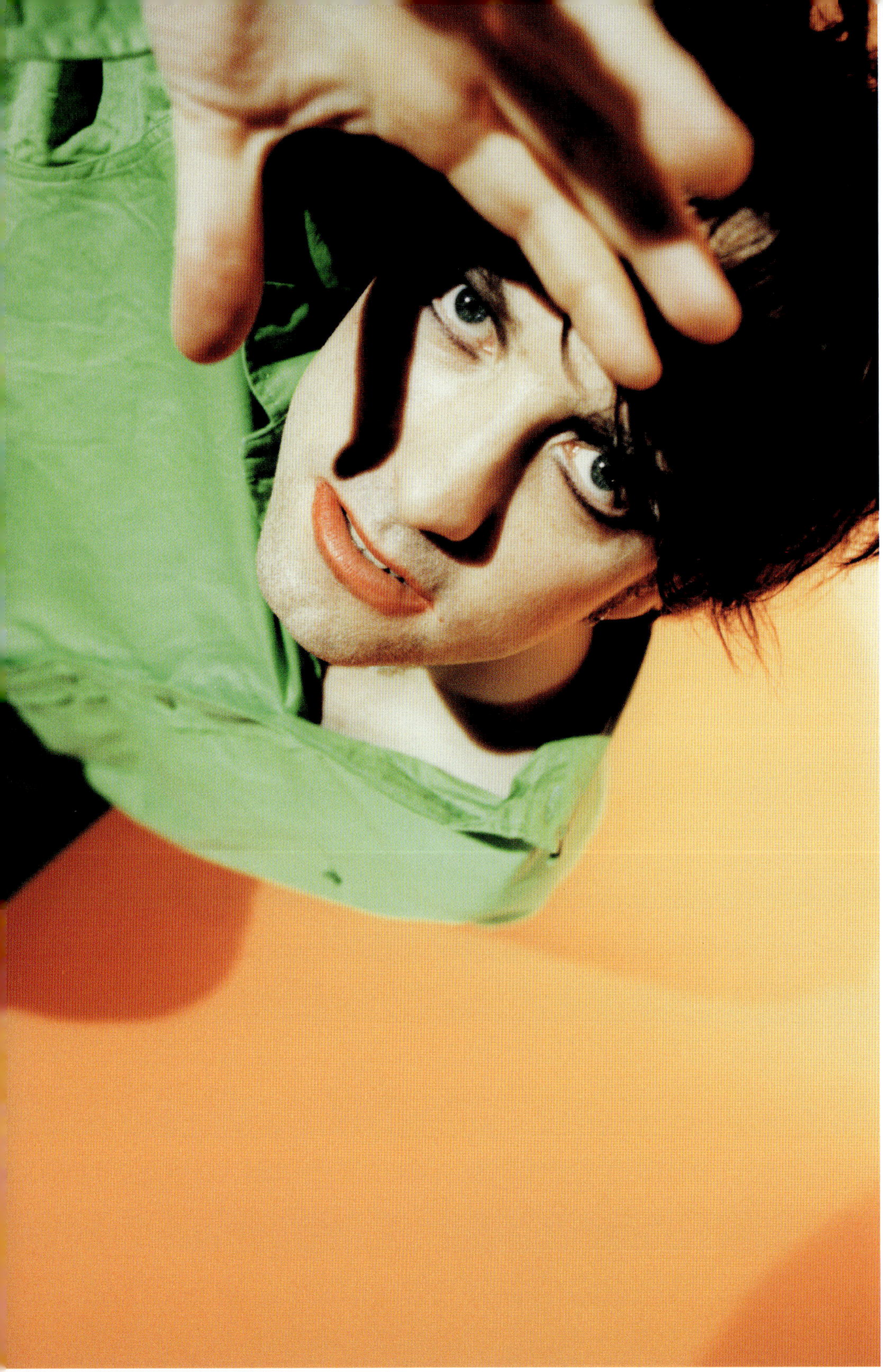

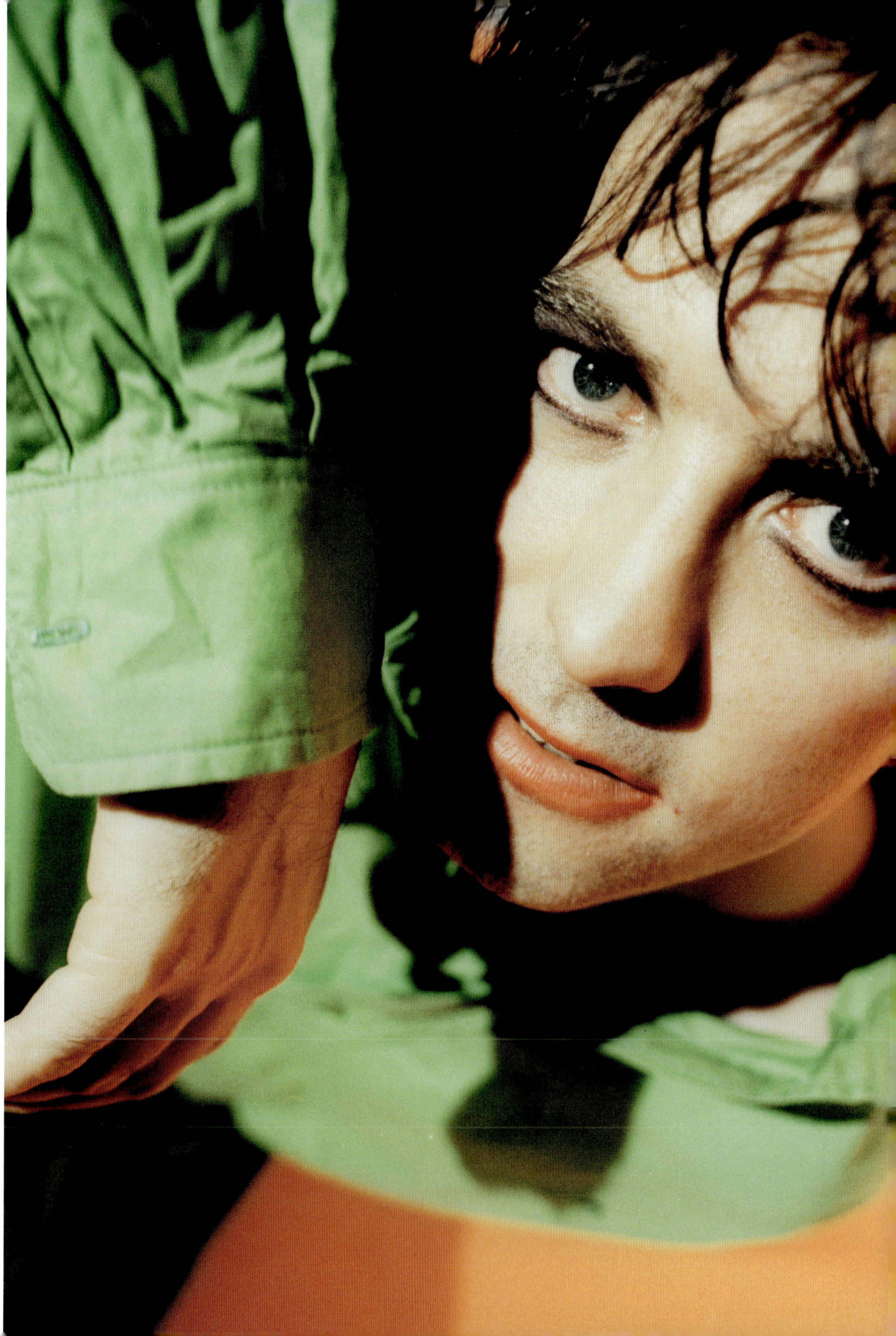

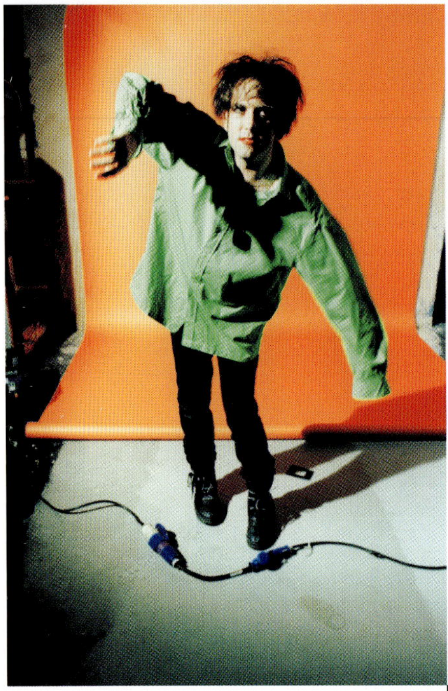

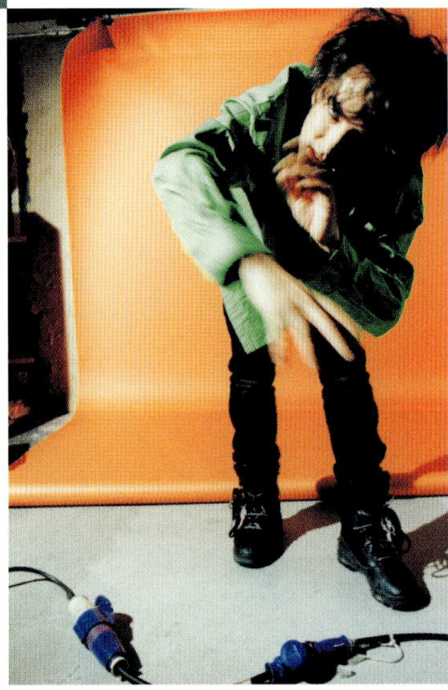

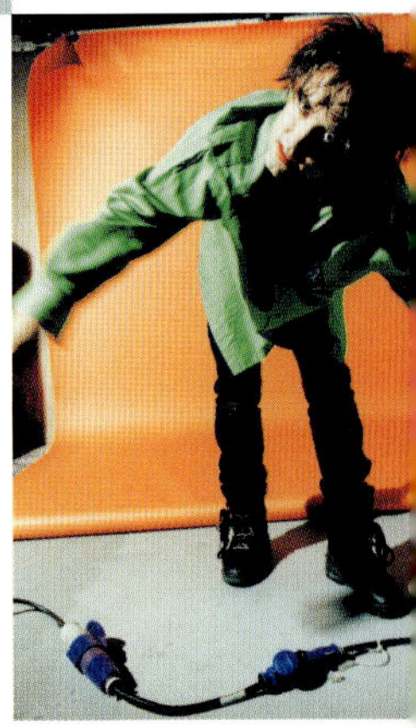

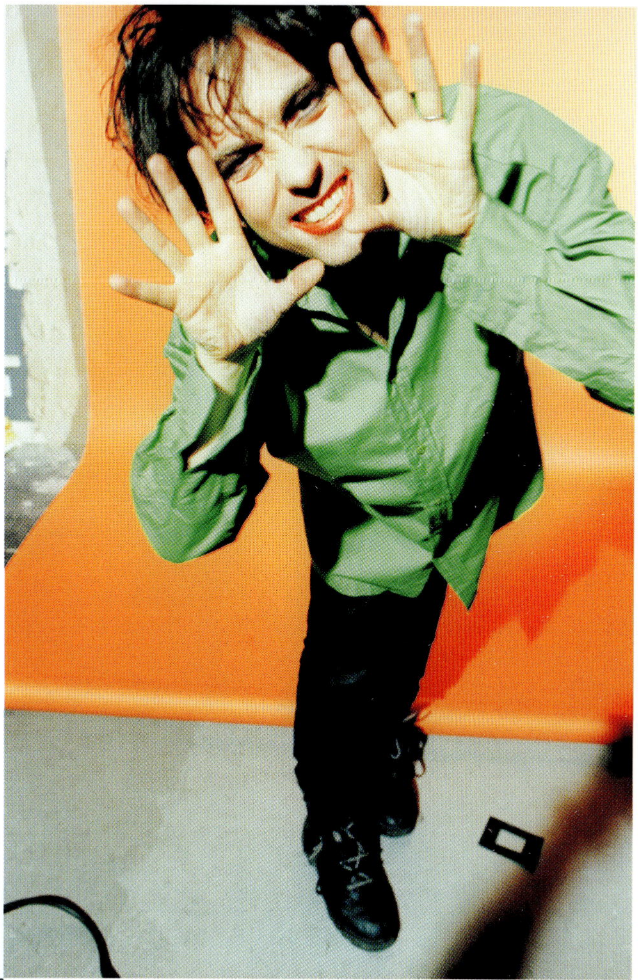

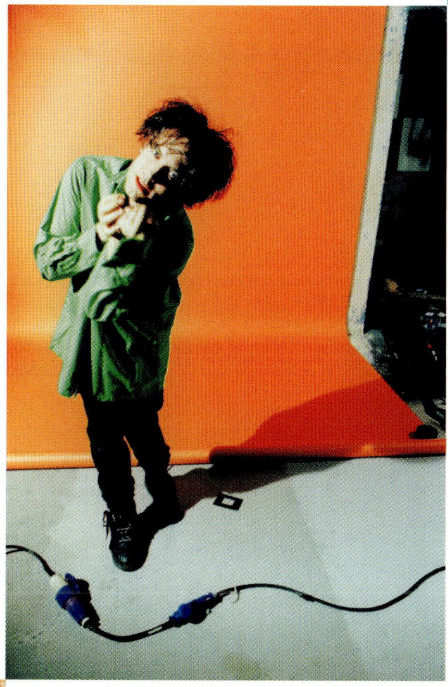

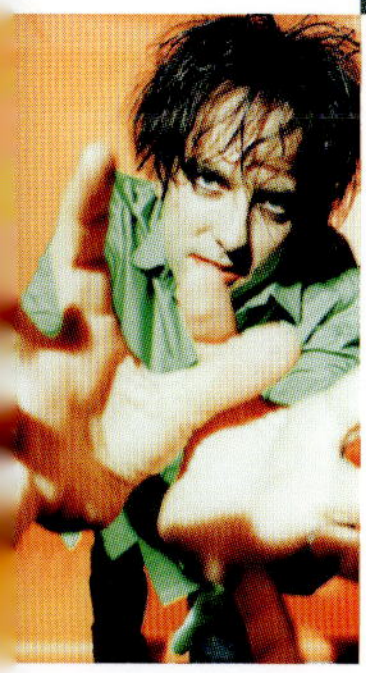

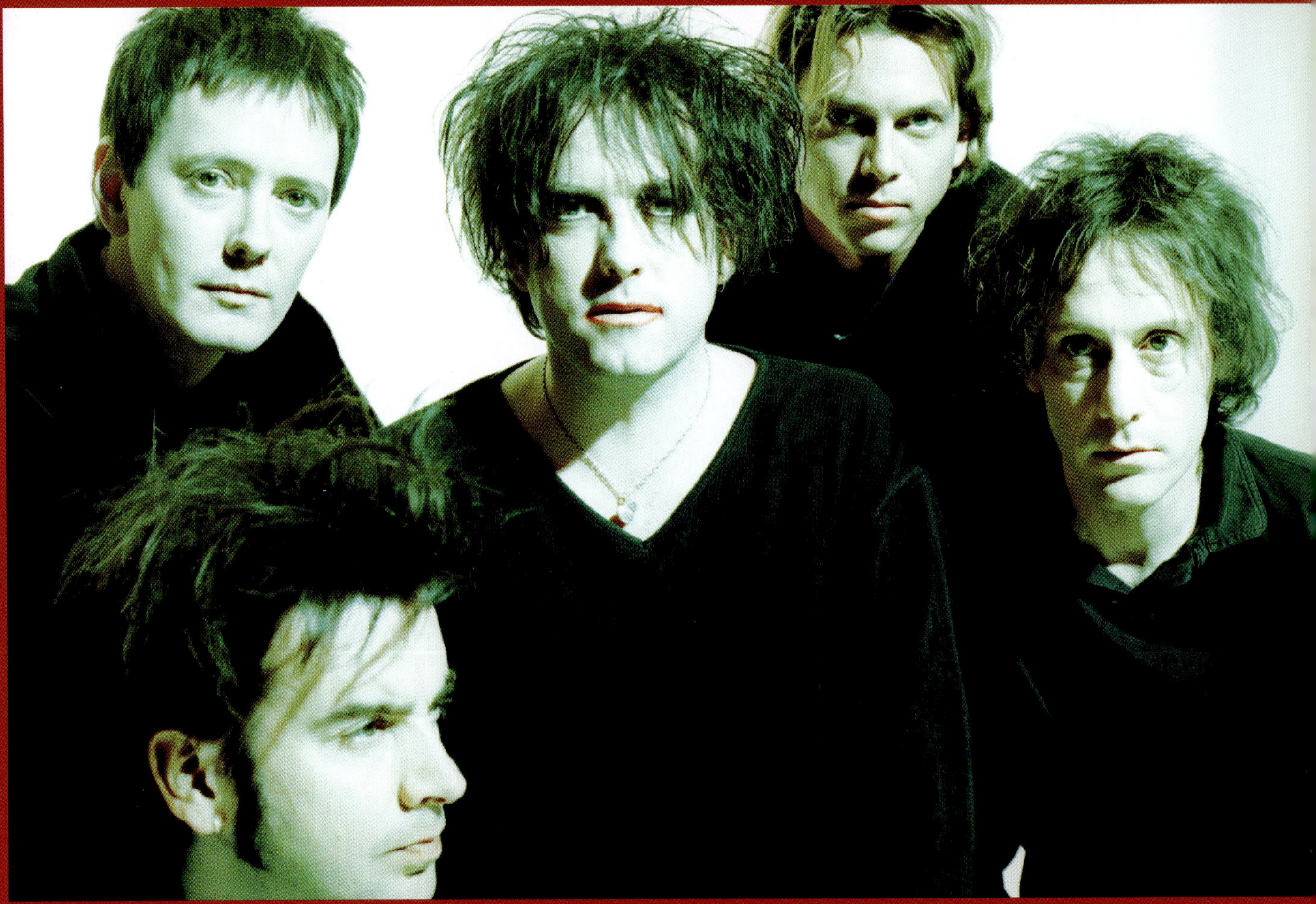

FULHAM STUDIO
[p.240 to 253]
1999

ROBERT: THIS SESSION WAS TO PROMOTE THE *BLOODFLOWERS* ALBUM 2000. THE BAND HAD A GREAT FEEL AROUND THIS TIME, BUT OUR VISUAL IDENTITY LOOKS LIKE IT IS REALLY COMING APART! THE P242-243 BAND SHOT BECAME KNOWN AS 'THE GARDEN CENTRE' SHOT, AS IT LOOKS LIKE WE SPENT AN AFTERNOON THERE CHOOSING OUR OUTFITS... THE UNDERWATER STUFF IS NICE THOUGH.

Paul: Around this time, the lease on my Fulham Studio came to an end, and sadly I had to leave. This session was for the *Bloodflowers* album 2000.
'Out of This World' was the inspiration for the space and stars backdrop, as well as the underwater shots. Red flowers were used as back and front projections.

ROBERT: THE END OF AN ERA...

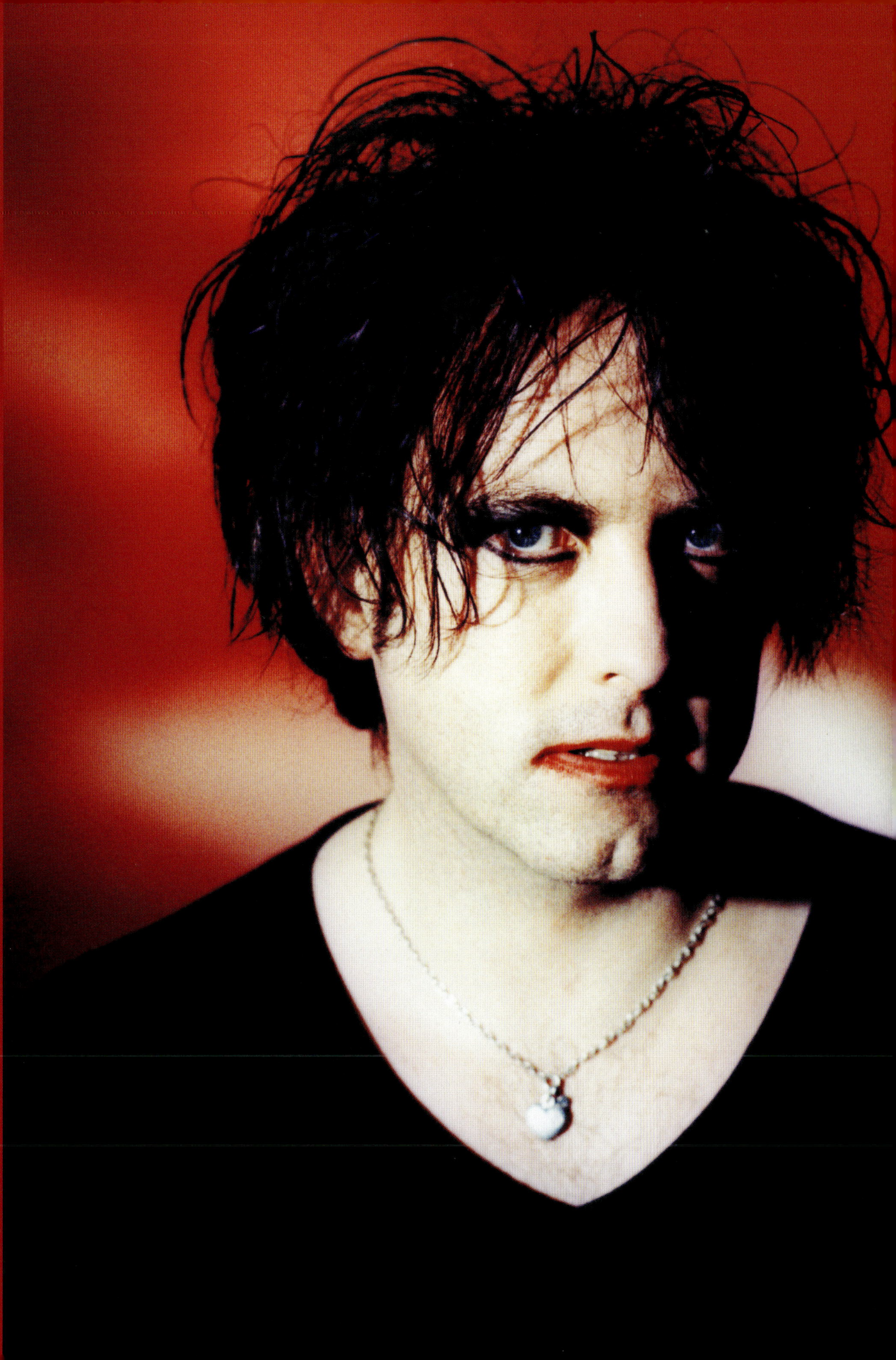

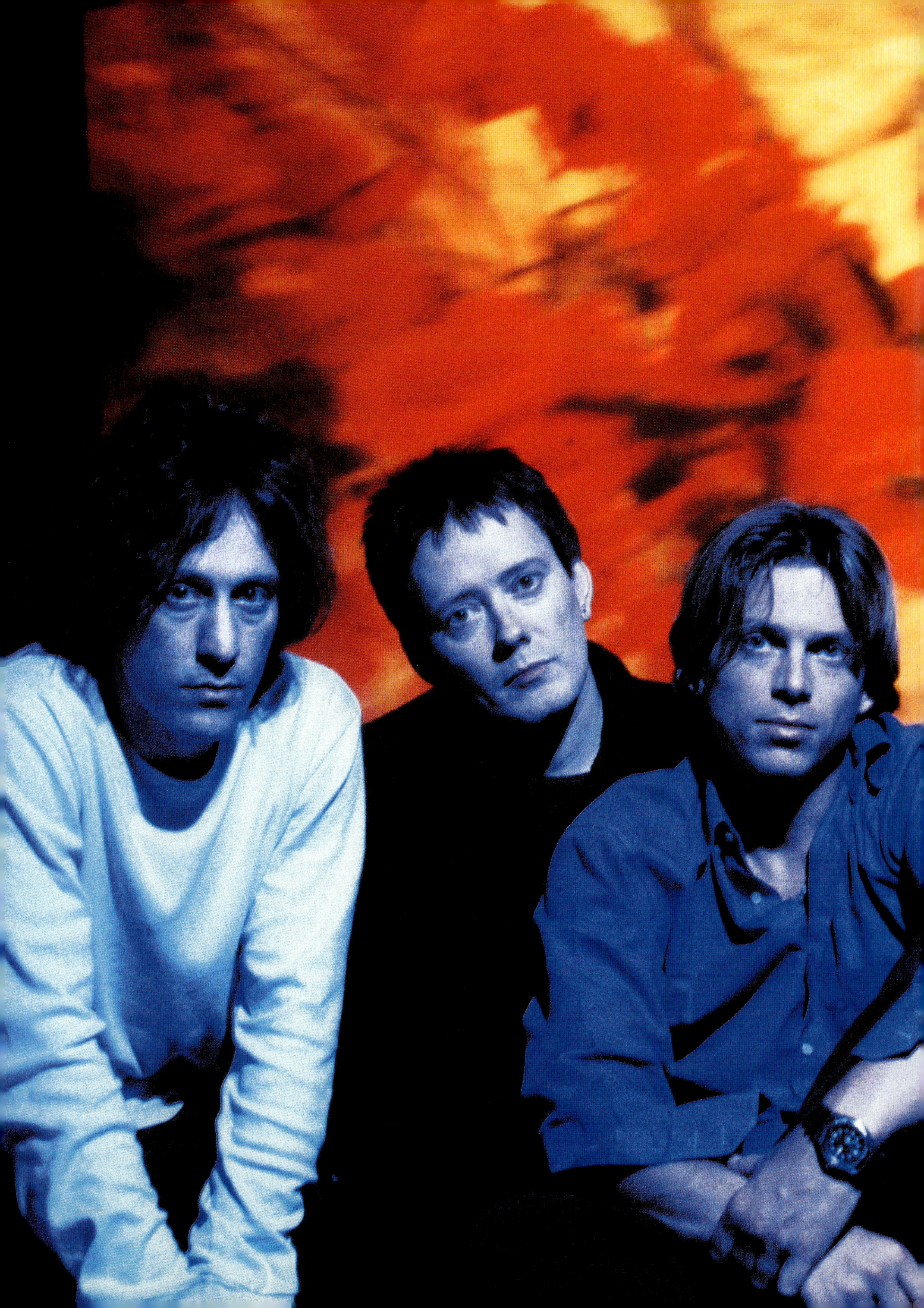

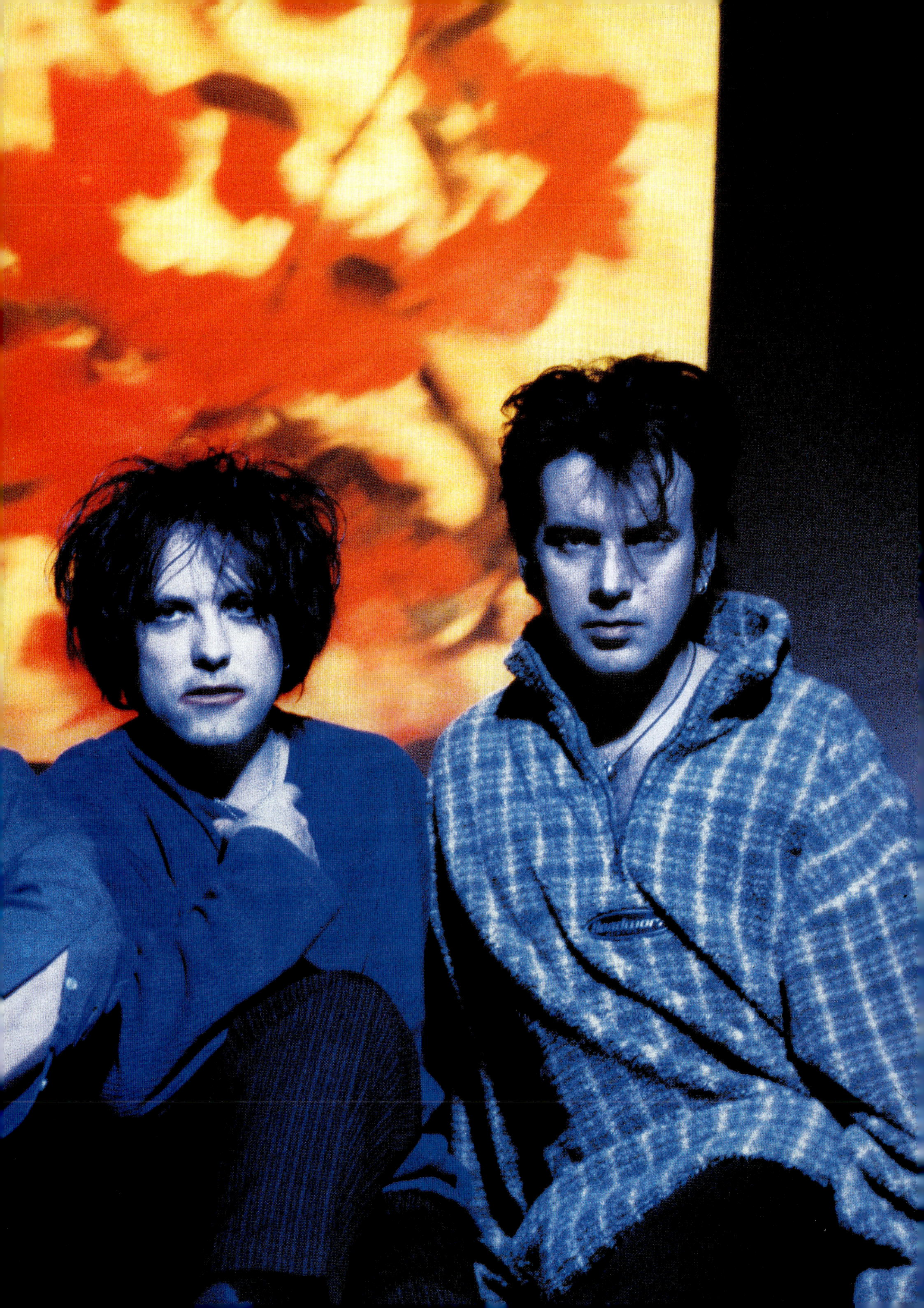

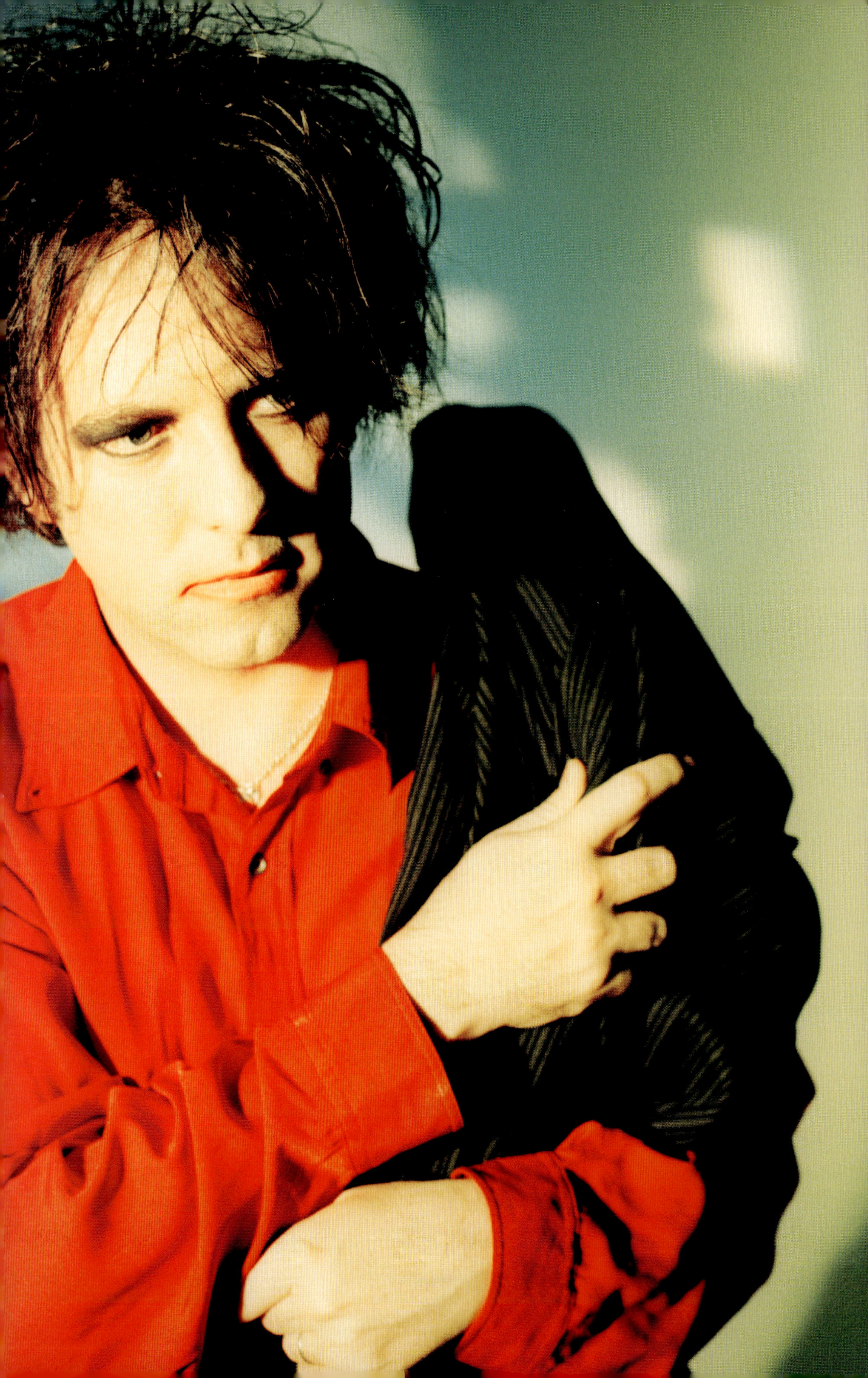

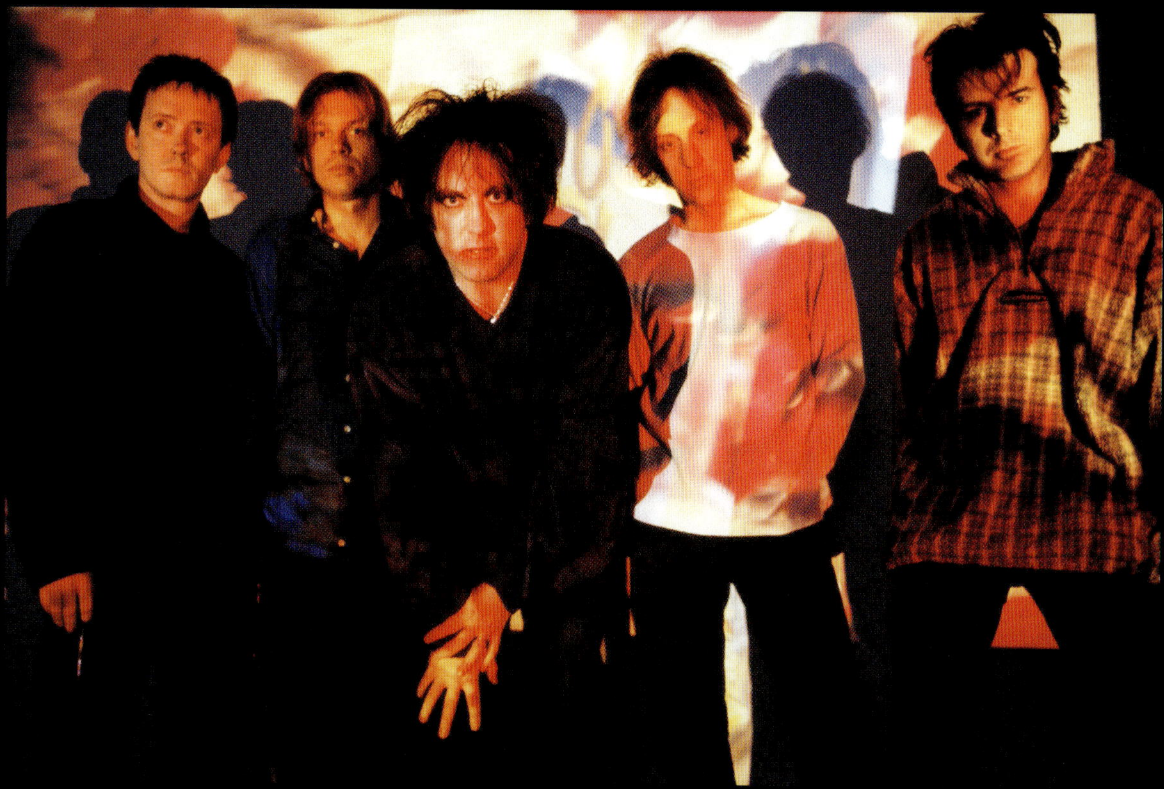

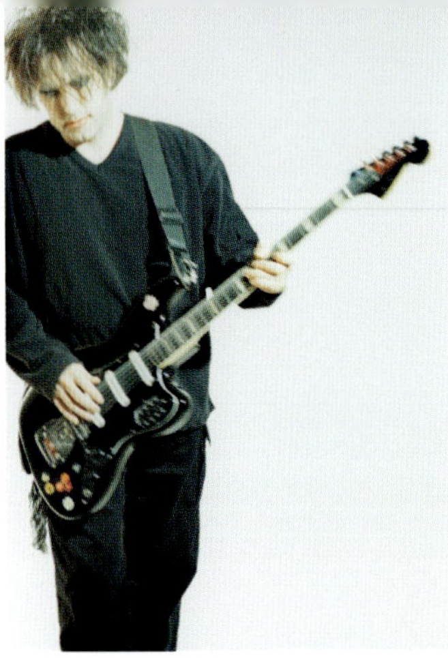

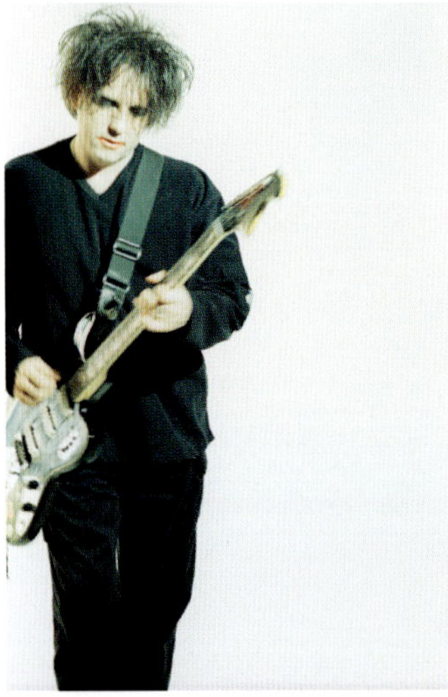

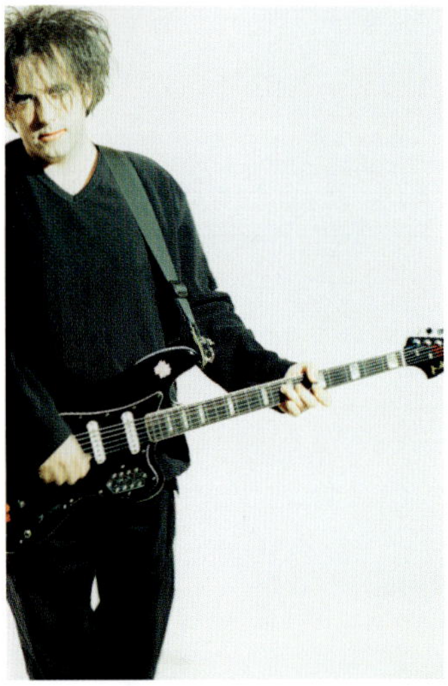

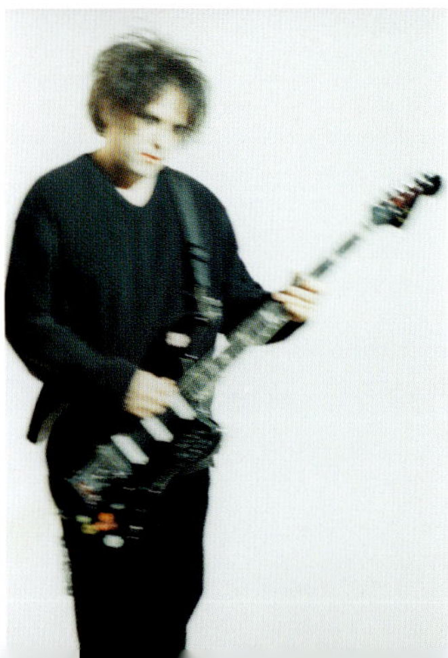

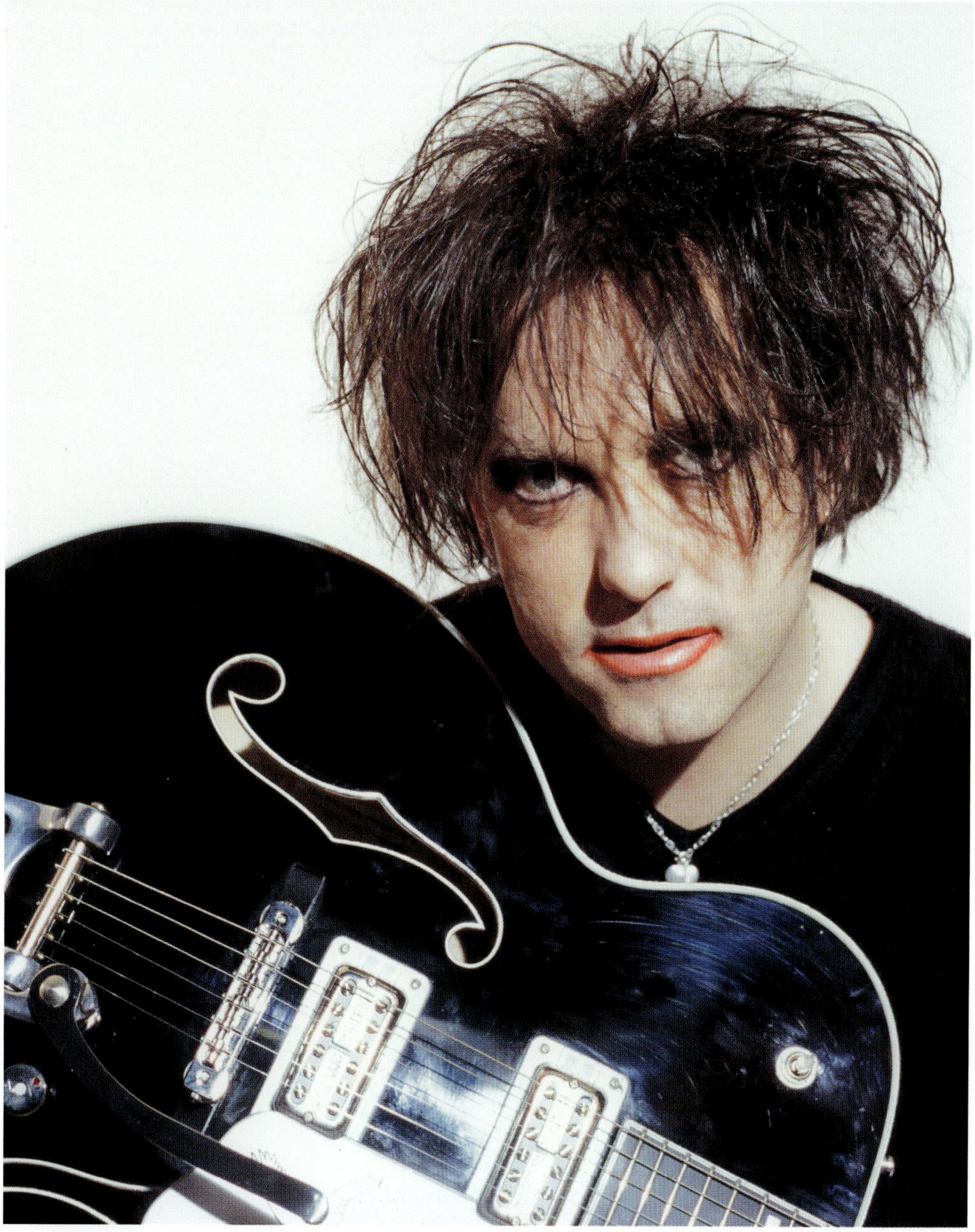

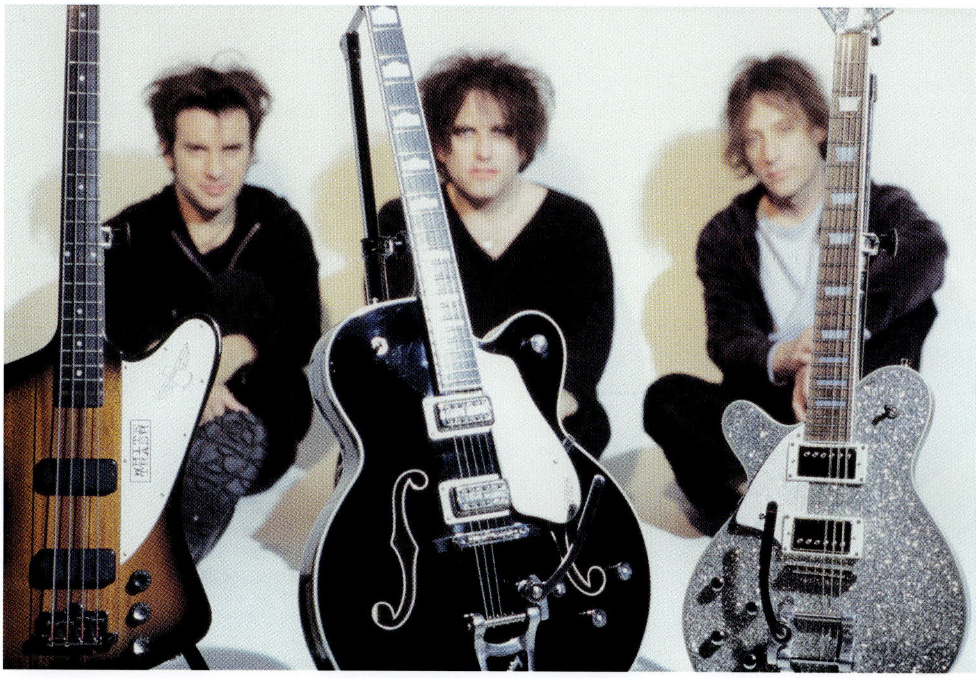

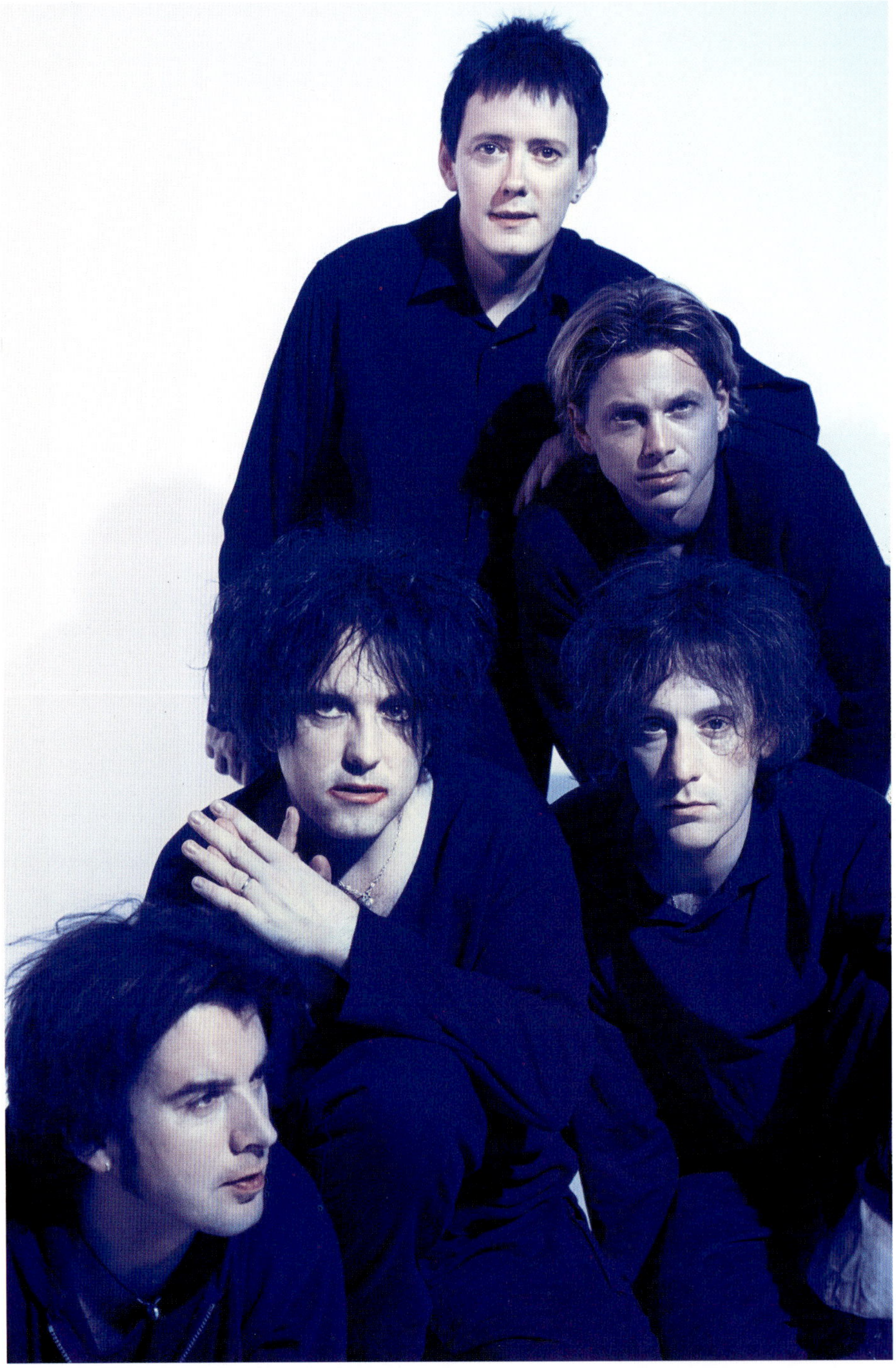

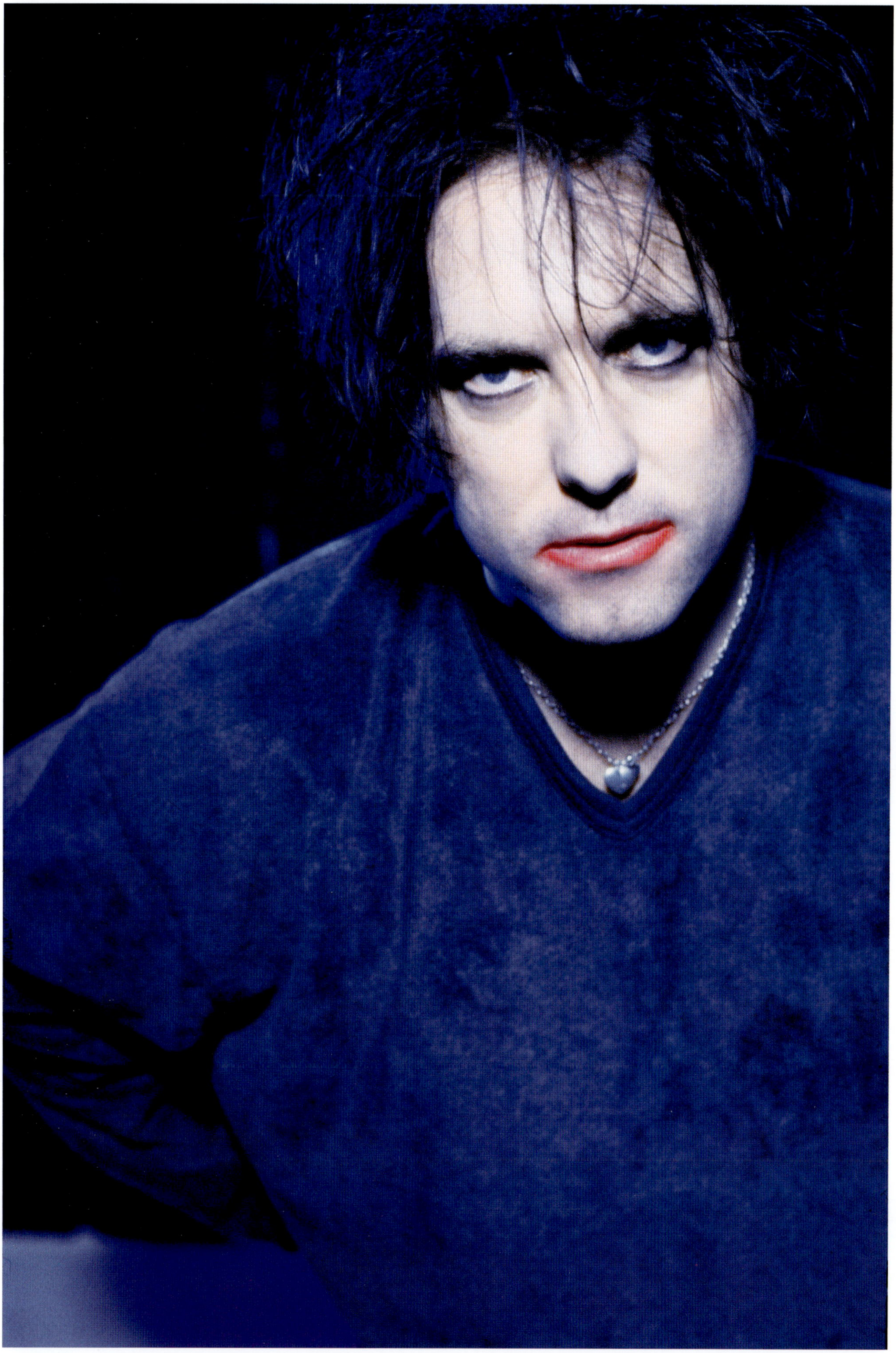

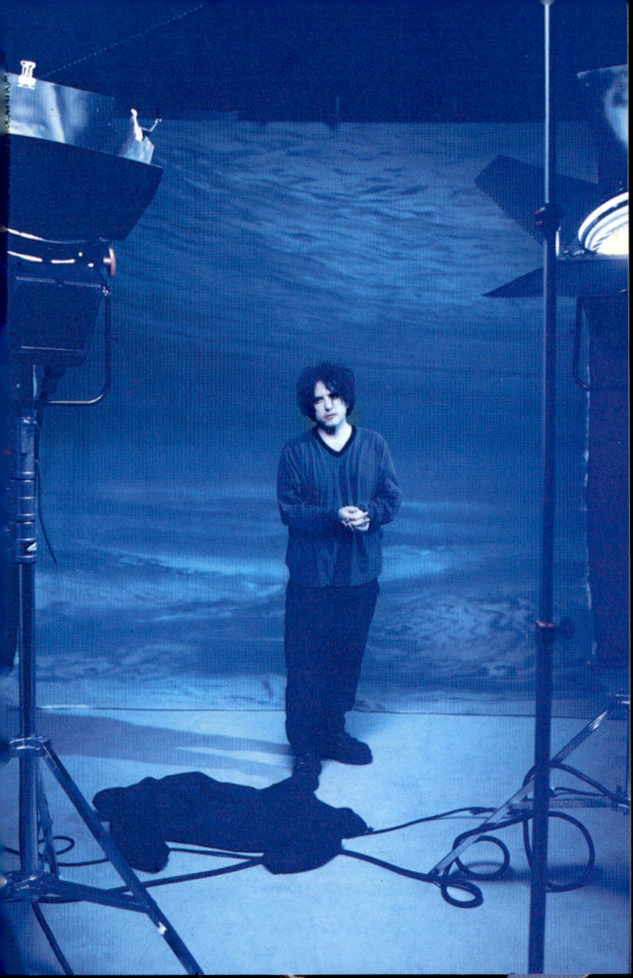

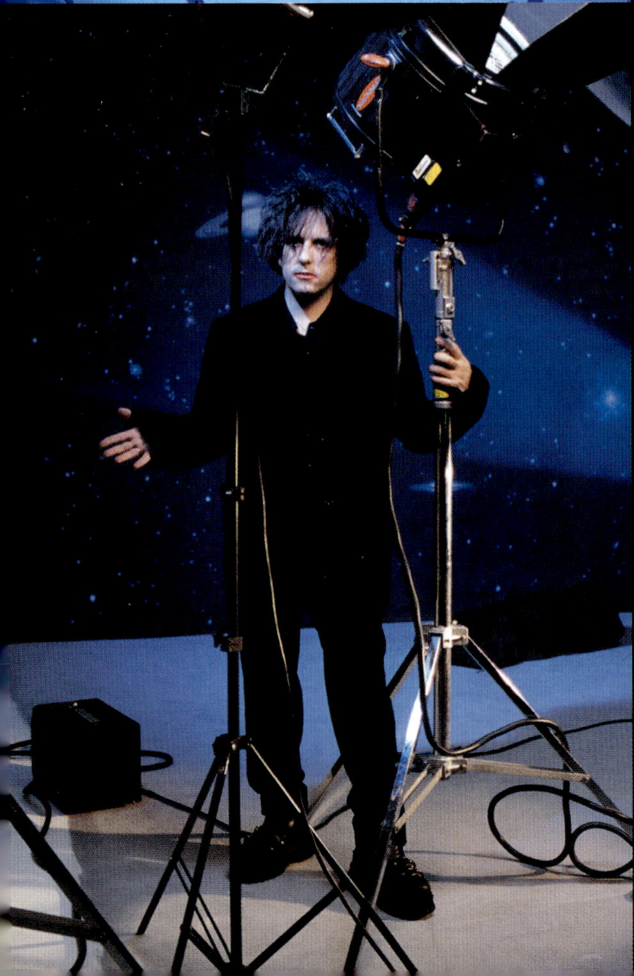

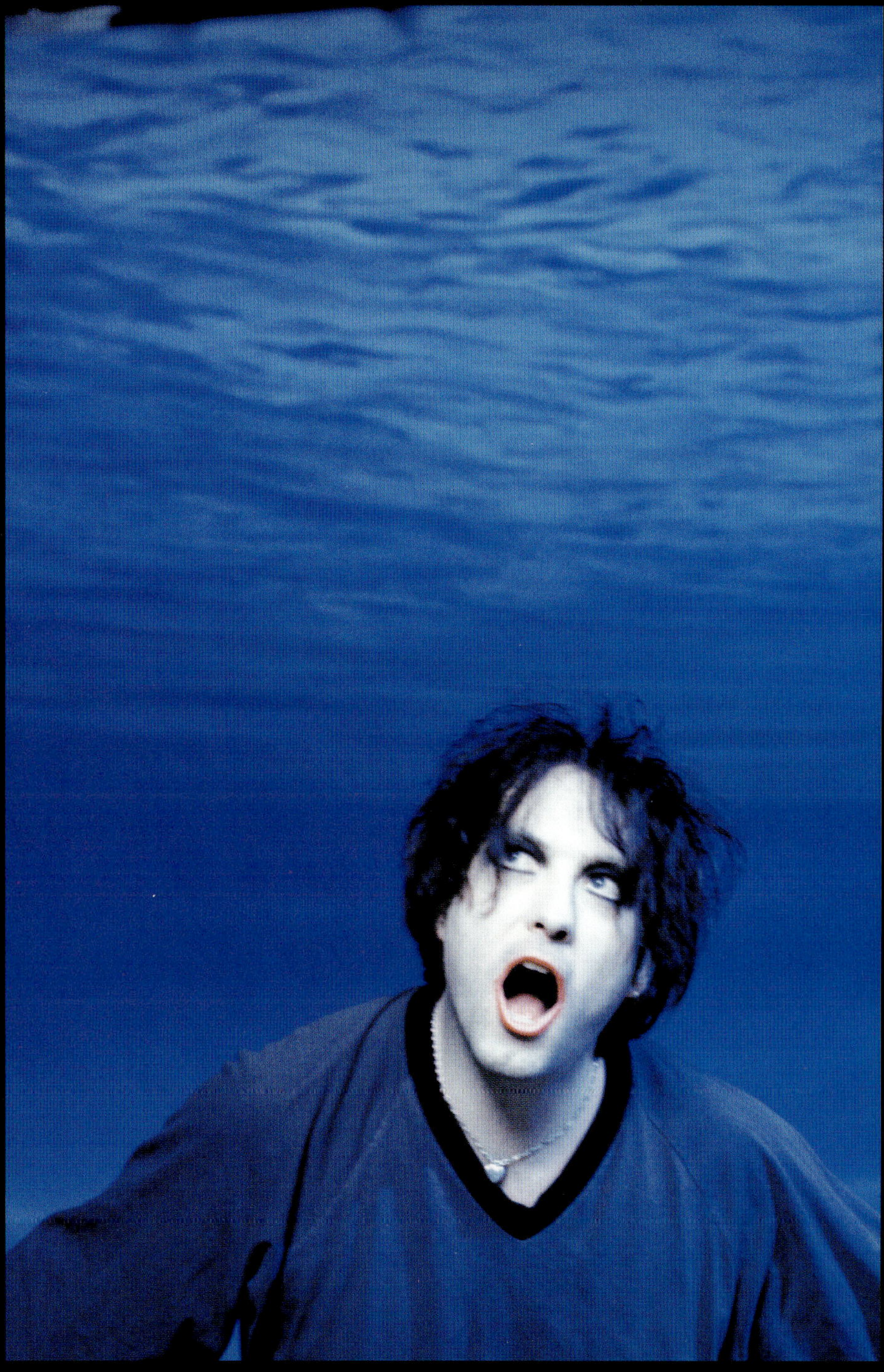

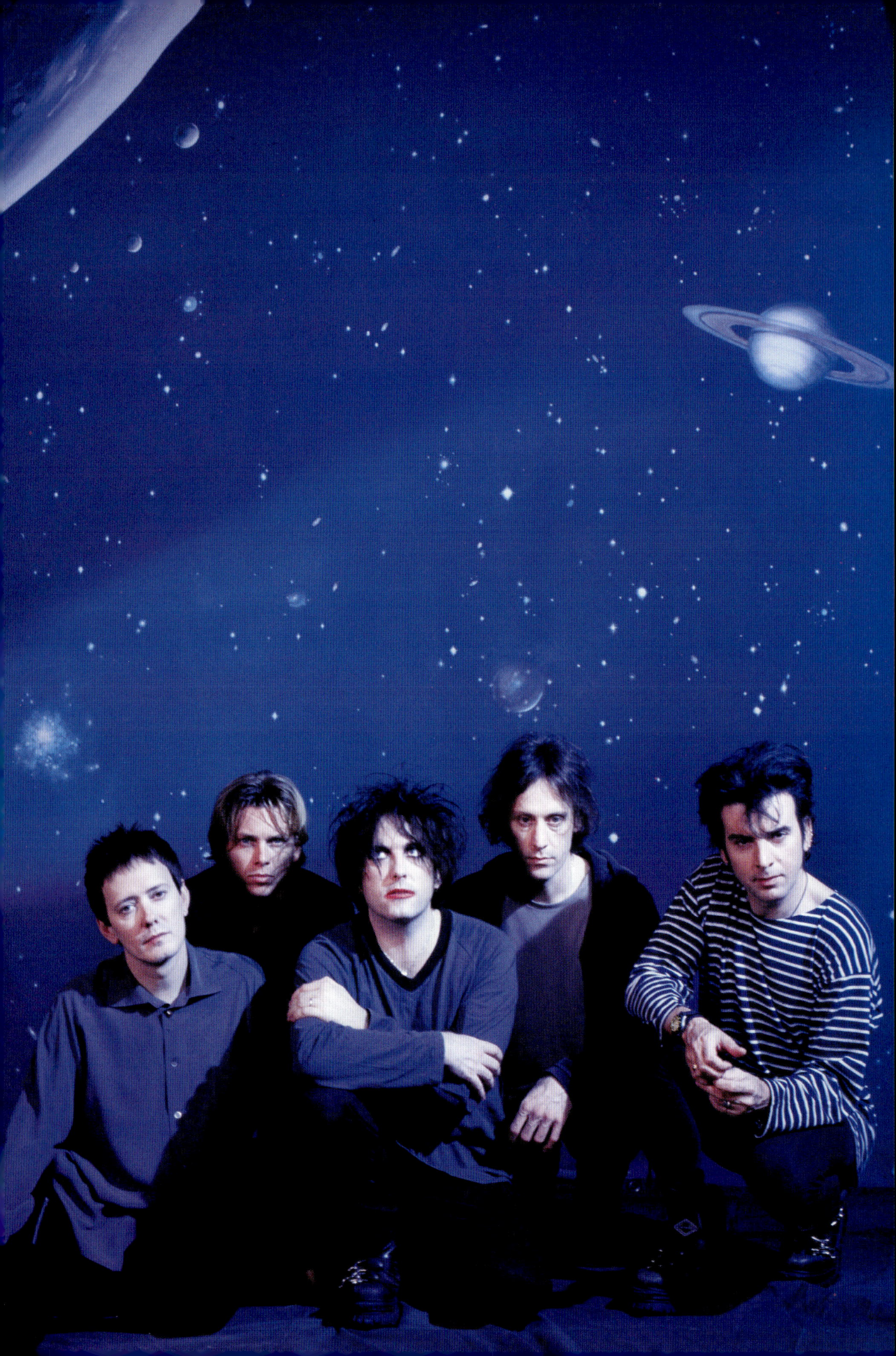

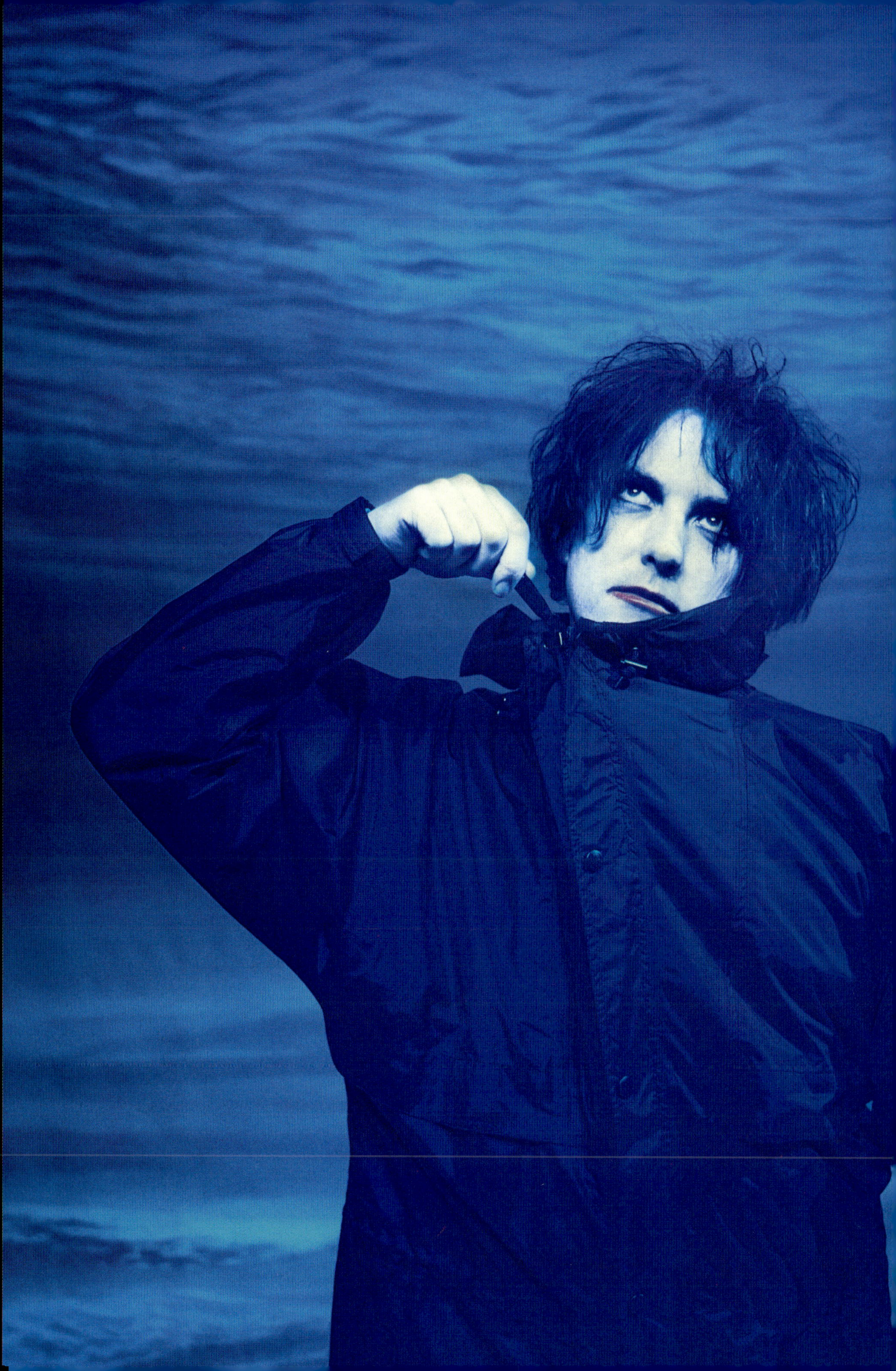

DEAR PAUL –

AS USUAL – EXCELLENT!

I'VE APPROVED FEWER THAN I COULD –
I FIND WHAT HAPPENS IS I APPROVE
100 AND THEN "THEY" PICK 10 – SO
THIS TIME I'VE APPROVED...

TRANNIES	COLOUR CONTACTS	B/W
58	50	9
(17 TO PRINT '6 X 4' FOR ME) (MARKED IN RED)	(19 TO PRINT '6 X 4' FOR ME) (MARKED IN RED)	(9 TO PRINT '6 X 4' FOR ME) (4 ASTERIXED IN RED – "GENERAL USE")

UMM... MORE THAN 100! BUT I'VE
USED AN "ASTERISK" SYSTEM FOR MY FAVOURITES –
I'M FAXING INSTRUCTIONS TO ANDY VELLA –

(ANDY VELLA – please put a copy of my instructions in here for Paul – thanks)

QUEEN ELIZABETH 2

Mr. Robert Smith
Cabin 8102

Thursday.

dear Paul

Posey paper or what!!!

Fab photos again — could you print up the ones boxed in white — 29 in total to about 9 x 6 — also one each of the portraits. Can you get Fiction to then re-courier them back to me in America: This way we'll choose and be able to mock up a calendar before returning to the UK.

Thankyou very much indeed

Land ahoy!

love Robert etc.

CUNARD

CREDITS

AUTHORS
Robert Smith
Paul Cox
Fabrice Couillerot

PHOTOGRAPHY
© Paul Cox
www.paulcoxphotos.co.uk
website © Holly Cox

PICTURE EDITORS
Paul Cox
Fabrice Couillerot

FOREWORDS
Robert Smith

INTRODUCTION
Lydie Barbarian / Helen Cox
Paul Cox

CAPTIONS
Robert Smith
Paul Cox

ARCHIVE MANAGEMENT
Ritchie Franklin

DESIGN
Fabrice Couillerot
www.moonboy.space

RINGMASTER
Cally (www.antar.cc)

LOGISTICS
Empress Litho

PROOFREADERS
Helen Cox
Etienne Foucher
Lawrence
Chris Tinker

PHOTOGRAVURE
Nathalie Cicurel @ Poisson Rouge, Paris

SPECIAL THANKS
Paul and Fabrice would like to especially thank Robert Smith for his creative input and time on this book.

Helen Cox, Etienne Foucher, Chris Tinker, Barnabé, Ernest and Firmin, David May, Lawrence, Nathalie Cicurel, Milo Cuffini and Solfegue Dobaria @ Poisson Rouge, Lydie Barbarian and Boris Colombier (http://wba.fr).

PAUL & FAB THANKS
For their help & support: Joe Black, Daren Butler, Millie, Charlotte and Holly Cox, Philip Yarranton and Scott Spurway, Charlotte Dorling and Dave Lavery, Lætitia Sadier, Jean Baptiste Garnero, and Ritchie Franklin.
Thanks to Snappy Snaps especially Magda in Soho, and Michael and Artur in Richmond.
Paul would like to thank all the great people who assisted and put up with him over the years and who have gone on to great things themselves: Lisa Devlin, Richard Fraser-Stansbie, Pete Mountain, Dan Smith, Ivan Bird and Paul Whitehill.

THE CURE
Robert Smith
Michael Dempsey
Lol Tolhurst
Simon Gallup
Matthieu Hartley
Phil Thornalley
Andy Anderson
Porl Thompson
Boris Williams
Roger O'Donnell
Perry Bamonte
Jason Cooper
Reeves Gabrels

Originally published in the UK by Moonboy Ltd
This edition published by ACC Art Books in 2024 by agreement with Moonboy Ltd

ISBN: 978 1 78884 274 7

A CIP catalogue record for this book is available from the British Library

The author and publisher gratefully acknowledge the permission granted to reproduce the copyright material in this book. Every effort has been made to trace copyright holders and to obtain their permission for the use of copyright material. The publisher apologises for any errors or omissions in the text and would be grateful if notified of any corrections that should be incorporated in future reprints or editions of this book.

ACC ART BOOKS

MIX
Paper | Supporting responsible forestry
FSC® C104723
FSC www.fsc.org

Printed in China
for ACC Art Books Ltd., Woodbridge, Suffolk, UK

www.accartbooks.com

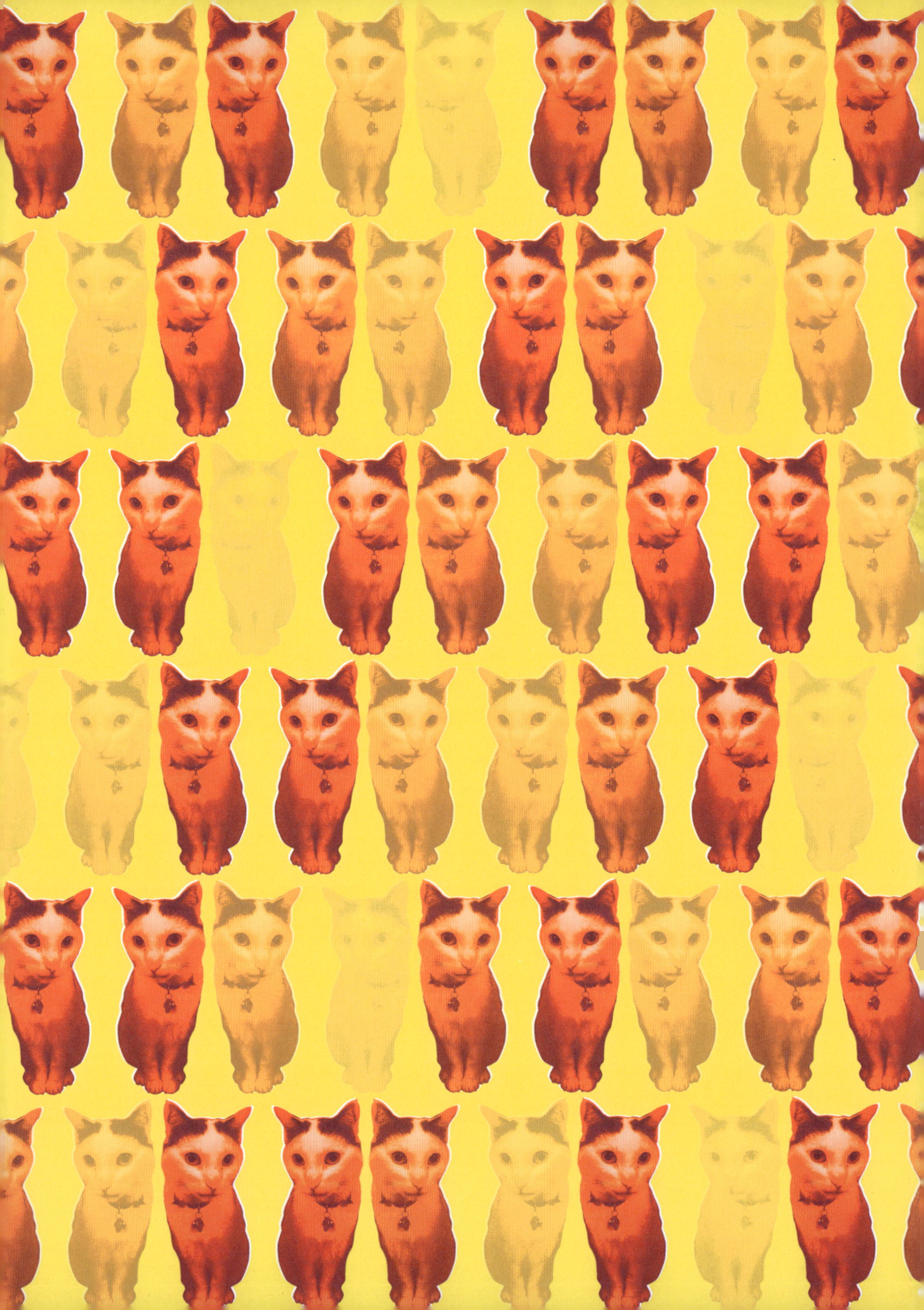